System Center 2012 R2 Virtual Machine Manager Cookbook

Second Edition

Over 70 recipes to help you design, configure, and manage a reliable and efficient virtual infrastructure with VMM 2012 R2

Edvaldo Alessandro Cardoso

[PACKT] enterprise 🞘

PUBLISHING

professional expertise distilled

BIRMINGHAM - MUMBAI

System Center 2012 R2 Virtual Machine Manager Cookbook

Second Edition

First published: March 2013

Second edition: June 2014

Production reference: 1180614

Published by Packt Publishing Ltd.
Livery Place
35 Livery Street
Birmingham B3 2PB, UK.

ISBN 978-1-78217-684-8

www.packtpub.com

Cover image by Ramon Reginald Vega (esrvega@yahoo.com)

Credits

About the Author

Edvaldo Alessandro Cardoso is passionate about technology, an evangelist, and a subject matter expert on cloud, virtualization, and management. He is an author and also a speaker at key technical events in Australia and New Zealand.

He has been the Microsoft Most Valuable Professional for Hyper-V since 2009. He leads major virtualization, UC&C, and AD and Exchange projects for large customers in APJ, closely collaborating and liaising with presales and sales teams to ensure client satisfaction and IT synergies. He has experience working within multigeographic and virtual teams.

He has in-depth knowledge across the Microsoft and VMware technologies stack. He holds the Microsoft MCSE+S and VMware VCP certifications. He also has experience leading complex global projects in his 24-year career in IT; he has worked in segments spanning the government, health, education, and IT services sectors.

He is an established manager with extensive leadership experience in all facets of IT management and functional management practices.

He recently authored the book, *Microsoft System Center Virtual Machine Manager 2012 Cookbook* (http://wp.me/p15Fu3-mK), and reviewed the books, *Windows Server 2012 Hyper-V Cookbook*, *Microsoft Hyper-V Cluster Design*, and *VMware vSphere 5.1 Cookbook*, all by Packt Publishing.

He is a blogger at http://cloudtidings.com/. You can also follow him on Twitter: @cloudtidings.

Acknowledgments

This book covers the newest VMM 2012 R2 version. Developing and updating this book was a real challenge. I have worked so hard to gather and put the content together, deploying the solutions, validating test scenarios, investigating, and also reporting issues back to MS, to provide you with a useful, accurate, and worth-the-time master resource. It has been an amazing journey, and I greatly appreciate all those who gave me their full support.

First and foremost, I would like to dedicate this book to my father, Olimpio, and the memory of my mother, Celcina, and especially to my kids—Matheus, Lucas, and Nicole—and my beautiful wife, Daniele, who cnoouraged me in all my endeavors. Thank you for the ongoing, full support, encouragement, inspiration, and for letting me take my time away from you to work on this project. I love you all.

I could not have finished this book without help from the Microsoft System Center and Microsoft Virtualization (Hyper-V) team in Redmond: Ben Armstrong and Travis Wright (now working for Cireson). In addition, as I wanted this book to be reviewed by the Microsoft System Center team, I would like to acknowledge and thank Nigel Cain and Carmen Summers from the Microsoft System Center and Virtualization team, not only for endorsing my participation in the TAP program, but also for their assistance; they worked beyond their work hours to review the book and provide great feedback, which helped me improve the content, adding substantial value to this book. I cannot forget Vijay Tewari and Christa Anderson. Thank you for the feedback on the first edition. The readers will truly appreciate that!

In addition, I would like to thank my fellow Hyper-V and System Center MVPs, as well as Tomica Kaniski, Richard Skinner, Steve Buchanan, Kristian Nese, and Marin Frankovic for their feedback.

I also had support from the Veeam team, who provided me with early access to the Veeam Management pack for SCOM and also gave great insights about their product.

I would also like to thank the Packt Publishing team involved in this project, especially those who helped and guided my efforts to make certain that the content was consistent and of a high quality. Thank you for the opportunity to work on this great project.

Finally, thank you for choosing and purchasing the *System Center 2012 R2 Virtual Machine Manager Cookbook, Second Edition*. It is a valuable resource to help you deploy and manage your own private cloud. I will be waiting for your feedback. You can follow my blog at `http://cloudtidings.com`, and my Twitter handle is `@cloudtidings`.

About the Reviewers

Marin Frankovic was born in 1976 in Makarska, Croatia, where he completed elementary and a part of high school. He graduated from high school in the U.S.A., where he attended his senior year as an exchange student. In 2003, he earned his Master of Economics (mag. oec.) degree from Faculty of Economics and Business, University of Zagreb, Croatia, where he majored in business computing. As a student, he volunteered in the faculty's IT department for a year as technical support. After obtaining his degree, Marin started as Microsoft MOC and an IBM ACE instructor in the largest private IT education company, Algebra. There, he also started as a consultant for infrastructure, virtualization, and cloud computing based on Microsoft technologies. Later on, when Algebra opened a private college for applied computing, he took on a position as the head of the operating systems department and took responsibility for creating course curriculums and managing several lecturers and assistants. He also gives lectures on several key courses in system administration track. Microsoft honored him with the MVP title for System Center and Datacenter Management five years in a row. He is a regular speaker at all regional conferences such as Windays, KulenDayz, MobilityDay, NT Konferenca, MS Network, DevArena, and so on.

In 2011, Marin was awarded with the Microsoft ISV award for his contribution to the Microsoft community. He regularly writes technical articles for the *Mreža IT* magazine. His main interests today are cloud computing, virtualization as its core component, and resource consolidation based on Microsoft technologies such as Windows Server and System Center applications.

Tomica Kaniski has been active in IT for about 10 years. He started out as a web designer and web developer, did some Windows development during his college days, and then finally discovered his true passion—systems administration on the Microsoft platform. Systems administration, virtualization, deployment, management... you name it, and he has been doing it since 2008, and also teaching about it since 2011 as a Microsoft Certified Trainer.

In 2009, he passed his first MCP exam and became a Microsoft Certified Professional. Certification is something that he continued doing through the years, and he now has certificates, titles, and knowledge about almost the entire Microsoft product portfolio. In 2010, he was awarded the Microsoft MVP title in Management Infrastructure expertise, and after two years, he switched to Virtual Machine, and is now a Hyper-V MVP. He is strongly engaged with communities worldwide—he is one of the community leads in Croatia and part of the Azure Insiders and Azure Advisors communities.

During this time, he has been continuously providing consultation, implementation, and support services for several companies, not necessarily located in Croatia or the region.

Nowadays, you can find him presenting at various local and regional conferences, user group meetings, and other events. You can say that he is fully engaged with Microsoft products and technologies (with a focus on Windows Server, virtualization, System Center, and Azure), and mostly interested in products that are yet to be released.

In his spare time, he plays the bass guitar and also likes to read and travel.

Tomica has also participated in the peer-reviewing of the book, *Introducing Windows Server 2012, Mitch Tulloch, Microsoft Press,* and done technical reviewing on Wiley's Windows Server 2012 MOAC courseware.

> I would like to thank my family and my girlfriend for their patience and constant support.

Richard Skinner has over 10 years of experience in the field of IT. Since starting as a software developer, he has had a varied career covering many aspects of IT, including Windows desktop deployment, SQL Server database administration, SAN implementation, document management, SharePoint, and Hyper-V. He is a blogger at `http://richardstk.com` and his Twitter handle is `@_richardstk`.

Carmen Summers has an extensive background in large-scale data center operations. Her experience includes program management, project management, and project engineering in the information technology and services and computer software industries. Before joining Microsoft, she served in the USAF for eight years, where she worked as an IT administrator within the Medical Information Systems field. After leaving the USAF, she joined a large-scale data center operations service provider, where she specialized in managing global patch management operations and was also an Account Chief Technologist. Carmen joined Microsoft in 2007 as a Senior Program Manager on System Center Virtual Machine Management, and in 2013, she transitioned to a customer-facing role that focuses on System Center, Windows Server, and Azure.

www.PacktPub.com

Support files, eBooks, discount offers and more

You might want to visit www.PacktPub.com for support files and downloads related to your book.

Did you know that Packt offers eBook versions of every book published, with PDF and ePub files available? You can upgrade to the eBook version at www.PacktPub.com and as a print book customer, you are entitled to a discount on the eBook copy. Get in touch with us at service@packtpub.com for more details.

At www.PacktPub.com, you can also read a collection of free technical articles, sign up for a range of free newsletters and receive exclusive discounts and offers on Packt books and eBooks.

PACKTLIB

http://PacktLib.PacktPub.com

Do you need instant solutions to your IT questions? PacktLib is Packt's online digital book library. Here, you can access, read and search across Packt's entire library of books.

Why Subscribe?

- ▶ Fully searchable across every book published by Packt
- ▶ Copy and paste, print and bookmark content
- ▶ On demand and accessible via web browser

Free Access for Packt account holders

If you have an account with Packt at www.PacktPub.com, you can use this to access PacktLib today and view nine entirely free books. Simply use your login credentials for immediate access.

Instant Updates on New Packt Books

Get notified! Find out when new books are published by following @PacktEnterprise on Twitter, or the *Packt Enterprise* Facebook page.

Table of Contents

Preface

Microsoft System Center 2012 is a comprehensive IT infrastructure, virtualization, and cloud management platform. With System Center 2012, you can easily and efficiently deploy, manage, and monitor a virtualized infrastructure, services, and applications across multiple hypervisors as well as public and private cloud infrastructures to deliver flexible and cost-effective IT services for your business.

This book has over 70 recipes to help you design, plan, and improve Virtual Machine Manager (VMM) deployment; integrate and manage fabric (compute, storage, gateway, and networking), services, and resources; deploy clusters from Bare Metal servers; configure integration with Operations Manager and App Controller; and carry out vital tasks quickly and easily.

What this book covers

Chapter 1, VMM 2012 Architecture, provides an understanding of the underlying VMM modular architecture, which is useful when troubleshooting VMM and improving implementation. Make sure you spend some time rewiring this chapter.

Chapter 2, Upgrading from Previous Versions, provides recipes that allow you to smooth the migration process from the previous versions of System Center to the new System Center 2012 R2 with tips and tricks.

Chapter 3, Installing VMM 2012 R2, provides tips to shorten and automate processes when installing VMM 2012 R2; it covers the SQL installation, the AD container for security and HA, and Run As accounts to automate and manage the credentials through VMM.

Chapter 4, Installing a High Available VMM Server, provides an understanding of how VMM has become a critical part of the private cloud infrastructure. This chapter walks you through the recipes to implement Highly Available VMM Server with useful tips and tricks.

Chapter 5, Configuring Fabric Resources in VMM, provides detailed recipes for Fabric Resources configuration and management, which is extremely powerful when configuring resources for hosts, virtual machines, and services. It provides information on configuring and managing the virtualization host, networking, storage, and library resources. The recipes allow you to get more out of this impressive feature and help you understand the logical flow, from preparing the infrastructure to making the infrastructure building blocks available to a private cloud.

Chapter 6, Deploying Virtual Machines and Services, provides information to help the administrator create, deploy, and manage private clouds, virtual machines, templates, and services in System Center VMM 2012; it provides recipes to assist you in getting the most out of deployment.

Chapter 7, Managing VMware ESXi and Citrix® XenServer® Hosts, provides tips and techniques to allow you to integrate VMM directly with VMware vCenter Server and Citrix XenServers, to manage and make their resources available to private cloud deployments. It provides recipes to help you manage the day-to-day operations of VMware ESX/ESXi and Citrix XenServers hosts and clusters, such as the discovery and management of hosts and the ability to create, manage, store, place, and deploy virtual machines and templates, all from the VMM console. It also provides a recipe to add VMware VCenter to VMM to manage VMware Hosts.

Chapter 8, Managing Hybrid Clouds, Fabric Updates, Resources, Clusters, and the New Features of R2, provides recipes with more improvements provided by the VMM 2012. The chapter also explores some of the key features of SP1 and R2, such as Linux VMs, the availability options, resource throttling, and IPAM integration. Additionally, it also provides recipes to integrate VMM with System Center 2012 R2 App Controller for Hybrid Cloud Management.

Chapter 9, Integration with System Center Operations Manager 2012 R2, provides tips and techniques to allow administrators to integrate SCOM 2012 R2 with VMM when monitoring the private cloud infrastructure.

Chapter 10, Scripting in Virtual Machine Manager, provides a useful understanding of VMM PowerShell scripts; they allow you to perform all VMM administrative functions using commands or scripts. You will also find some useful sample scripts in this chapter.

What you need for this book

Depending on your scenario, you will need System Center 2012 R2 Virtual Machine Manager as well as SQL Server (I recommend the 2012 version) installed, as a minimum requirement. The book also covers System Center 2012 R2 Operations Manager and SC App Controller; they will be required depending on the complexity of your scenario. You will also need VMware vCenter if you plan to integrate and manage ESXi hosts as well as Veeam Management Pack to monitor them.

Finally, to integrate with Azure, you will need an Azure subscription (for development/test purposes, you can use the ones that come with the MSDN subscription).

Who this book is for

This book has been written for solutions architects, technical consultants, administrators, and any other virtualization enthusiasts who need to use Microsoft System Center Virtual Machine Manager in a real-world environment. It is assumed that you have previous experience with Windows 2012 R2 and Hyper-V.

Conventions

In this book, you will find a number of styles of text that distinguish between different kinds of information. Here are some examples of these styles, and an explanation of their meaning.

Code words in text, database table names, folder names, filenames, file extensions, pathnames, dummy URLs, user input, and Twitter handles are shown as follows: "Send the ETL file located in `%SystemDrive%\VMMlogs\DebugTrace_%computername%.ETL` to Microsoft."

A block of code is set as follows:

```
;SQL Server 2012 Configuration File
[OPTIONS]
; Setup work flow: INSTALL, UNINSTALL, or UPGRADE.
ACTION="Install"
; Language.
ENU="True"
```

Any command-line input or output is written as follows:

```
winrm qc -q
winrm set winrm/config/service/auth @{CredSSP="True"}
winrm set winrm/config/winrs @{AllowRemoteShellAccess="True"}
winrm set winrm/config/winrs @{MaxMemoryPerShellMB="2048"}
```

New terms and **important words** are shown in bold. Words that you see on the screen, in menus or dialog boxes for example, appear in the text like this: "In the **Server Manager** window, click on **Tools**."

> Warnings or important notes appear in a box like this.

> Tips and tricks appear like this.

Reader feedback

Feedback from our readers is always welcome. Let us know what you think about this book—what you liked or may have disliked. Reader feedback is important for us to develop titles that you really get the most out of.

To send us general feedback, simply send an e-mail to feedback@packtpub.com, and mention the book title via the subject of your message.

If there is a topic that you have expertise in and you are interested in either writing or contributing to a book, see our author guide on www.packtpub.com/authors.

Customer support

Now that you are the proud owner of a Packt book, we have a number of things to help you to get the most from your purchase.

Errata

Although we have taken every care to ensure the accuracy of our content, mistakes do happen. If you find a mistake in one of our books—maybe a mistake in the text or the code—we would be grateful if you would report this to us. By doing so, you can save other readers from frustration and help us improve subsequent versions of this book. If you find any errata, please report them by visiting http://www.packtpub.com/submit-errata, selecting your book, clicking on the **errata submission form** link, and entering the details of your errata. Once your errata are verified, your submission will be accepted and the errata will be uploaded on our website, or added to any list of existing errata, under the Errata section of that title. Any existing errata can be viewed by selecting your title from http://www.packtpub.com/support.

Piracy

Piracy of copyright material on the Internet is an ongoing problem across all media. At Packt, we take the protection of our copyright and licenses very seriously. If you come across any illegal copies of our works, in any form, on the Internet, please provide us with the location address or website name immediately so that we can pursue a remedy.

Please contact us at copyright@packtpub.com with a link to the suspected pirated material.

We appreciate your help in protecting our authors, and our ability to bring you valuable content.

Questions

You can contact us at questions@packtpub.com if you are having a problem with any aspect of the book, and we will do our best to address it.

1

VMM 2012 Architecture

In this chapter, we will cover the following:

- ▶ Understanding each component for a real-world implementation
- ▶ Planning for High Availability
- ▶ Designing the VMM server, database, and console implementation
- ▶ Specifying the correct system requirements for a real-world scenario
- ▶ Licensing the System Center
- ▶ Troubleshooting VMM and supporting technologies

Introduction

This chapter has been designed to provide an understanding of the underlying **Virtual Machine Manager** (**VMM**) modular architecture, which is useful for improving implementation and troubleshooting VMM.

As a reference, this book is based on the System Center 2012 R2 Virtual Machine Manager version.

The first version of VMM was launched in 2007 and was designed to manage virtual machines. The VMM 2012 version is a huge product change that will now give you the power to manage your own private cloud.

The focus of VMM 2012 is the ability to create and manage private clouds, retain the characteristics of public clouds by allowing tenants and delegated VMM administrators to perform functions, and abstract the underlying fabric to let them deploy the VM's applications and services. Although they have no visibility into the underlying hardware, there is a uniform resource pooling that allows you to add or remove the capacity as your environment grows. VMM also supports private clouds across supported hypervisors, such as Hyper-V, Citrix, and VMware.

The main strategies of VMM 2012 are as follows:

- **Application focus**: VMM abstracts fabric (host servers, storage, and networking) into a unified pool of resources. It also gives you the ability to use Server App-V to deploy applications and SQL Server profiles to deploy customized database servers.

- **Service consumer**: One of the powerful features of VMM 2012 is its capability to deploy a service to a private cloud. These services are dependent on multiple VMs that are tied together (for example, web frontend servers, application servers, and backend database servers). These services can be provisioned as simply as provisioning a VM, but they all should be provisioned together.

- **Dynamic Optimization**: This strategy will balance the workload in a cluster, while a feature called **Power Optimization** can turn off physical virtualization host servers when they are not needed. It can then turn them back on when the load increases. This process will automatically move VMs between hosts to balance the load.

- **Multivendor hypervisor support**: The list of managed hypervisors has been extended. VMM 2012 now manages Hyper-V, VMware, and Citrix XenServer, covering all of the major hypervisors on the market.

The following figure highlights VMM Multivendor hypervisor support:

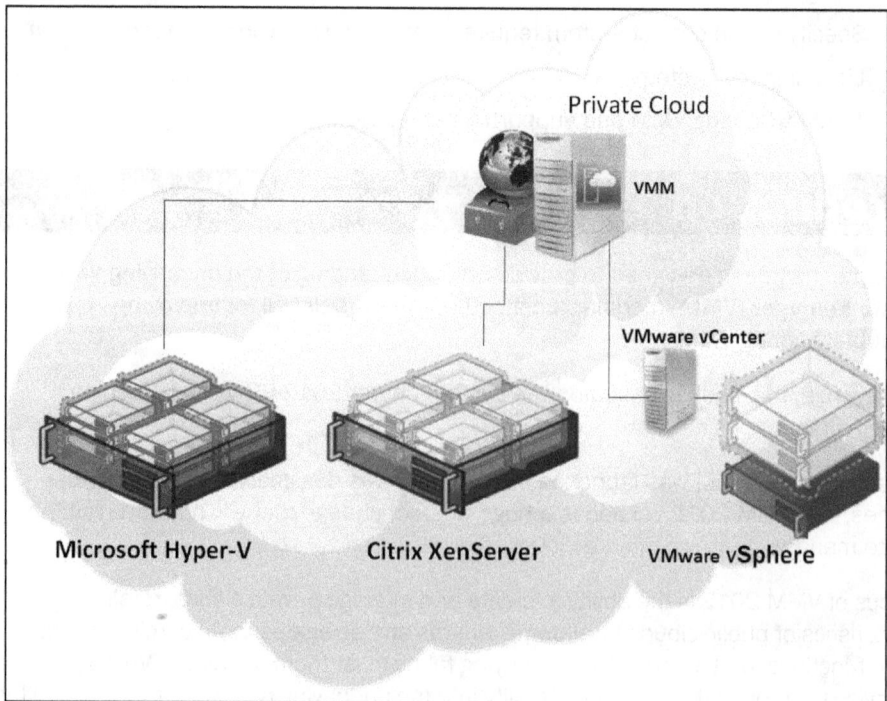

Knowing your current environment – assessment

This is the first step. You need to do an assessment of your current environment to find out how and where the caveats are. You can use the **Microsoft Assessment and Planning** (**MAP**) toolkit (download it from `http://www.microsoft.com/en-us/download/details.aspx?id=7826`) or any other assessment tool to help you carry out a report assessment by querying the hardware, OS, application, and services. It is important to define what you can and need to address and, sometimes, what you cannot virtualize.

> The MAP toolkit will assess your environment using agentless technology to collect data (inventory and performance) to provide reports. Server Consolidation, VMware Discovery , Microsoft Workload Discovery, and Microsoft Private Cloud Fast Track Onboarding Assessment are some of the useful reports that will enable your IT infrastructure planning. For more information, refer to `http://social.technet.microsoft.com/wiki/contents/articles/1640.microsoft-assessment-and-planning-toolkit.aspx`.

Currently, Microsoft supports the virtualization of all MS infrastructure technologies (for example, SQL, Exchange, AD, Lync, IIS, and file server).

Designing the solution

With the assessment report in hand, it is recommended that you spend a reasonable amount of time on the solution design and architecture, and you will have a solid and consistent implementation. The following figure highlights the new VMM 2012 features for you to take into consideration when working on your private cloud design:

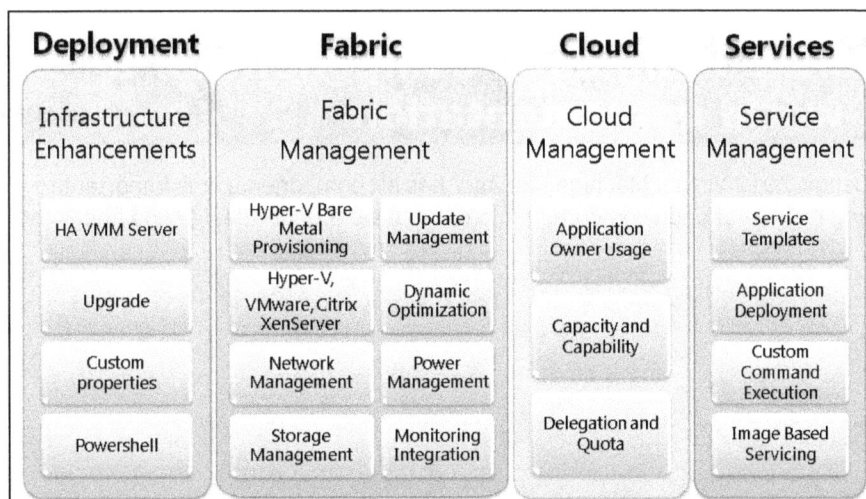

Deployment	Fabric		Cloud	Services
Infrastructure Enhancements	Fabric Management		Cloud Management	Service Management
HA VMM Server	Hyper-V Bare Metal Provisioning	Update Management	Application Owner Usage	Service Templates
Upgrade	Hyper-V, VMware, Citrix XenServer	Dynamic Optimization	Capacity and Capability	Application Deployment
Custom properties	Network Management	Power Management		Custom Command Execution
Powershell	Storage Management	Monitoring Integration	Delegation and Quota	Image Based Servicing

Creating the private cloud fabric

In VMM, before deploying VMs and services to a private cloud, you need to set up the **private cloud fabric**. There are three resources that are included in the fabric in VMM 2012, which are as follows:

- ▸ **Servers**: These contain virtualization hosts (Hyper-V, VMware, and Citrix servers) and groups, **Preboot eXecution Environment** (**PXE**), update servers (that is, Windows Server Update Services), and other servers.

- ▸ **Networking**: This contains the network fabric and devices' configuration (for example, gateways, virtual switches, and network virtualization); it presents the wiring between resource repositories, running instances, VMs, and services.

- ▸ **Storage**: This contains the configuration for storage connectivity and management, simplifying storage complexities, and the way storage is virtualized. It is here that you configure the SMI-S and SMP providers or a Windows 2012 SMB 3.0 file server.

If you are really serious about setting up a private cloud, you should carry out a virtualization assessment using MAP, as discussed earlier, and work on a detailed design document that covers the hardware, hypervisor, fabric, and management. With this in mind, the implementation will be pretty straightforward.

System Center 2012 will help you install, configure, manage, and monitor your private cloud from the fabric to the hypervisor and up to the service deployment. It will also allow you to manage the public cloud (Azure).

> Refer to the *Designing the VMM server, database, and console implementation* recipe in this chapter for further information.

Understanding each component for a real-world implementation

System Center 2012 Virtual Machine Manager has six components. It is important to understand the role of each component in order to have a better design and implementation.

Getting ready

For small deployments, test environments, or a proof of concept, you can install all of the components in one server, but as is the best practice in the production environments, you should consider separating the components.

How to do it...

Let's start by reviewing each component of VMM 2012 and understanding the role it plays:

- ▶ **VMM console**: This application connects to the VMM management server to allow you to manage VMM, centrally view and manage physical and virtual resources (for example, hosts, VMs, services, fabric, and library resources), and carry out tasks on a daily basis, such as VM and services deployment, monitoring, and reporting.

  By using the VMM console from your desktop, you will be able to manage your private cloud without needing to remotely connect it to the VMM management server.

> It is recommended that you install the VMM console on the administrator desktop machine, taking into account the OS and prerequisites, such as a firewall and preinstalled software. See the *Specifying the correct system requirements for a real-world scenario* recipe in this chapter.

- ▶ **The management server**: The management server is the core of VMM. It is the server on which the Virtual Machine Manager service runs to process commands and control communications with the VMM console, the database, the library server, and the hosts.

  Think of the VMM management server as the heart, which means that you need to design your computer resources accordingly to accommodate such an important service.

> For **High Availability** (**HA**), VMM Management Server must be deployed as an HA service on Windows Server Failover Cluster. Note, though, that SQL Server, where the VMM database will be installed and the file share for the library share must also be highly available. For more information, check the *Planning for High Availability* recipe and *Chapter 4, Installing a High Available VMM Server*.

The following figure shows the Windows Failover Cluster Manager console. For HA, you will need to have at minimum two VMM servers on a cluster.

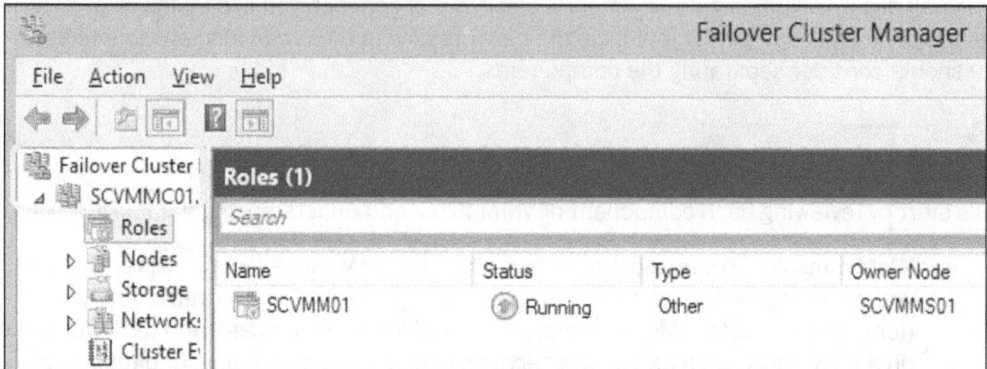

As is the best practice for medium and enterprise production environments, keep the VMM management server on a separate cluster from the production cluster, due to its crucial importance for your private cloud.

▶ **Database**: The database server runs SQL Server and contains all of the VMM data. It plays an important role when you have a clustered VMM deployment by keeping the shared data. The best practice is to also have the SQL database in a cluster.

> When running VMM in a cluster, you cannot install SQL Server in one of the VMM management servers. Instead, you will need to have it on another machine.

▶ **VMM library**: The VMM library servers are file shares, a catalog that stores resources, such as VM templates, virtual hard drive files, ISOs, scripts, and custom resources with a `.cr` extension, which will all be visible and indexed by VMM and then shared among application packages, tenants, and self-service users in private clouds.

The library has been enhanced to support services and the sharing of resources. It is a store for drivers for Bare Metal deployments, **SQL data-tier applications** (**SQL DAC**), and Web Deploy packages.

In a distributed environment, you can group equivalent sets of resources and make them available in different locations by using resource groups. You can also store a resource in a storage group that will allow you to reference that group in profiles and templates rather than in a specific **Virtual Hard Disk** (**VHD**). This is especially important when you have multiple sites, and VMM will automatically select the right resource from a single reference object. This essentially enables one template that can reference an object that can be obtained from multiple locations.

You can also have **application profiles** and **SQL** profiles (answer files for the configuration of the application or SQL) to support the deployment of applications and databases to VM after the base image is deployed. Application profiles can be Server App-V packages, web applications, or a SQL data-tier.

▸ **Self Service Portal**: The web-based Self Service Portal was removed from SC 2012 VMM.

> The Self Service Portal's replacement is SC App Controller.

▸ **VMM command shell**: VMM is based on PowerShell. Everything you can do on the GUI, you can do by using PowerShell. VMM PowerShell extensions make available the cmdlets that perform all of the functions in VMM 2012.

> When working with complex environments, or if you need to automate some process, the PowerShell cmdlets will make your work easier. When performing wizard-based tasks on the GUI, save the PowerShell script for future use and automation.

How it works...

As you may have noticed, although the VMM management is the core, each component is required in order to provide a better VMM experience. In addition to this, for a real-world deployment, you also need to consider implementing other System Center family components to complement your design. Every System Center component is designed to provide part of the private cloud solution. The Microsoft private cloud solution includes the implementation of VMM 2012 plus the following utilities:

▸ **System Center 2012 App Controller**: This provides a common self-service experience across private and public clouds that can help application owners easily build, configure, deploy, and manage services

▸ **System Center 2012 Configuration Manager**: This provides comprehensive configuration management for the Microsoft platform that can help users with the devices and applications they need in order to be productive while maintaining corporate compliance and control

▸ **System Center 2012 Data Protection Manager**: This provides unified data protection for the Windows environment, delivering protection and restore scenarios from the disk, tape, off premise, and cloud

▶ **System Center 2012 Endpoint Protection**: This is built on the System Center Configuration Manager and provides threat detection of malware and exploits as part of a unified infrastructure to manage client security and compliance to simplify and improve the endpoint protection

▶ **System Center 2012 Operations Manager**: This provides deep application diagnostics and infrastructure monitoring to ensure the predictable performance and availability of vital applications, and it offers a comprehensive view of the data center, private cloud, and public clouds

▶ **System Center 2012 Orchestrator**: This provides the orchestration, integration, and automation of IT processes through the creation of **runbooks** to define and standardize best practices and improve operational efficiency

▶ **System Center 2012 Service Manager**: This provides flexible self-service experiences and standardized data center processes to integrate people, workflows, and knowledge across enterprise infrastructure and applications

There's more...

When deploying System Center, there are some other systems and configurations you need to consider.

Windows Azure Pack

Windows Azure Pack (**WAP**) is an administrator portal to manage resources that integrate with System Center and Windows Server to provide a customizable self-service portal to manage services such as websites, Virtual Machines, and Service Bus; it also includes capabilities for automating and integrating additional custom services. For more information, refer to `http://www.microsoft.com/en-us/server-cloud/products/windows-azure-pack/`.

Service Reporting

Service Reporting, an optional component of System Center 2012 R2, enables IT (particularly hosting providers) to create detailed views of the virtual machines' consumption of the resources (CPU, memory, storage, and networking) for each customer (tenant). For more information, refer to `http://technet.microsoft.com/en-us/library/dn251058.aspx`.

Domain controllers

Although the domain controller is not part of the System Center family and is not a VMM component, it plays an important role in the deployment of a private cloud as VMM requires it to be installed on a domain environment.

This requirement is for the System Center VMM. You can have the managed hosts on a workgroup mode or even on a trusted domain other than the System Center domain. We will discuss this later in the chapter.

Windows Server Update Service

Windows Server Update Service (WSUS) plays an important role with reference to the private cloud as it is used to update the Hyper-V hosts, library servers, or any other role for compliance and remediation.

In SC 2012 R2, you can use WSUS for other System Center family components as well.

System Center App Controller

The App Controller provides a self-service experience through a web portal that can help you easily configure, deploy, and manage VMs and services across private, third-party hosters (that support Microsoft Hyper-V) and public clouds (Azure). For example, moving a VM from a private cloud to Azure, creating checkpoints, granting access, scaling out deployed services, and so on.

The App Controller is a replacement for the VMM Self-Service Portal since SC 2012 SP1 and it is the key for Cloud mobility.

System Center components' scenarios

The following table will guide you through choosing the System Center component that is necessary as per your deployment:

Although Configuration Manager (SCCM) is not mentioned in the following table, it plays an important role when it comes to patching Virtual Machine and now you can use SCCM **Task Sequence (TS)**, which is a new feature in SC 2012 R2, on a single process to deploy an OS to a Virtual Hard Disk. For more information, refer to http://technet.microsoft.com/en-us/library/dn448591.aspx.

You should also check Service Management Automation, which will enable Orchestrated offline VM Patching. For more information, refer to http://blogs.technet.com/b/privatecloud/archive/2013/12/07/orchestrated-vm-patching.aspx.

Scenarios	Enabling technologies				
	AppCtrl	Operations Manager	Orchestrator	Service Manager	VMM
The fabric provider					
Bare Metal deploy					√
Integration with network and storage			√		√
Host patching					√
Host Optimization/Power Optimization					√
Monitoring of the fabric		√			√
Capacity reporting		√			√
The service provider					
Service templates (offerings)					√
Service and VM catalog	√			√	√
Life cycle (create, upgrade, and retire)	√		√	√	√
Application and SLA monitoring		√			
SLA and capacity reporting		√		√	
The service consumer					
Request quote or capacity (cloud)			√	√	√
Request/deploy VM	√	√	√	√	√
Request/deploy service	√	√	√	√	√
Quota enforcement	√				√
Request approvals			√	√	

See also

▸ The *Planning for High Availability* recipe

▸ *Chapter 9, Integration with System Center Operations Manager 2012 R2*

▸ *Chapter 10, Scripting in Virtual Machine Manager*

Planning for High Availability

High Availability is important when your business requires minimum or no downtime, and planning for it in advance is very important.

Getting ready

Based on what we learned about each component, we now need to plan the HA for each VMM component.

How to do it...

Start by planning the HA for the core component, followed by every VMM component of your design. It is important to consider the hardware and other System Center components as well the OS and software licenses.

How it works...

When planning for highly available VMM management servers, you should first consider where you can place the VMM cluster. As per best practices, the recommendation is to install the VMM cluster on a management cluster, preferably on physical servers, if using a converged network for your virtual network. However, if you plan to install highly available VMM management servers on the managed cluster, you need to take into consideration the following points:

▶ Only one highly available VMM management server is allowed per failover cluster.

▶ Despite the possibility of having a VMM management server installed on all cluster nodes, only one node can be active at a time.

▶ To perform a planned failover, use **Failover Cluster Manager**. The use of the VMM console is not supported.

▶ In a planned failover situation, ensure that there are no running tasks on the VMM management server, as it will fail during a failover operation and will not automatically restart after the failover operation.

▶ Any connection to a highly available VMM management server from the VMM console will be disconnected during a failover operation, and it will be reconnected right after.

▶ The failover cluster must run Windows Server v2012 or higher in order to be supported.

▶ The highly available VMM management server must meet the system requirements. For information about system requirements for VMM, see the *Specifying the correct system requirements for a real-world scenario* recipe in this chapter.

- ▸ In a highly available VMM management deployment, you will need a domain account to install and run the VMM management service. You are required to use **Distributed Key Management** (**DKM**) to store the encryption keys in Active Directory.

- ▸ A dedicated and supported version of Microsoft SQL Server should be installed. For supported versions of SQL Server for the VMM database, refer to the *Specifying the correct system requirements for a real-world scenario* recipe.

There's more...

The following sections are the considerations for SQL Server and the VMM library in an HA environment.

SQL Server

In an enterprise deployment of VMM, it is recommended that you have a SQL Server cluster to support the HA VMM, preferably on a cluster separated from the VMM cluster. VMM 2012 R2 supports SQL Server **AlwaysOn Availability Groups**. The following link will show you a good example of how you can set it up:

```
http://blogs.technet.com/b/scvmm/archive/2012/10/24/how-to-configure-
sql-2012-alwayson-availability-groups-in-system-center-2012-virtual-
machine-manager-service-pack-1.aspx.
```

The VMM library

As the best practice in an enterprise deployment, it is highly recommended that you use a highly available file server to host the VMM library shares, as VMM does not provide a method to replicate files in the VMM library, and they need to be replicated outside of VMM.

As a suggestion, you can use the Microsoft Robocopy tool to replicate the VMM library files, if necessary.

Designing the VMM server, database, and console implementation

When planning a VMM 2012 design for deployment, consider the different VMM roles, keeping in mind that VMM is part of the Microsoft private cloud solution. If you are considering a private cloud, you will need to integrate VMM with the other System Center family components.

> By integrating VMM 2012 with Microsoft Server App-V, you can create application profiles that will provide instructions for installing Microsoft App-V applications, Microsoft Web Deploy applications, and Microsoft SQL Server data-tier applications. The profiles will also provide instructions for running scripts when deploying a virtual machine as part of a service. It is important to note that if you use Server App-V, you should confirm with the application owner whether the app will be supported if it's sequenced. Web Deploy and SQL DAC would not have the same issue.

In VMM, you can create the hardware, guest operating system, SQL Server, and application profiles that will be used in a template to deploy virtual machines. These profiles are essentially answer files to configure the application or SQL during the setup.

Getting ready

You can create a private cloud by combining hosts, even from different hypervisors (for example, Hyper-V, VMware, and Citrix) with networking, storage, and library resources.

To start deploying VMs and services, you first need to configure the fabric.

How to do it...

Create a spreadsheet with the server names and the IP settings of every System Center component you plan to deploy, as shown in the following table. This will help you manage and integrate the solution.

Server name	Role	IP settings
Vmm-mgmt01	VMM Management Server 01	IP: 10.16.254.20/24
		GW: 10.16.254.1
		DNS: 10.16.254.2
Vmm-mgmt02	VMM Management Server 02	IP: 10.16.254.22/24
		GW: 10.16.254.1
		DNS: 10.16.254.1
Vmm-consol01	VMM console	IP: 10.16.254.50/24
		GW: 10.16.254.1
		DNS: 10.16.254.2
Vmm-lib01	VMM library	IP: 10.16.254.25/24
		GW: 10.16.254.1
		DNS: 10.16.254.2

Server name	Role	IP settings
w2012-sql	SQL Server 2012	IP: 10.16.254.40/24
		GW: 10.16.254.1
		DNS: 10.16.254.2

How it works...

The following rules need to be considered when planning a VMM 2012 deployment:

▶ The computer name cannot contain the character string "SCVMM" (for example, srv-scvmm-01) and cannot exceed 15 characters.

▶ Your VMM database must use a supported version of SQL Server to perform a VMM 2012 deployment. Express editions of Microsoft SQL Server are no longer supported for the VMM 2012 database. For more information, check the system requirements specified in the *Specifying the correct system requirements for a real- world scenario* recipe in this chapter.

> For a full High Available VMM, not only must VMM be deployed on a Failover Cluster (minimum two servers), but the SQL Server must also be deployed on a cluster (minimum two servers).

▶ VMM 2012 R2 does not support a library server on a computer that runs Windows Server 2003/2008; it now requires Windows Server 2012 as a minimum, but for consistence and standardization, I do recommend that you install it on Windows Server 2012 R2.

▶ VMM 2012 no longer supports Microsoft Virtual Server 2005 R2 Hosts. If you are upgrading from a previous version of VMM that has Virtual Server hosts, they will be removed from the VMM 2012 database. If you do not want these hosts to be removed automatically, remove the hosts manually before you start the upgrade process.

▶ Hosts that run the following versions of VMware ESX and VMware vCenter Server are supported:

  ❑ ESX 3.x

  ❑ ESX 4.1

  ❑ ESX 5.0, ESX 5.1

▶ Upgrading a previous version of VMM to a highly available VMM 2012 requires additional preparation. Refer to *Chapter 2, Upgrading from Previous Versions,* for this purpose.

- If you're planning for High Availability of VMM 2012, be sure to install SQL Server on a Cluster and on separate servers as it cannot physically be located on the same servers as your VMM 2012 management server.

- The VMM management server must be a member of a domain. (This rule does not apply to the managed hosts, which can be on a workgroup.)

- The startup RAM for the VMM management server (if running on VM with dynamic memory enabled) must be at least 2048 MB.

- The VMM library does not support **DFS Namespaces** (**DFSN**) or **DFS Replication** (**DFSR**).

- VMM does not support file servers configured with the case-insensitive option for Windows Services for Unix as the network filesystem case control is set to `ignore`. Refer to the *Windows Services for UNIX 2.0 NFS Case Control* article available at `http://go.microsoft.com/fwlink/p/?LinkId=102944` to learn more.

- The VMM console machine must be a member of a domain.

There's more...

For a complete design solution, there are more items you need to consider.

Storage providers – SMI-S and SMP

VMM provides support for both block-level storage (fibre channel, iSCSI, and **Serial Attached SCSI** (**SAS**) connections) and file storage (on SMB 3.0 network shares, residing on a Windows file server or on a NAS device).

By using storage providers, VMM enables discovery, provision, classification, allocation, and decommissioning.

Storage classifications enable you to assign user-defined storage classifications to discovered storage pools for **Quality of Service** (**QoS**) or chargeback purposes.

> You can, for example, assign a classification of GOLD to storage pools that have the highest performance and availability, SILVER for high performance, and BRONZE for low performance.

In order to use this feature, you will need the SMI-S provider.

VMM 2012 R2 can discover and communicate with **Storage Area Network** (**SAN**) arrays through the **Storage Management Initiative** (**SMI-S**) provider and SMP provider.

If your storage is SMI-S compatible, you must install the storage provider on a separately available server (do not install the VMM management server) and then add the provider to the VMM management. If your storage is compatible with SMP, it does not require a provider installation.

> Each vendor has its own SMI-S setup process. My recommendation is that you contact the storage vendor to ask for a storage provider compatible with VMM 2012 R2.

CIM-XML is used by VMM to communicate with the underlying SMI-S providers since VMM never communicates with the SAN arrays itself.

By using the storage provider to integrate with the storage, VMM can create LUNs (both GPT and MBR) and assign storage to hosts or clusters.

> Do not install a storage provider other than the WMI SMP providers from Dell EqualLogic and Nexsan in the VMM Management Server as they are not supported.

VMM 2012 also supports the SAN snapshot and clone feature, allowing you to duplicate a **Logical Unit Number** (**LUN**) through a SAN copy-capable template to provide for new VMs, if you are hosting them in a Hyper-V platform. You will need to provision the outside of VMM for any other VMs hosted with VMware or Citrix hosts.

Bare Metal

This capability enables VMM 2012 to identify the hardware, install the **Operating System** (**OS**), enable the Hyper-V role, and add the machine to a target-host group with streamlined operations in an automated process.

> You can now deploy Bare Metal File Servers (clusters), which are new to SC 2012 R2.

The PXE capability is required and is an integral component of the server pool. The target server will need to have a **Baseboard Management Controller** (**BMC**) that supports one of the following management protocols:

- ▶ **Data Center Management Interface** (**DCMI**) 1.0
- ▶ **Systems Management Architecture for Server Hardware** (**SMASH**) 1.0
- ▶ **Intelligent Platform Management Interface** (**IPMI**) 1.5 or 2.0
- ▶ HP **Integrated Lights-Out** (**iLO**) 2.0

Enterprise and hosting companies will benefit from the ability to provide new Hyper-V servers without having to install the Operating System manually on each machine. By using BMC and integrating with **Windows Deployment Services** (**WDS**), VMM deploys the OS to designated hosts through the boot from the VHD(X) feature.

Configuring security

To ensure that users can perform only assigned actions on selected resources, create tenants, self-service users, delegated administrators, and read-only administrators in VMM using the VMM console. You will need to create **Run As** accounts to provide necessary credentials for performing operations in VMM (for example, adding hosts).

Run As accounts in VMM

Run As accounts are a very useful addition to enterprise environments. These accounts are used to store credentials that allow you to delegate tasks to other administrators and self-service users *without exposing sensitive credentials*.

> By using Windows **Data Protection API** (**DPAPI**), VMM provides OS-level data protection when storing and retrieving the Run As account.

There are several different categories of Run As accounts, which are listed as follows:

- **Host computer**: This is used to provide access to Hyper-V, VMware ESX, and Citrix XenServer hosts

- **BMC**: This is used to communicate with BMC on the host computer for out-of-band management

- **Network device**: This is used to connect to network load balancers

- **Profile**: This is to be used for service creation in the OS and application profiles as well as SQL and host profiles

- **External**: This is to be used for external systems such as System Center Operations Manager

Only administrators or delegated administrators can create and manage Run As accounts.

> During the installation of the VMM management server, you will be requested to use **DKM** to store encryption keys in **Active Directory Domain Services** (**AD DS**).

Ports' communications and protocols for firewall configuration

When designing the VMM implementation, you need to plan which ports you are going to use for communication and file transfers between VMM components. Based on the chosen ports, you will also need to configure your host and external firewalls. Refer to the *Configuring ports and protocols on the host firewall for each VMM component* recipe in *Chapter 3, Installing VMM 2012 R2*.

> Not all of the ports can be changed through VMM. Hosts and library servers must have access to the VMM management server on the ports specified during the setup. This means that all firewalls, whether software-based or hardware-based, must be previously configured.

The VM storage placement

My recommendation is to create a big CSV volume spread across multiple disk spindles, as it will give great storage performance for VMs, as opposed to creating volumes based on the VHD purpose (for example, OS, data, and logs).

Management clusters

The best practice is to have a separate management cluster to manage the production, test, and development clusters.

In addition to this, although you can virtualize the domain controllers with Windows 2012, it is not the best practice to have all the domain controllers running on the management clusters, as the cluster and System Center components highly depend on the domain controllers.

The following figure shows you a two-node management cluster with System Center 2012 and SQL Server cluster installed in separate VMs to manage the production cluster:

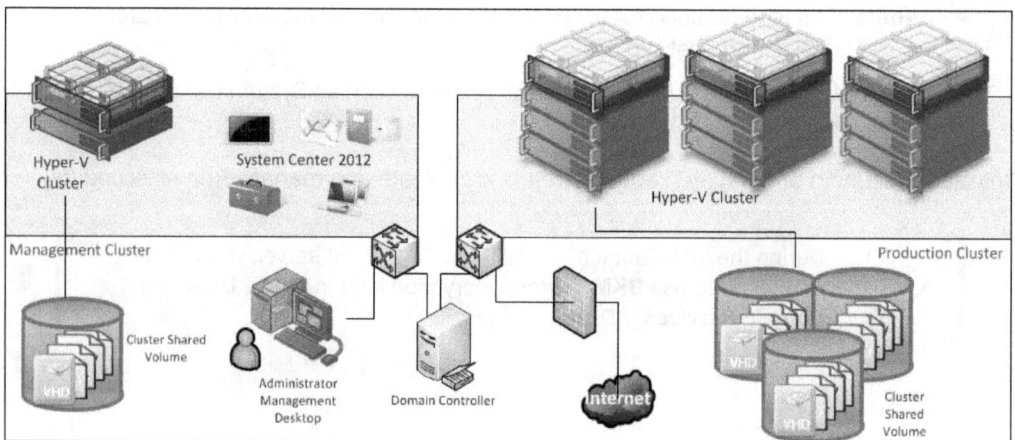

Small environment

In a small environment, you can have all the VMM components located on the same server. A small business may or may not have High Availability in place as VMM 2012 is now a critical component for your private cloud deployment.

Start by selecting the VMM server's location, which could be a physical server or a virtual machine.

You can install SQL Server on the VMM server as well, but as VMM 2012 does not support SQL Express editions, you will need to install SQL Server first and then proceed with the VMM installation.

If you are managing more than 10 hosts in the production environment, my recommendation would be that you have SQL Server running on a separate machine.

It is important to understand that when deploying VMM in production environments (real-world scenarios), the business will require a reliable system that it can trust.

The following figure illustrates a real-world deployment where all VMM 2012 components are installed on the same VM and SQL is running on a separate VM:

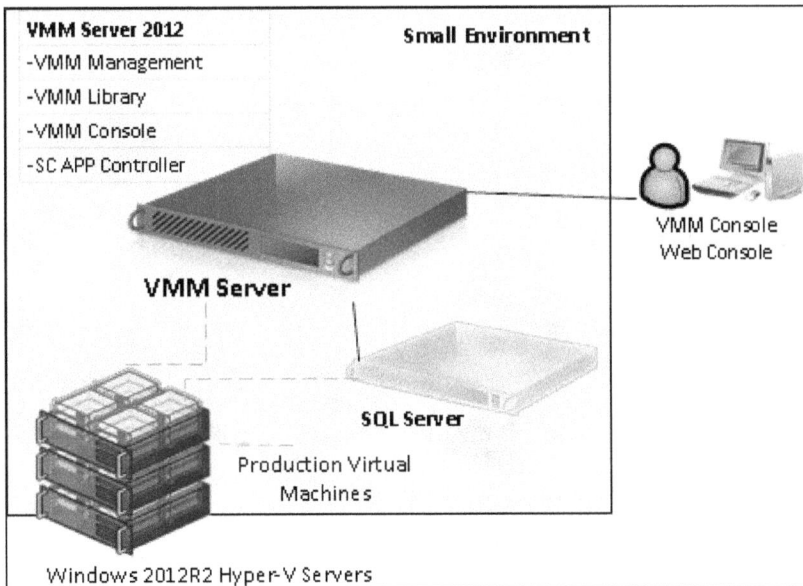

> This deployment won't allow for converged network if no dedicated network adapter is provided for VMM Management.

Lab environments

I would recommend up to 50 hosts in a lab environment with SQL Server and all VMM components installed on a single VM. This will work well, but I would not recommend this installation in a production environment.

Medium and enterprise environments

In a medium- or large-scale environment, the best practice is to split the roles across multiple servers or virtual machines. By splitting the components, you can scale out and introduce High Availability to the System Center environment.

In the following design, you can see each component and what role it performs in the System Center Virtual Machine Manager environment:

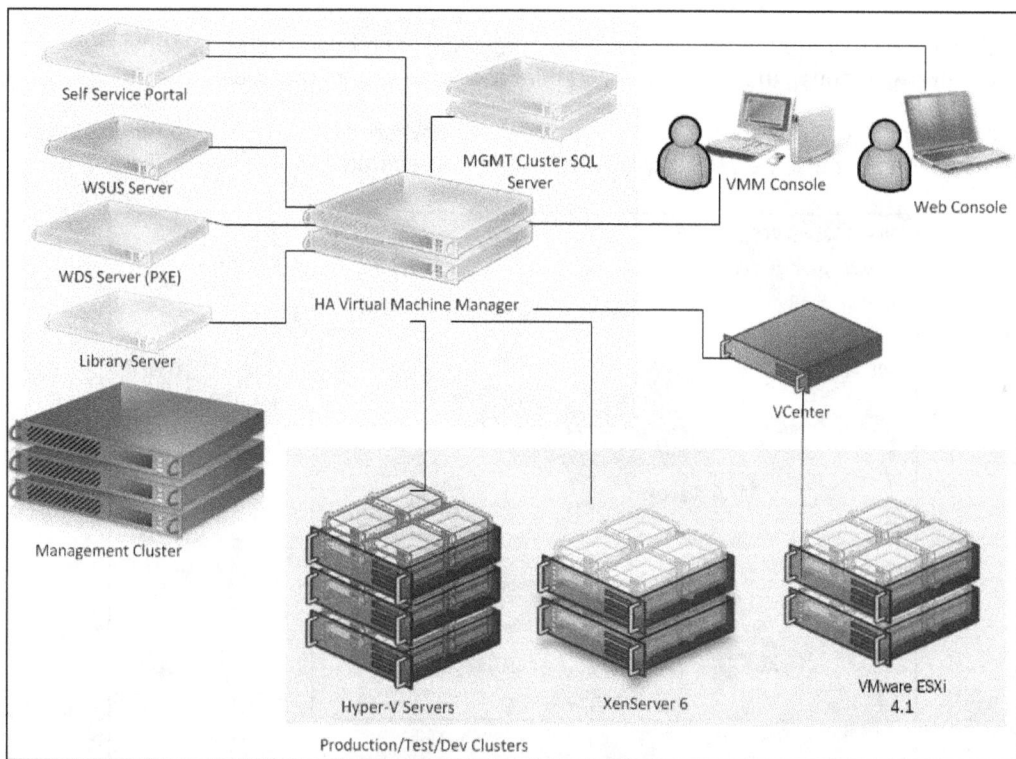

When designing an enterprise private cloud infrastructure, you should take into consideration some key factors such as business requirements, company policies, applications, services, workloads, current hardware, network infrastructure, storage, security, and users.

Private cloud sample infrastructure

The following is a sample of a real-world infrastructure that can support up to 3000 VMs and 64 server nodes that run Windows 2012 R2 Hyper-V.

The number of VMs you can run on an implementation such as this will depend on some key factors. Do not take the following configuration as a mirror for your deployment but as a starting point. My recommendation is that you start understanding the environment, and then run a capacity planner such as a MAP toolkit. It will help you gather information that you can use to design your private cloud.

I am assuming a ratio of 50 VMs per node cluster with 3 GB of RAM, which has been configured to use **Dynamic Memory (DM)**.

- **Servers**
    - 64 servers (4 clusters x 16 nodes)
    - A dual processor of 6 cores, which makes it 12 cores in total
    - 192 GB RAM
    - 2 x 146 GB local HDD (ideally SDD) in Raid 1

- **Storage**

    Switch and host redundancy

    - A fibre channel or iSCSI
    - An array with the capacity to support customer workloads
    - A switch with connectivity for all hosts

- **Network**

    A switch that provides switch redundancy and sufficient port density and connectivity to all hosts. It provides support for VLAN tagging and trunking. NIC Team and VLAN are recommended for better network availability, security, and performance achievement.

- **Storage connectivity**
    - **If it uses a fibre channel**: 2 x 4 GB HBAs
    - **If it uses ISCSI**: 2 x dedicated NICs (recommended 10 GbE)

- **Network connectivity**
    - **If it maintains a 1 GbE connectivity**: 6 dedicated 1 GbE (live migration, CSV, management, virtual machines' traffic)
    - **If it maintains a 10 GbE connectivity**: 3 dedicated NICs 10 GbE (live migration, CSV, management, and virtual machines' traffic)

Hosting environments

System Center 2012 SP1 VMM introduced multi-tenancy. This is one of the most important features for hosting companies as they only need to install a single copy of System Center VMM and then centralize their customer management, each running in a controlled environment in their own domain. Hosting companies want to maximize their compute capacity and a VLAN segmented on hardware won't allow for that. Network virtualization moves the isolation up to the software stack, enabling the hoster to maximize all the capacity and isolate customers via software-defined networking.

New networking features in VMM 2012 R2

VMM 2012 R2 brings a new networking feature: network virtualization. Taking advantage of Windows Server 2012 R2's new features, VMM now delivers site-to-site NVGRE gateway for Hyper-V network virtualization. This new capability will now enable you to use network virtualization to support multiple site-to-site tunnels and direct access through a NAT firewall. **Networking Virtualization** (**NV**) now uses the NVGRE protocol, allowing network load balancers to act as NV gateways. Plus, switch extensions can make use of NV policies to interpret the IP information in packets being sent, and the communication between Cisco switches and VMM is now expanded to support Hyper-V NV.

See also

- ▶ The *Planning for High Availability* recipe
- ▶ The *Configuring ports and protocols on the host firewall for each VMM component* recipe in *Chapter 3, Installing VMM 2012 R2*
- ▶ The *Rapid Provisioning of Virtual Machines Using SAN Copy Overview* article at `http://technet.microsoft.com/en-us/library/gg610594.aspx`
- ▶ The *Understanding Generation 1 and Generation 2 Virtual Machines in VMM* article at `http://technet.microsoft.com/en-us/library/dn440675.aspx`
- ▶ For more information on SMI-S, refer to the link at `http://www.snia.org/ctp/conformingproviders/index.html`
- ▶ For more information on DPAPI architecture and security, visit the link at `http://go.microsoft.com/fwlink/p/?LinkID=213089`

Specifying the correct system requirements for a real-world scenario

In a real-world production environment, you need to specify a system according to the design and business requirements.

Getting ready

When specifying the hardware for your private cloud deployment, take into consideration future growth needs. It is also important to apply the latest OS and software updates.

How to do it...

Use the following tables to carry out an extensive documentation of the hardware and software requirements for your deployment.

Create a document that outlines every solution component, describing the system requirements, before starting to implement it.

How it works...

The following table shows you the supported OS and servers for SC 2012 R2:

Component	OS/Server supported	Version
VMM server	Windows Server 2012	64 bit (Standard and Datacenter)
	Windows Server 2012 R2	
VMM database	SQL Server 2008 R2 SP1 or higher	Standard, Enterprise, and Datacenter
	SQL Server 2012 and SQL Server 2012 SP1	
VMM console	Windows Server 2008 R2 SP1	64 bit (Standard, Enterprise, and Datacenter)
	Windows Server 2012 and Windows 2012 R2	64 bit (Standard and Datacenter)
	Windows 7 SP1	x86 and x64 Enterprise and Ultimate
	Windows 8 and Windows 8.1	x86 and x64

Component	OS/Server supported	Version
VMM library	Windows Server 2008 R2 SP1	Standard, Enterprise, and Datacenter
	Windows Server 2012 and Windows 2012 R2	(full installation or Server Core installation)
SC App Controller	Windows Server 2008 R2 SP1	Standard, Enterprise, and Datacenter
	Windows Server 2012 and Windows 2012 R2	64 bit (Standard and Datacenter)
WSUS	Windows Server 2012 and Windows 2012 R2 - WSUS 3.0 SP2	64 bit (Standard and Datacenter)
PXE	Windows Server 2008 R2, Windows Server 2012, or Windows Server 2012 R2	64 bit (Standard and Datacenter)

For any procedure that uses `.vhdx`, the library server must be running on Windows Server 2012.

The following are the hardware requirements to consider when specifying your VMM environment. The minimum values are the Microsoft-recommended values.

The first scenarios would be for up to 50 hosts, SMB environments, POC, and demos (all components installed on a single server). Although, for this type of scenario, you can have SQL installed on the VMM management server, the recommendation is to have SQL Server installed on another server:

Hardware component	Minimum	Recommended
Processor	One Processor, 2 GHz (x64)	Dual processor, dual core, 2.8 GHz (x64) or higher
RAM	4 GB	6 GB [*2]
Hard disk space (recommended OS partition) [*4]	20 GB	40 GB or higher
Hard disk space (VMM components) [*1] [*4]	80 GB [*2]	150 GB [*2]
Hard disk space (VMM library) [*1] [*4]	As a minimum, I recommend 80 GB, taking into consideration some samples from real-world implementation. However, this will vary depending on business requirements, the number and size of the files stored, and especially when working with templates.	

Hardware component	Minimum	Recommended
Roles	VMM management	
	VMM library	
	VMM console	
	VMM database (SQL Server full version—Standard or Enterprise) [3]	

[1] Excluding OS partition

[2] With a full version of Microsoft SQL Server installed on the same server

[3] The recommendation is to have SQL Server installed on another server

[4] The recommended minimum total hard disk space for this deployment with full SQL is 270 GB

The second scenario would be for up to 150 hosts. In this scenario, the recommendation is to have each component installed on a separate server, especially the VMM library server. Although (and this is not recommended) you can install SQL Server on the VMM management server as well.

The following table will give you hardware requirements for the VMM management server:

Hardware component	Minimum	Recommended
Processor	Pentium 4, 2 GHz (x64)	Dual processor, dual core, 2.8 GHz (x64) or greater
RAM	2 GB	4 GB [2] / 6 GB [3]
Hard disk space [1]	2 GB [2]/ 80 GB [3]	40 GB [2] / 150 GB [3]

[1] Excluding OS partition

[2] Without a local VMM database (SQL Server installed)

[3] With a local VMM database (Microsoft SQL Server installed on the same server)

The following table will give you hardware requirements for the VMM database server:

Hardware component	Minimum	Recommended
Processor	Pentium 4, 2.8 GHz	Dual core 64 bit, 2 GHz
RAM	2 GB	4 GB
Hard disk space*	80 GB	150 GB

* Excluding OS partition

The following table will give you hardware requirements for the VMM console:

Hardware component	Minimum	Recommended
Processor	Pentium 4, 550 MHz	Pentium 4, 1 GHz or higher
RAM	512 MB	1 GB
Hard disk space *	512 MB	2 GB
* Excluding OS partition		

The following table will give you hardware requirements for the VMM library server.

The minimum and recommended requirements for a VMM library server will be determined by the quantity and size of the files that will be stored.

Hardware component	Minimum	Recommended
Processor	Pentium 4, 2.8 GHz	Dual core 64 bit, 3.2 GHz or higher
RAM	2 GB	2 GB
Hard disk space	As a minimum, I recommend 80 GB, taking into consideration the following table that contains some samples of real image sizes. However, the recommended size will vary depending on business requirements and on the number and size of files stored, especially when working with templates.	

The following table will give you sizes of different ISO images:

Image	ISO size	Application
en_windows_server_2008_r2_with_sp1_vl_build_x64_dvd_617403	2.94 GB	Windows 2008 R2
en_install_disc_windows_small_business_server_2011_standard_x64_dvd_611535	6.35 GB	SBS 2001
en_office_professional_plus_2010_x86_515486	650 MB	Office 2010

The following table will give you hardware requirements for the VMM management server:

Hardware component	Minimum	Recommended
Processor	Pentium 4, 2.8 GHz (x64)	Dual processor, dual core, 3.6 GHz or higher (x64)
RAM	4 GB	8 GB
Hard disk space*	10 GB	50 GB
* Excluding OS partition		

The following table will give you hardware requirements for the VMM database server:

Hardware component	Minimum	Recommended
Processor	Dual-Core 64-bit, 2 GHz	Dual core 64 bit, 2.8 GHz
RAM	4 GB	8 GB
Hard disk space *	150 GB	200 GB
* Excluding OS partition		

The following table will give you hardware requirements for the VMM console:

Hardware component	Minimum	Recommended
Processor	Pentium 4, 1 GHz	Pentium 4, 2 GHz or higher
RAM	1 GB	2 GB
Hard disk space *	512 MB	4 GB
* Excluding OS partition		

The following table will give you hardware requirements for the VMM library server.

The minimum and recommended requirements for a VMM library server will be determined by the quantity and size of the files that will be stored.

Hardware component	Minimum	Recommended
Processor	Pentium 4, 2.8 GHz	Dual core 64 bit, 3.2 GHz or higher
RAM	2 GB	2 GB
Hard disk space	As a minimum, I recommend 80 GB*, taking into consideration the following table that contains some samples of real image sizes. However, the recommended size will vary depending on business requirements and the number and size of files stored, especially when working with templates.	
* Excluding OS partition		

The following table shows you the software requirements for the VMM management for SC 2012 R2:

Software requirement	Notes
Windows Remote Management (WinRM) 2.0	The WinRM service is set to start automatically (delayed start). If it is not configured in this way (manually modified or by GPO), you must configure and start it before installing VMM.
Microsoft .NET Framework 4.0, or Microsoft .NET Framework 4.5	This is included in Windows Server 2012/ R2. Microsoft .NET Framework 4.5 is available at `http://go.microsoft.com/fwlink/p/?LinkId=267119`.
Windows Automated Installation Kit (AIK)	To install the Windows AIK, you need to download the ISO from `http://go.microsoft.com/fwlink/p/?LinkID=194654`, burn the ISO file to a DVD or map the ISO if VMM is a VM, and then install the Windows AIK. **Important** Windows ADK replaced Windows Automated Installation (Windows AIK) as a VMM prerequisite in VMM 2012 R2.
A supported version of SQL Server (if you're installing SQL on the VMM management server)	Refer to the first table in this section for the supported OS's and servers for SC 2012 R2.
SQL Server 2012 Command Line Utilities	The SQLCMD utility allows users to connect to, send Transact-SQL batches from, and output row set information from SQL Server 2005, SQL Server 2008, SQL Server 2008 R2, and SQL Server 2012 instances (`http://go.microsoft.com/fwlink/?LinkID=239650&clcid=0x409`).
Microsoft SQL Server Native Client	This contains runtime support for applications using native code APIs (ODBC, OLE DB, and ADO) to connect to Microsoft SQL Server 2005, 2008, 2008 R2, and SQL Server 2012. SQL Server Native Client is used to enhance applications that need to take advantage of new SQL Server 2012 features (`http://go.microsoft.com/fwlink/?LinkID=239648&clcid=0x409`).

The following table shows the requirement for the VMM console:

Software requirement	Notes
Windows PowerShell 2.0	This is included in Windows Server 2008 R2 and Windows 7
At least Microsoft .NET Framework 3.5 Service Pack 1 (SP1)	On a computer that runs Windows 7, .NET Framework 3.5.1 will be installed by default.
	On a computer that runs Windows Server 2008 R2, if the .NET Framework 3.5.1 feature is not installed (not installed by default), the VMM setup wizard will install it.

The following table shows the requirement for the VMM library:

Software requirement	Notes
Windows Remote Management (WinRM) 1.1 or 2.0	Version 1.1 is included in Windows Server 2008
	Version 2.0 is included in Windows Server 2008 R2
	By default, the WinRM (WS-Management) service is set to start automatically (delayed start). If it is not configured in this way (manually modified or by GPO), it must be configured and started before the setup can continue.

See also

▶ Download the Windows Assessment and Deployment Kit (ADK) for Windows 8.1 at `http://www.microsoft.com/en-us/download/details.aspx?id=39982`

Licensing the System Center

System Center 2012 is licensed with two versions, Standard and Datacenter. The same capabilities across editions are differentiated only by virtualization rights. All System Center components are included in these two editions.

Getting ready

The license is now required only to manage endpoints. No additional licenses are required for management consoles and they are available exclusively with Software Assurance.

How to do it...

As part of the private cloud design solution, you need to define the license that you will need, based on your solution design and business requirements.

[For updated information about licensing, go to `https://www.microsoft.com/licensing/about-licensing/SystemCenter2012-R2.aspx`.]

How it works...

The following is the license summary for System Center 2012 R2:

  ▸ **For endpoints being managed**: No additional licenses are needed for management servers or SQL Server technology

  ▸ **Consistent licensing model across editions**: Processor-based license that covers server management (up to two processors). User-based or OS environment (OSE)-based license for client management

System Center 2012 editions	Datacenter	Standard
Recommendation	For highly virtualized environments	For lightly or non-virtualized environments
Virtualization rights	Unlimited	Two Operating Systems
Capabilities	All SC components and all workload types	All SC components and all workload types
License type	Covers up to two processors	

Troubleshooting VMM and supporting technologies

This recipe will take you through the process of troubleshooting VMM and its supporting technologies for a successful VMM deployment.

Getting ready

Having an understanding of the core technologies that VMM depends on in order to work correctly is the initial step to troubleshooting VMM:

► WS Management (WinRM)

► WMI

► BITS

► DCOM

► WCF

Troubleshooting is never an easy task, but VMM 2012 provides tools and ways to help you find and remediate an issue.

How to do it...

The following are some techniques you can use to troubleshoot:

► **Event logs**: A good starting point is to look at the event logs. Look for OS- and VMM-related errors or failures. A problem with the Operating System or one of its core services could result or lead to a problem in VMM.

  For example, if you are running SQL Server on the same server and it did not start, the VMM management service will not start either and VMM operations will fail as a direct result of this. You can easily find this by looking for errors in the system or application logs or errors that would indicate, in this example, that the service is not running (for this example, you can also check `Services.msc`).

► **VM manager log**: When looking for VMM errors, it is recommended that you look at the VM Manager log as well. To do so, perform the following steps on the VMM server that runs Windows 2012:

  1. In the **Server Manager** window, click on **Tools**.

  2. Select **Event Viewer**, expand **Applications and Services logs**, and then select the **VM Manager** log.

- **VMM installation-related troubleshooting logs**: VMM records information about the VMM agent installation. However, if the installation logging is not sufficient to determine the cause of failure, you can enable tracing by using the VMM MPS Reports tool and then restart the installation.

- **VMM server setup logging**: Installation logs are written, by default, to the `C:\ProgramData\VMMLogs` hidden folder.

- **VMM agent installation logging**: When installing an MSI package, such as installing the VMM agent manually, you can enable logging using the following syntax:

  ```
  msiexec /I <MSIPackageName.msi> /L*V <path\logfilename>.log
  ```

  For example, using the syntax, we can come up with something like the following command:

  ```
  msiexec /I "C:\setup\vmmAgent.msi" /L*V vmmagent.log
  ```

  The local agent installation information is logged in the `C:\ProgramData\VMMLogs` hidden folders.

  Look for the log file, `vmmAgent.msi_<m-d-yyyy_hh-mm-dss>.log`.

> In logs, it is common to see errors shown as **Carmine** errors. Carmine was a VMM project name code during its development process.

- **Troubleshooting WinRM**: To check whether WinRM has remote access, check the following:

  - The **Security Identifier** (**SID**) in **RootSDDL** maps to the **Virtual Machine Manager Servers** local group on each Hyper-V host
  - The local group contains the account that VMM management service runs as a service

How it works...

A good understanding of what a successful installation log contains from a POC or a pilot environment is important to identify possible issues, especially if it appears when deploying VMM on a production environment, as you can then compare both logs.

There's more...

Run the following command on the Hyper-V host:

```
winrm id
```

This should produce an output similar to the following one:

```
IdentifyResponse
ProtocolVersion = http://schemas.dmtf.org/wbem/wsman/1/wsman.xsd
ProductVendor = Microsoft Corporation
ProductVersion = OS: 6.1.7201 SP: 0.0 Stack: 2.0
```

If the result shows an error, run the following command for a quick configuration of WinRM:

```
winrm qc
```

If prompted, answer Yes. You will receive a response similar to the following one:

```
WinRM already is set up to receive requests on this machine.
WinRM is not set up to allow remote access to this machine for
management.
The following changes must be made:
Enable the WinRM firewall exception

Make these changes [y/n]?
WinRM has been updated for remote management.
WinRM firewall exception enabled.
WinRM can now be tested again by typing 'winrm id' as before
```

Now, check the listener with the following command:

```
winrm enum winrm/config/listener
```

Run the following command on the VMM management server:

```
winrm id -r:http://HyperVHost.yourdomain.local:5985  -
u:YOURDOMAIN\AdminUser
```

The result will be similar to the following one:

```
IdentifyResponse
ProtocolVersion = http://schemas.dmtf.org/wbem/wsman/1/wsman.xsd
ProductVendor = Microsoft Corporation
ProductVersion = OS: 6.1.7201 SP: 0.0 Stack: 2.0
```

Otherwise, you will receive the following error:

```
Error number: -2144108526 0x80338012
The Client cannot connect to the destination specified in the request
```

This could indicate communication issues, so check your network, host firewall, and connectivity.

Most WinRM-related events appear in the system or application event logs. The Service Control Manager often contains the error, as the WinRM service has terminated or restarted for some reason.

During the VMM installation, you will get the following error:

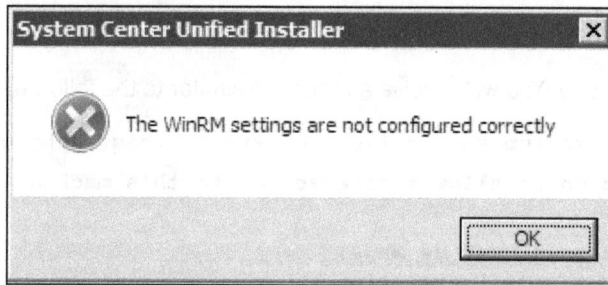

To avoid this scenario, conduct the following checks:

> ▸ Make sure that you have installed all of the prerequisites

> ▸ Check the firewall rules and make sure the ports are configured correctly

> ▸ Open the command prompt (**Run as Administrator**) and type the following commands:

```
winrm qc -q
winrm set winrm/config/service/auth @{CredSSP="True"}
winrm set winrm/config/winrs @{AllowRemoteShellAccess="True"}
winrm set winrm/config/winrs @{MaxMemoryPerShellMB="2048"}
```

Verifying WMI providers

You can check whether the WinRM can communicate with OS WMI providers by running the following command:

```
winrm enum wmi/root/cimv2/Win32_ComputerSystem -
r:http://servername:5985 [-u:YOURDOMAIN\AdminUser]
```

By running the following command, you can check whether the WinRM can communicate with Hyper-V WMI providers:

```
winrm enum wmi/root/virtualization/msvm_computersystem

-r:http://servername:5985 [-u:YOURDOMAIN\AdminUser]
```

Also, to check whether WinRM can communicate with the VMM agent WMI provider, run the following command:

```
winrm invoke GetVersion wmi/root/scvmm/AgentManagement
-r:servername [-u:YOURDOMAIN\AdminUser] @{}
```

> If you are using VMM services, do not remove and re-add the host. Instead, evacuate the host before removing it or, on the host, uninstall and then reinstall the agent manually, and then reassociate it in VMM.

Troubleshooting tools

The following are the troubleshooting tools available for use:

- **Windows Management Instrumentation Tester** (wbemtest.exe): The wbemtest. exe tool gives you the ability to query WMI namespaces on local or remote servers.

  Connecting to a namespace locally indicates that it is properly registered and is accessible via the WMI service. By connecting to a remote server additionally, it also indicates that the WMI connectivity between the two machines is working.

  For more information about wbemtest, refer to the link at http://technet. microsoft.com/en-us/library/cc785775.aspx.

- **WMI Service Control Utility**: This tool configures and controls the WMI service, allowing namespace permissions to be modified.

  To open this tool, type in the following command in the command prompt:

  ```
  winmgmt.msc
  ```

  Then, perform the following steps:

  1. Right-click on **WMI Control (Local)**.
  2. Select **Properties**.
  3. Click on the **Security** tab, and then select **Root**.
  4. Click on the **Security** button to check the permissions.

Background Intelligent Transfer Service troubleshooting

Background Intelligent Transfer Service (**BITS**) transfers files between machines, providing information about the operation's progress. The transfer can be asynchronous.

In VMM, BITS is used for encrypted data transfer between managed computers. Encryption is done by using a self-signed certificate that is generated when the Hyper-V host is added to VMM.

You can use **BITSadmin** to verify that BITS is working properly outside of VMM. BITSadmin can be downloaded at `http://msdn.microsoft.com/en-us/library/aa362813(VS.85).aspx`.

You can also find some examples of BITSadmin at `http://msdn.microsoft.com/en-us/library/aa362812(VS.85).aspx`.

Data collection tools

The following tools are used to collect data surrounding VMM issues:

▶ **VMM tracing tools**: VMM tracing tools provide the ability to manage, collect, and view various traces and diagnostic information in a VMM environment.

When you face an issue and need to report it to Microsoft, you can gather the trace by performing the following steps:

1. In the VMM server, open the command prompt with administrative rights and type in the following command:

   ```
   logman create trace
   ```

   ```
   VMMDebug -v mmddhhmm -o %SystemDrive%\VMMlogs\
   DebugTrace_%computername%.ETL -cnf 01:00:00 -p Microsoft-
   VirtualMachineManager-Debug
   ```

2. Start the trace collection by executing the following command:

   ```
   logman start VMMDebug
   ```

3. Next, try to reproduce the issue, and at the end, stop the trace collection by executing the following command:

   ```
   logman stop VMMDebug
   ```

4. Send the ETL file located in `%SystemDrive%\VMMlogs\DebugTrace_%computerna;me%.ETL` to Microsoft.

5. Delete the debug information by executing the following command:

   ```
   logman delete VMMDebug
   ```

▸ **The VMM TraceViewer utility**: After gathering the trace, you can use **TraceViewer** on the traces. This tool converts the ETL binary trace logs into CAR files that can be viewed in both the TraceViewer and other trace parsing tools and provides basic trace parsing.

To convert the ETL file, perform the following steps:

1. In the TraceViewer, drag the trace file into the open pane.

2. Provide the location to where you want to save the CAR file. Once the file has been saved, TraceViewer will open the converted ETL file for analysis.

3. You can download the tool from `http://blogs.technet.com/b/ jonjor/archive/2011/01/07/vmmtrace-simplified-scvmm- tracing.aspx`.

See also

▸ The *Configuring ports and protocols on the host firewall for each VMM component* recipe in *Chapter 3, Installing VMM 2012 R2*

2
Upgrading from Previous Versions

In this chapter, we will cover the following:

- ▸ Reviewing the upgrade options
- ▸ Checking the VMM system requirements and preparing for the upgrade
- ▸ Upgrading to VMM 2012 R2
- ▸ Reassociating hosts after upgrading
- ▸ Updating the VMM agents
- ▸ Performing other post-upgrade tasks

Introduction

This chapter is about guiding you through the requirements and steps necessary to upgrade your VMM 2008 R2 SP1 to VMM 2012 R2.

> There is no direct upgrade path from VMM 2008 R2 SP1 to VMM 2012 R2. You must first upgrade to VMM 2012 and then to VMM 2012 R2. VMM 2008 R2 SP1-> VMM 2012-> SCVMM 2012 SP1 -> VMM 2012 R2 is the correct upgrade path.

Upgrade notes:

- ▸ VMM 2012 cannot be upgraded directly to VMM 2012 R2. Upgrading it to VMM 2012 SP1 is required

- VMM 2012 can be installed on a Windows 2008 Server

- VMM 2012 SP1 requires Windows 2012

- VMM 2012 R2 requires minimum Windows 2012 (Windows 2012 R2 is recommended)

- Windows 2012 hosts can be managed by VMM 2012 SP1

- Windows 2012 R2 hosts require VMM 2012 R2

- System Center App Controller versions must match the VMM version

> To debug a VMM installation, the logs are located in `%ProgramData%\VMMLogs`, and you can use the `CMTrace.exe` tool to monitor the content of the files in real time, including `SetupWizard.log` and `vmmServer.log`.

As discussed in *Chapter 1, VMM 2012 Architecture*, VMM 2012 is a huge product upgrade, and there have been many improvements; go through the chapter for more details.

This chapter only covers the VMM upgrade.

> If you have a previous version of System Center family components installed on your environment, make sure you follow the upgrade and installation. System Center 2012 R2 has some new components, in which the installation order is also critical. It is critical that you take the steps documented by Microsoft in *Upgrade Sequencing for System Center 2012 R2* at `http://go.microsoft.com/fwlink/?LinkId=328675` and use the following upgrade order:
>
> - Service Management Automation
> - Orchestrator
> - Service Manager
> - Data Protection Manager (DPM)
> - Operations Manager
> - Configuration Manager
> - Virtual Machine Manager (VMM)
> - App Controller
> - Service Provider Foundation
> - Windows Azure Pack for Windows Server
> - Service Bus Clouds
> - Windows Azure Pack
> - Service Reporting
>
> Before we start, I recommend that you go through *Chapter 1, VMM 2012 Architecture*, and pay special attention to the *Specifying the correct system requirements for a real-world scenario* recipe.

Reviewing the upgrade options

This recipe will guide you through the upgrade options for VMM 2012 R2. Keep in mind that there is no direct upgrade path from VMM 2008 R2 to VMM 2012 R2.

How to do it...

Read through the following recommendations in order to upgrade your current VMM installation.

In-place upgrade from VMM 2008 R2 SP1 to VMM 2012

Use this method if your system meets the requirements for a VMM 2012 upgrade and you want to deploy it on the same server. The supported VMM version to upgrade from is VMM 2008 R2 SP1. If you need to upgrade VMM 2008 R2 to VMM 2008 R2 SP1, refer to http://go.microsoft.com/fwlink/?LinkID=197099.

In addition, keep in mind that if you are running the SQL Server Express version, you will need to upgrade SQL Server to a fully supported version beforehand as the Express version is not supported in VMM 2012. Refer to *Chapter 3, Installing VMM 2012 R2*.

Once the system requirements are met and all of the prerequisites are installed, the upgrade process is straightforward. To follow the detailed recipe, refer to the *Upgrading to VMM 2012 R2* recipe.

Upgrading from 2008 R2 SP1 to VMM 2012 on a different computer

Sometimes, you may not be able to do an in-place upgrade to VMM 2012 or even to VMM 2012 SP1. In this case, it is recommended that you use the following instructions:

1. Uninstall the current VMM that retains the database and then restore the database on a supported version of SQL Server.
2. Next, install the VMM 2012 prerequisites on a new server (or on the same server, as long it meets the hardware and OS requirements).

3. Finally, install VMM 2012, providing the retained database information on the **Database configuration** dialog, and the VMM setup will upgrade the database. When the install process is finished, upgrade the **Hyper-V** hosts with the latest VMM agents.

The following figure illustrates the upgrade process from VMM 2008 R2 SP1 to VMM 2012:

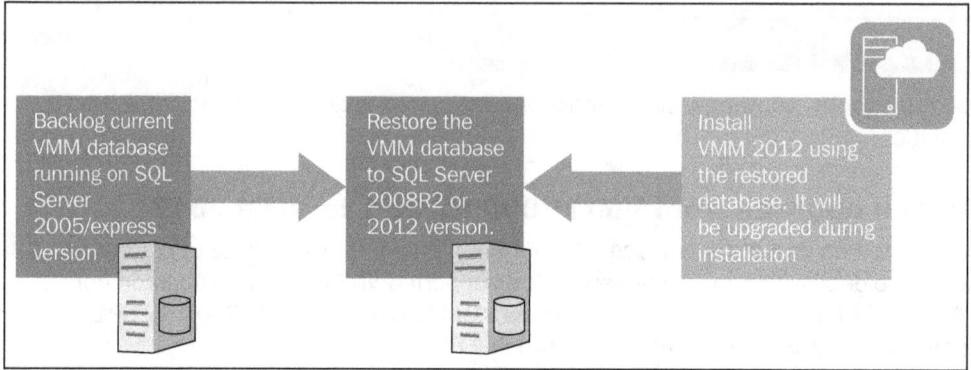

When performing an upgrade from VMM 2008 R2 SP1 with a local VMM database to a different server, the encrypted data will not be preserved as the encryption keys are stored locally. The same rule applies when upgrading from VMM 2012 to VMM 2012 SP1 and from VMM 2012 SP1 to VMM 2012 R2 and not using **Distributed Key Management** (**DKM**) in VMM 2012.

Upgrading from VMM 2012 to VMM 2012 SP1

To upgrade to VMM 2012 SP1, you should already have VMM 2012 up and running. VMM 2012 SP1 requires a Windows Server 2012 and Windows ADK 8.0. If planning an in-place upgrade, back up the VMM database; uninstall VMM 2012 and App Controller (if applicable), retaining the database; perform an OS upgrade; and then install VMM 2012 SP1 and App Controller.

Upgrading from VMM 2012 SP1 to VMM 2012 R2

To upgrade to VMM 2012 R2, you should already have VMM 2012 SP1 up and running. VMM 2012 R2 requires minimum Windows Server 2012 as the OS (Windows 2012 R2 is recommended) and Windows ADK 8.1. If planning an in-place upgrade, back up the VMM database; uninstall VMM 2012 SP1 and App Controller (if applicable), retaining the database; perform an OS upgrade; and then install VMM 2012 R2 and App Controller.

Some more planning considerations are as follows:

▶ **Virtual Server 2005 R2**: VMM 2012 does not support Microsoft Virtual Server 2005 R2 anymore.

> If you have Virtual Server 2005 R2 or an unsupported ESXi version running and have not removed these hosts before the upgrade, they will be removed automatically during the upgrade process.

▸ **VMware ESX and vCenter**: For VMM 2012, the supported versions of VMware are from ESXi 3.5 to ESXi 4.1 and vCenter 4.1. For VMM 2012 SP1/R2, the supported VMware versions are from ESXi 4.1 to ESXi 5.1, and vCenter 4.1 to 5.0.

▸ **SQL Server Express**: This is not supported since VMM 2012. A full version is required. For more details, go through *Chapter 1, VMM 2012 Architecture*.

▸ **Performance and Resource Optimization (PRO)**: The PRO configurations are not retained during an upgrade to VMM 2012. If you have an Operations Manager (**SCOM**) integration configured, it will be removed during the upgrade process. Once the upgrade process is finished, you can integrate SCOM with VMM.

▸ **Library server**: Since VMM 2012, VMM does not support a library server on Windows Server 2003. If you have it running and continue with the upgrade, you will not be able to use it. To use the same library server in VMM 2012, move it to a server running a supported OS before starting the upgrade.

▸ **Choosing a service account and DKM settings during an upgrade**: During an upgrade to VMM 2012, on the **Configure service account and distributed key management** page of the setup, you are required to create a VMM service account (preferably a domain account) and choose whether you want to use DKM to store the encryption keys in **Active Directory** (**AD**).

▸ **Make sure to log on with the same account that was used during the VMM 2008 R2 installation**: This needs to be done because, in some situations after the upgrade, the encrypted data (for example, the passwords in the templates) may not be available depending on the selected VMM service account, and you will be required to re-enter it manually.

▸ **For the service account, you can use either the Local System account or a domain account**: This is the recommended option, but when deploying a highly available VMM management server, the only option available is a domain account.

> Note that DKM is not available with the versions prior to VMM 2012.

▸ **Upgrading to a highly available VMM 2012**: If you're thinking of upgrading to a High Available (HA) VMM, consider the following:

  ❑ **Failover Cluster**: You must deploy the failover cluster before starting the upgrade.

❑ **VMM database**: You cannot deploy the SQL Server for the VMM database on highly available VMM management servers. If you plan on upgrading the current VMM Server to an HA VMM, you need to first move the database to another server. As a best practice, it is recommended that you have the SQL Server cluster separated from the VMM cluster.

❑ **Library server**: In a production or High Available environment, you need to consider all of the VMM components to be High Available as well, and not only the VMM management server. After upgrading to an HA VMM management server, it is recommended, as a best practice, that you relocate the VMM library to a clustered file server. In order to keep the custom fields and properties of the saved VMs, deploy those VMs to a host and save them to a new VMM 2012 library.

❑ **VMM Self-Service Portal**: This is not supported since VMM 2012 SP1. It is recommended that you install System Center App Controller instead.

How it works...

There are two methods to upgrade to VMM 2012 from VMM 2008 R2 SP1: an in-place upgrade and upgrading to another server. Before starting, review the initial steps and the VMM 2012 prerequisites and perform a full backup of the VMM database.

Uninstall VMM 2008 R2 SP1 (retaining the data) and restore the VMM database to another SQL Server running a supported version. During the installation, point to that database in order to have it upgraded. After the upgrade is finished, upgrade the host agents.

> VMM will be rolled back automatically in the event of a failure during the upgrade process and reverted to its original installation/configuration.

There's more...

The names of the VMM services have been changed in VMM 2012. If you have any applications or scripts that refer to these service names, update them accordingly as shown in the following table:

VMM version	VMM service display name	Service name
2008 R2 SP1	Virtual Machine Manager	vmmservice
	Virtual Machine Manager Agent	vmmagent
2012 / 2012 SP1 / 2012 R2	System Center Virtual Machine Manager	scvmmservice
	System Center Virtual Machine Manager Agent	scvmmagent

See also

▸ The *Software requirements* section in the *Specifying the correct system requirements for a real-world scenario* recipe in *Chapter 1, VMM 2012 Architecture*

▸ To move the file-based resources (for example, ISO images, scripts, and VHD/VHDX), refer to `http://technet.microsoft.com/en-us/library/hh406929`

▸ To move the virtual machine templates, refer to *Exporting and Importing Service Templates in VMM* at `http://go.microsoft.com/fwlink/p/?LinkID=212431`

Checking the VMM system requirements and preparing for the upgrade

This recipe will guide you through the steps required to check if your current VMM 2008 R2 SP1 installation meets the requirements for an upgrade to VMM 2012. The recipe will also help you with the initial steps that you need to carry out to prepare the environment for a VMM 2012 in-place upgrade.

Getting ready

First, you need to know that upgrades from the Beta versions and the versions prior to VMM 2008 R2 SP1 are not supported.

Confirm that your system meets the requirements for the installation. Refer to the *Supported OS and Servers* section of the *Specifying the correct system requirements for a real-world scenario* recipe in *Chapter 1, VMM 2012 Architecture*.

> A direct upgrade from VMM 2008 R2 SP1 to VMM 2012 R2 is not supported. You need to first upgrade to VMM 2012.

How to do it...

Carry out the following steps to check if your environment meets the system requirements, and to perform the initial steps for an in-place upgrade to VMM 2012:

1. Remove the integration of SCOM with VMM.

2. Remove the integration of VMM with VMware vCenter.

3. Wait for the completion of all of the jobs running in VMM.

4. Close the VMM console, the VMM command shell, and the VMM Self-Service Portal.

5. Perform a full backup of the VMM database (refer to http://go.microsoft.com/fwlink/?LinkID=162661).

6. If your VMM library is running on another machine, make sure that the OS version meets the minimum requirements. Upgrade the OS if necessary.

7. Update the server by running Windows Update.

8. Verify that there are no pending restarts on the server. Restart the server if necessary.

> The job history will be deleted during the upgrade.

Uninstalling previous versions of Windows Automated Installation Kit (WAIK)

VMM 2012 requires WAIK for Windows 7. In VMM 2012 SP1 and VMM 2012 R2, Windows ADK replaced WAIK as a VMM prerequisite. To uninstall WAIK, follow the ensuing instructions:

1. Navigate to **Control Panel | Programs | Programs and Features** and select **Windows Automated Installation Kit**.

2. Click on **Uninstall** and then follow the wizard to uninstall the program.

3. Click on **Yes** to confirm, then click on **Finish**.

4. Restart the server.

Checking whether Windows Remote Management (WinRM) is working

It is a prerequisite to have the WinRM service running and set to **Automatic**. Perform the following steps for assistance with this:

1. In the **Services** console (services.msc), locate and select the **Windows Remote Management (WS-Management)** service. If **Status** is not showing as **Started** and/or **Startup Type** is showing as **Manual**, change the settings by right-clicking on the service and then clicking on **Properties**. This is shown in the following screenshot:

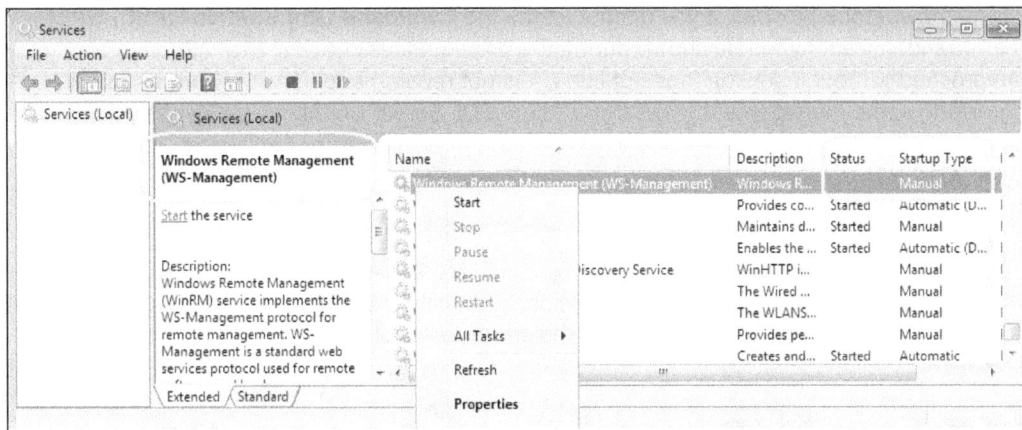

2. In the **Properties** dialog box, change the **Startup Type** to **Automatic**, click on **Start** to initiate the service, and then click on **OK**.

How it works...

If your VMM 2008 R2 does not have the SP1 update applied to it, start by applying it for it to be supported for the upgrade to VMM 2012. If you are planning to do an in-place upgrade to VMM 2012 SP1 and running Windows Server 2008 R2, you need to carry this out in the following two phases:

1. **Upgrade from VMM 2008 R2 SP1 to VMM 2012**: Carry out a VMM database backup, remove VMM 2008 R2 SP1 (choosing to retain the data), and then during the VMM 2012 installation, provide the previously saved database. VMM 2012 will upgrade the database during the installation.

2. **Upgrade from VMM 2012 to VMM 2012 SP1**: As VMM 2012 SP1 requires Windows Server 2012, first run an in-place upgrade of the OS to Windows Server 2012 (refer to *Installing Windows 2012* at `http://technet.microsoft.com/en-us/library/jj134246.aspx`), install the prerequisites, and then carry out the upgrade from VMM 2012 to VMM 2012 SP1.

3. **Upgrade from VMM 2012 SP1 to VMM 2012 R2**: As Windows 2012 R2 is recommended for VMM 2012 R2, first run an in-place upgrade of the OS to Windows Server 2012 R2 (refer to *Installing Windows 2012* at `http://technet.microsoft.com/en-us/library/jj134246.aspx`), install the prerequisites, and then carry out the upgrade from VMM 2012 SP1 to VMM 2012 R2.

During the upgrade process, if you did not install the **Command Line Utilities** for SQL Server beforehand, a warning will be shown during the prerequisites check phase. Although you can proceed without installing these utilities, it is not recommended as they are required to perform some management tasks (refer to the *SQL Server Connectivity Feature Pack components* section under the *Installing VMM dependencies* recipe in *Chapter 3, Installing VMM 2012 R2*).

> The Windows Remote Management (WS-Management) service must be started and set to automatic before the upgrade is started; otherwise, an error will appear during the prerequisites check.

There's more...

Review the software requirements for the VMM management server as given in *Chapter 1, VMM 2012 Architecture,* under the *Specifying the correct system requirements for a real-world scenario* recipe.

Install the following prerequisites as well:

▸ Windows Assessment and Deployment Kit (8.0 for SP1 and 8.1 for VMM 2012 R2)

▸ SQL Server Command Line Utilities (for the supported and installed version of SQL)

▸ Microsoft SQL Server Native Client

Upgrading to VMM 2012 R2

This recipe will guide you through the tasks required to upgrade VMM 2008 R2 SP1 to VMM 2012, showcasing the possible options and actions. It will then highlight the upgrade path to VMM 2012 R2.

> To upgrade from VMM 2012 to 2012 R2, refer to the *Upgrading from VMM 2012 SP1 to VMM 2012 R2* section in the *Reviewing the upgrade options* recipe.

Getting ready

Go through the *Checking the VMM system requirements and preparing for the upgrade* recipe after deciding the upgrade method (an in-place upgrade or upgrade to another server), and make sure you've installed all of the prerequisites.

If you're planning an in-place upgrade of VMM 2008 R2 SP1 running on a server with an OS other than the supported version, first upgrade the OS and then carry out the steps to upgrade to VMM 2012, as described in this recipe.

How to do it...

To upgrade to VMM 2012 R2 from VMM 2008 R2, you first need to carry out the following steps:

1. On the VMM 2008 R2 SP1 console, click on **General** in the **Administration** view. Next, click on **Back up Virtual Machine Manager** in the **Actions** pane. All of these are depicted in the following screenshot:

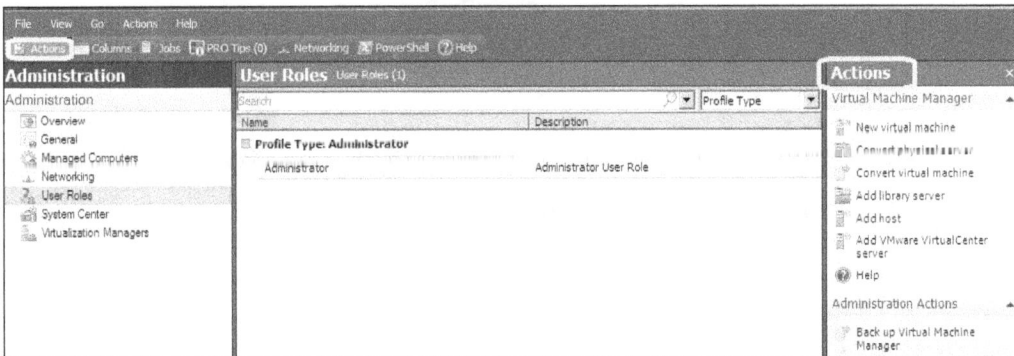

2. In the **Virtual Machine Manager Backup** dialog box, type in the path for the destination folder of the backup file. The folder must not be a root directory, and it must be accessible to the SQL Server database.

3. Take note of the backup location as we will need it later during the VMM 2012 upgrade.

4. If you're doing an in-place upgrade and running a full version of SQL Server, go directly to step 7.

5. If you're upgrading to another server or running SQL Server Express, uninstall SCVMM 2008 R2 SP1, remove all of the components, and choose **Retain Database** during the removal of the SCVMM 2008 R2 SP1 Server service.

6. If you're running SQL Server 2005 Express Edition, do the following:

    i. Click on **Start**, and in the **Search programs and files** box, or in the **Run** window, type in `services.msc` and press *Enter*. Stop the **SQL Server (MICROSOFTVMM)** service.

    ii. Copy **VirtualManagerDB** and **VirtualManagerDB_log** from `C:\Program Files(x86)\Microsoft SQL Server\MSSQL.1\MSSQL\Data` to a backup folder (for example, `C:\backup`).

iii. Navigate to **Control Panel | Programs | Programs and Features**, select **Microsoft SQL Server 2005,** and then click on **Uninstall**, as shown in the following screenshot:

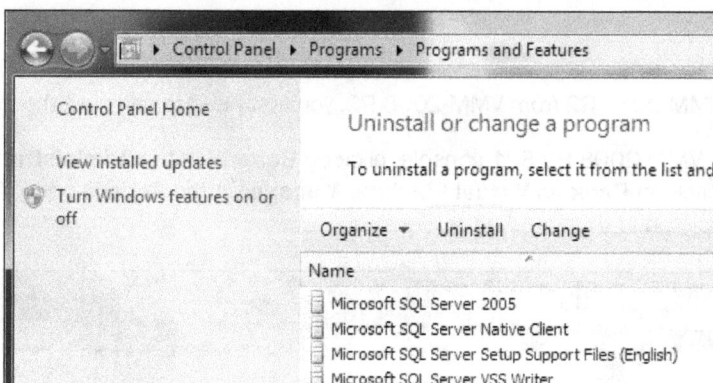

iv. On the **Component Selection** page, select the **Remove SQL Server 2005 instance components** checkbox and also the **Workstation Components** checkbox.

v. On the confirmation page, click on **Finish** to complete the uninstall process.

vi. In **Add or Remove Programs**, select **Microsoft SQL Native Client** and then click on **Remove**.

vii. In the confirmation dialog box, click on **Yes**. Install a full version of SQL Server (it is recommended that you install it on another server). Refer to the *Deploying a Microsoft SQL Server for a VMM implementation* recipe in *Chapter 3, Installing VMM 2012 R2*.

viii. Restore the VMM database backup to SQL Server. To do this, open SQL Server Management Studio and select **Restore Database**. On the **Specify Backup** window, click on **Add** and navigate to C:\backup. Enter VirtualManagerDB as the new name. Select **Restore** and click on **OK**. On successful restoration, a pop up will be displayed. Click on **OK** and close SQL Server Management Studio.

7. Browse to the installation media and double-click on setup.exe.

8. On the main setup page, click on **Install**.

9. Click on **Yes** to confirm the upgrade to VMM 2012 as shown in the following screenshot:

> **Microsoft System Center VMM Setup** ☒
>
> ⚠ An existing installation of System Center Virtual Machine Manager has been detected. Do you want to upgrade that installation to System Center 2012 Virtual Machine Manager?
>
> [Yes] [No]

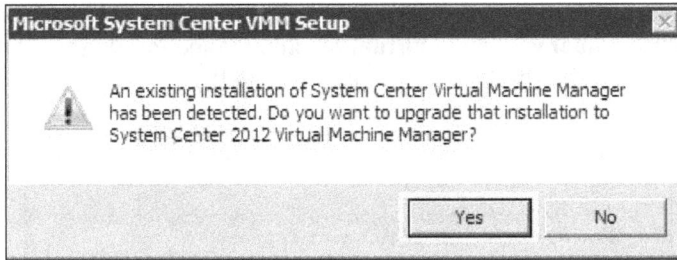

10. On the **Features to be upgraded** page, confirm that **VMM management** and **VMM console** are selected and click on **Next**.

11. On the **Product registration information** page, enter the VMM product key and then click on **Next** (if you don't provide a product key, VMM 2012 will be installed as a trial version).

12. On the **Please read this license agreement** page, tick the **I have read, understood, and agree with the terms of the license agreement** chookbox and oliok on **Noxt**.

13. On the **Join the Customer Experience Improvement Program (CEIP)...** page, choose either **Yes** or **No** and click on **Next**.

14. On the **Microsoft Update** page, select **On (recommended)** to use Microsoft Update and click on **Next**.

15. On the **Installation location** page, provide the path for the installation and then click on **Next**.

> 💡 My recommendation is that you use the OS partition (C:) only for the operating system. It is recommended that you place the VMM program files on a separate drive.

16. On the **Database Configuration** page, specify the name in the **Server name** field of the SQL Server and the **Instance name** field, for example, **MSSQLSERVER**.

17. Select **Existing database** and choose **VirtualManagerDB** (or whichever name the restored database has) from the drop-down menu, as shown in the following screenshot:

Select an existing database or create a new database.

- ○ New database: [   ]
- ● Existing database: [VirtualManagerDB] ▼

18. Click on **Next**, and then click on **Yes** when you get the **The selected database is created by an older version of Virtual Machine Manager. Do you want to upgrade it?** message, as shown in the following screenshot:

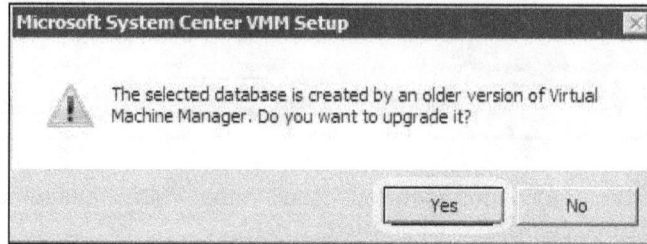

19. On the **Configure service account and distributed key management** page (shown in the next screenshot), select the account for Virtual Machine Manager Service.

20. If your selection is **Domain Account**, type in the username and domain in the `domain\user` format, enter the password, and click on **Next**.

> You will not be able to change the account after the VMM installation is complete as this is not supported.

21. In the **Distributed Key Management** section, select **Store my keys in Active Directory** if you decide to use DKM (recommended approach):

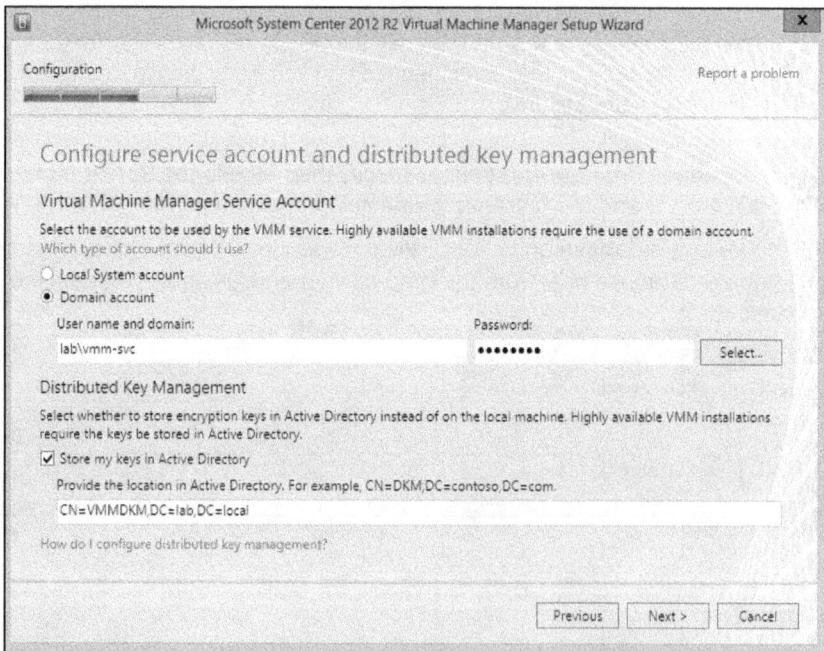

22. On the **Port configuration** page, leave the default port numbers unchanged or provide a unique value for each feature, then click on **Next**.

> Plan and document the ports before choosing them as you will not be able to change them again; it would require reinstalling VMM.

23. You might find certain issues listed on the page that says **Upgrade compatibility report**. In this case, you can either click on **Next** to proceed with the upgrade or click on **Cancel** to cancel the upgrade and resolve the issues.

24. On the **Installation summary** page, click on **Install** and then on **Close** to finish.

How it works...

Just like all upgrade processes, the VMM upgrade process requires planning. Start by confirming that the current server/VM meets the system requirements for VMM 2012.

Decide the upgrade method you wish to use between the in-place upgrade and upgrading to another server. An in-place upgrade will not be successful if the database version is not supported.

Back up the current VMM database. If you're running SQL Express Edition, you will need to uninstall VMM 2008 R2 SP1, retaining the data. You will then need to install a fully supported SQL version, restore the VMM database, and then start the VMM 2012 upgrade process.

> If you are running a small VMM 2012 installation, you can install SQL on the same server as long it is not an HA VMM, as discussed in *Chapter 1, VMM 2012 Architecture*.

Start the VMM 2012 installer and carry out the upgrade steps, reviewing and paying special attention to the database and DKM configuration and confirming your options in all of the upgrade dialogs. At the end of the process, open the VMM console to confirm the upgrade and update the agent hosts to VMM 2012.

During the migration process, if the database is not compatible, the following pop-up dialog box (that shows an error) will appear:

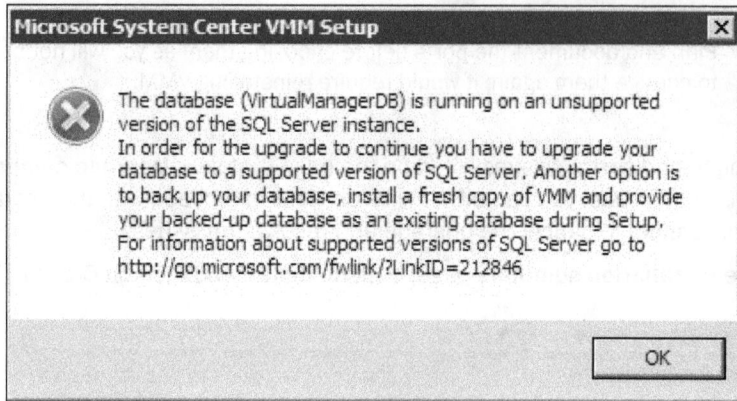

```
┌─────────────────────────────────────────────────────────────┐
│ Microsoft System Center VMM Setup                       [X] │
├─────────────────────────────────────────────────────────────┤
│                                                             │
│    ⊗   The database (VirtualManagerDB) is running on an     │
│        unsupported version of the SQL Server instance.      │
│        In order for the upgrade to continue you have to     │
│        upgrade your database to a supported version of SQL  │
│        Server. Another option is to back up your database,  │
│        install a fresh copy of VMM and provide your         │
│        backed-up database as an existing database during    │
│        Setup. For information about supported versions of   │
│        SQL Server go to                                     │
│        http://go.microsoft.com/fwlink/?LinkID=212846        │
│                                                             │
│                                          ┌──────────┐       │
│                                          │    OK    │       │
│                                          └──────────┘       │
└─────────────────────────────────────────────────────────────┘
```

There's more...

Now, let's talk about the VMM 2012 SP1/R2 upgrade and other VMM components.

Upgrading to VMM 2012 SP1 or VMM 2012 R2

If you are running VMM 2012, you can upgrade to VMM 2012 SP1. As VMM 2012 SP1 requires Windows Server 2012, you will need to upgrade the OS beforehand.

If you are running VMM 2012 SP1, you can upgrade to VMM 2012 R2. As VMM 2012 R2 requires minimum Windows Server 2012, you don't need to upgrade the OS beforehand, although I recommend that you upgrade the OS to Windows Server 2012 R2.

> You can follow the steps for either VMM 2012 to VMM 2012 SP1 or VMM 2012 SP1 to VMM 2012 R2

Make sure you take a backup of the VMM database. Next, I would recommend that you uninstall VMM 2012, retaining the database, followed by the installation of the VMM 2012 SP1/R2 prerequisites.

Database options

Please select if you want to remove or retain the VMM database when you uninstall the VMM management server.

⦿ Retain database

Choose this option if you plan to reinstall VMM and want to resume managing virtual machines in the same host environment.

◯ Remove database

Choose this option to delete the VMM database and all associated configuration and status information.

If access to the database requires credentials different than the current user's, enter the required credentials below.

☐ Use the following credentials

User name and domain:

Format: Domain\UserName

Password:

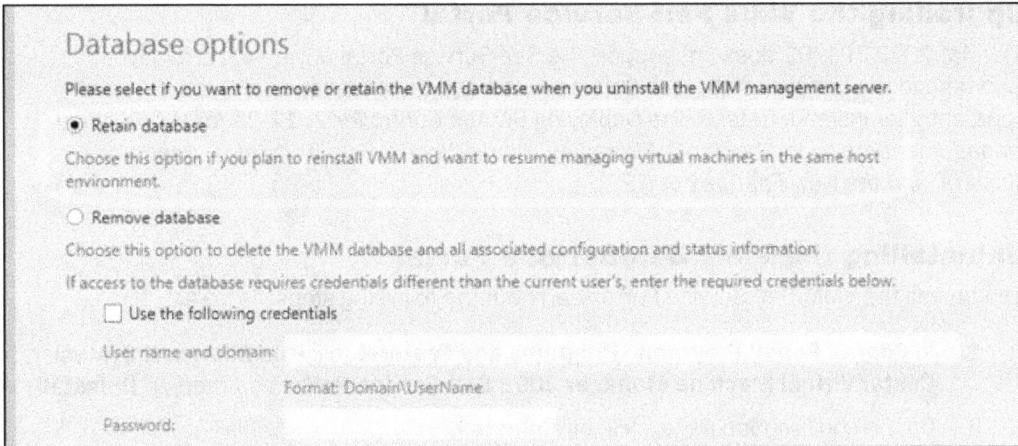

Proceed with the VMM 2012 SP1/R2 installation using the same database. For more details on installing VMM 2012 SP1/R2, refer to the *Installing a VMM management server* recipe in *Chapter 3, Installing VMM 2012 R2*.

Upgrading a VMM console

Close VMM Administrator Console and VMM Command Shell (if open), and then pick one of the following options:

▸ **Option 1**: An in-place upgrade

▸ **Option 2**: The uninstallation of the VMM 2008 R2 SP1 console

If you picked option 1, carry out the following steps:

1. Browse to the installation media and run the setup file.

2. On the main setup page, click on **Install**.

3. Go through the installation steps.

If you picked option 2, carry out the following steps:

1. In **Control Panel | Programs | Programs and Features**, click on **Microsoft System Center Virtual Machine Manager 2008 Administrator Console** and then on **Uninstall**.

2. On the confirmation page, click on **Uninstall**.

3. Browse to the VMM 2012 media and double-click on the setup file to run it.

4. On the main setup page, click on **Install**.

5. Go through the installation steps.

Upgrading the VMM Self-Service Portal

As VMM 2012 SP1/R2 does not support the Self-Service Portal anymore, I strongly recommend the removal of the Self-Service Portal and the installation of System Center App Controller instead. Refer to the *Deploying SC App Controller 2012 R2 for hybrid cloud management* recipe in *Chapter 8, Managing Hybrid Clouds, Fabric Updates, Resources, Clusters, and the New Features of R2*.

Uninstalling the VMM Self-Service Portal

To uninstall the VMM Self-Service Portal, carry out the following steps:

1. In **Control Panel\Programs\Programs and Features**, click on **Microsoft System Center Virtual Machine Manager 2008 Self-Service Portal** and then on **Uninstall**.

2. On the confirmation page, click on **Uninstall**.

See also

▶ The *Deploying a Microsoft SQL Server for a VMM implementation* recipe in *Chapter 3, Installing VMM 2012 R2*

▶ The *Reassociating hosts after upgrading* recipe

▶ The *Updating the VMM agents* recipe

▶ The *Performing other post-upgrade tasks* recipe

Reassociating hosts after upgrading

After upgrading to a new version of VMM, you will need to reassociate the Hyper-V hosts. This recipe will guide you through the steps required to do so.

How to do it...

To reassociate hosts and library servers, carry out the following steps after you have upgraded VMM:

1. In the **Fabric** workspace on the VMM console, expand **Servers**. Under **Servers**, expand **All Hosts**. In the **Hosts** pane, right-click on the column header and select **Agent Status**.

> If a host needs to be reassociated, the **Host Status** column will display **Needs Attention** and the **Agent Status** column will display **Access Denied**.

Select the host(s) to reassociate (use the *Shift* or the *Ctrl* key if you need to select multiple hosts), then right-click on the host(s), and click on **Reassociate**.

2. In the **Reassociate Agent** dialog box, type in the account name and password.

3. Click on **OK**. The **Agent Status** column will display **Reassociating**.

4. After the host has been reassociated successfully, it will display **Responding**.

5. On the **Hosts** tab in the ribbon, click on **Refresh**. The **Host Status** will display **OK**.

How it works...

After upgrading to VMM 2012, you will need to reassociate the Hyper-V servers and VMM library servers with VMM. If a host needs to be reassociated, the **Host Status** column will exhibit **Needs Attention** and the **Agent Status** column will exhibit **Access Denied**.

Library agents are treated in the same way that host agents are, and therefore, the same procedure needs to be followed for them as well. Reassociate the VMM library server using the same steps. To view a list of the VMM library servers, in the **Fabric** workspace, expand **Servers** and then click on **Library Servers**.

> After reassociation, all the agents will display the status, **Update Needed**.

There's more...

DMZ and other untrusted domain hosts will display an **Access Denied** state. They can't be reassociated; they will need to be removed and re-added to the VMM 2012 management.

See also

▸ The *Updating the VMM agents* recipe

▸ The *Performing other post-upgrade tasks* recipe

Updating the VMM agents

After upgrading to a new version of VMM, you will also need to update the VMM agents running on the Hyper-V server hosts. This recipe will guide you through the steps to do so.

How to do it...

To update the VMM agent of a host, carry out the following steps after upgrading:

1. In the **Fabric** workspace on the VMM console, expand **Servers** and then go to **All Hosts**. In the **Hosts** pane, right-click on the column header and select **Agent Status**.

2. On the **Hosts** tab in the ribbon, click on **Refresh**.

> If a host requires the VMM agent to be updated, it will display **Needs Attention** in the **Host Status** column and **Upgrade Available** in the **Agent Version Status** column.

3. To update the VMM agent, select and right-click on the host and then click on **Update Agent**.

4. In the **Update Agent** dialog box, type in the user credentials and click on **OK**.

5. The **Agent Version Status** column will exhibit **Upgrading**, which will then change to **Up-to-date** once the update process has been completed successfully.

6. On the **Hosts** tab in the ribbon, click on **Refresh**. The **Host Status** column for the host will display **OK**.

> Use the same steps as the ones used before to update the VMM agent on a VMM library server. To view a list of the VMM library servers, in the **Fabric** workspace, expand **Servers** and then click on **Library Servers**.

How it works...

After upgrading to VMM 2012, you are required to update the VMM agent on the Hyper-V hosts and VMM library servers. Although this process does not require immediate action after the upgrade (as the previous VMM agent versions are supported by VMM 2012), take into account that the previous versions do not provide the functionalities that the new VMM agent does. The following is a list of the older versions of the VMM agent supported by VMM 2012:

▸ VMM 2008 R2 SP1 (2.0.4521.0)

▸ VMM 2008 R2 QFE4 (2.0.4275.0)

- ► VMM 2008 R2 QFE3 (2.0.4273.0)
- ► VMM 2008 R2 (2.0.4271.0)

See also

- ► The *Reassociating hosts after upgrading* recipe
- ► The *Performing other post-upgrade tasks* recipe

Performing other post-upgrade tasks

There are some others tasks that need to be performed after you have upgraded to VMM 2012. This recipe will guide you through them.

How to do it...

To update a VM template, carry out the following steps after you have upgraded VMM:

1. On the VMM console, in the **Library** workspace, expand **Templates** and click on **VM Templates**.
2. In the **Templates** pane, right-click on the VM template to be updated and select **Properties**.
3. On the **Hardware Configuration** page, configure the following:

   ❑ **VLAN ID**: Configure this if you have previously configured it in a hardware profile.

   > In VMM 2012, the VLAN ID will be resolved automatically based on the logical network specified when deploying a VM from a template.

   ❑ **Logical Network/VM Network**: Ensure that the correct network is specified in the hardware profile.

How it works...

The VM template settings specifying the VHD file that contains the OS are not preserved during the VMM upgrade. After upgrading to VMM 2012 SP1/R2, you will have to update the upgraded VM templates to specify which VHD file contains the OS.

There's more...

There are a couple of other tasks that you need to perform if you had driver packages in the previous version.

Updating driver packages

After upgrading to VMM 2012, remove any previously added driver packages and then add them again so that they are correctly discovered. Use the following steps to add the driver packages to the library:

1. Locate a driver package, and create a folder in the VMM library share to store the drivers (for example, you could create a folder named **Drivers**).

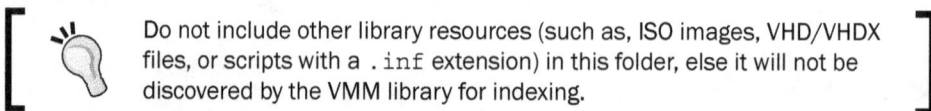

   > Do not include other library resources (such as, ISO images, VHD/VHDX files, or scripts with a .inf extension) in this folder, else it will not be discovered by the VMM library for indexing.

2. Copy the driver package to a folder within this folder; that is, create a separate subfolder for every driver package.

3. In the **Library** workspace on the VMM console, expand **Library Servers** in the **Library** pane. Select and right-click on the new folder (for example, **Drivers**), and then click on **Refresh** to update the display and show the newly created folder.

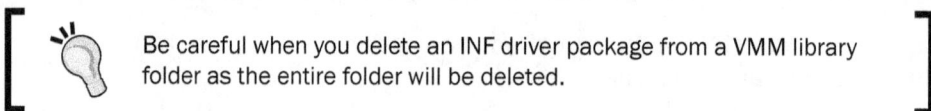

   > Be careful when you delete an INF driver package from a VMM library folder as the entire folder will be deleted.

Relocating the VMM Library

If you're upgrading to an HA VMM management server, the best practice is to relocate the VMM library to a cluster file server, create a new VMM library, and move the resources. Carry out the following steps to import the physical resources:

1. On the VMM console, in the **Library** workspace, click on **Import Physical Resource** on the **Home** tab and choose one of the following:

   - **Add a custom resource** to import a folder and its contents. If you select a folder with a .cr extension, it will be imported as a custom resource package. Without a .cr extension, only the supported file types will show up in the VMM library.

[🔅 You can use Windows Explorer to access the VMM library share in order to access all the files in the folder (if your account has the requisite access rights).]

   ❑ **Add resource** to import the file(s) of a supported type from another library location.

2. Under **Select library server and destination for the imported resources,** click on **Browse**.

3. Select the library server, library share, and folder location (optional), and click on **OK** and then on **Import**.

See also

▸ The *Upgrading Virtual Machine Manager and App Controller* article at `http://technet.microsoft.com/en-us/library/dn521014.aspx`

▸ The *Troubleshooting a VMM Upgrade* article at `http://technet.microsoft.com/en-us/library/jj870885.aspx`

▸ The *How to Export a Service Template in VMM* article at `http://technet.microsoft.com/en-US/library/gg675114.aspx`

▸ The *How to Import a Service Template in VMM* article at `http://technet.microsoft.com/en-US/library/gg675092.aspx`

▸ The *How to Add File-Based Resources to the VMM Library* article at `http://technet.microsoft.com/library/gg610607.aspx`

3
Installing VMM 2012 R2

In this chapter, we will cover the following:

- ▶ Creating service accounts
- ▶ Deploying a Microsoft SQL Server for a VMM implementation
- ▶ Installing VMM dependencies
- ▶ Configuring Distributed Key management
- ▶ Installing a VMM management server
- ▶ Installing the VMM console
- ▶ Connecting to a VMM management server using the VMM console
- ▶ Creating credentials for a Run As account in VMM
- ▶ Configuring ports and protocols on the host firewall for each VMM component

Introduction

Based on what we learned in the previous chapter, you now know that in order to start our System Center 2012 R2 **Virtual Machine Manager** (**VMM**) deployment, we need to create the install accounts and deploy the SQL database.

As discussed, VMM is required to be an Active Directory member server.

In addition, it is up to you to decide where you will deploy the SQL database based on the business requirements and your design. However, as previously stated in *Chapter 1*, *VMM 2012 Architecture*, you should always have SQL installed on a separate server. This way, you are safe to grow, and you will have scalability and high availability on the database side (if installing a SQL Cluster).

For the purpose of this chapter, we will be referring to the following infrastructure:

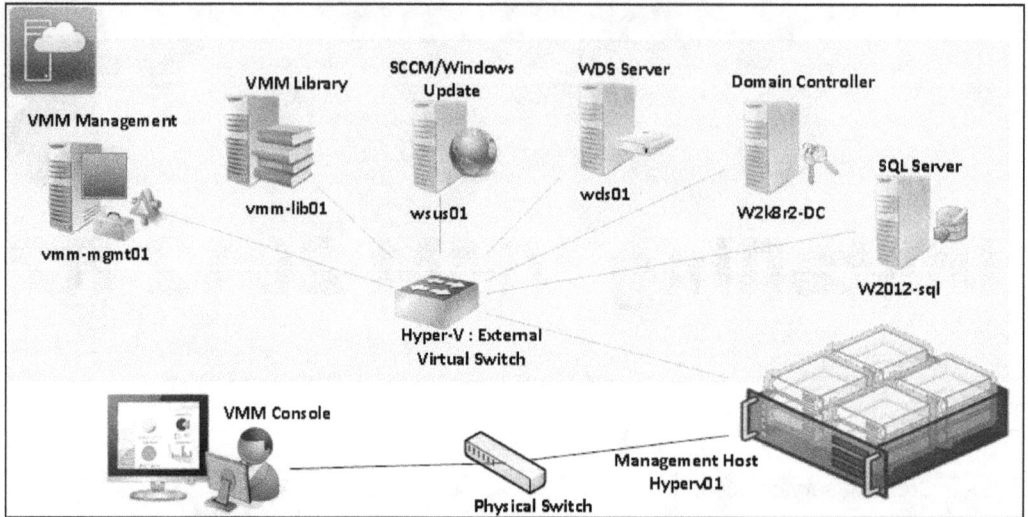

Creating service accounts

Let's start our private cloud deployment. First, we need to create a service account.

In order to install, configure, and manage SQL and Virtual Machine Manager and its components, we need to create the user and service accounts. My recommendation is to keep the account names alike, but the naming convention is up to your business to decide.

Getting ready

To perform this recipe, you need to have domain administrator rights or delegate permissions assigned to your account. You will also need to connect to the domain controller, **w2kr8-DC,** (in our sample infrastructure) using **Remote Desktop Connection** (**RDC**), or use the **Remote Administrative Tools** (**RSAT**) to open the Active Directory Users and Computers.

> If you do not have the domain admin rights or delegate permissions to execute the following recipe, ask the domain administrator to do it.
>
> We are also using LAB.local as our domain. Replace it with your own domain.

How to do it...

Carry out the following steps using Active Directory Users and Computer MMC (ADUC) to create a service account:

1. Create the following accounts and groups in your domain; you may name them according to your naming convention as follows:

   ❑ SCVMM Service user account: `LAB\vmm-svc`

   ❑ SCVMM Run As user account: `LAB\vmm-admin`

   ❑ SCVMM administrators' security group: `LAB\vmm-admins`

   ❑ SQL Service user account: `LAB\sql-svc`

   ❑ SQL Server system administrators' user account: `LAB\sql-admin`

> I normally create these accounts under a previously created **Organisational Unit** (**OU**): Service Accounts.

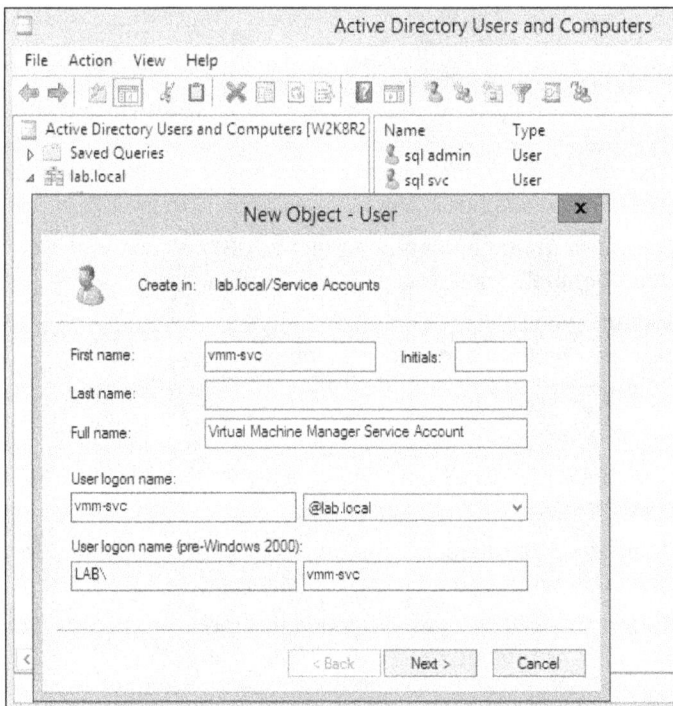

Optionally, you can use the following PowerShell commands to create the accounts:

```
Import-Module ServerManager

Add-WindowsFeature -Name "RSAT-AD-PowerShell"

New-ADUser -Name "SCVMM Service" -SamAccountName
"vmm-svc" -DisplayName "SCVMM Service Acct" -Enabled
$true -ChangePasswordAtLogon $false -AccountPassword
(ConvertTo-SecureString "type here the password" -AsPlainText
-force) -PasswordNeverExpires $true

$admgroup = [ADSI] "WinNT://./Administrators,group"

$admgroup.Psbase.Invoke("Add",([ADSI] "WinNT://lab/
vmm-svc").Path)
```

2. After creating the accounts, double-click on the **vmm-admins** security group.

> Make sure that the **Password never expires** and **User cannot change password** options are checked for these accounts. Also, make sure that there is no **Group Policy** (**GPO**) applied that changes these settings. Note, though, that **Group Managed Service Account** (**GMSA**) is not supported by VMM.

3. Select the **Members** tab and then click on **Add**.

4. Enter vmm-svc and click on **OK**.

5. Log in to the VMM management server (vmm-mgmt01) with an account that has local administrator rights (for example, LAB\Administrator).

6. Launch **Computer Management** (on Server 2008) and open the **Start** menu. Right-click on **Computer** and then click on **Manage**.

7. Expand **System Tools**, select **Local Users and Groups**, double-click on **Administrators**, and then add vmm-admins.

8. Repeat steps 5 through 7 for all of the VMM servers: vmm-console, vmm-lib01, and vmm-ssportal01.

9. Log in to SQL Server (w2012-sql) with an account that has local administrator rights (for example, LAB\Administrator).

10. Launch **Computer Management** (on Server 2008) and open the **Start** menu. Right-click on **Computer** and then click on **Manage**.

11. Expand **System Tools**, select **Local Users and Groups**, double-click on **Administrators**, and then add sql-svc and sql-admin.

> You can use the domain policy to assign these accounts to the local Administrators group on the VMM and SQL servers. For more information, go to http://social.technet.microsoft.com/wiki/contents/articles/7833.how-to-make-domain-user-as-a-local-administrator-for-all-pcs.aspx.

How it works...

These accounts will be used to install, configure, and manage SQL Server. They will also be used to install, configure, and manage VMM 2012 R2 to communicate with SQL and other System Center components. The accounts will be used by VMM to manage the Hyper-V hosts as well.

There's more...

During the VMM management server installation, on the **Configure service account and distributed key management** page, you will be required to provide an account for the Virtual Machine Manager service account. The account could be either the local system or a domain account (recommended):

▶ The domain account that you create specifically to be used for this purpose, as per best practice, must be a member of the local Administrators group on the computer.

▶ You are required to use a domain account for the VMM service if you want to use shared ISO images with Hyper-V VMs.

▶ You are required to use a domain account if you want to use a disjointed namespace.

▶ You are required to use a domain account if you want to install a highly available VMM management server.

▶ Changing the account identity of the Virtual Machine Manager service after the completion of the VMM installation is not supported. If you need to change it, you must uninstall VMM and then select the **Retain data** option to keep the SQL Server database and the data, and then reinstall VMM using the new service account.

You might get the following warning at the end of the installation:

"The Service Principal Name (SPN) could not be registered in Active Directory Domain Services (AD DS) for the VMM management server"

If you get this warning, perform the following steps to register **Service Principal Name** (**SPN**) and **Service Connection Point** (**SCP**), else no computers will be able to connect to the VMM management server, including the VMM console:

1. Open a command prompt with administrative rights (Run As).

2. Create the SPN for the VMM management server by running the following command:

    ```
    "C:\Windows\system32\setspn.exe -S SCVMM/vmmmgmt01.lab.local
    va\vmm-svc".
    ```

3. Add the SPN values (REG_SZ) to the registry key, VmmServicePrincipalNames, by navigating to Software\Microsoft\Microsoft System Center Virtual Machine Manager Server\Setup, as shown in the following screenshot:

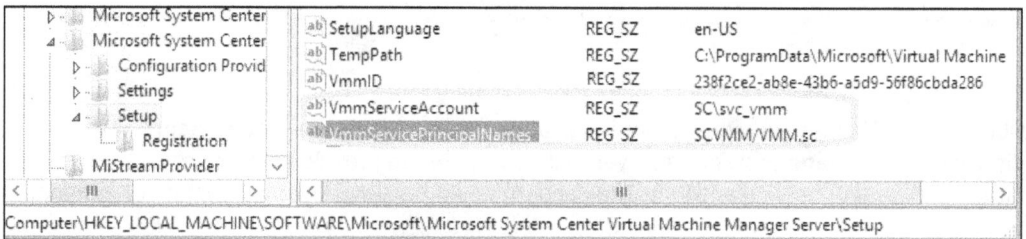

4. Configure the SCP by running the following command:

    ```
    Run "C:\Program Files\Microsoft System Center 2012 R2\Virtual
    Machine Manager\setup\ConfigureSCPTool.exe -install"
    ```

Deploying a Microsoft SQL Server for a VMM implementation

In this recipe, we will see how to install SQL Server 2012.

> For more information on the SQL Server versions supported by Virtual Machine Manager 2012 R2, refer to the *Specifying the correct system requirements for a real-world scenario* recipe in *Chapter 1, VMM 2012 Architecture*.

Getting ready

Assuming you have already installed the operating system according to the SQL Server requirements of the SQL version you are installing, connect to the SQL Server machine (for example, vm2012-sql).

> SQL 2012 and SQL 2012 SP1 are only supported by VMM 2012 SP1/R2.

Before starting, make sure the machine is a member of the domain, and refer to the following Microsoft articles for the hardware and software requirements for SQL Server:

- SQL 2012 and SQL 2012 SP1:

  `msdn.microsoft.com/en-us/library/ms143506.aspx`

- SQL 2008 R2:

  `http://technet.microsoft.com/en-us/library/`
  `ms143506(v=sql.105).aspx`

> To provide high availability, it is recommended that you deploy a clustered SQL Server. SQL AlwaysOn is supported by VMM and would be my recommendation. Check the following articles for more information on this:
> - *Getting Started with AlwaysOn Availability Groups (SQL Server)*: `http://technet.microsoft.com/en-us/library/` `gg509118.aspx`
> - *AlwaysOn Failover Cluster Instances (SQL Server)*: `http://` `technet.microsoft.com/en-us/library/ms189134.aspx`
> - *How to configure SQL Always On for System Center*: `http://` `blogs.technet.com/b/scvmm/archive/2012/10/24/` `how-to-configure-sql-2012-alwayson-availability-` `groups-in-system-center-2012-virtual-machine-` `manager-service-pack-1.aspx`

There are three ways to install SQL 2012: through a wizard, a configuration file, or the command prompt. The following section will guide you through the process of installing SQL 2012 using the configuration file method, which is quite simple to carry out. Using this method, after you have deployed the proof of concept, you will use the same file to replicate the SQL installation onto production or test sites.

How to do it...

The following configuration will install SQL Server 2012 with the following components: Database Engine, Reporting Services, and client tools:

> Full Text is required by OpsMgr.

1. Log in as `LAB\SQL-admin` or another account that has SQL system admin rights.

2. Create a folder named `Setup` in `C:\`.

3. Open Notepad and copy the following content on a new file:

```
;SQL Server 2012 Configuration File
[OPTIONS]
; Setup work flow: INSTALL, UNINSTALL, or UPGRADE.
ACTION="Install"
; Language.
ENU="True"
; Display progress only, no user interaction.
QUIETSIMPLE="True"
; Include product updates: True and False or 1 and 0.
UpdateEnabled="True"
; Features: SQL, AS, RS, IS, MDS, and Tools.
FEATURES=SQL,RS,Tools
; Detailed Setup log to show on the console.
INDICATEPROGRESS="False"
; 32-bit.
X86="False"
; Installation folder for shared components.
INSTALLSHAREDDIR="C:\Program Files\Microsoft SQL Server"
; Installation folder for the WOW64 shared components.
INSTALLSHAREDWOWDIR="C:\Program Files (x86)\Microsoft SQL
Server"
; Named instance. MSSQLSERVER is the default
INSTANCENAME="MSSQLSERVER"
; Instance ID
INSTANCEID="MSSQLSERVER"
; Data collected can be sent to Microsoft. True and False
or 1 and 0.
SQMREPORTING="False"
; Reporting Services Mode
RSINSTALLMODE="DefaultNativeMode"
; Installation directory.
INSTANCEDIR="C:\Program Files\Microsoft SQL Server"
; Agent account name
AGTSVCACCOUNT="LAB\sql-svc"
; Service start mode.
AGTSVCSTARTUPTYPE="Automatic"
; Startup type for Integration Services.
ISSVCSTARTUPTYPE="Automatic"
; Account for Integration Services: Domain\User or system
account.
```

```
ISSVCACCOUNT="LAB\sql-svc"
; Startup type for the SQL Server service.
SQLSVCSTARTUPTYPE="Automatic"
; Level to enable FILESTREAM feature at (0, 1, 2 or 3).
FILESTREAMLEVEL="0"
; Windows collation or an SQL collation to use for the
Database Engine.
SQLCOLLATION="SQL_Latin1_General_CP1_CI_AS"
; Account for SQL Server service: Domain\User or system
account.
SQLSVCACCOUNT="LAB\sql-svc"
; Windows account(s) to provision as SQL Server system
administrators.
SQLSYSADMINACCOUNTS="LAB\sql-svc" "LAB\sql-admin"
; Provision current user as a Database Engine system
administrator.
ADDCURRENTUSERASSQLADMIN="true"
; Specify 0 to disable or 1 to enable the TCP/IP protocol.
TCPENABLED="1"
; Specify 0 to disable or 1 to enable the Named Pipes protocol.
NPENABLED="0"
; Startup type for Browser Service.
BROWSERSVCSTARTUPTYPE="Automatic"
; Account the report server NT service should execute
under.  RSSVCACCOUNT="LAB\sql-svc"
; Startup mode of the report server service : Manual,
Automatic, Disabled
RSSVCSTARTUPTYPE="Automatic"
; FTSVCACCOUNT
FTSVCACCOUNT="NT Service\MSSQLFDLauncher"
IAcceptSQLServerLicenseTerms="True"
```

4. Save the file as `SQLConfigurationFile.ini` in `c:\setup`.

   Now that you have created the configuration file, proceed with the installation of SQL 2012 using this file.

5. Open the command prompt with administrative rights (**Run as administrator**).

6. Navigate to the SQL Server Source Media path and type in the following command:

```
Setup.exe /SQLSVCPASSWORD="P@ssword"
/AGTSVCPASSWORD="P@ssword" /ASSVCPASSWORD="P@ssword"
/ISSVCPASSWORD="P@ssword" /RSSVCPASSWORD="P@ssword"
/ConfigurationFile=c:\setup\SQLConfigurationFile.INI
```

7. Press *Enter* to start the installation.

You should see a window showing the installation progress, as shown in the following screenshot. The installation will proceed without user input.

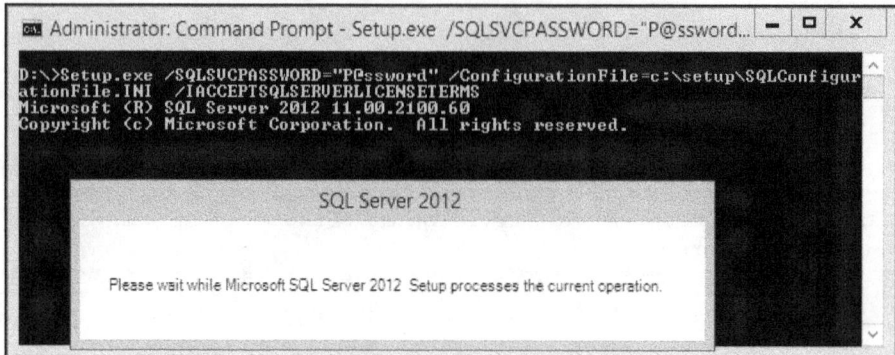

How it works...

The configuration file is a text file with parameters and descriptive comments, which can be useful to standardize SQL deployments. It is processed in the following order:

▸ The values in the configuration file replace the default values

▸ Command-line values replace the default and configuration file values

For security reasons, it is recommended that you specify the passwords at the command prompt instead of in the configuration file.

The SQL parameter can install SQL Server Database Engine, Reporting Services, Replication, Full Text, and Data Quality Services. The RS parameter will install all the Reporting Services components, and the Tools parameter will install the client tools.

In this sample configuration file, LAB is the domain, and you need to replace it with your own domain.

The following table enlists the various service accounts and password parameters:

SQL component	Account parameter	Password parameter	Startup type
SQL Server Agent	/AGTSVCACCOUNT	/AGTSVCPASSWORD	/AGTSVCSTARTUPTYPE
Analysis Services	/ASSVCACCOUNT	/ASSVCPASSWORD	/ASSVCSTARTUPTYPE
Database Engine	/SQLSVCACCOUNT	/SQLSVCPASSWORD	/SQLSVCSTARTUPTYPE
Integration Services	/ISSVCACCOUNT	/ISSVCPASSWORD	/ISSVCSTARTUPTYPE
Reporting Services	/RSSVCACCOUNT	/RSSVCPASSWORD	/RSSVCSTARTUPTYPE

There's more...

Optionally, you can generate the configuration file using SQL 2012 Wizard. To do this, carry out the following steps:

1. Browse to the SQL Server installation media.

2. Select and double-click on `Setup.exe`.

3. Follow the SQL setup wizard through to the **Ready to Install** page, and write down the configuration file path in the **configuration file path** section.

4. At this point, click on **Cancel** to cancel the setup as we are just looking to generate the configuration file.

5. Browse through the configuration path folder for the generated INI file as shown in the following screenshot:

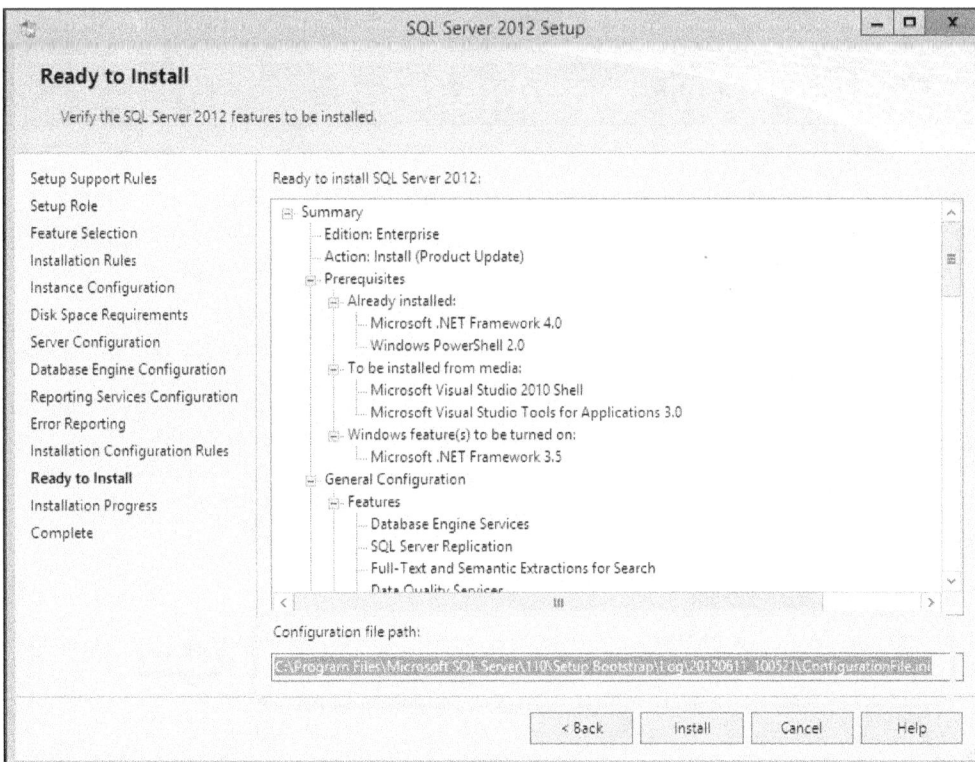

See also

▸ The *SQL Server Failover Cluster Installation* article at `http://msdn.microsoft.com/en-us/library/hh231721`

▸ The *Install SQL Server 2012 from the Installation Wizard (Setup)* article at `http://msdn.microsoft.com/en-us/library/ms143219`

▸ The *Install SQL Server 2012 from the Command Prompt* article at `http://msdn.microsoft.com/en-us/library/ms144259.aspx`

▸ The *Configure Windows Service Accounts and Permissions* article at `http://msdn.microsoft.com/en-us/library/ms143504`

▸ The *Run DQSInstaller.exe to Complete Data Quality Server Installation* article at `http://msdn.microsoft.com/en-us/library/hh231682`

▸ The *Configure the Windows Firewall to Allow SQL Server Access* article at `http://msdn.microsoft.com/en-us/library/cc646023.aspx`

Installing VMM dependencies

Before installing a VMM, we need to ensure that the server meets the minimum system requirements and that all of the prerequisite software is installed. For more information, check the software requirements specified in the *Specifying the correct system requirements for a real-world scenario* recipe in *Chapter 1, VMM 2012 Architecture*.

The previous versions of Windows Server introduced Windows PowerShell support, and Windows Server 2012 was improved with over 2,300 cmdlets to manage the platform.

You can use Windows PowerShell to automate all of the IT tasks around cloud datacenter deployment and management, starting with deploying your cloud infrastructure servers through to onboarding virtual machines to that infrastructure, and ending with monitoring your datacenter environment and collecting information about how it performs.

Getting ready

Virtual Machine Manager 2012 has automated almost all of the prerequisites, but you will need to install the Windows **Assessment and Deployment Kit** (**ADK**) for Windows 8.1 and SQL features (if you are not running SQL on the management server).

> I also recommend that you install the Telnet client feature as it is very useful for testing or troubleshooting on all servers.

To download the Windows Assessment and Deployment Kit for Windows 8.1, go to `http://go.microsoft.com/fwlink/?LinkId=293840`.

How to do it...

To install ADK, carry out the following steps:

1. Download and run the `adksetup.exe` file.

2. Select **Install the Assessment and Deployment Kit on this computer** and click on **Next**.

3. On the **Customer Experience Improvement Program** page, select **Yes** to join the Customer Experience program and click on **Next**. Then, click on **Accept**.

4. Select **Deployment Tools** and **Windows Preinstallation Environment (Windows PE)**, as shown in the following screenshot, and click on **Install**:

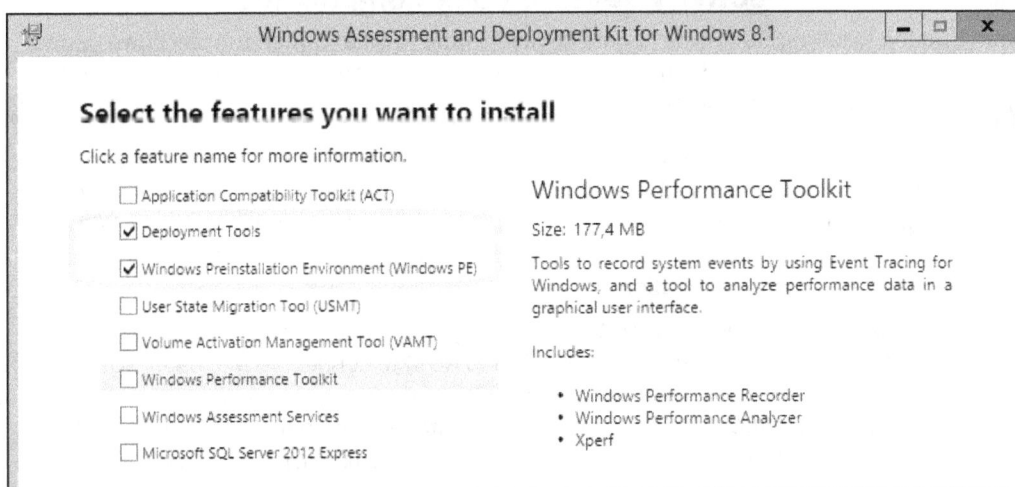

> For the complete installation options, go to `http://go.microsoft.com/fwlink/?LinkId=234980`.

How it works...

The Windows ADK for Windows 8.1, which is a collection of tools you can use to customize, assess, and deploy Windows operating systems to new computers, is a prerequisite for VMM 2012 R2 and is used for the Bare Metal deployment of Hyper-V servers.

It includes Windows Preinstallation Environment, Deployment Imaging, Servicing and Management, and Windows System Image Manager.

Right after starting the installation, at the **Assessment and Deployment** kit page, select **Deployment Tools** and **Windows Preinstallation Environment (Windows PE)** and then follow the wizard to complete the installation.

There's more...

There are more items that you need to install, which we will take a look at in the following sections.

SQL Server Connectivity Feature Pack components

Download the following SQL Server Connectivity Feature Pack and then run the downloaded file to install that package. Note, though, that you need the feature pack for the SQL version that the VMM database is running on.

▸ **SQL Server 2012 Command Line Utilities**: The SQLCMD utility allows users to connect to, send Transact-SQL batches from, and output row set information from SQL Server 2005, SQL Server 2008, SQL Server 2008 R2, and SQL Server 2012 instances. Visit http://go.microsoft.com/fwlink/?LinkID=239650&clcid =0x409 for more information.

▸ **Microsoft SQL Server Native Client**: This contains runtime support for applications using native code APIs (ODBC, OLE DB, and ADO) to connect to Microsoft SQL Server 2005, 2008, 2008 R2, and SQL Server 2012. SQL Server Native Client is used to enhance applications that need to take advantage of the new SQL Server 2012 features. Visit http://go.microsoft.com/fwlink/?LinkID=239648&clcid= 0x409 for more information.

The Telnet client

Install the Telnet client as it is very useful for testing and troubleshooting. The following are the steps to install the Telnet client:

1. On the Windows 2012 start screen, right-click on the tile for Windows PowerShell. Next, on the app bar, click on **Run as administrator**.

2. Type in the following command and hit *Enter*:

```
Install-WindowsFeature TelnetClient
```

See also

▸ The *Installing the Windows ADK* article at http://go.microsoft.com/ fwlink/?LinkId=234980

Configuring Distributed Key Management

Distributed Key Management (**DKM**) is used to store VMM encryption keys in **Active Directory Domain Services** (**AD DS**).

When installing VMM, for security reasons (recommended, as it encrypts the information on AD) and when deploying HA VMM (required), choose to use DKM on the **Configure service account and distributed key management** page.

Why do we need the DKM? By default, VMM encrypts some data in the VMM database using the **Windows Data Protection API** (**DPAPI**)—for example, the Run As account's credentials and passwords—and this data is tied to the VMM server and the service account used by VMM. However, with DKM, different machines can securely access the shared data.

Once an HA VMM node fails over to another node, it will access the VMM database and use the encryption keys conveniently stored under a container in AD to decrypt the data in the VMM database.

Getting ready

The following are some considerations to use distributed key management in VMM 2012:

▶ When installing a highly available VMM management server, DKM is required.

▶ The VMDK container should be created in AD starting with the VMM setup, if you do not have domain administrator rights when installing VMM.

▶ You need to create the VMDK container and the Virtual Machine Manager Service account in the same domain as the VMM management server.

▶ The installation account requires **Full Control** permissions to the VMDK container in AD DS. Also, in the **Apply to** drop-down menu, you need to choose the **This object and all descendant objects** option.

▶ On the **Configure service account and distributed key management** page, you need to specify the location of the container in AD DS (for example, `CN=VMMDKM,DC=lab,DC=local`).

> If you do not have the domain admin rights or delegate permissions to execute the following recipe, ask the domain administrator to do it.

How to do it...

Carry out the following steps to configure the DKM:

1. Log in as the domain administrator on your domain controller (for example, `W2k8r2-DC`), or log in from the administrator desktop if you have installed RSAT.

2. Type in `adsiedit.msc` in the **Run** window.

3. When the **ADSI Edit** window opens, right-click on **adsiedit** and select **Connect to**.

4. Click on **Select a well known Naming Context** and select **Default naming context**.

5. Click on **OK** and expand **Default naming context**, as shown in the following screenshot:

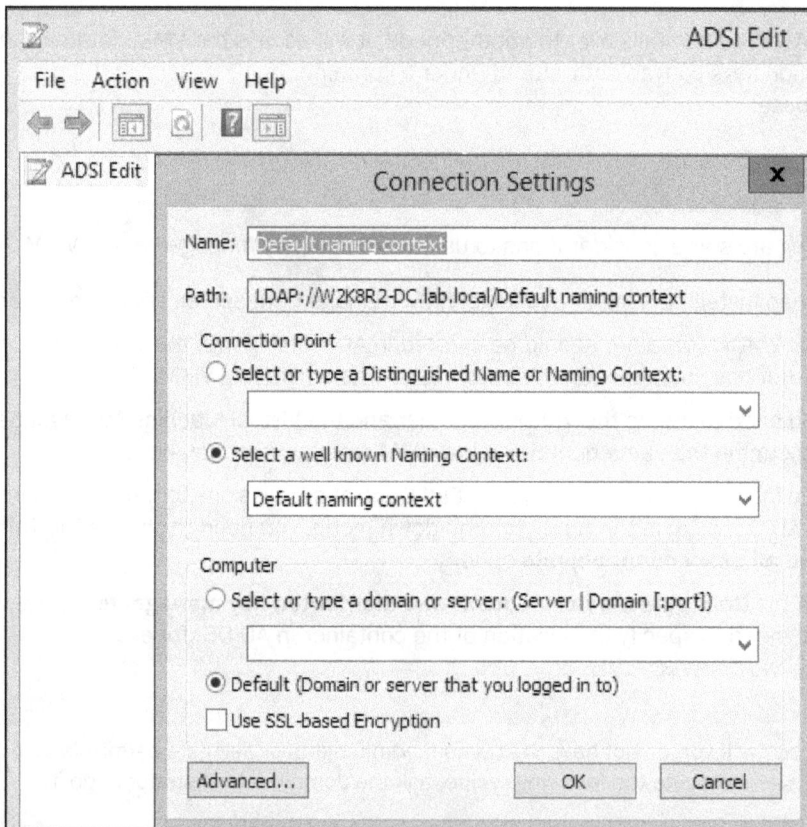

6. Expand **DC=lab,DC=local**.

7. Right-click on **DC=lab,DC=local** and select **New**, then select **Object**.

8. Select **container** and click on **Next**, as shown in the following screenshot:

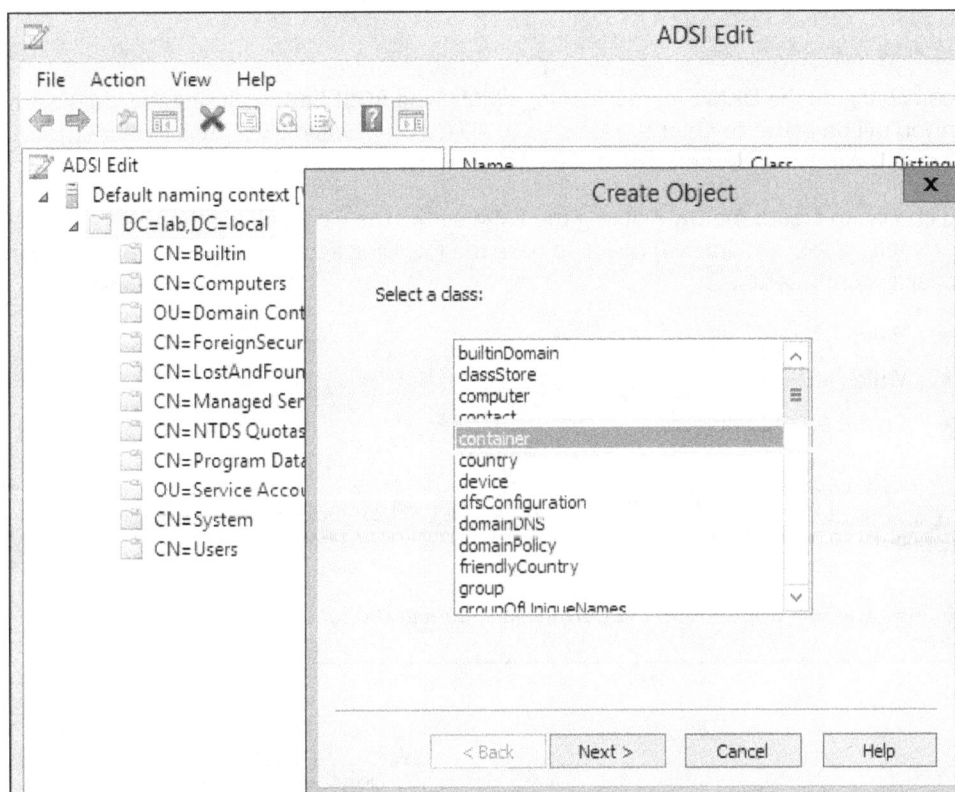

9. In the **Value** textbox, type in VMMDKM and click on **Next**.

10. Click on **Finish** and close the **ADSI Edit** window.

11. In the **Active Directory Users and Computers** window, in the top menu, click on **View** and then select **Advanced Features**.

12. Right-click on the **VMMDKM** container and click on **Properties**.

13. Click on the **Security** tab and then on **Add**.

14. Type in the name of the VMM administrators group, that is, lab\vmm-admins.

15. Check the **Read**, **Write**, and **Create all child objects** options.

16. Click on **Advanced**.

17. Select **VMM Admins** and click on **Edit**.

18. In the **Apply to** drop-down menu, select **This object and all descendant objects**.

19. Click on **OK**.

How it works...

You can configure the DKM before installing VMM using **ADSI Edit**, or during the VMM setup, when you will be asked to enter the location in AD that you would like to use to store the encryption keys. The location is the distinguished name of the container.

If you choose to create the DKM during the VMM setup, the user running the VMM installation (for example, `lab\vmm-admin`) needs to have the following access rights on the location that you specify during setup:

▶ Read

▶ Write

▶ Create all child objects

> If you are creating DKM under the root level, you will need these rights at the domain level.

The following screenshot shows the permissions configured for the VMM account:

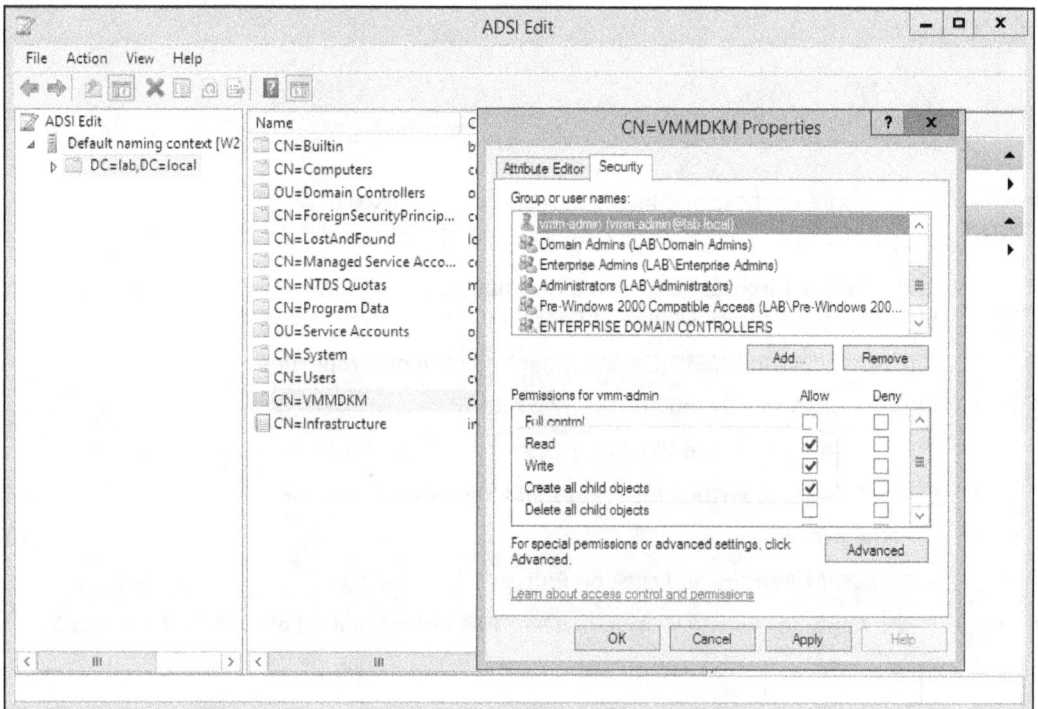

If the user running the setup has the right to create a container in AD DS, the VMM setup will check if a DKM container is created and then do either of the following:

▸ If a DKM container has already been created in AD, the VMM setup will create a new container under **VMMDKM** and give the necessary permissions to the VMM service account for this new container

▸ If a DKM container has not been created in AD, the VMM setup will create the container

> Note that the VMM service account is also selected on this wizard page. For HA VMM installations, the local system account is disabled.

See also

▸ The *KB. System Center 2012 Virtual Machine Manager Setup fails to create child objects for DKM* article at `http://blogs.technet.com/b/scvmm/archive/2012/06/18/kb-system-center-2012-virtual-machine-manager-setup-fails-to-create-child-objects-for-dkm.aspx`

▸ The *Configuring Distributed Key Management in VMM* article at `http://go.microsoft.com/fwlink/p/?LinkID=209609`

Installing a VMM management server

As discussed in *Chapter 1, VMM 2012 Architecture*, the VMM management server is the core of VMM. In this recipe, we will install the VMM management component. Again, it is important to look at your design first to find out where you are going to deploy this component. This should be the first component that you install.

Getting ready

Before you start with the installation of the VMM management server, ensure that your SQL server is up and running.

> From the VMM server, run the following command at the command prompt:
>
> `Telnet SQL-Server 1433`
>
> If you get a black screen after typing the preceding command and pressing *Enter*, it means that communication has been established. If you receive the message, **Could not open connection to the host**, the connection has failed and you need to look at SQL services or the firewall rules of your SQL Server and then proceed with the VMM installation. You can close the black screen.

Update your computer by running Windows Update and restarting it, if requested, before continuing with the VMM installation.

Ensure the following:

- ▸ The server meets the minimum system requirements.

- ▸ You have created the domain account that will be used by the Virtual Machine Manager Service (for example, `lab\vmm-svc`). *Do not log in with this account.* The VMM service account will be used on the **VMMDKM** wizard page.

- ▸ The installation account (for example, `lab\vmm-admin`) is a member of the local `Administrators` group. The account you are going to use for VMM needs to be a member of the local `Administrators` group on the computer you are installing VMM on. Add `LAB\vmm-svc` as well, which is the account we created previously to be the SCVMM service account.

- ▸ You have closed any open applications and there is no pending restart on the server.

- ▸ The computer is a member of the domain. In our case, we are using `LAB.LOCAL` as the domain.

- ▸ You have created a DKM container in AD DS before installing VMM. Otherwise, if the user account (`LAB\vmm-admin`) running the setup has the right to create the `VMMDKM` container in AD DS, you don't need to create it beforehand.

> If the setup was not completed successfully, check the logs in the `%SYSTEMDRIVE%\ProgramData\VMMLogs` folder.

How to do it...

Carry out the following steps to install the VMM management server:

1. Log in as `LAB\vmm-admin` or with an account that has administrator rights.

2. Browse to the VMM setup folder, right-click on **setup**, and then select **Run as administrator**.

3. Click on **Install** on the setup page and select **VMM Management server** on the **Select features to install** page, and then click on **Next** as follows:

> Microsoft System Center 2012 R2 Virtual Machine Manager Setup Wizard ☒
>
> Getting started   Report a problem
>
> ## Select features to install
>
> ☑ VMM management server
>
> Installs the Virtual Machine Manager service, which processes commands and controls communications with the VMM database, library servers, and virtual machine hosts.
> This feature requires a SQL Server database and Windows Assessment and Deployment Kit (ADK) for Windows 8.1. (View all installation requirements)
>
> ☑ VMM console
>
> Installs a program that allows you to connect to a VMM management server to centrally view and manage resources, such as hosts, virtual machines, private clouds, and services. (View all installation requirements)
>
>   Previous   Next >   Cancel

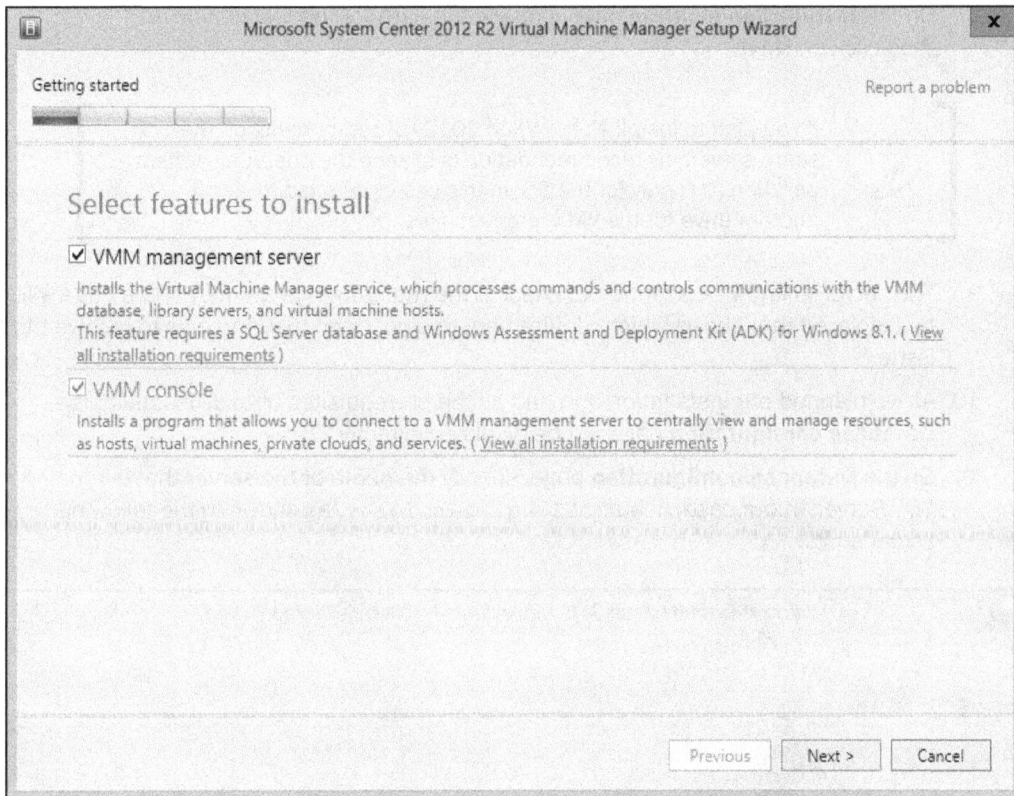

The VMM Self-Service Portal has not been available since VMM 2012 SP1 and was replaced by System Center App Controller. Refer to the *Deploying SC App Controller 2012 R2 for hybrid cloud management* recipe in *Chapter 8, Managing Hybrid Clouds, Fabric Updates, Resources, Clusters, and the New Features of R2*.

The VMM console option will be selected and installed when you select **VMM management server**.

4. On the **Product registration information** page, type in the key and then click on **Next**.

5. On the **Please read this license agreement** page, check the **I have read, understood, and agree with the terms of the license agreement** checkbox and then click on **Next**.

6. On the **Customer Experience Improvement Program** page, choose **Yes** to participate or **No**, and then click on **Next**.

7. On the **Microsoft Update** page, check the checkbox **ON** (recommended) to look at Microsoft Update for the latest updates, and then click on **Next**.

8. On the **Installation location** page, provide the path for the installation and then click on **Next**.

> If you plan to install all the VMM 2012 R2 components on the same server, my recommendation is to keep the operating system partition (C:) only for the OS. In this case, you need to select another drive for the VMM program files.

9. The server will now be scanned to check if the requirements are met and a page will be displayed that shows which requirement has not been met and how to resolve the issue.

10. As we planned our installation and had all the prerequisites already installed, the **Database configuration** page will be displayed directly.

11. On the **Database configuration** page, specify the name of the server that is running SQL Server. In our case, it is w2012-sql.lab.local, as shown in the following screenshot:

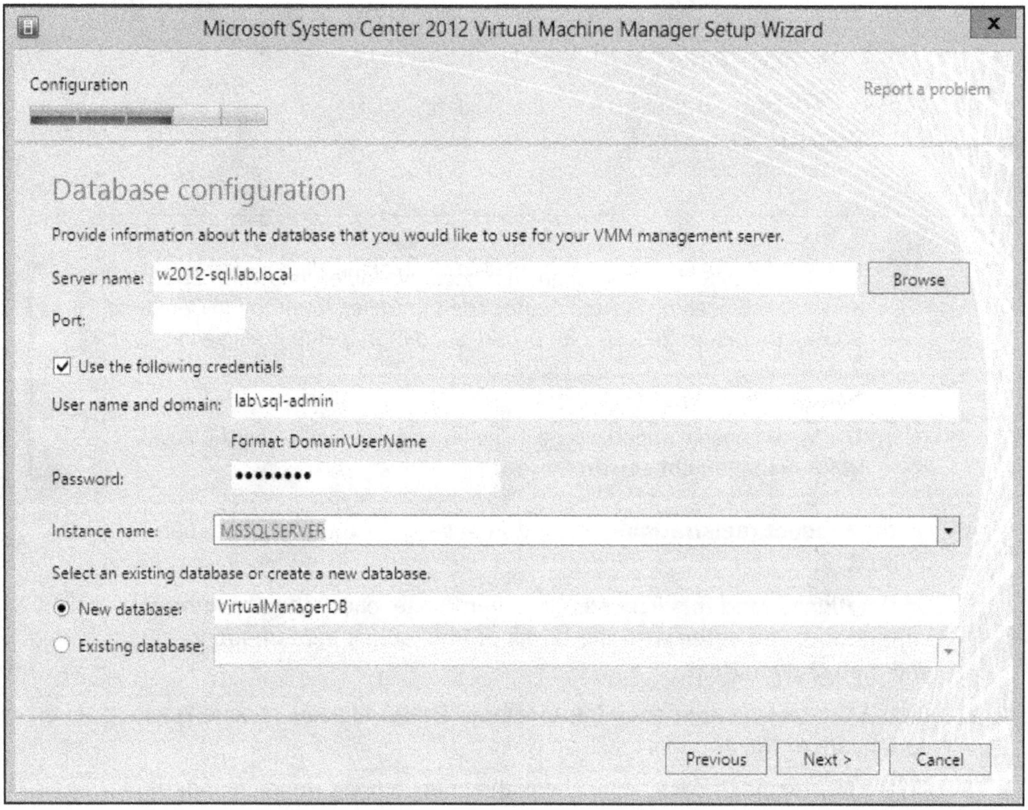

> If SQL Server is running on the same server, which is not a recommended approach, you can type in `localhost` or the name of the computer (for example, `vmm-mgmt01.lab.local`).

12. You don't need to specify the port used for SQL communication unless *all* of the following conditions are true for SQL:

    ❑ SQL Server is running on another server (recommended)

    ❑ The SQL Server Browser service is not started

    ❑ Not using the default port of 1433

13. In the **Instance name** field, provide the SQL Server instance or select the default, that is, **MSSQLSERVER**.

> If the **Instance** name does not show the SQL instances to be selected, confirm whether the SQL Server Browser service is running and check the inbound firewall rules on SQL Server.

14. Agree to create a new database (new VMM installation) or use an existing database (for example, a recover situation), and click on **Next**.

15. On the **Configure service account and distributed key management** page, select the account for Virtual Machine Manager Service.

16. If the selection is **Domain Account**, type in the user domain account in the `domain\user` format, type in the password, and click on **Next**.

> You will not be able to change the account after the VMM installation is complete (as it is not supported). Refer to the *Creating service accounts* recipe in this chapter.

17. In the **Distributed Key Management** section, select **Store my keys in Active Directory** if you have decided to use DKM (recommended approach), as shown in the following screenshot:

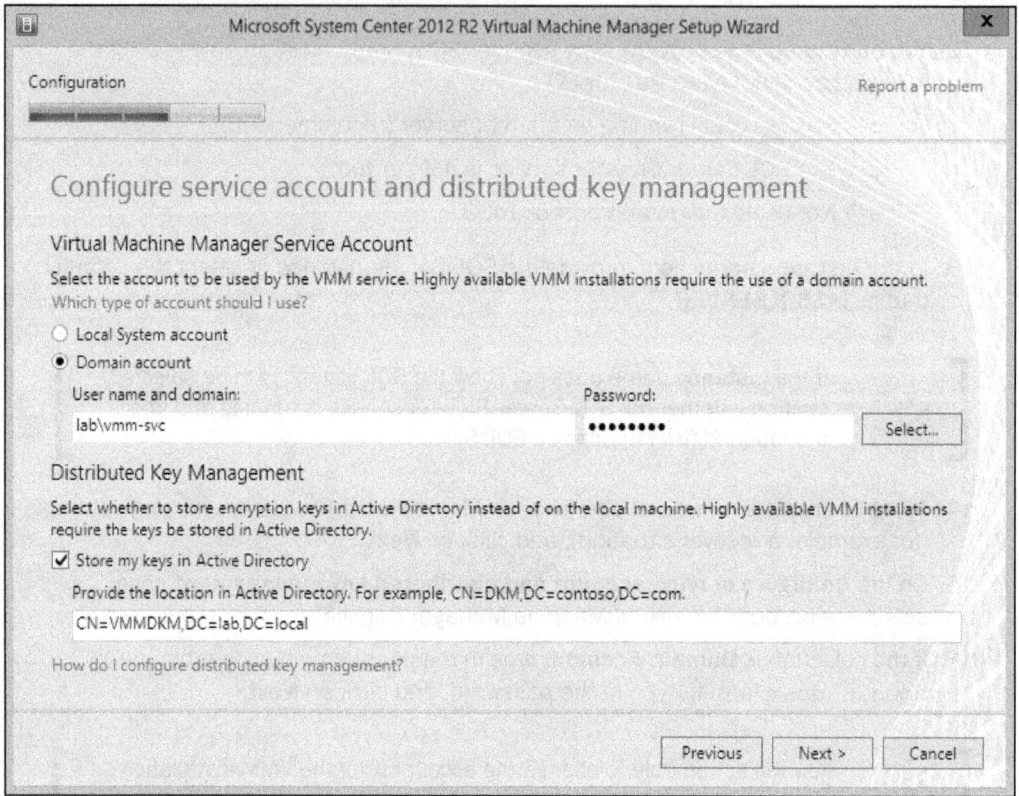

| Microsoft System Center 2012 R2 Virtual Machine Manager Setup Wizard | ☒ |

Configuration   Report a problem

Configure service account and distributed key management

Virtual Machine Manager Service Account

Select the account to be used by the VMM service. Highly available VMM installations require the use of a domain account.
Which type of account should I use?

○ Local System account
● Domain account

| User name and domain: | Password: |
| lab\vmm-svc | •••••••• | Select... |

Distributed Key Management

Select whether to store encryption keys in Active Directory instead of on the local machine. Highly available VMM installations require the keys be stored in Active Directory.

☑ Store my keys in Active Directory

Provide the location in Active Directory. For example, CN=DKM,DC=contoso,DC=com.

CN=VMMDKM,DC=lab,DC=local

How do I configure distributed key management?

Previous | Next > | Cancel

> It is strongly recommended that you select to store in Active Directory; this is required when installing a highly available VMM server.

18. On the **Port configuration** page, leave the default port numbers or provide a unique value for each feature, and then click on **Next** as shown in the following screenshot:

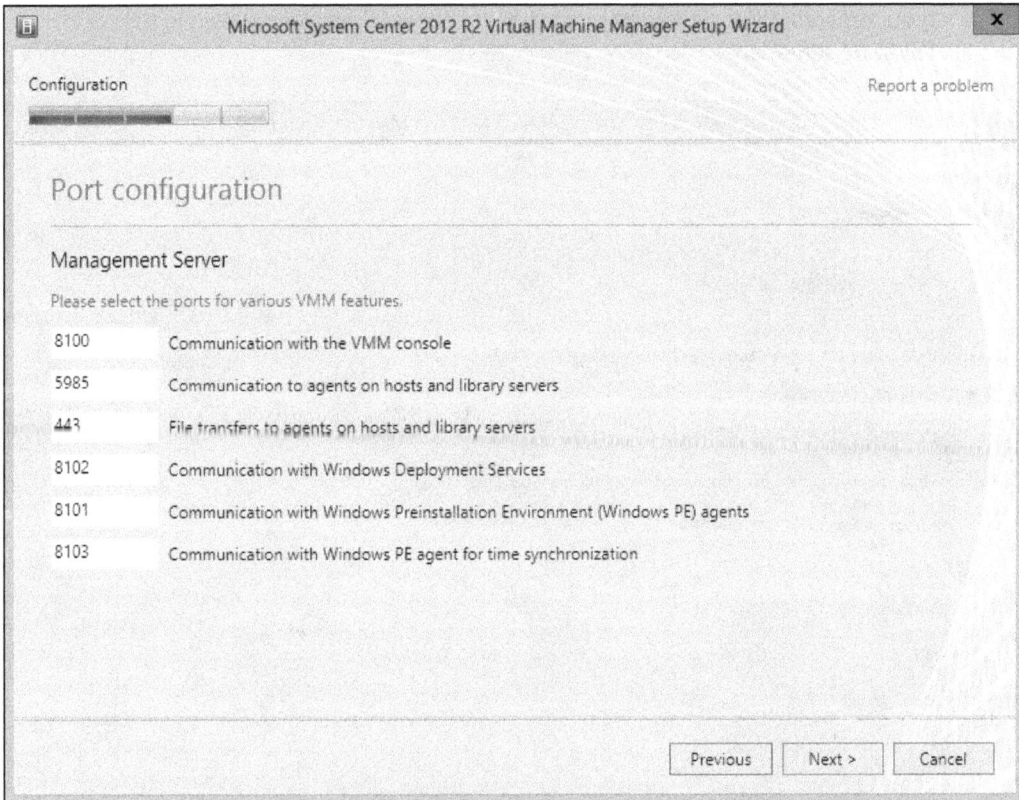

Microsoft System Center 2012 R2 Virtual Machine Manager Setup Wizard	x

Configuration   Report a problem

Port configuration

Management Server

Please select the ports for various VMM features.

Port	Description
8100	Communication with the VMM console
5985	Communication to agents on hosts and library servers
443	File transfers to agents on hosts and library servers
8102	Communication with Windows Deployment Services
8101	Communication with Windows Preinstallation Environment (Windows PE) agents
8103	Communication with Windows PE agent for time synchronization

Previous	Next >	Cancel

Document and plan the ports before choosing them as you cannot change the ports without reinstalling VMM.

19. On the **Library configuration** page, select the **Create a new library share** option if you want to create a new library share; or, select the **Use an existing library share** option if you want to use the existing library share, depending upon your requirements. Click on **Select** to specify the share location as shown in the following screenshot:

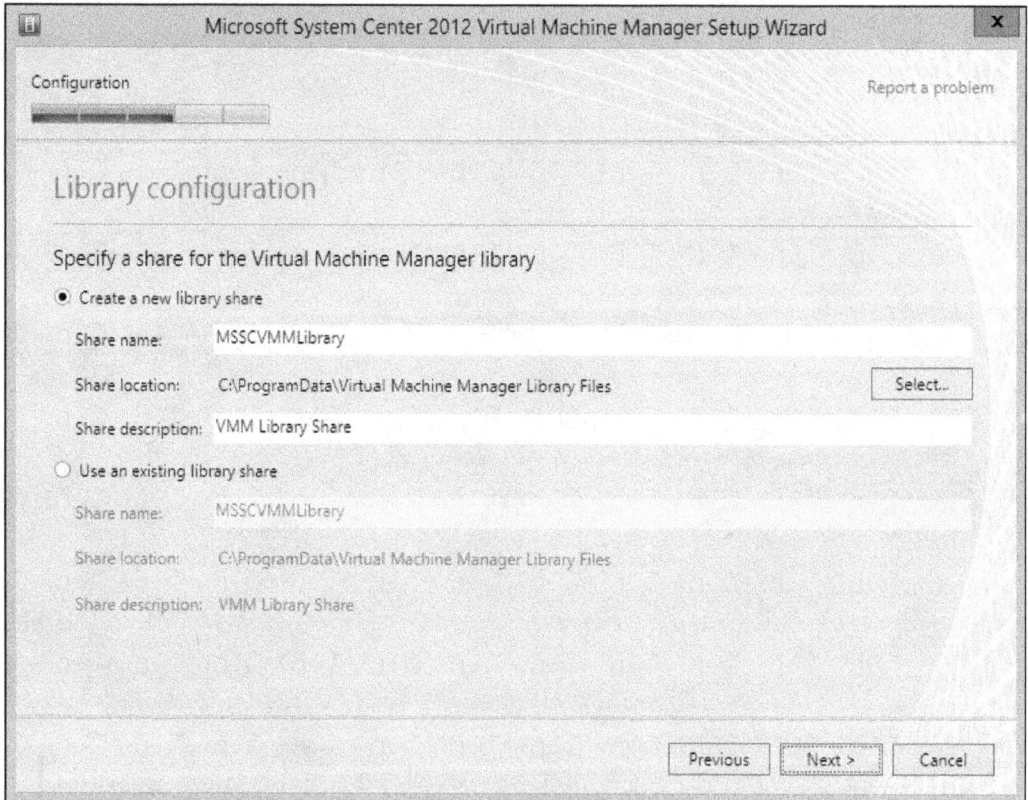

Microsoft System Center 2012 Virtual Machine Manager Setup Wizard ☒

Configuration   Report a problem

Library configuration

Specify a share for the Virtual Machine Manager library

● Create a new library share

    Share name: MSSCVMMLibrary

    Share location: C:\ProgramData\Virtual Machine Manager Library Files   Select...

    Share description: VMM Library Share

○ Use an existing library share

    Share name: MSSCVMMLibrary

    Share location: C:\ProgramData\Virtual Machine Manager Library Files

    Share description: VMM Library Share

Previous   Next >   Cancel

---

20. Click on **Next** to continue.

21. On the **Installation summary** page, review your selections. Click on **Previous** if you want to change any selections.

22. Click on **Install** to start the installation, and an installation progress bar will be displayed.

23. On the **Setup completed successfully** page, click on **Close**.

How it works...

The installation of VMM Management Server 2012 is straightforward because it has enhancements added that simplify the installation process. When you click on **Install** on the main setup page, this version will install some of the prerequisites for you, if necessary. In addition, if you are installing VMM on a cluster node, you will be prompted to make it highly available. For more information, refer to *Chapter 4, Installing a High Available VMM Server*.

If the user account running the VMM setup (LAB\vmm-admin) has the right to create the VMMDKM container in AD DS, you don't necessarily need to create it beforehand; although, it is recommended because of the following:

▸ The VMM setup checks if the VMMDKM container is present in AD. If it is present, it creates a new container under VMMDKM.

▸ If the VMMDKM container does not exist, the setup tries to create it.

When creating the container, VMM will give the VMM service domain account's selected permissions to it (informed on the same page).

> When installing HA VMM, you cannot select the local system account as it is not supported.

If your account does not have the CREATE permissions option on the SQL database server, or if you are not a database administrator, you can ask the administrator to create the VMM database beforehand. Alternatively, you can provide an account with permissions to create a database on SQL Server during the installation process by selecting the **Use the following credentials** checkbox and then providing the username and password.

During installation, you will be required to create the VMM library. The default share is MSSCVMMLibrary, and the folder is located at %SYSTEMDRIVE%\ProgramData\Virtual Machine Manager Library Files, which is a hidden folder.

> After the installation, you will be able to add additional library shares or servers on the VMM console using the VMM command shell.

See also

▸ The *Designing the VMM server, database, and console implementation* recipe in *Chapter 1, VMM 2012 Architecture*

Installing the VMM console

After installing the VMM management server, we need to install the VMM console to manage VMM from the desktop.

The VMM console is the GUI interface to the VMM management server. For example, you will be using it to manage the cloud, fabric, storage, and resources.

Getting ready

Before you start with installing the VMM console, ensure that the VMM management server is up and running. Also, check if your machine fulfills all the prerequisites for the VMM console installation.

> Consult the logfiles in the `%SYSTEMDRIVE%\ProgramData\VMMLogs` folder. Check `ProgramData` if you find issues at the time of installation.

Make sure you log in with an account that is a member of the local `Administrators` group before starting with the installation.

How to do it...

Carry out the following steps to install the VMM console:

1. Log in as `lab\vmm-admin` or with administrator rights.

2. Browse to the VMM setup folder, right-click on **setup**, and then select **Run as administrator**.

3. On the setup page, click on **Install**.

4. On the **Select features to install** page, select only **VMM console** (as shown in the following screenshot), and then click on **Next**:

```
┌──────────────────────────────────────────────────────────────────────┐
│ 🔲     Microsoft System Center 2012 R2 Virtual Machine Manager Setup Wizard    │ x │
├──────────────────────────────────────────────────────────────────────┤
│ Getting started                                              Report a problem │
│ ▬▬▬                                                                    │
│                                                                        │
│   Select features to install                                          │
│                                                                        │
│   ☐ VMM management server   ⟸ uncheck this option                     │
│   Installs the Virtual Machine Manager service, which processes commands and controls communications with the VMM │
│   database, library servers, and virtual machine hosts.               │
│   This feature requires a SQL Server database and Windows Assessment and Deployment Kit (ADK) for Windows 8.1. ( View │
│   all installation requirements )                                     │
│                                                                        │
│   ☑ VMM console                                                       │
│   Installs a program that allows you to connect to a VMM management server to centrally view and manage resources, such │
│   as hosts, virtual machines, private clouds, and services. ( View all installation requirements ) │
└──────────────────────────────────────────────────────────────────────┘
```

5. On the **Please read this license agreement** page, check the **I have read, understood, and agree with the terms of the license agreement** checkbox and then click on **Next**.

6. On the **Join the Customer Experience Improvement Program (CEIP)** page, choose **Yes** to participate or **No**, and then click on **Next**.

7. On the **Microsoft Update** page, check the checkbox **ON** (recommended) to look at Microsoft Update for the latest updates, and then click on **Next**.

8. On the **Installation location** page, provide the path for the installation and then click on **Next**.

9. On the **Port configuration** page, type in the port that the VMM console will use to communicate with the VMM management server, and then click on **Next**.

> You already configured this port setting during the installation of the VMM management server. The default port setting is 8100.

10. On the **Installation summary** page, click on **Previous** if you want to change any selections, or on **Install** to proceed with the installation.

> To open the VMM console at the end of the installation, select **Open the VMM console when this wizard closes**.

11. On the **Setup completed successfully** page, click on **Close**.

How it works...

The installation process will install the VMM console on your desktop machine. By doing this, you will be able to connect to and perform all VMM-related activities remotely from your computer.

The installation process will scan the computer to make sure the requirements are met, and a page will be displayed that shows any prerequisites that have not been met.

Connecting to a VMM management server using the VMM console

The VMM console is the GUI interface to the VMM management server. You will be using it, for example, to manage virtual machines, services, the private cloud, fabric, storage, and resources.

You can use this recipe to configure the VMM console to connect to a VMM management server.

The VMM console will enable you to manage VMM remotely from your desktop without the need of RDP into the VMM server.

How to do it...

Carry out the following steps in order to complete this recipe:

1. In the **Server name** box that is in the **Connect to Server** dialog box of the **Virtual Machine Manager Console** window, type in the name of the VMM management server (for example, `vmm-mgmt01:8100`, where `8100` is the default port).

2. To connect, click on **Specify credentials** and then type the user credentials (for example, `lab\vmm-admin`), or click on **Use current Microsoft Windows Identity**.

3. Click on **Connect**.

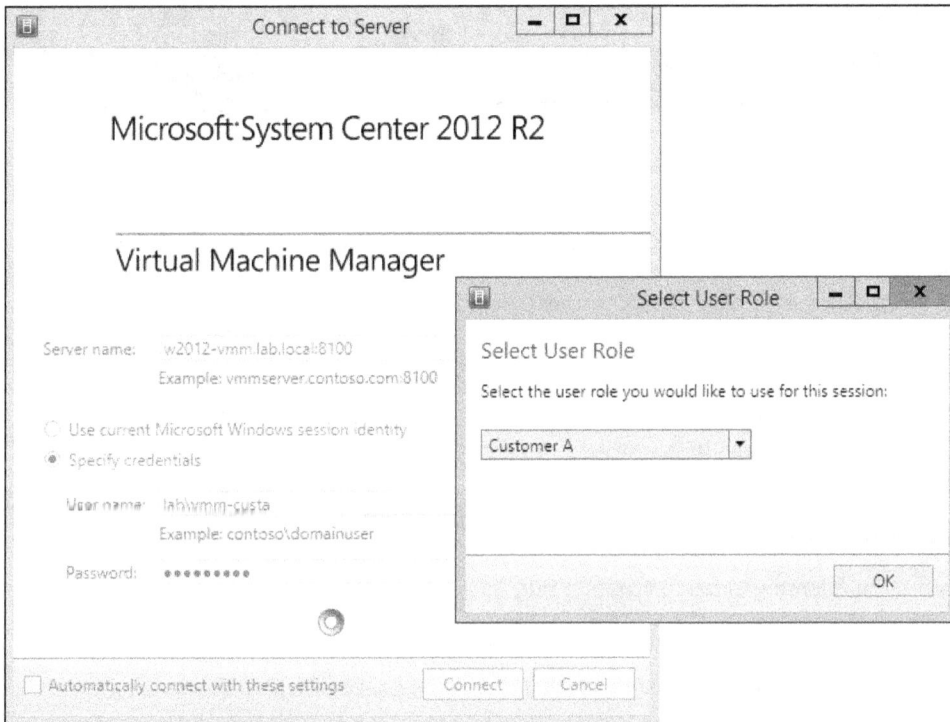

How it works...

You can use the logged Windows login credentials to connect to VMM if the user is allowed to connect, or you can specify an account.

You will need to specify the user credentials on a multitenant environment or if the user account is not on the same domain as the VMM management server.

If the account has multiple user roles (for example, Tenant Administrator and Self-Service User), you will be prompted to select the user role that you can log in with.

See also

▶ The *Creating user roles in VMM* recipe in *Chapter 6, Deploying Virtual Machines and Services*

Creating credentials for a Run As account in VMM

This recipe will guide you through the process of configuring security in VMM using Run As accounts.

In VMM 2012, the credentials that a user enters for any process can be provided by a Run As account.

Only administrators or delegated administrators have the rights to create and manage Run As accounts.

If within their scope, read-only administrators will be able to read a user's account name related to the Run As account.

How to do it...

Carry out the following steps to create a Run As account's credentials in VMM:

1. In Windows, click on the **Start** menu and then on the VMM console.

2. On the VMM 2012 console, in the left-bottom corner, click on the **Settings** workspace.

3. In the **Home** tab, on the top ribbon, click on **Create Run As Account**.

4. In the **Create Run As Account** dialog box, type in the name for the Run As account (for example, `Hyper-V Host Administration Account`).

5. Optionally, enter a description for the account.

6. Provide the user account that will be used by the Run As account in the **User name** field (for example, `lab\vmm-admin`), as shown in the following screenshot:

> You can use a domain user or group or a local credential.

Provide the details for this Run As account

Name: Host Admin
Description:

User name: lab\vmm-HostAdmin
               Example: contoso\domainuser or localuser
Password: |
Confirm password:
☑ Validate domain credentials

7. Type in the password.

> ![note] Unselect **Validate domain credentials** if you are sure that the username
> and password are correct.

8. Click on **OK** to create the account.

How it works...

The creation of a Run As account starts when we create the account on the Active Directory
that will be used for the association.

A Run As account is an account securely stored in VMM that will be used to perform VMM
administrative tasks, such as adding hosts, adding clusters, and performing Bare Metal
deployments. If using the Run As account, you will not need to provide a username and
password while performing tasks that require credentials. There is no limit to the number
of Run As accounts you can have.

There's more...

Administrators and delegated administrators can create, delete, and make a Run As account temporarily unavailable in VMM. They can do the last by disabling the account and then enabling it to have it available again.

> Delegated administrators can only perform these actions within their scope.

Disabling a Run As account

Carry out the following steps to disable a Run As account:

1. In the VMM 2012 R2 console, in the left-bottom corner, click on the **Settings** workspace.

2. On the **Settings** pane, click on **Security**, and then click on **Run As Accounts**.

3. On the **Run As Accounts** main pane, click on the enabled Run As account to be disabled.

4. In the **Home** tab, on the top ribbon, click on **Disable**; you will see the **Enabled** status change to a red **X**.

> The account will be unavailable until you enable it again.

Enabling a disabled Run As account

Carry out the following steps to enable a Run As account:

1. In the VMM 2012 R2 console, in the left-bottom corner, click on the **Settings** workspace.

2. On the **Settings** pane, click on **Security** and then click on **Run As Accounts**.

3. On the **Run As Accounts** main pane, click on the disabled Run As account to be enabled.

4. In the **Home** tab, on the top ribbon, click on **Enable**; you will see the status change to **Enabled**.

Deleting a Run As account

Use the following steps to delete a Run As account that is not being used by any VMM running task:

1. In the VMM 2012 console, in the left-bottom corner, click on the **Settings** workspace.

2. On the **Settings** pane, click on **Security**, and then click on **Run As Accounts**.

3. On the **Run As Accounts** main pane, click on the Run As account to be deleted.

4. In the **Home** tab, on the top ribbon, click on **Delete** and then click on **Yes** to confirm the removal.

Configuring ports and protocols on the host firewall for each VMM component

When designing the VMM implementation, you need to plan which ports you are going to use for communication and file transfers between the VMM components. Based on the chosen ports, you also need to configure the host firewall and external firewalls to enable these ports.

Getting ready

Take note of the following ports to create firewall exceptions. Depending on your environment, you will need to configure the following exceptions on the host firewall as well as on your external firewall (for example, if you have a DMZ in place).

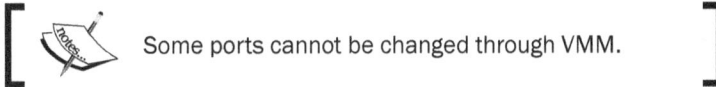

> Some ports cannot be changed through VMM.

The following table lists the default port settings and the place to change, if it is possible:

Connection from and to	Protocol	Default port	To change the port settings
SFTP file transfer from VMware ESX Server 3.0 to VMware ESX Server 3.5 hosts	SFTP	22	Cannot be changed.
The VMM management server to the P2V source agent (control channel)	DCOM	135	Cannot be changed.
The VMM management server to load balancer	HTTP/HTTPS	80/443	Load balancer configuration provider.

Connection from and to	Protocol	Default port	To change the port settings
The VMM management server to the WSUS server (data channel)	HTTP/HTTPS	80/8530 (non-SSL) and 443/8531 (with SSL)	These ports are the IIS port bindings with WSUS. They cannot be changed from the VMM.
The VMM management server to the WSUS server (control channel)	HTTP/HTTPS	80/8530 (non-SSL) and 443/8531 (with SSL)	These ports are the IIS port bindings with WSUS. They cannot be changed from the VMM.
The BITS port for VMM transfers (data channel)	BITS	443	During VMM setup.
The VMM library server to the hosts (file transfer)	BITS	443 (maximum value: 32768)	During VMM setup.
VMM host-to-host file transfer	BITS	443 (maximum value: 32768)	Cannot be changed.
VMware Web Services communication	HTTPS	443	VMM console.
SFTP file transfer from the VMM management server to VMware ESX Server 3i hosts	HTTPS	443	Cannot be changed.
OOB Connection: SMASH over WS-Man	HTTPS	443	On BMC.
The VMM management server to the in-guest agent (VMM to the virtual machine data channel)	HTTPS (using BITS)	443	Cannot be changed.
The VMM management server to the VMM agent on the host based on Windows Server (data channel for file transfers)	HTTPS (using BITS)	443 (maximum value: 32768)	Cannot be changed.
OOB connection IPMI	IPMI	623	On BMC.
The VMM management server to the remote Microsoft SQL Server database	TDS	1433	Cannot be changed.
Console connections (RDP) to virtual machines through Hyper-V hosts (VMConnect)	RDP	2179	VMM console.

Connection from and to	Protocol	Default port	To change the port settings
The VMM management server to the Citrix XenServer host (customization data channel)	iSCSI	3260	On XenServer in transfer VM.
Remote Desktop to virtual machines	RDP	3389	On the virtual machine.
The VMM management server to the VMM agent on Windows -Server-based host (control channel)	WS-Management	5985	During the VMM setup.
The VMM management server to the in-guest agent (VMM to the virtual machine control channel)	WS-Management	5985	Cannot be changed.
The VMM management server to the VMM agent on the Windows -Server-based host (control channel: SSL)	WS-Management	5986	Cannot be changed.
The VMM management server to the XenServer host (control channel)	HTTPS	5989	On the XenServer host in `/opt/cimserver/cimserver_planned.conf`.
The VMM console to the VMM management server	WCF	8100	During VMM setup.
The VMM console to the VMM management server (HTTPS)	WCF	8101	During VMM setup.
The Windows PE agent to the VMM management server (control channel)	WCF	8101	During VMM setup.
The VMM console to the VMM management server (Net.TCP)	WCF	8102	During VMM setup.
The WDS provider to the VMM management server	WCF	8102	During VMM setup.
The VMM console to the VMM management server (HTTP)	WCF	8103	During VMM setup.
The Windows PE agent to the VMM management server (time sync)	WCF	8103	During VMM setup.
The VMM management server to Storage Management Service	WMI	Local call	Cannot be changed.

Connection from and to	Protocol	Default port	To change the port settings
The VMM management server to the Cluster PowerShell interface	PowerShell	N/A	Cannot be changed.
Storage Management Service to the SMI-S provider	CIM-XML	Provider-specific port	Cannot be changed.
The VMM management server to the P2V source agent (data channel)	BITS	User defined	P2V cmdlet option.

How to do it...

Carry out the following steps to change the firewall rules:

1. On the server where you need to configure the firewall exceptions, click on **Start**. Next, click on **Administrative Tools** and then click on **Windows Firewall with Advanced Security**.

2. On the **Windows Firewall with Advanced Security on Local Computer** pane, click on **Inbound Rules**.

3. On the **Actions** pane, under **Inbound Rules**, click on **New Rule**.

4. In the **New Inbound Rule Wizard** window, under **Rule Type**, click on **Port** and then click on **Next**.

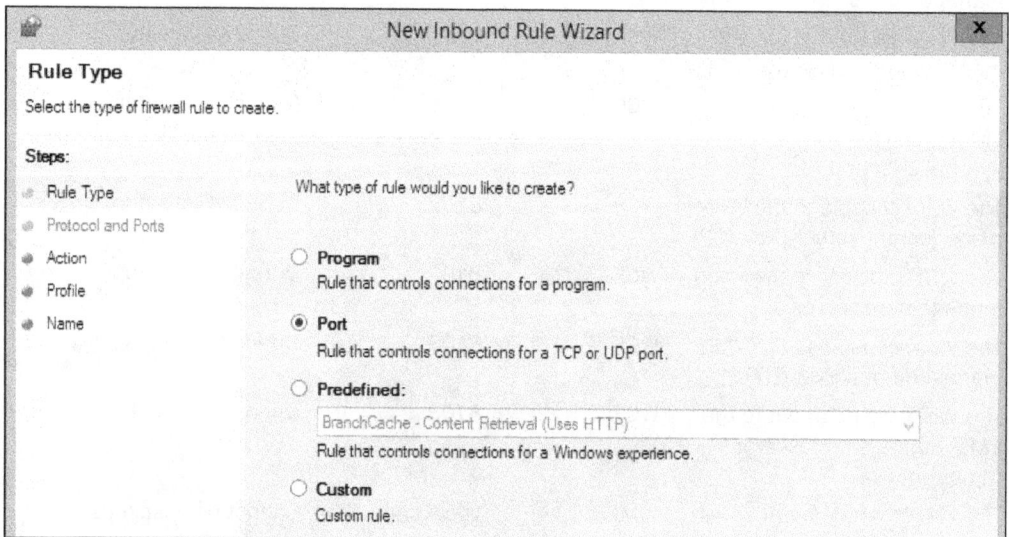

5. In **Protocol and Ports**, click on **TCP**.

6. Click on **Specific local ports** and type the port number (for example, 8100); then, click on **Next**.

7. On the **Action** page, click on **Next**.

8. On the **Profile** page, click on **Next**.

9. On the **Name** page, type in the description (for example, VMM console TCP 8100).

10. Click on **Finish** to create the rule.

> Repeat steps 3 through 10 for each port number that you need to configure.

1. Close **Windows Firewall with Advanced Security**.

See also

► The *Configure the Windows Firewall to Allow SQL Server Access* article at http://msdn.microsoft.com/en-us/library/cc646023.aspx

► The *SCVMM 2012 Ports Communications for Firewall Configuration* article at http://social.technet.microsoft.com/wiki/contents/articles/4581.scvmm-2012-ports-communications-for-firewall-configuration.aspx

► The *Technical Documentation Download for System Center 2012 – Operations Manager* article at http://www.microsoft.com/en-au/download/details.aspx?id=29256

4
Installing a High Available VMM Server

In this chapter, we will cover the following:

- ▶ Installing a highly available VMM management server
- ▶ Installing a VMM management server on the additional node of a cluster
- ▶ Connecting to a highly available VMM management server using the VMM console
- ▶ Deploying a highly available library server on a file server cluster
- ▶ Uninstalling a highly available VMM management server

Introduction

Understanding how VMM has become a critical part of private cloud infrastructure is very important. This chapter will walk you through the recipes to implement a highly available VMM server, which is especially useful in enterprise and datacenter environments.

VMM plays a critical role in managing private cloud and datacenter infrastructure, which means that keeping the VMM infrastructure always available is crucial to preserving a service's continuity, to provisioning, and to monitoring VMs to respond to fluctuations in usage.

Before VMM 2012, it was not possible to have an HA VMM management server, which resulted in an unavailable service if a VM stopped responding or if the host server restarted, failed, or needed to be shut down for maintenance or patching.

VMM 2012 now allows you to deploy the VMM server on a failover cluster, resulting in highly available services. You can then plan the failover for maintenance purposes, and in the event of a failure, it will automatically fail over to a running node to ensure the VMM service remains online.

Keep in mind that the VMM library needs to be made accessible by all cluster nodes as the VMM server requires access to the library, irrespective of which cluster node it is running on. This can be achieved by placing the VMM library files on a clustered file server.

Installing a highly available VMM management server

This recipe will provide the steps to install a high available VMM management server.

The HA VMM installation is very similar to a standalone installation, and it is integrated into the usual standalone installation.

To install VMM in an HA, you just need to start the installation of VMM management in one of the nodes of the cluster and then select **Install**.

Important VMM 2012 R2 high available notes:

This is a fault-tolerant service feature, but it does not mean that it will increase the scale or performance.

Of a maximum of 16 nodes, only one VMM management node will be active at any time.

Connecting to a node name is not allowed. You will have to type the HA VMM service cluster name in the VMM console login when prompted for a VMM server name and port number.

To run a VMM-planned failover, say, for server patching, use the failover cluster UI and not the VMM console.

In SP1, high availability with N_Port ID Virtualization (NPIV) is not supported, although VMM does support Virtual Fibre Channel configured for VMs in Windows 2012/R2 Hyper-V.

Designing and planning the failover cluster is the first thing you need to do before beginning the installation of a highly available VMM management server. You can install a VMM management server on either a physical cluster or guest cluster.

The best practice—and my recommendation—for production hosting and datacenter operations would be to install the VMM management server on a cluster with dedicated physical servers, as you will be running critical solutions.

The figures in this section show the architecture design for a guest cluster using Share VHDX or Virtual Fibre Channel, which are explained as follows:

▸ **Shared VHDX**: Configuration using a Shared VHDX disk stored on an iSCSI/FC/file server storage

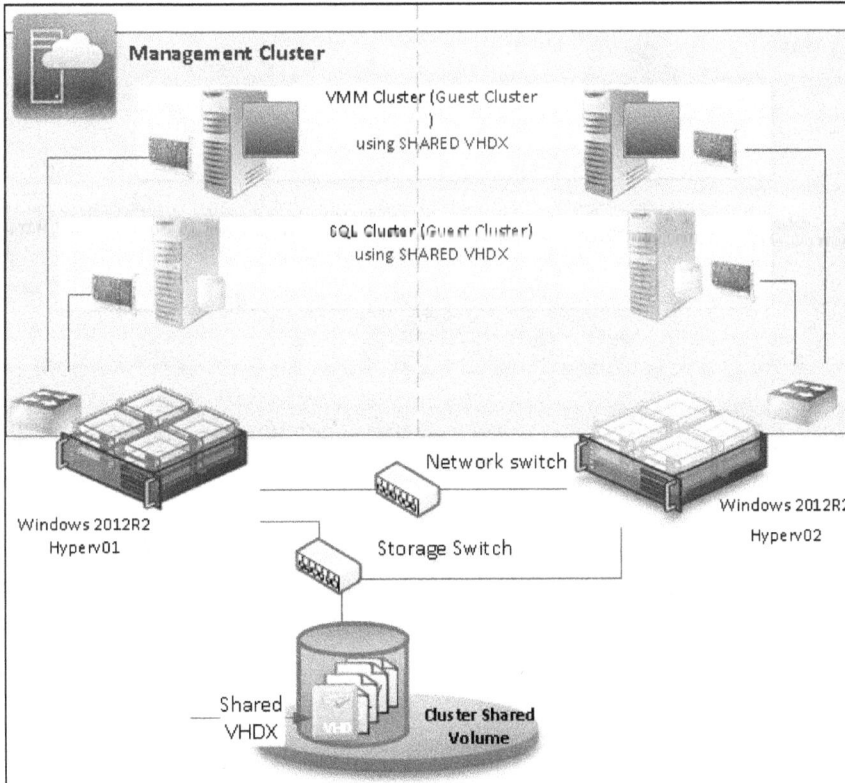

▶ **Virtual Fibre Channel**: As a new feature in Windows 2012, if your storage is Fibre Channel and supports NPIV, you can use it to create a guest cluster using Virtual Fibre Channel connectivity directly with the storage:

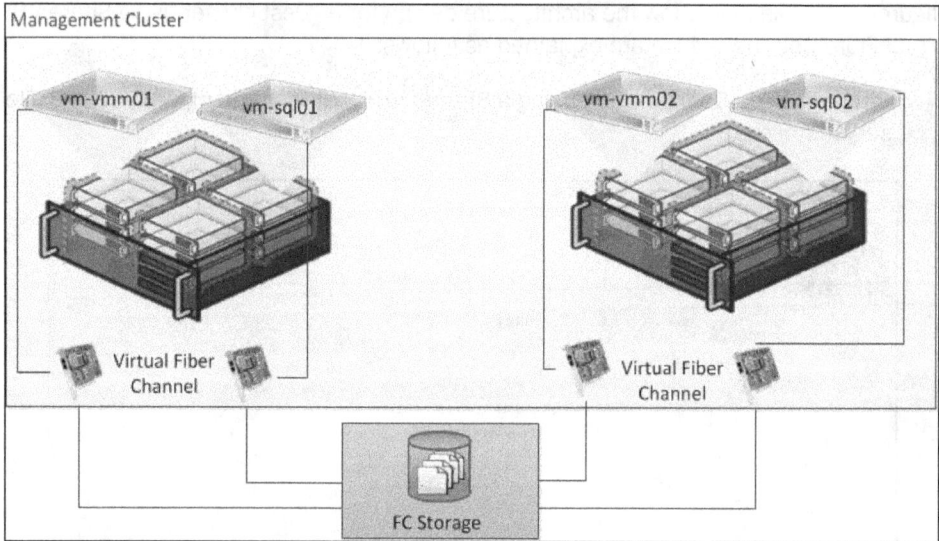

> VMM 2012 R2 supports NPIV, but VMM 2012 SP1 does not. You can still deploy it with the Hyper-V Manager console if you are using VMM 2012 SP1.

Getting ready

Update your computer by running Windows Update and restarting it, if requested, before continuing with the VMM installation.

Ensure the following:

▶ The server meets the minimum system requirements; they are as follows:

  ❏ The failover cluster should be created and configured.

> For information on how to create a failover cluster, visit `http://technet.microsoft.com/en-us/library/dn505754.aspx`.

  ❏ The SQL Server should be deployed and ready. The recommendation and best practice is to have a clustered SQL Server.

☐ The **Distributed key management** (**DKM**) container should be created earlier on Active Directory or on an installation account that has permission on the Active Directory container.

▸ The domain account that will be used by the VMM service (for example, `Lab\vmm-svc`) is created. *Do not log in with this account*. The VMM service account will be used on the VMMDKM wizard page. For HA VMM installations, the local system account is disabled.

▸ The installation account (for example, `Lab\vmm-admin`) is a member of the local `Administrators` group on the computer that you are installing VMM on. Add the `Lab\vmm-svc` account, as well, which is the account we previously created to be the SCVMM Service Account.

▸ You have closed any open applications, and there is no pending restart on the server.

▸ The computer is a member of the domain. In our case, we are using `LAB.LOCAL` as the domain.

▸ You have installed all the VMM prerequisites.

> If the setup was not completed successfully, check the logfiles for details. The logfiles are present in the `%SYSTEMDRIVE%\ProgramData\VMMLogs` folder.
>
> Note that the `ProgramData` folder is a hidden folder.

How to do it...

Carry out the following steps to install an HA VMM management server:

1. Log in as `lab\vmm-admin` or with an account that has administrator rights.

2. Browse to the VMM installation media, right-click on `setup`, and select **Run as administrator**.

3. On the main **Setup** page, click on **Install**; the install process will detect whether it is running on a cluster node and then ask if you want to make it highly available.

4. Click on **Yes** to start the HA VMM installation.

> If you click on **No**, VMM will be installed as a standalone VMM server.

5. Click on **VMM management server** to select it and then click on **Next >**:

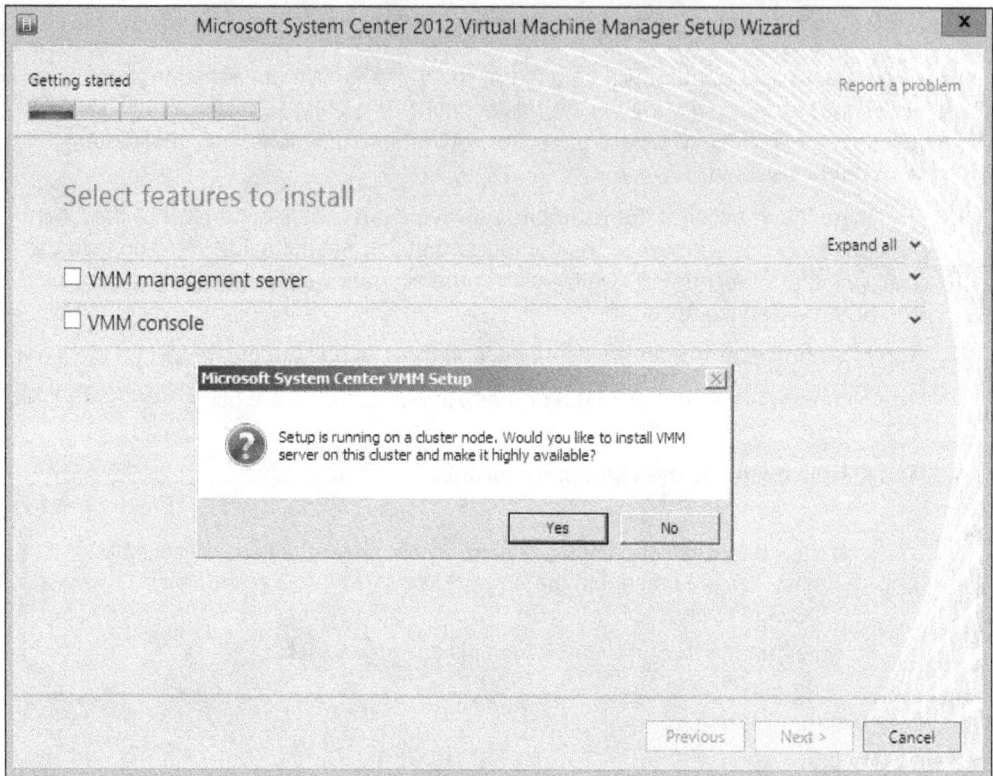

> The VMM Self-Service Portal is not available for installation since VMM 2012 SP1, as it has now been replaced by System Center App Controller.
>
> Also note that the VMM console gets selected automatically when you select a VMM management server.

6. On the **Product registration information** page, type the VMM key and click on **Next**.

7. On the **Please read this license agreement** page, accept the license and click on **Next**.

8. On the **Join the Customer Experience Improvement Program (CEIP)** page, choose **Yes** or **No** and click on **Next**.

9. On the **Microsoft Update** page, select **On (recommended)** to use Microsoft Update and click on **Next**.

10. On the **Installation location** page, provide the path for the installation and then click on **Next**.

> It is recommended that you keep the OS partition (C:) only for the operating system and allot another drive for the VMM program files.

11. The server will now be scanned to check whether the requirements have been met. A page will be displayed that shows which requirement has not been met and how to resolve the issue.

12. As we have planned our installation and have all of the prerequisites already installed, the **Database configuration** page will be displayed.

> As per best practice, and for a full high-availability deployment of VMM, it is recommended that you use a clustered SQL Server. Refer to the *Planning for High Availability* recipe in *Chapter 1, VMM 2012 Architecture*.

13. On the **Database configuration** page, specify the name of the server that is running SQL Server. In our case, it is **w2012-sql.lab.local**, as shown in the following screenshot:

> You cannot have SQL Server on the same machine that is running the high available VMM management server. SQL Server needs to be available from both cluster nodes.

14. You don't need to specify the port used for SQL communication unless *all* of the following conditions are true for SQL:

    ❑ The SQL Server is running on another server (recommended).

    ❑ The SQL Server Browser service has not been started.

    ❑ You are not using the default port, 1433.

15. In the **Instance name** field, provide the SQL Server instance or select the default, that is, **MSSQLSERVER**.

> If the **Instance name** field does not show the SQL instances to be selected, check whether **SQL Browser service** is running on the SQL Server and whether the inbound firewall rules on the SQL Server are running, as well.

16. Specify whether you want to create a new database or use an existing database and click on **Next**.

17. On the **Cluster Configuration** page, specify the cluster name, and if required, the network configuration (for example, if the IP has been provided by DHCP servers, the network configuration will not be requested).

> The cluster name is an AD object name. Make sure the cluster name is a unique name.

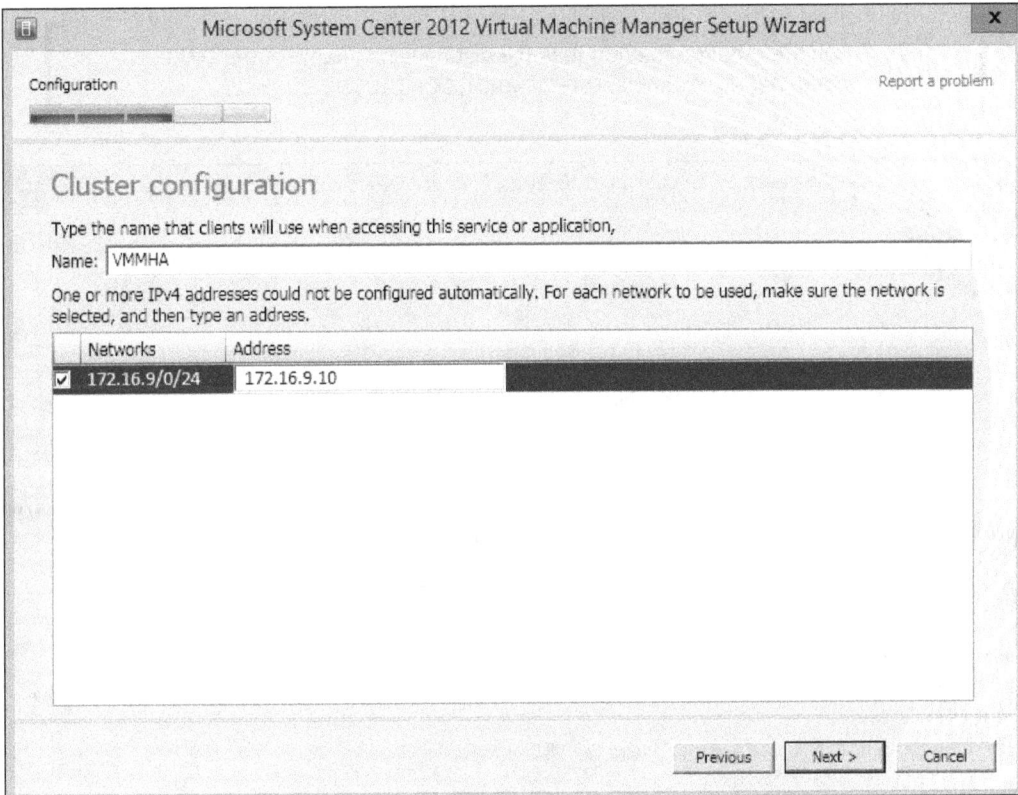

18. On the **Configure service account and distributed key management** page, provide the domain account for the VMM service.

> Create a dedicated domain account for VMM as a service account (for example, **LAB\vmm-svc**).
>
> It is important to know that you will not be able to change the account after the VMM installation is complete (as it is not supported). Refer to the *Creating service accounts* recipe in *Chapter 3, Installing VMM 2012 R2*.

19. In the **Distributed Key Management** section, select **Store my keys in Active Directory,** as it is required by the HA VMM deployment.

[You are required to enter it as the distinguished name of the DKM
container (for example, `CN=VMMDKM,DC=lab,DC=local`).]

Microsoft System Center 2012 Virtual Machine Manager Setup Wizard   X

Configuration   Report a problem

Configure service account and distributed key management

Virtual Machine Manager Service Account

Select the account to be used by the VMM service. Highly available VMM installations require the use of a domain account.
Which type of account should I use?

○ Local System account
◉ Domain account

User name and domain: Password:

lab\vmm-svc   ••••••••   Select...

Distributed Key Management

Select whether to store encryption keys in Active Directory instead of on the local machine. Highly available VMM installations require the keys be stored in Active Directory.

☑ Store my keys in Active Directory

Provide the location in Active Directory. For example, CN=DKM,DC=contoso,DC=com.

CN=VMMDKM,DC=lab,DC=local

How do I configure distributed key management?

                  Previous   Next >   Cancel

---

20. On the **Port configuration** page, leave the default port numbers or provide a unique value for each feature, as shown in the following screenshot, and then click on **Next**:

> Document and plan the ports before choosing, as you cannot change the ports without reinstalling VMM.

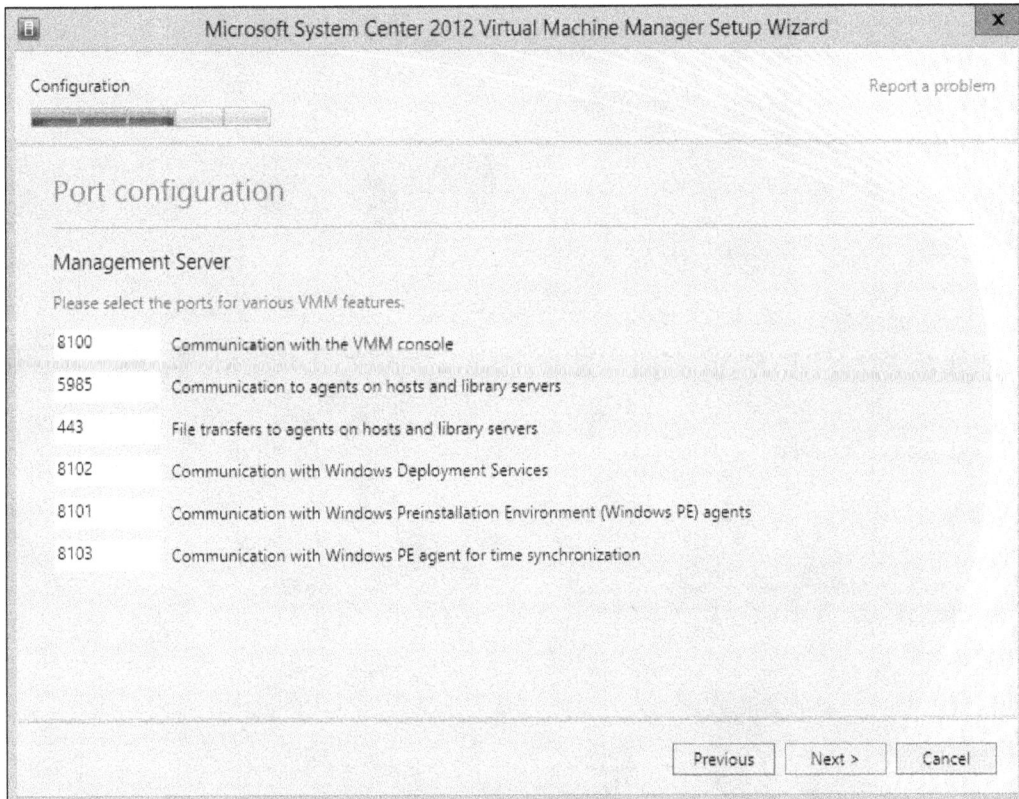

| Microsoft System Center 2012 Virtual Machine Manager Setup Wizard | x |

Configuration   Report a problem

Port configuration

Management Server

Please select the ports for various VMM features.

8100	Communication with the VMM console
5985	Communication to agents on hosts and library servers
443	File transfers to agents on hosts and library servers
8102	Communication with Windows Deployment Services
8101	Communication with Windows Preinstallation Environment (Windows PE) agents
8103	Communication with Windows PE agent for time synchronization

Previous   Next >   Cancel

---

21. On the **Library configuration** page, click on **Next**.

> The setup does not create a default library share on the HA VMM installation, as you cannot have a VMM library running on the VMM management cluster.

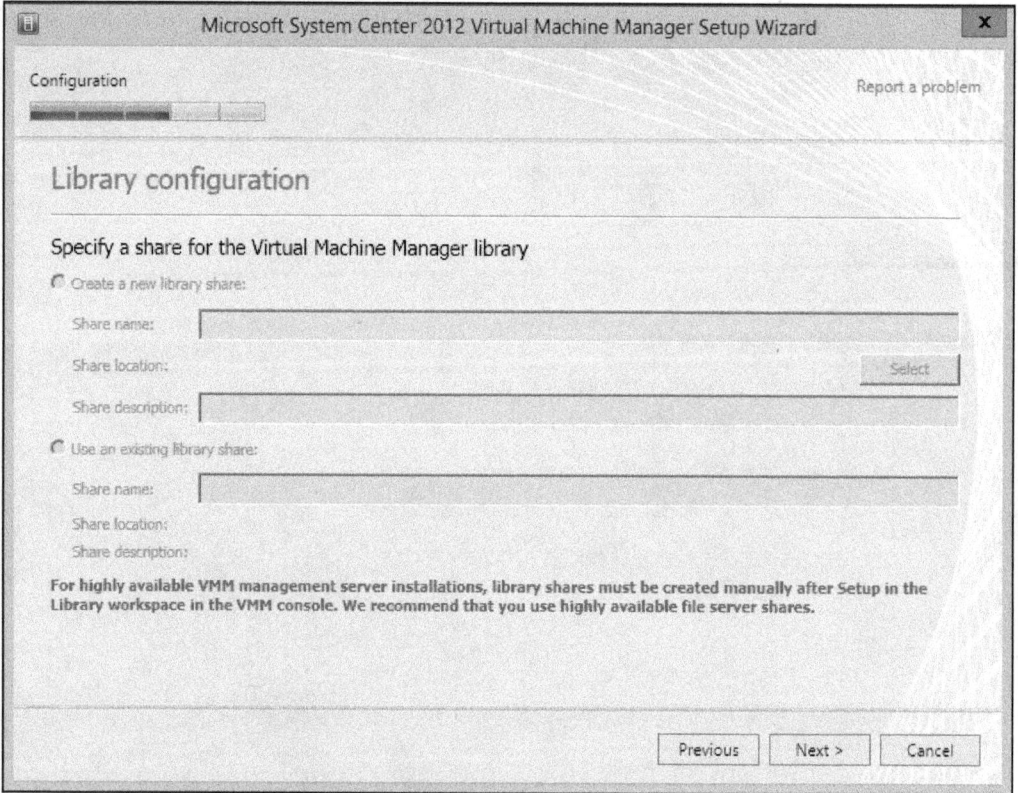

Microsoft System Center 2012 Virtual Machine Manager Setup Wizard	**X**

Configuration   Report a problem

Library configuration

Specify a share for the Virtual Machine Manager library

○ Create a new library share:

    Share name:

    Share location: Select

    Share description:

○ Use an existing library share:

    Share name:

    Share location:

    Share description:

For highly available VMM management server installations, library shares must be created manually after Setup in the Library workspace in the VMM console. We recommend that you use highly available file server shares.

                                                              Previous   Next >   Cancel

---

22. On the **Installation summary** page, review your selections. Click on **Previous** if you want to change any selections.

23. Click on **Install** to start the installation, and the installation progress will be displayed.

24. On the **Setup completed successfully** page, click on **Close**.

> Because the installation was completed successfully, you can now install VMM on the other cluster nodes.

How it works...

The installation of the VMM management server is straightforward, with added enhancements that simplify the installation process. The VMM 2012/R2 version will install some of the prerequisites for you, if that's necessary. When you click on **Install** on the main **Setup** page, the setup process will prompt you to install the missing prerequisites.

As you install the VMM management server on a cluster node, you will be prompted to make the VMM management server highly available. Click on **Yes** to install an HA VMM or on **No** to install it as a standalone VMM running on a cluster.

If the user account (in our case, LAB\vmm-admin) running the VMM setup has the right to create the VMMDKM container in AD DS, you don't need to create it, as mentioned previously, as the VMM setup checks and creates the VMMDKM container. The DKM container allows users and processes running on diverse servers to share data securely. On an HA VMM, if a VMM management service fails over to another node on the cluster, the active node will access the VMM database using the encryption keys stored in the DKM container to decrypt the encrypted data that is being held securely in the VMM database.

If your account does not have the **CREATE** permission on the SQL database server, or you are not a database administrator, you can ask them to create the VMM database beforehand. Alternatively, you can provide an account with permissions to create a database on the SQL Server during the install process by selecting the **Use the following credentials** checkbox and then providing the username and password.

When performing an HA VMM installation, although the **Library Configuration** page does appear, click on **Next,** as it will not create the default VMM library, and you will be required to create an HA library after the installation is complete using the VMM console.

There's more...

When carrying out a planned failover for VMM, make sure you note the following points:

▸ Any connection from the VMM console to the VMM management server will be lost in a failover operation but will reconnect after the failover, as the connection is made through the VMM cluster service name and not to a particular node. Keep this in mind and communicate with the VMM admin/users beforehand.

▸ Active running jobs will fail in a failover operation. You will need to restart an active running job manually if it does support restart; otherwise, you will need to start the job/task from the beginning.

Finally, the following are some of the best practices to deploy highly available VMM management servers:

- ▸ Use a SQL Server cluster for database high availability
- ▸ If deploying on a highly available production environment, ensure the SQL Server cluster is on a distinct cluster rather than the VMM cluster
- ▸ Use a file server to host the library shares

See also

- ▸ *Windows Server 2012 Scale-Out File Server for SQL Server 2012 – Step-by-step Installation* (`http://blogs.technet.com/b/josebda/archive/2012/08/23/windows-server-2012-scale-out-file-server-for-sql-server-2012-step-by-step-installation.aspx`)
- ▸ *How to Build SQL Server 2012 Always On Hyper-V Virtual Machines* (`http://social.technet.microsoft.com/wiki/contents/articles/6198.how-to-build-sql-server-2012-alwayson-hyper-v-virtual-machines-for-demos-emu-build.aspx`)
- ▸ The *Configuring Distributed Key Management* recipe in *Chapter 3, Installing VMM 2012 R2*
- ▸ *What's New in Failover Clustering* (`http://technet.microsoft.com/en-us/library/hh831414.aspx`)
- ▸ *Introduction of iSCSI Target in Windows Server 2012* (`http://blogs.technet.com/b/filecab/archive/2012/05/21/introduction-of-iscsi-target-in-windows-server-2012.aspx`)

Installing a VMM management server on the additional node of a cluster

Now that we have our first node running, we are going to deploy the second node of the VMM cluster. This recipe will guide you on how to add additional VMM nodes to an existing VMM management cluster.

You can install VMM management servers on up to 16 nodes on a cluster, but keep in mind that only one VMM management service will be active at a time.

The VMM console, in the event of a failover, will reconnect to the VMM management server automatically, as you are using the cluster service name to connect.

Getting ready

Before you start installing an additional node for VMM 2012/R2, close any connections (VMM console, PowerShell, or any web portal) to the primary VMM management node. Also, make sure there are no pending restarts on the current and primary VMM management nodes.

How to do it...

Carry out the following steps to add another VMM node to the VMM cluster:

1. On an additional node of your cluster, log in as `lab\vmm-admin` or with administrator rights.

2. Browse to the VMM installation media, right-click on **Setup**, and select **Run as administrator**.

3. On the main **Setup** page, click on **Install**, and on the **Select features to install** page, select **VMM management server**, as shown in the following screenshot:

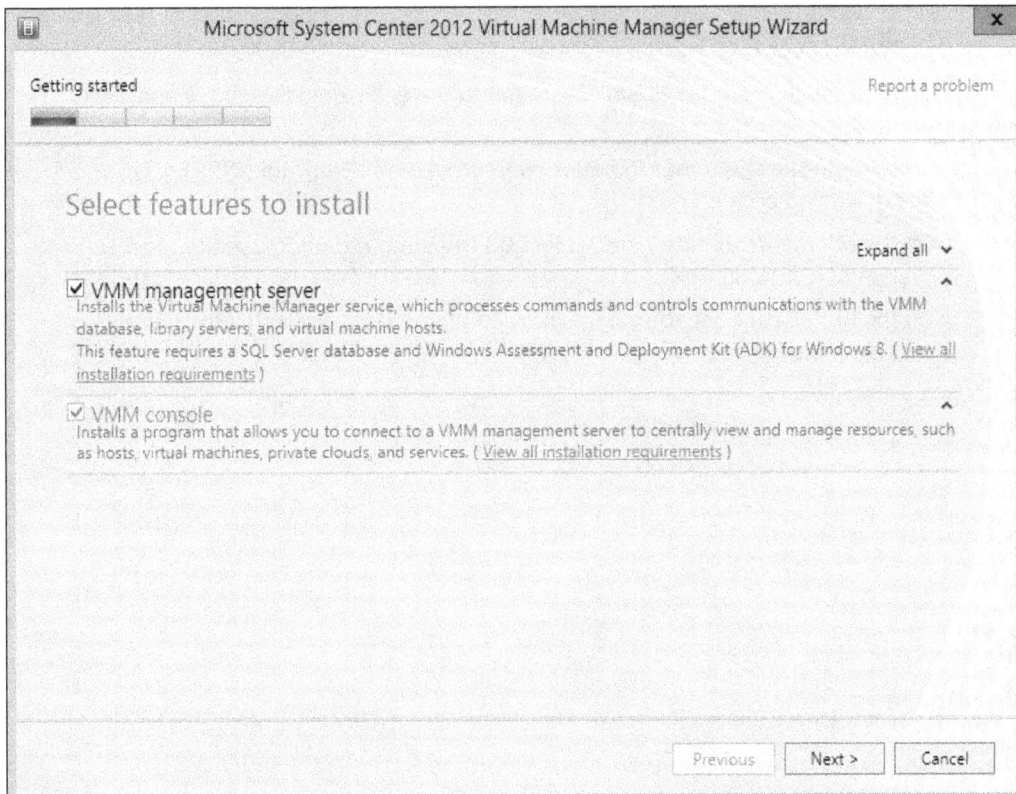

> The VMM console option will be selected and installed when you select **VMM management server**.

4. Click on **Yes** when the **Highly available VMM already installed** window pops up (refer to the following screenshot) to proceed with the installation, and then click on **Next**:

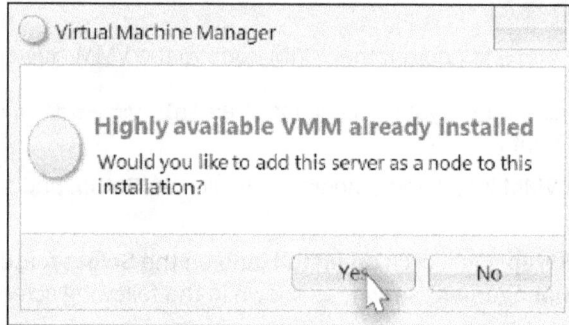

5. On the **Product registration information** page, type the VMM key and click on **Next**.

6. On the **Please read this license agreement** page, accept the license and click on **Next**.

7. On the **Join the Customer Experience Improvement Program (CEIP)** page, choose **Yes** or **No** and click on **Next**.

8. On the **Microsoft Update** page, select **On (recommended)** to use the Microsoft Update and click on **Next**.

9. On the **Installation location** page, provide the path for the installation and then click on **Next**.

> It is recommended that you keep the OS partition (C:) only for the operating system and have another drive for the VMM program files.

10. The server will now be scanned to check if the requirements are met, and a page will be displayed that shows which requirement has not been met and how to resolve the issue.

11. On the **Database configuration** page, click on **Next**.

> Because we are installing an additional VMM management server on a cluster node and they both share the same SQL database, this page is only informational.

12. On the **Configure service account and distributed key management** page, provide the password for the VMM service.

13. On the **Port configuration** page, click on **Next**.

14. On the **Library configuration** page, click on **Next,** as you cannot have a VMM library running on the VMM management cluster.

15. On the **Installation summary** page, review your selections. Click on **Previous** if you want to change any selections.

16. Click on **Install** to start the installation, and an installation progress bar will be displayed.

17. On the **Setup completed successfully** page, click on **Close**.

How it works...

With VMM 2012/R2, you can now deploy the management server on a cluster.

Installing an additional node of the VMM management server on a cluster is straightforward, with added enhancements that simplify the installation process.

To start with, make sure you have the required hardware and software. System Center 2012 R2 only supports Windows 2012/R2 as the deployment OS. Check *Chapter 1, VMM 2012 Architecture*, for more information about the hardware and software required for VMM.

The VMM 2012/R2 version will install some of the prerequisites for you, if necessary. When you click on **Install** on the main **Setup** page, the setup process will prompt you to install the missing prerequisites.

The setup process will detect that you are running on a cluster; then, you will be prompted to choose whether you want to add the installation server to the existing highly available VMM management server or not. Click on **Yes** to confirm the additional node.

On the database page, since you already informed the SQL Server about whether you want to add the installation server or not during the deployment of the first VMM node, you will not be prompted to do so again, and the page will be a read-only page.

As for the VMM library, you cannot have it running on the VMM management cluster. The page will only be for informational purposes.

See also

- The *Planning for High Availability* recipe in *Chapter 1, VMM 2012 Architecture*
- The *Specifying the correct system requirements for a real world scenario* recipe in *Chapter 1, VMM 2012 Architecture*

Connecting to a highly available VMM management server using the VMM console

The VMM console is the GUI interface of the VMM management server. You will be using it to manage the cloud, fabric, storage, and resources.

You can use this recipe to configure the VMM console to connect to a highly available VMM management server.

Getting ready

To ensure best practice, install the VMM console on a machine rather than on clustered VMM servers. It is recommended that you install it on the management desktop, and from there, connect to the HA VMM cluster, as it will prevent a connection loss in one of the VMM management nodes in the event of failure.

> Review the *Installing the VMM console* recipe in *Chapter 3, Installing VMM 2012 R2*, for information about installing the VMM console, and *Chapter 1, VMM 2012 Architecture*, for the system prerequisites.

The VMM console will enable you to manage VMM remotely from your desktop without requiring you to use RDP in the VMM server.

How to do it...

Carry out the following steps to connect to an HA VMM management server:

1. On a computer that the VMM console is installed on, start the VMM console.

2. On the login screen, in the **Server name** box (shown in the following screenshot), type the VMM cluster service name, followed by a colon and the port (for example, vmmha:8100).

> The default port for the VMM console connection is `8100`.

3. To connect, click on **Specify credentials** and then type the user's credentials (for example, type the username, `lab\vmm-admin`) or select **Use current Microsoft Windows session identity**.

> You will need to specify the user credentials on a multitenant environment, or if the user account is not on the same domain as the VMM management server.

4. Click on **Connect**.

5. If the account has multiple user roles (for example, **Tenant Administrator** or **Self-Service User**), you will be prompted to select the user role that you want to log in with. In this case, select the role, **Customer A**, and click on **OK**.

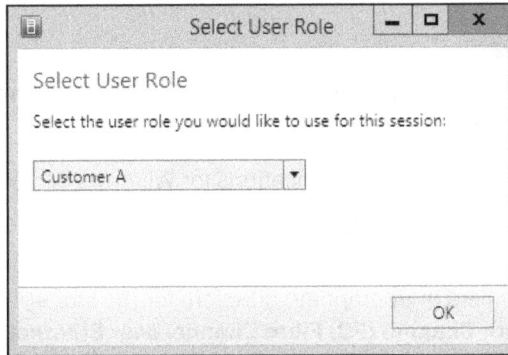

How it works...

After installing the VMM server on a cluster, to manage it using the GUI, you will need to use the VMM console to connect to the VMM management server.

It is preferable to install the VMM console on the administrator desktop and then follow this recipe to connect to the HA VMM management service by providing the VMM cluster service name (mentioned during the installation of the first VMM cluster node on the **Cluster configuration** page). Do not type a particular VMM computer server name.

The VMM console will reconnect automatically to the HA VMM service using the VMM cluster service name.

See also

▸ The *Installing the VMM console* recipe in *Chapter 3, Installing VMM 2012 R2*

Deploying a highly available library server on a file server cluster

Following the deployment of a VMM management server in a cluster and with the knowledge that VMM 2012 does not automatically create the VMM library when installed in a high-availability mode, we now need to deploy the VMM library. Since we are talking about a high available deployment, the VMM library will have to be HA, as well.

In this recipe, we will go through the deployment of a file server cluster to be used as the VMM library. You can use an existing file server cluster as the library as long as it meets the system requirements for SC 2012 R2.

VMM 2012 R2 includes support for designated network file shares on Windows 2012 servers as the storage location for the VMM library.

Getting ready

To start with, make sure your hardware meets the VMM library requirements, as discussed in *Chapter 1, VMM 2012 Architecture,* and note the following points:

- The hardware must meet the qualifications for Windows Server 2012.

- The storage should be attached to all of the nodes in the cluster if you are using shared storage.

- The device controllers or appropriate adapters for the storage must be one of these types: **iSCSI, Fibre Channel (FC, Fibre Channel over Ethernet (FCoE)**, or **Serial Attached SCSI (SAS)**.

- The cluster configuration (servers, network, and storage) should pass all of the cluster validation tests.

- VMM does not support a clustered file share for the VMM library running on the VMM cluster. You need to deploy the cluster file share on another cluster.

The following figure is a sample design scenario for a highly available VMM library over an SMB 3.0 file server deployment:

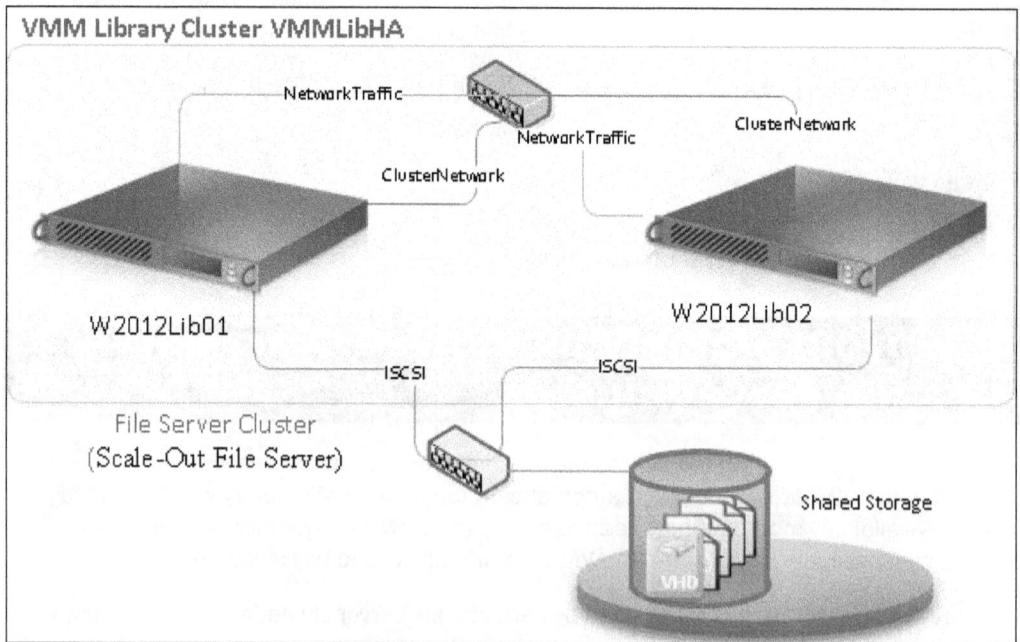

How to do it...

Let's start by setting up the file server cluster.

> For this recipe, I have used two dedicated physical servers for the file server cluster. However, you can set up a Hyper-V guest cluster, as well.

First, we will have a look at how to install, validate, and configure the failover clustering feature using PowerShell. Carry out the following steps in order to deploy the HA VMM library:

1. Log in on the first cluster node.

2. Open the Windows PowerShell command prompt with administrator rights and type the following command:

   ```
   Add-WindowsFeature -name File-Services,Failover-Clustering -
   IncludeManagementTools
   ```

3. Validate and create the cluster using PowerShell:

   ```
   Test-Cluster -Node w2012Lib01, w2012Lib02

   New-Cluster -Name vmmLibHA -Node w2012Lib01, w2012Lib02
   ```

> w2012Lib01 and w2012Lib02 are the physical servers' names, and vmmLibHA is the cluster name.

4. Configure the cluster networks in such a way as to use the ClusterNetwork network and exclude the NetworkTraffic one, as shown in the following configuration:

   ```
   (Get-ClusterNetwork | ? Address -like 10.16.1.*).Name =
   "ClusterNetwork"

   (Get-ClusterNetwork | ? Name -notlike Internal*).Name =
   "NetworkTraffic"

   (Get-ClusterNetwork ClusterNetwork).Role = 3

   (Get-ClusterNetwork NetworkTraffic).Role = 1


   # Confirm the configuration was successful
   Get-ClusterNetwork | Select *
   ```

> NetworkTraffic and ClusterNetwork are the network names that were previously renamed. You can use any denomination, but for consistency, remember to rename the cluster networks to match the network names used previously.

5. Add storage using the following PowerShell command:

```
Add-ClusterSharedVolume
```

This command can be used in the following manner:

```
Get-ClusterResource | ? OwnerGroup -like Available* | Add-ClusterSharedVolume
```

The following screenshot is an example of how storage can be added using a PowerShell command:

```
                                           Administrator: Windows PowerShell

PS C:\Windows> Get-ClusterResource *disk* | Add-ClusterSharedVolume

Name                                      State
----                                      -----
Cluster Disk 2                            Online
Cluster Disk 3                            Online
```

6. You can also use the GUI to perform these tasks. For more information, refer to http://technet.microsoft.com/en-us/library/hh831478.aspx.

Next, we will need to configure the file server. Carry out the following steps after installing and configuring the failover cluster:

1. On the **Failover Cluster Management** page, select the main node on the tree, and in the **Actions** menu on the right pane, click on **Configure Role**.

2. When the **High Availability Wizard** starts, click on **Next** to continue.

3. On the **Select Role** page, select **File Server** and click on **Next**.

4. On the **File Server Type** page, select **File Server for General Use**.

5. On the **Client Access Point** page, type the name of the clustered file server (for example, VMMLibFS) and IP address (for example, 10.1.2.100), if needed, and click on **Next**.

6. On the **Select Storage** page, select the disks to be assigned to this clustered file server and click on **Next**.

7. On the **Confirmation** page, click on **Next**.

8. On the **Summary** page, click on **Finish**.

Next, create a file share on the cluster shared volume by carrying out the following steps:

1. In the **Failover Cluster Management** window, click on the cluster, then expand it, and click on **Roles**.

2. Select the file server, right-click on it, and then click on **Add File Share**.

3. On the **Select the profile** page, select **SMB Share – Applications** and click on **Next**.

4. On the **Share location** page, click on the volume to create the CSV file and click on **Next**.

5. On the **Share name** page, type the share name (for example, VMMLibShare) and click on **Next**.

6. On the **Configure share settings** page, select **Enable continuous availability** and click on **Next**.

> For more information on Windows Server 2012, see *Windows Server 2012, File Servers and SMB 3.0 – Simpler and Easier by Design* (http://blogs.technet.com/b/josebda/archive/2012/10/08/windows-server-2012-file-servers-and-smb-3-0-simpler-and-easier-by-design.aspx) and *Scale-Out File Server for Application Data Overview* (http://technet.microsoft.com/en-us/library/hh831349.aspx).

7. On the **Specify permissions to control access** page, click on **Customize permissions** to grant full control on the share and security filesystem to the **SYSTEM** account, **Administrators**, and **VMM administrators**.

8. Click on **Next**.

9. On the **Confirm selection** page, click on **Create** and then on **Close**.

Next, add a VMM library share by performing the following steps:

1. Start the VMM console.

2. On the login screen, in the **Server name** box, type the VMM cluster service name followed by a colon and the port (for example, vmmha:8100).

3. In the bottom-left pane, click on the **Library** workspace.

4. Click on the **Home** tab, and then click on the **Add Library Server** option in the ribbon, as shown in the following screenshot:

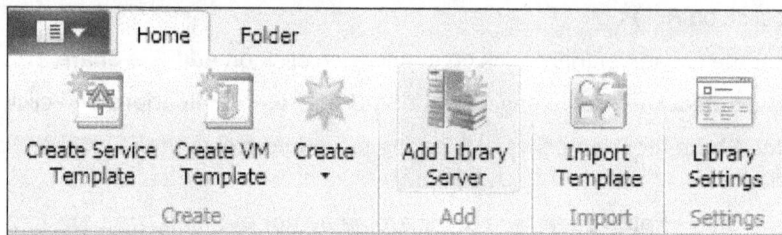

5. In the **Add Library Server** wizard, type a domain account that has administrative rights on the library servers (for example, LAB\vmm-admin) and click on **Next**.

> As discussed in *Chapter 3, Installing VMM 2012 R2*, it is recommended as best practice that you use a **Run As** account, which you can create by clicking on **Browse**. For more information, see the *Creating credentials for a Run As account in VMM* recipe of *Chapter 3, Installing VMM 2012 R2*.

6. On the **Select Library Servers** page, type the library server domain name (for example, LAB.local).

7. In the **Computer name** box, type the name of the HA file server cluster (for example, vmmLibHA) or click on **Search** to find it in AD.

8. Click on **Add** and then click on **Next**

9. In the **Add Library Shares** page, select the library shares from the file server cluster to be added to VMM (for example, **VMMLibShare**).

10. If you select **Add Default Resources**, the default library resources will be added to the share that is being used for the services. In addition, it will add the ApplicationFrameworks folder to the library share.

11. Click on **Next**, and on the **Summary** page, click on **Add Library Servers** to add the selected servers and shares.

How it works...

This recipe guided us through the steps on how to set up a Windows 2012 file server cluster and how to add a VMM library server to VMM management.

VMM does not offer the ability to replicate physical files stored in the VMM library or metadata for objects stored in the VMM database. As a recommendation, you should use a file server cluster for high availability.

In a clustered file server, when you take the associated file server resource offline, all of the shared folders in that resource go offline. This means that all of the shared folders will be affected.

You can set up the file server cluster on a physical server or Windows 2012 cluster using Hyper-V guest cluster options.

When adding a library server to VMM management, VMM automatically installs the agent on the new library server.

The minimum required permission for the local system (**SYSTEM**) account is **Full Control** permissions for the **Share** and **NTFS filesystem** levels (this is the default setting).

> Make sure you assign the correct access control permissions, full control share, and NTFS permissions to the **Administrators** group.

See also

The *Failover Clustering Overview* article (`http://go.microsoft.com/fwlink/p/?LinkId=243991`)

Uninstalling a highly available VMM management server

When you have a highly available VMM server, to uninstall the high availability completely, you will need to uninstall the VMM management server from each node in the cluster.

Before uninstalling the VMM management server, ensure that any connections to the server are closed.

How to do it...

Carry out the following steps to remove an additional node from a VMM:

1. On a VMM highly available server node, in the `Programs and Features` folder (**Control | Panel | Programs**), click on **Microsoft System Center 2012 Virtual Machine Manager,** and then on **Remove features**.

2. On the **Select features to remove** page, click on **VMM management server** and then click on **Next**.

3. On the **Database options** page, click on **Next**.

4. On the **Summary** page, click on **Uninstall** and then on **Close**.

How it works...

The preceding steps show you how to remove a VMM server installed as an HA VMM server, for which you need to either be a member of the local **Administrators** group or have equivalent rights on the VMM server node that you are removing.

Make sure beforehand that the node is not currently the owner of the HA VMM service in Failover Cluster Manager; move it to another node in the event that it is the owner, then proceed with the removal.

During the removal steps, you can select the VMM console to be removed, as well.

There's more...

Uninstall the last node of a highly available VMM management server using the following steps:

1. On a VMM highly available server node, in the `Programs and Features` folder (**Control | Panel | Programs**), click on **Microsoft System Center 2012 Virtual Machine Manager** and then on **Remove features**.

2. In the **Select features to remove** page, click on the **VMM management server** and then on **Next**.

3. Click on **Yes** when prompted to uninstall the last node of the highly available VMM management server and then on **Next**.

4. On the **Database options** page, choose whether you want to retain or remove the VMM database.

> By selecting **Retain database**, keep in mind that you will only be able to use this database for an HA VMM deployment.

5. Click on **Next**.

6. On the **Summary** page, click on **Uninstall** and then on **Close**.

5
Configuring Fabric Resources in VMM

In this chapter, we will cover the following:

- ▶ Creating host groups
- ▶ Setting up a VMM library
- ▶ Configuring networks in VMM
- ▶ Networking – configuring logical networks
- ▶ Networking – configuring VM networks and gateways
- ▶ Networking – configuring logical switches, port profiles, and port classifications
- ▶ Integrating and configuring the storage
- ▶ Creating a physical computer profile (host profile)
- ▶ Provisioning a physical computer as a Hyper-V host – Bare Metal host deployment
- ▶ Adding and managing Hyper-V hosts and host clusters

Introduction

This chapter is all about configuring the fabric resources infrastructure that you can use in your private cloud deployment. The following design shows the VMM components' infrastructure deployed as VMs on a Hyper-V server. You can use this as an example for your lab or small deployments.

Note that, on this design sample, there is no guest-cluster implementation; VMM is neither implemented as HA, nor as SQL:

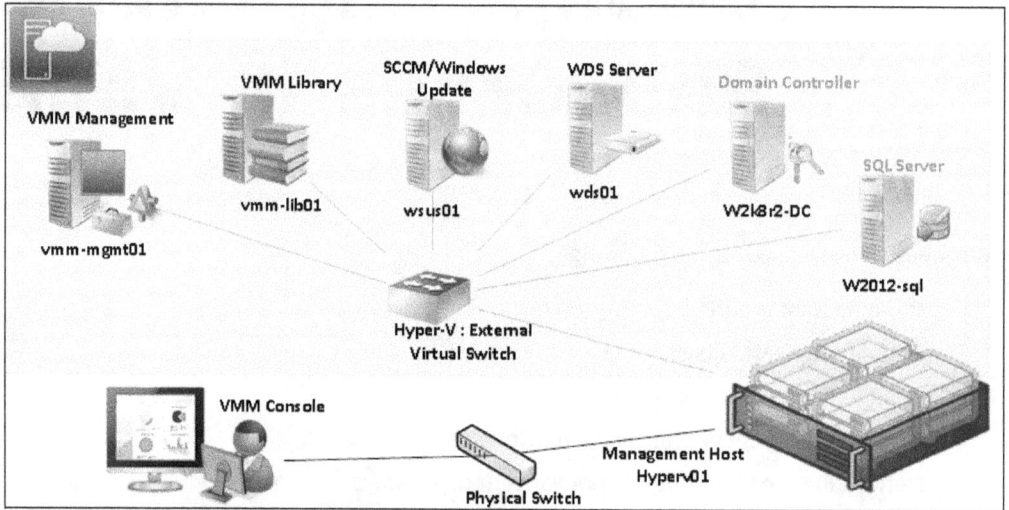

VMM 2012 fabric resources are powerful when configuring resources for private clouds, hosts, VMs, and services. This chapter will give you the necessary guidance to deploy physical servers as Hyper-V hosts and to configure and manage networking, storage, and VMM library resources. These recipes will empower you to get more out of this feature and help you understand the steps required to create the necessary infrastructure for your private cloud deployment.

The fabric resources are the infrastructure needed in order to manage the private cloud, hosts, VMs, or services. The following recipes will guide you when creating those resources.

The following figure illustrates the fabric resources that can be managed by VMM:

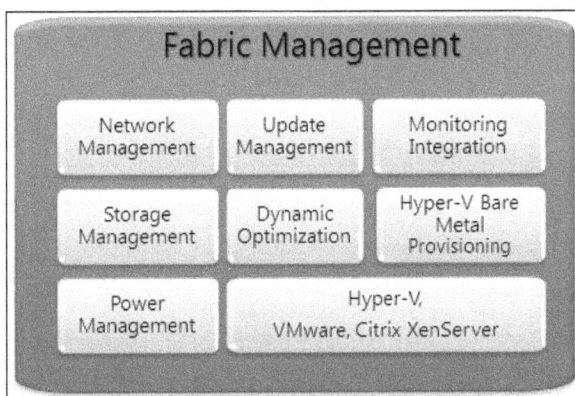

Creating host groups

Based on site location or resource allocation, host groups are designed to group virtual machine hosts.

Getting ready

When you have a host group structure, the following settings and resources will be allocated at the host group level:

- Placement rules
- Host reserve settings (CPU, memory, disk I/O, disk space, and network I/O)
- Dynamic Optimization and Power Optimization settings
- Network resources
- Storage capacity allocation
- PRO configuration
- Custom properties

A host group will also allow you to do the following:

- Assign the groups to delegated administrators and the read-only administrators' roles, and then members of these user roles will be able to view and/or assign fabric resources

> ► Create a private cloud, assign host groups to it, and then allocate resources from the assigned host groups to that private cloud

> For this recipe, we will create a host group based on site location and system capabilities. You should create it based on your solution design.

How to do it...

Carry out the following steps:

1. Connect to the VMM 2012 R2 console using the VMM admin account previously created (`lab\vmm-admin`), and then on the bottom-left pane, click on **Fabric** to open the Fabric workspace.

2. On the left-hand-side pane called **Fabric**, expand **Servers**, right-click on **All Hosts**, and then click on **Create Host Group**.

3. Type in the name for the host group, for example, `Sydney`.

The following steps will help you create a child host group:

1. In the **Fabric** pane, expand the parent host group for which you want to create the child, right-click on it, and then click on **Create Host Group**.

2. Type in the name for the host group, for example, `Hyper-V`.

3. Repeat steps 1 and 2 to create your host group structure. The host group creation is illustrated in the following screenshot:

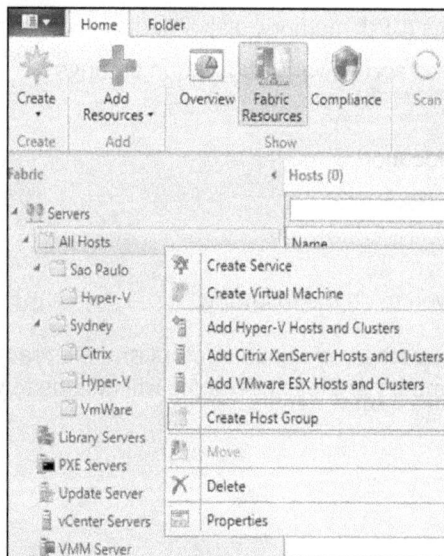

How it works...

By default, child host groups inherit settings from the parent host group, but it is possible to override those settings in the host properties.

Optionally, you can create a host group by clicking on **All Hosts**, then on the **Folder** tab, and finally on **Create Host Group**. VMM will create a new host group, initially named **New host group**, with the host group name highlighted. Right-click on that, click on **Rename**, and type in the name you want for the host group.

For guidance, you can create the host group structure based on location, hardware capabilities, applications, server roles, type of hypervisors, the business unit, or the delegation model.

There's more...

With the host group created, you can then configure its properties.

Moving a host group to another location

Carry out the following steps to move the host group location:

1. In the VMM 2012 R2 console, in the **Fabric** workspace, expand **Servers** on the left-hand side, and then expand **All Hosts**.
2. Drag-and-drop the host group to its new location in the tree or click to select the host group; then, perform the following steps:
    1. Click on the **Folder** tab.
    2. Click on **Move** on the top ribbon.
    3. Click to select the target parent host group.
    4. Click on **OK**.

Configuring host group properties

Carry out the following steps to set up the host group properties:

1. In the VMM 2012 R2 console, in the **Fabric** pane, expand **Servers**, expand **All Hosts**, and then click on the host group to configure.

2. In the **Folder** tab, click on **Properties** on the ribbon, as shown in the following screenshot:

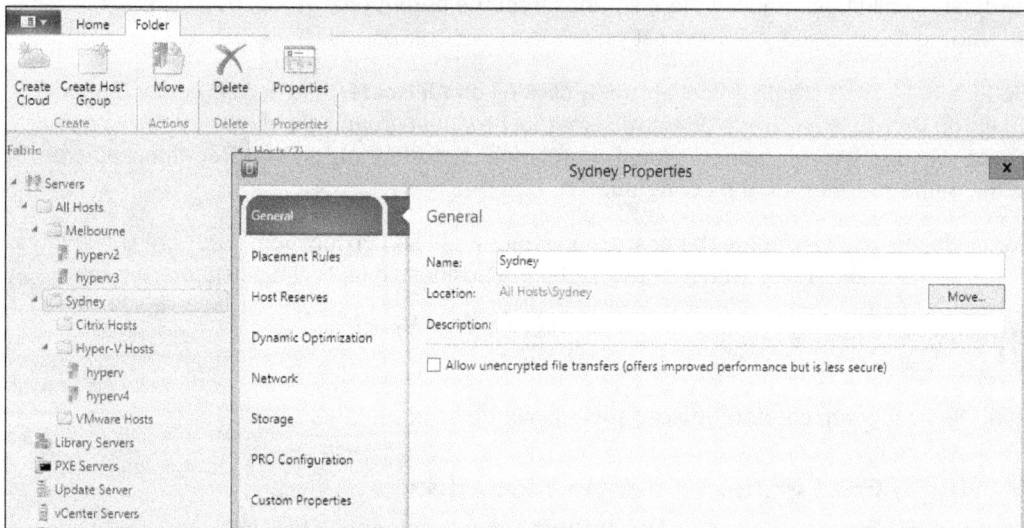

3. Click on the **General** tab and provide the host group name. Optionally, type in a description and click on **Allow unencrypted file transfers**; this will improve the transfer performance but will be less secure.

4. Click on the **Host Reserves** tab, as shown in the following screenshot, if you want to configure reserve values (**CPU**, **Memory**, **Disk I/O**, **Disk space**, and **Network I/O**):

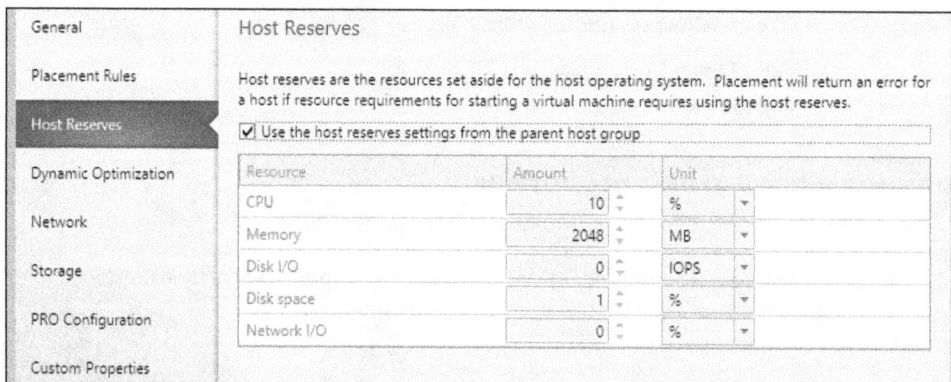

5. Click on the **Placement Rules** tab if you want to specify custom placement rules for this host group.

> By default, a host group inherits the placement settings from its parent host group.

6. Click on the **Dynamic Optimization** tab to configure Dynamic Optimization (aggressiveness and thresholds) and Power Optimization settings.

7. Click on the **Network** tab to view the associated network resource type and optionally configure the **Inherit network logical resources from parent host groups** setting.

8. Click on the **Storage** tab to view and allocate **storage pools** and **storage units**.

9. Click on **PRO Configuration** (if VMM is integrated with OpsMgr) to configure the host PRO monitor.

10. Click on the **Custom Properties** tab (as shown in the previous screenshot) to assign custom properties for **Virtual Machine, Virtual Machine Template, Host, Host Cluster, Host Group, Service Template, Service Instance, Computer Tier**, and **Cloud**. The custom properties are shown in the following screenshot:

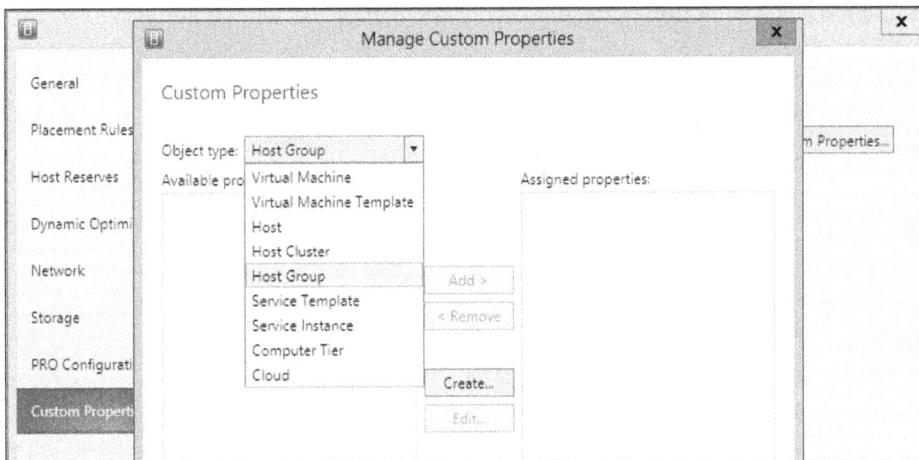

See also

▸ The *How to Allocate Storage Logical Units to a Host Group in VMM* article at
   `http://technet.microsoft.com/en-us/library/gg610686.aspx`

▸ The *How to Allocate Storage Pools to a Host Group in VMM* article at
   `http://technet.microsoft.com/en-us/library/gg610635.aspx`

▸ The *Configuring Dynamic Optimization and Power Optimization in VMM* article at
   `http://technet.microsoft.com/en-us/library/gg675109.aspx`

Setting up a VMM library

A default VMM library is configured when you install a VMM management server. However, you can add more VMM libraries later on.

> For high availability, it is recommended that you deploy a high available VMM library. For more information, see *Chapter 4, Installing a High Available VMM Server.*

In VMM 2012, the library can store file-based resources, custom resources, templates and profiles, equivalent objects, private cloud libraries, self-service user content, stored virtual machines and services, orphaned resources and update catalogs, and baseline files.

> It is strongly recommended that you use the Windows 2012 R2 server for the Library Server OS, as the VHDX does require at least Windows Server 2012.

This recipe will guide you through the process of configuring the VMM library.

Getting ready

The following table shows the configuration that we are going to use in this recipe:

Resource	Name
VMM management server	`vmm-mgmt01.lab.local`
Library share added during VMM management server installation	`vmm-mgmt01\MSSCVMMLibrary`
Library server and share in the Sydney office	`vmm-lib01\VMMSYD-Library`
Second library share in the Sydney office	`vmm-lib01\ISO-Library`
Library server and share in the Seattle office	`vmm-lib02\VMMSEA-Library`

During the VMM setup, you can accept the default `MSSCVMMLibrary` library, provide a new name to be created, or specify an existing share.

> The library server must be on the same domain as VMM, or in a two-way trusted domain.

How to do it...

Carry out the following steps to add a library server:

1. Connect to the VMM 2012 console by using the VMM admin account previously created (lab\vmm-admin), or use an account with VMM administrator rights.

2. On the bottom-left pane, click on **Library** to open the library workspace.

3. Click on the **Home** tab, and then click on the **Add Library Server** button on the ribbon, as shown in the following screenshot:

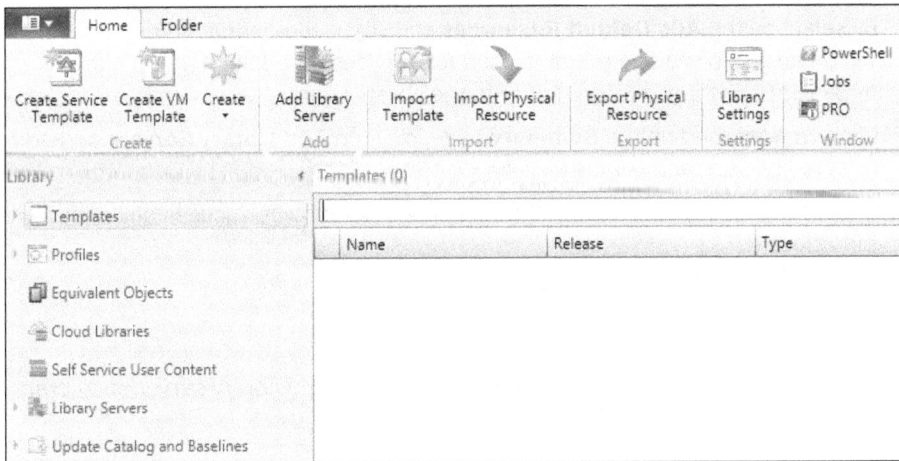

4. When the **Add Library Server** wizard opens, in the **Enter Credentials** page, type in a domain account that has administrator rights on the library servers, for example, LAB\vmm-admin, and then click on **Next**.

> You can also specify a Run As account. Create one by clicking on **Browse**, or manually type in the user credentials in the domain\username format.

5. In the **Select Library Servers** page, in the **Domain** box, type in the library server domain name, for example, LAB.local, and then click on **Add**.

6. In the **Computer name** box, type in the name of the library server, for example, `vmm-lib01`, or click on **Search** to look for the library server in Active Directory.

> Although not recommended, if you are sure about the name, you can click on **Skip Active Directory name verification**. By skipping the name verification, you need to manually certify the computer is a domain member.

7. In the **Add Library Shares** page, select the library shares to add, for example, **VMMSYD-Library**.

8. By selecting the **Add Default Resources** checkbox, the default library resources will be added to the share that is used for services. In addition, it will add the `ApplicationFrameworks` folder to the library share.

9. Click on **Next**, and on the **Summary** page, click on **Add Library Servers** and add the selected servers and shares.

10. In the **Jobs** dialog box, confirm that the library server was successfully added and then close it.

How it works...

The preceding steps guided us through the process of adding a library server and library shares to an existing VMM 2012 R2 installation.

When adding a library server to VMM, it automatically installs the agent on the new library server.

The minimum required permission is the local system account with full control permission in the file share and NTFS filesystem (the **Security** tab), which is the default setting.

> Make sure you assign the correct access control permissions and assign Full Control share and NTFS permissions to the local **Administrators** group.

There's more...

You can also add library shares or file-based resources to a library share.

Adding a library share

Carry out the following steps to add a VMM library share:

1. Connect to the VMM 2012 R2 console by using the VMM admin account previously created (`lab\vmm-admin`), or use an account with VMM administrator rights.

2. In the library workspace, on the **Library** pane to the left, expand **Library Servers**. Next, select the library server that has a library share to be added.

3. Click on the **Library Server** tab on the ribbon and then click on **Add Library Shares** (or right-click on the library server and then on **Add Library Shares**).

4. On the **Add Library Shares** page, select the library share and then click on **Next**.

5. On the **Summary** page, confirm the settings and click on **Add Library Shares**.

6. In the **Jobs** dialog box, confirm that the library was successfully added and then close it.

Adding file-based resources to a VMM library share

Carry out one of the following steps to add file-based resources to an existing VMM library share, and then manually refresh it.

> When you add files to a VMM library share, they will not show up until VMM indexes them in the next library refresh.

1. In Windows Explorer, copy the new files to the library share. You can also use **Robocopy** or any other copy method. For more information about using Robocopy, see `http://technet.microsoft.com/en-us/library/cc733145(v=ws.10).aspx`.

2. Now, using the VMM console in the library workspace, on the left-hand pane, expand **Library Servers** and then select the library server. Right-click on the library share, click on **Explore**, and start copying the files to the library share.

> To manually refresh the VMM library, right-click on the library server or library share and then click on **Refresh**.

3. Click on the **Home** tab, and then click on **Import Physical Resource** or **Export Physical Resource** to import/export file-based resources between library shares.

> You can change the library refresh interval from the left-hand-side pane in the library workspace, under **Library Settings**. The default and the minimum value is one hour.

Creating or modifying equivalent objects in the VMM library

You can mark (create) a similar file type library object in different sites as an equivalent object. This will enable VMM to use any instance of the object when deploying it.

If you have a VHD file that is stored in a library share, for example, in Sydney as well as in Sao Paulo, and if you mark it as an equivalent object, when you create a new VM template and then specify that VHD for the template, VMM will interpret it as a global object instead of a site-specific object. This allows you to create single templates across multiple locations.

> To mark resources as equivalent, they must be of the same file type (same family name, release value, and namespace).

The next sections will guide you through creating and modifying library resources as equivalent objects in VMM.

Marking (creating) objects as equivalent

Carry out the following steps to create an object as equivalent:

1. In the VMM console, in the library workspace and in the **Library** pane to the left, click on **Library Servers** (or, if connected using a self-service user, expand **Self Service User Content** and click on the data path).

2. In the **Physical Library Objects** main pane (or the **Self Service User Objects** pane if connected as a self-service user), click on **Type** on the column header to sort the library resources by type.

3. Next, to select the resources to mark as equivalent, carry out one of the following steps:

   - Select the first resource to mark, press and hold the *Ctrl* key, and then click on the other resources that you want to mark as equivalent

   - Select the first resource to mark, press and hold the *Shift* key, and then click on the last resource

4. Right-click on the objects and then click on **Mark Equivalent**, as shown in the following screenshot:

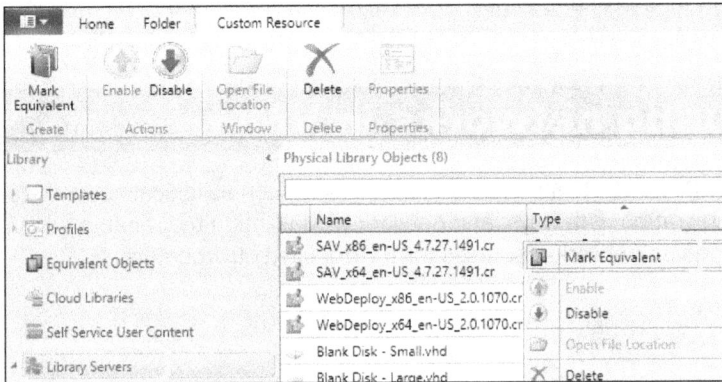

5. In the **Equivalent Library Objects** dialog, type in the family name in the **Family** list (for example, W2012R2 STD) and a release value (string) in the **Release** list (for example, March 2014).

6. Click on **OK** and verify that the objects show in the **Equivalent Objects** pane. They will be grouped by family name.

> The namespace will automatically be assigned by VMM: a Global namespace if created by an administrator, or a namespace that matches the self-service username if created by a self-service user.

Modifying equivalent objects

If you need to modify equivalent objects, carry out the following steps:

1. In the library workspace, in the **Library** pane to the left, click on **Equivalent Objects**.

2. In the **Equivalent Objects** main pane, expand the family name and the release value, right-click on the equivalent object, and then click on **Properties**.

3. In the **General** tab, add/modify the values.

> Delete the family name and release values if you need to remove an object from an equivalent objects set.

4. Click on **OK** to confirm.

See also

▸ The *How to Import and Export Physical Resources To and From the Library* article at http://go.microsoft.com/fwlink/p/?LinkId=227739

Configuring networks in VMM

Networking in VMM 2012 R2 includes enhancements such as logical networks, network load balance integration, gateways, and network virtualization that enable administrators to efficiently provision network resources for a virtualized environment.

How to do it...

You first need to define the model/design you will choose for your network. Planning is the first important task you need to execute to carry on.

The following should be considered:

▸ Physical and virtual networks

▸ Make sure your hardware (servers, switch, storage) support the network design model

▸ Will QoS be put in place? Does your physical network device support QoS?

▸ Is your environment going to support customers/tenants?

▸ How will you isolate the traffic: physical separation, network virtualization, or VLAN?

The following figure illustrates the steps to configure the network in VMM 2012 R2:

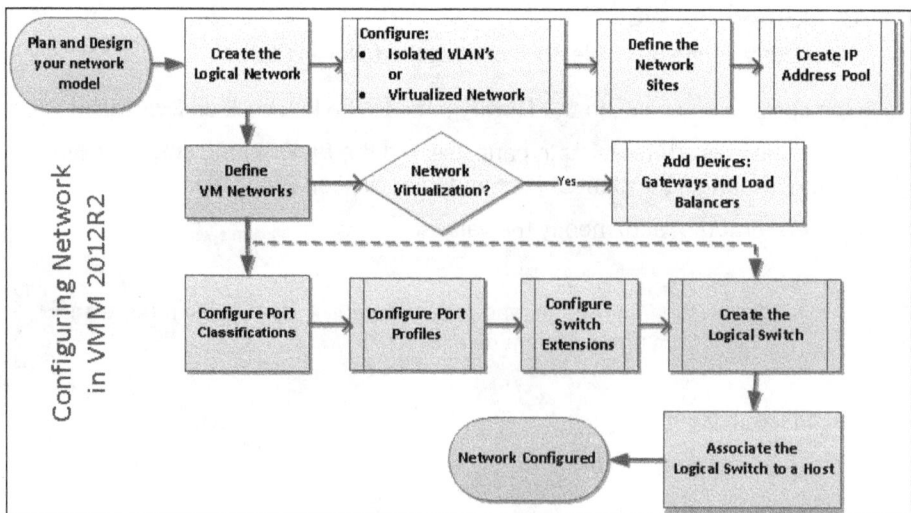

There's more...

Nowadays, servers with 2 x 10GB physical network cards are quite common. In this scenario, the new **converged network** approach simplifies the solution and reduces the implementation and running costs. But there are many other design scenarios for converged networks.

Designing for converged networks

Converged network is a Windows Server 2012/R2 feature that allows the creation of virtual network adapters, meaning that you can partition the physical NIC in many virtual NICs (useful to create the live migration, CSV, management, and guest VM NICs). We'll now discuss the advantages and disadvantages of using a converged network architecture. You need to consider these to avoid potential performance issues. Let's start with the advantages.

VMM 2012 R2 can be used for setting up the network, traffic partitioning, VMs QoS, and NIC Teaming.

QoS based on weight can be configured to enhance resource utilization based on the need and the priority. You will need, for example, to guarantee a minimum bandwidth for the live migration and CSV vNICs to secure the cluster reliability and stability.

If the physical network switch does support LACP, you can team the two or add more physical NICs and use LACP configuration, although you need to pay attention to the number of queues versus VMs (if you run more VMs than queues, then LACP may not be the best decision).

> If you plan accordingly and there isn't an expectation for more than 10 GB throughput to be used for a particular VM, the Switch Independent / Hyper-V Port would be my recommended configuration.

SMB Multichannel can be used to increase the bandwidth as it uses more CPU cores to improve network throughput for the same traffic. As illustrated in the following figure, 2 x 10 GB physical network cards are dedicated to the virtual machine and host management traffic. Those NICs are teamed using Windows 2012/R2 team capability, which will provide fault tolerance and load balancing. The other two NICs are RDMA cards, which will provide SMB multichannel capabilities and will offer great performance, but can't be teamed or used on a virtual switch.

[🔍 RDMA offers high throughput and density and low latency and CPU utilization.]

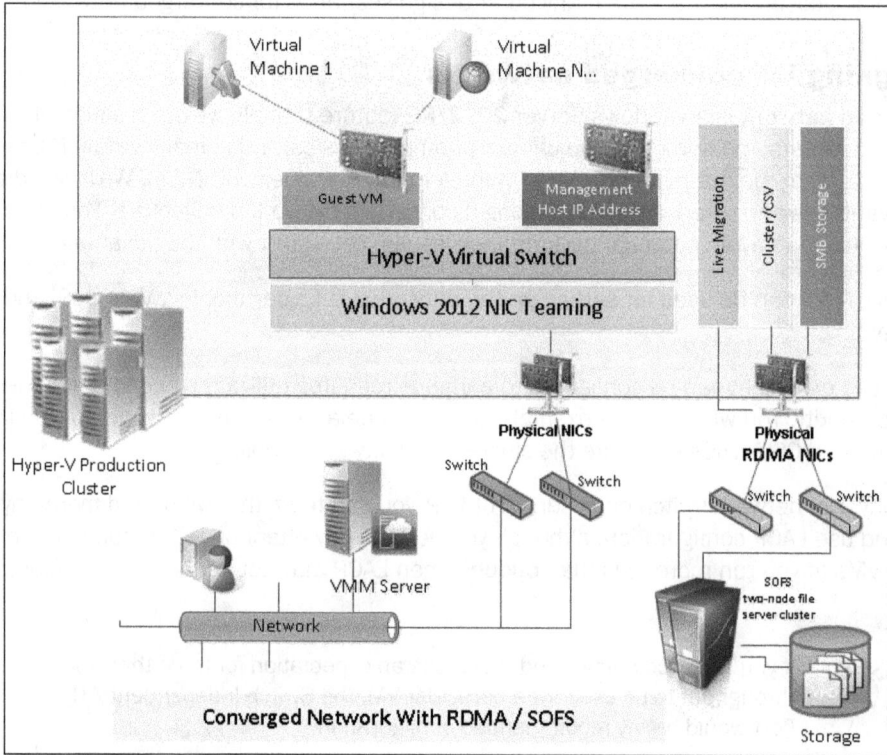

The next figure shows a network with 2 x 10GB NICs that offers a single dual-port network adapter per host. Network failures are usually related to cables and switches, not the NIC itself. It the NIC does fail, failover clustering on the Hyper-V or storage side would kick in. Configuring two network adapters, each with one port, is also an option.

[🔍 Network QoS (partitioning) should be used to prioritize the traffic. **VMM Port Profiles** should be used to define the configuration for the virtual NICs: offload settings, security settings, and bandwidth settings.]

Depending on your requirements and design configuration, you may find that creating more vNICs would increase the throughput, as the vNICs do not support **Receive Side Scaling** (**RSS**), whose main benefit is that it allows you to spread the CPU burden of network activity to the many cores.

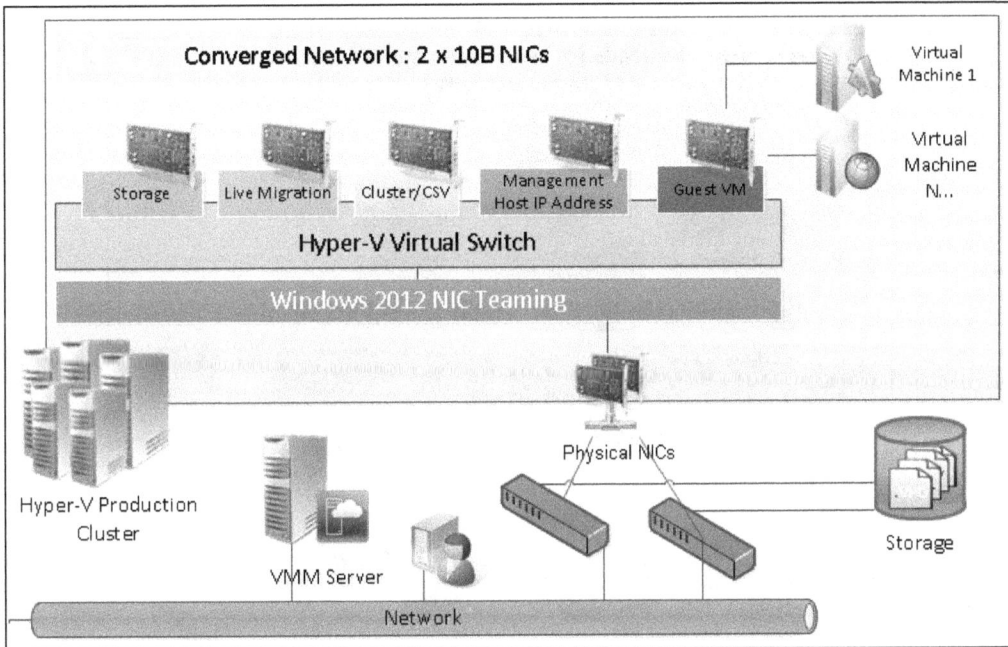

If the physical host network adapter is RDMA-capable, for this particular scenario (the one mentioned just now), where you have NIC teaming and the virtual switch configured, the RDMA capabilities won't be leveraged, as the physical NIC will be hidden behind the team and virtual switch.

In the following figure, we have 2 x 10GB NICs on teaming, providing fault tolerance and load balancing for the guest virtual machines' traffic. We also have 2 x 10B on NIC teaming for the Management OS, which includes host management, live migration, and CSV, and two NICs dedicated to storage, which can be RDMA (if you are looking for high throughput), iSCSI, or fibre channel.

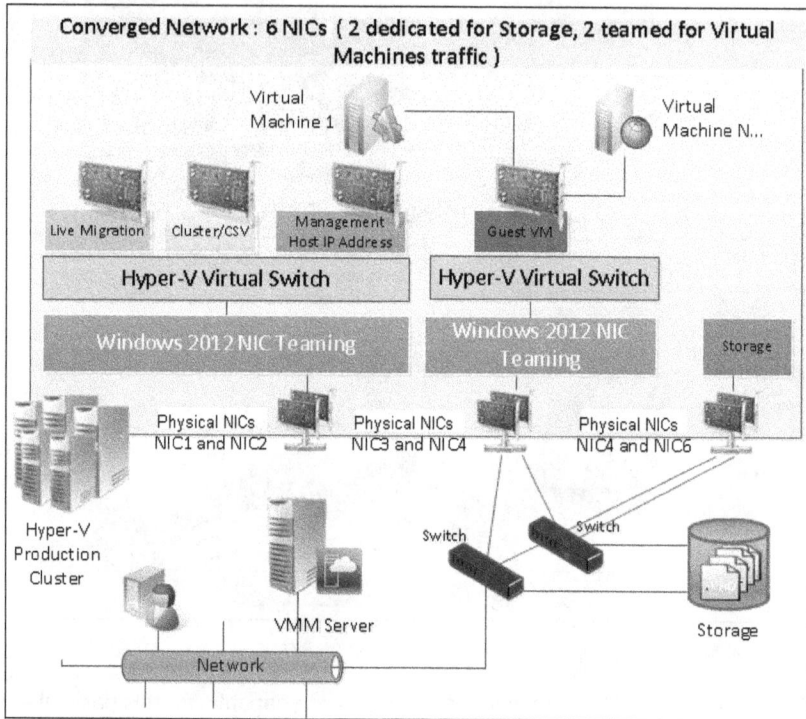

Network QoS (partitioning) should be used to prioritize the traffic for live migration, host management, and CSV. **VMM Port Profiles** should be used to define the configuration for the virtual NICs: offload settings, security settings, and bandwidth settings.

Networking – configuring logical networks

Logical network is a container that contains elements that defines the underlying networking infrastructure. It contains a group of IP subnets and/or VLANs.

In this recipe, we will go through the logical network configuration.

Getting ready

A logical network linked to a network site is a user-defined group of IP subnets, VLANs, or IP subnet/VLAN pairs that is used to organize and simplify network assignments. It can be used to label networks with different purposes, for traffic isolation, and to provision networks for different types of **service-level agreements** (**SLAs**).

> As VMs move across Hyper-V servers, make sure that the virtual network switches are named exactly the same in all Hyper-V servers (as they are associated with VMs). Additionally, if you plan to use a Hyper-V host as part of a cluster node, make sure you have at least two external virtual network switches per node. For more information about virtual switches, see `http://technet.microsoft.com/en-us/library/hh831823.aspx`.

To make a logical network available to a host, you must associate the logical network with a physical network adapter on the host.

> You cannot associate a logical network with a Hyper-V internal or private vSwitch.

For the purposes of this section, we will be assuming that the physical servers do have 4 x 10GB physical network ports, and two of those are dedicated to storage, while the other two will be teamed and portioned to create the host management, as shown in the following figure:

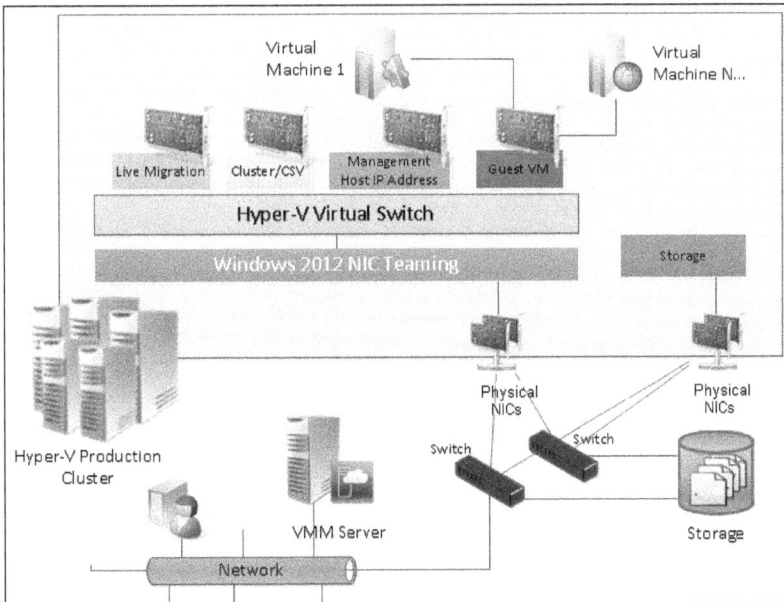

The following table shows the configuration that we will be using for our deployment:

Physical NIC	Team/MPIO	Can it be associated with a logical network?
10 gigabit NIC #1	Team	Yes
10 gigabit NIC #2		
ISCSI #1	MPIO	No
ISCSI #2		

In this section, we will create the logical network management that will be used for host management, guest VMs, live migration, and CSV traffic, as shown in the previous figure.

Some other possible examples of logical networks would include DMZ, backend, frontend, backup, cluster, and extranet.

How to do it...

Carry out the following steps to create a logical network and an associated network site:

1. Connect to the VMM 2012 R2 console by using the VMM admin account previously created (lab\vmm-admin), and then, on the bottom-left pane, click on **Fabric** to open the fabric workspace.

2. Click on the **Home** tab on the ribbon, and then click on **Fabric Resources**.

3. Expand **Networking** in the **Fabric** pane to the left, and then click on **Logical Networks**.

4. On the **Home** tab, click on **Create Logical Network**.

5. When the **Create Logical Network Wizard** window opens, type in the logical
   network name (for example, Management) on the **Name** page, as shown in the
   following screenshot:

> You may optionally type in a description for the logical network, for
> example, Management OS network traffic - Used by
> Guest VMs, Hosts mgmt., Live Migration, and CSV.

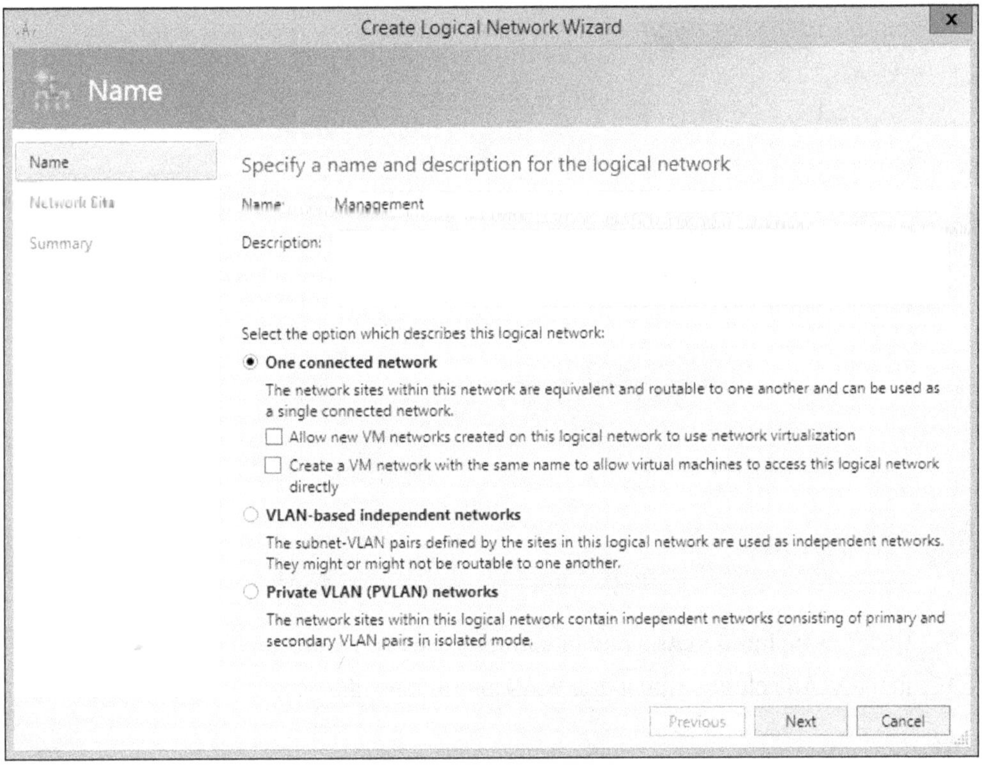

6. Select the option that describes the logical network and click on **Next**.
7. In the **Network Site** page, click on the **Add** button.

8. For **Host groups that can use this network site**, select the host group(s) to make available for this logical network. For example, **Sydney**, as shown in the following screenshot:

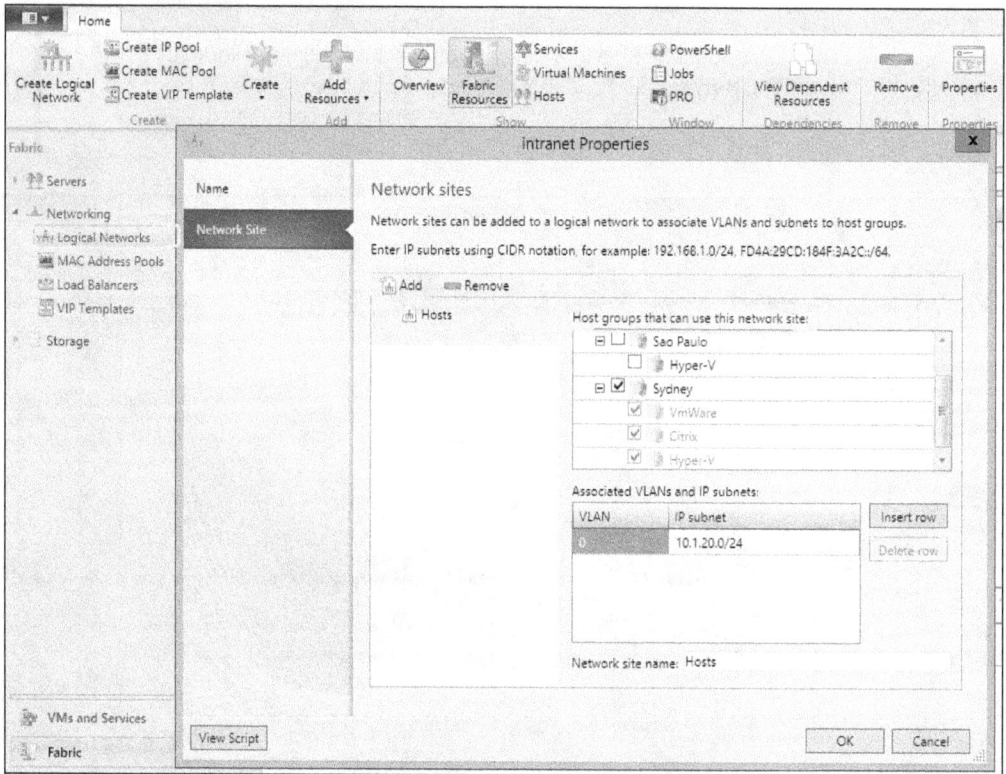

9. Under **Associated VLANs and IP subnets**, click on **Insert row**.

10. In the **VLAN** column, type in the VLAN information, if any.

> Leave it blank if there is no VLAN, or type in 10, for example, to create VLAN 10.

11. Under **IP subnet**, type in the IP address, for example, 10.1.10.0/24.

12. In the **Network Site Name** box, type in the network site name, for example, Hosts, and then click on **Next**.

13. Repeat steps 6 through 12 to add the live migration, CSV, and guest VM network sites.

14. In the **Summary** page, click on **Finish**.

> Repeat steps 4 through 12 to create more logical networks, if required.

How it works...

This recipe describes the process of creating a logical network and associating it with a site (normally a physical location) and an IP subnet and VLANs (if any).

For VMM to automatically assign static IP addresses, you need to create IP address pools from an IP subnet associated with a network site.

When you add a Hyper-V host to VMM, if the physical network adapter is not associated with a logical network, VMM will then automatically create and associate a logical network that matches the DNS suffix of the connection (the first one). Refer to the *How to Configure Global Network Settings in VMM* article at `http://technet.microsoft.com/en-us/library/gg610695.aspx`.

If you decide to assign an IP address from an VMM IP address pool to the management network of the Hyper-V hosts, be prepared to manually enter the MAC address of the physical NIC that is used for PXE or use the VMM **deep discovery** feature to retrieve the information. CDN provides the physical NIC's name, but not the MAC addresses.

Certify that you have at least one physical network adapter available for communication between the host and the VMM management server when associating a logical network with a physical network adapter.

> If working with **Full Converged** networks, it is recommended that you have a VMM management server outside of the production cluster, on a separate and dedicated cluster.

There's more...

Now, let's create the IP address pool for the logical network and then associate the logical network to a physical network adapter.

Creating an IP address pool

Now that you have created the logical networks, you need to carry out the following steps to create an IP address pool for the logical network:

1. Open the **Fabric** workspace and then click on the **Home** tab on the ribbon.

2. Click on **Fabric Resources**, expand **Networking** in the **Fabric** pane to the left, and then click on **Logical Networks**.

3. In the **Logical Networks and IP Pools** main pane, click on the logical network to create the IP address pool (**Management**, in our example).

4. On the **Home** tab on the ribbon, click on **Create IP Pool**; the following wizard appears:

5. When **Create Static IP Address Pool Wizard** opens, on the **Name** page type in the name and description (optional) for the IP address pool, for example, HostsIPAddressPool.

6. On the **Network Site** page, click on **Use an existing network site**.

7. Enter the correct IP address range and click on **Next**.

8. Enter the correct gateway and metric and click on **Next**.

9. Enter the correct DNS server address and DNS suffix (if any) and click on **Next**.

10. Enter the correct WINS (if any) and click on **Next**.

11. On the **Summary** page, review the settings and click on **Finish**.

> You can specify one or more IP addresses from the address range in the IP subnet to create a **virtual IP** (**VIP**) address or reserve one for other purposes.

After completing the logical network and IP pool creation, on the **Fabric** workspace, expand **Networking** and then click on **Logical Networks** to confirm that the logical networks you just created are listed.

Automating the network configuration

In VMM 2012 R2, you can optionally use **Global Networking Settings** to automate the creation of logical networks and its association with a physical network adapter and the creation of external virtual networks. Carry out the following steps in order to configure it:

1. On the VMM console, in the **Settings** workspace and in the **Settings** pane, click on **General**.

2. Double-click on **Network Settings** and configure the logical networking settings from the drop-down menu: **DNS**, **Network Connection Name**, and **Virtual Network Switch Name**.

> In VMM 2012 R2, the setting **Create virtual networks automatically** is enabled by default, which means that when you add a Hyper-V host to VMM, and no logical network is assigned with any physical NIC, VMM will automatically create a logical network.

Associating the VMM Logical Network with the physical adapter

Carry out the following steps to associate the VMM logical network with the physical adapter on the hypervisor host:

> In VMM 2012 SP1 and R2 versions, if there is no logical network associated to a physical network adapter when adding the Hyper-V host, VMM will, by default, create and then associate a logical network matching the first DNS suffix of the connection and a VM network configured with No Isolation.

3. In the **Fabric** workspace, on the **Fabric** pane to the left, navigate to **Servers | All Hosts** and then expand the host group, for example, **Hyper-V**.

4. In the **Hosts** main pane, select the host to configure, for example, **hyperv02**.

> In order to proceed with this step, you should have added the Hyper-V server to the host group first. See the *Adding and managing Hyper-V hosts and host clusters* recipe in this chapter.

5. In the **Host** tab on the ribbon, click on **Properties** (or right-click on the host and click on **Properties**).

6. In the **Host Name Properties** dialog box, navigate to **Hardware | Network Adapters**, and select the physical network adapter to be associated.

> Wireless network adapters will not be displayed, as this technology is not supported.

7. On the **Logical network connectivity** page, select the logical network to associate with the physical adapter, for example, **Management**, as shown in the following screenshot:

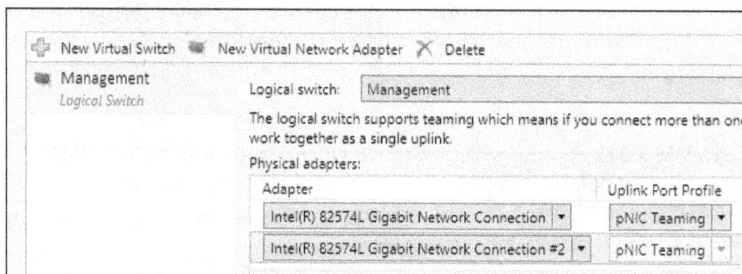

> To team two or more physical network adapters, make sure the **Uplink Port Profile** mode setting is configured to **Team** and then apply the same logical switch and uplink port profile.

8. Select **Uplink Port Profile** from the list.

> If a profile displays no port, review the logical switch configuration.

9. Click on **OK** to complete.

[💡 Repeat these steps on every host of the host group that's using the same logical network.]

See also

▶ The *How to Create IP Address Pools for Logical Networks in VMM* article at
   `http://go.microsoft.com/fwlink/p/?LinkID=212422`

▶ The *How to Configure Network Settings on a Hyper-V Host in VMM* article at
   `http://go.microsoft.com/fwlink/p/?LinkID=212537`

▶ The *How to Configure Global Network Settings in VMM* article at `technet.`
   `microsoft.com/en-us/library/gg610695.aspx`

Networking – configuring VM networks and gateways

A VM network is created on top of a logical network, enabling you to create multiple virtualization networks. Network virtualization and gateway devices are new features in VMM 2012 R2, and are only available on Windows Server 2012/R2 Hyper-V hosts. The types of VM networks in VMM 2012 R2 are as follows:

▶ **Isolation** (network virtualization): Without the VLAN constraints, isolation enables VM deployment flexibility as the VM keeps its IP address independent of the host it is placed on, removing the necessity of physical IP subnet hierarchies or VLANs.

It allows you to configure numerous virtual network infrastructures (they can even have the same **customer IP address** (**CA**) that are connected to the same physical network. A likely scenario is either a hosting environment, with customers sharing the same physical fabric infrastructure, or an enterprise environment with different teams that have different objectives that also share the same physical fabric infrastructure or even on a software house having test, stage, and production environments sharing the physical infrastructure. There are many other different scenarios where the network virtualization will enable each virtual network infrastructure to work as unique, but in fact it will be running on a shared physical network.

▶ **No Isolation**: In the No Isolation mode, the VM network will act as the associated logical network, and you only have one VM network configured with no isolation per logical network.

> When creating the logical network, click on **One connected network** and then select **Create a VM network with the same name to allow virtual machines to access this logical network directly**, and if using network virtualization, check the box for allowing network virtualization.

- **VLAN-based**: If your environment makes use of a VLAN for network isolation, you can use VMM to manage it. In most cases, select **VLAN-based independent networks**. However, if you are using private VLAN technology, select **Private VLAN (PVLAN) networks**.

- **External networks implemented through a vendor network-management console**: If you have configured the network through a vendor management software console, you can use VMM to import the data settings (for example, for logical networks, network sites, and VM networks) by installing the vendor-specific virtual switch extension manager.

  If running a multitenant environment, such as a hosted datacenter with multiple customers, the feature will give you a powerful advantage. For more information on how to add a virtual switch extension or network manager in System Center 2012 R2, see `http://technet.microsoft.com/en-us/library/dn249411.aspx`.

  Network virtualization in Windows Server 2012 R2 is designed to remove the constraints of VLAN and hierarchical IP address assignment for virtual machine provisioning. This enables flexibility in virtual machine placement because the virtual machine can keep its IP address regardless of what host it is placed on. Placement is no longer limited by physical IP subnet hierarchies or VLAN configurations.

- **Gateways**: The likely scenario for this implementation is when you want to configure a VPN tunnel directly on your gateway device and then connect it directly to a VM by selecting **Remote Networks** when creating the VM network. Note, though, that a gateway device software provider is required on the VMM management server. In the VMM model, the Hyper-V Network Virtualization gateway is managed via a PowerShell plugin module (which will communicate the policy to the gateway). You will need to request a PowerShell plugin module from your vendor to install on the VMM server.

Getting ready

Network virtualization only works on Windows Server 2012/R2 Hyper-V hosts and VMM 2012 R2.

Make sure you've created the logical network in VMM before you start creating the VM network because VMM will use it to assign the **provider addresses** (**PAs**).

VMM 2012 R2 uses the IP address pools that are associated with a VM network to assign customized addresses to virtual machines by using network virtualization.

IP address virtualization uses **Network Virtualization with Generic Routing Encapsulation** (**NVGRE**).

For our deployment, we have two customers with the same IP range sharing the same logical network, as shown in the following table:

Logical network	Associated Hyper-V switch	VM network	Customer IP address
Customers	vExternal	VM-CustA	172.16.2.0/24
Customers	vExternal	VM-CustB	172.16.2.0/24

How to do it...

Carry out the following steps to create a VM network with isolation:

1. In the VMM console, click on **VMs and Services** in the bottom-left area to open the **VMs and Services** workspace, and then click on the **Home** tab on the ribbon.

2. Click on **Create VM Network**, and in **Create VM Network Wizard**, type in the name for the VM network (for example, VM-CustA) and an optional description.

3. In the **Logical network** list, select a previously created logical network (following our sample infrastructure, select **Internet**).

4. On the **Isolation** page, click on **Isolate using Hyper-V network virtualization**, and then, click on **Next**.

> If you select **No isolation**, the **VM Subnets and Gateway** page configuration will not appear.

5. On the **VM Subnets** page, click on **Add** and type in a name for the VM subnet, for example, VM-Network-Internal-Servers.

6. In the **Subnet** box, type in an IP subnet address (for example, 172.16.2.0/24) followed by the **Classless Inter-Domain Routing** (**CDIR**) notation.

7. On the **Connectivity** page, if the **No network service that specifies a gateway has been added to VMM** message appears, click on **Next**; alternatively, configure the gateway in the following manner:

> Do not select any option if you are planning to set up the gateway settings for this VM network later.

- Select the option, **No connectivity if the VM's will communicate only within this VM network**.

- Select the option, **Connect to another network through a VPN tunnel** if the VMs will communicate with other networks through a VPN tunnel or if the device will make use of the **Border Gateway Protocol**. Then, if applicable, select and confirm the VPN Gateway device.

> The **VPN Connections** wizard will show up if the VPN gateway is selected. The **Border Gateway Protocol** wizard will be shown if selected. Enter the VPN endpoint, bandwidth, and other requested information.

- Select the option, **Connect directly to an additional logical network** if the VMs will communicate with other VMs in other networks; then, select either **Direct routing** or **Network address translation (NAT)**. Select and confirm the gateway device.

8. Click on **Next**. Then, on the **Summary** page, click on **Finish**.

> To create an IP pool, select the VM network (for example, **VM-intranet**), right-click on it, click on **Create IP Pool**, and then follow the steps provided in the *Creating an IP address pool* subsection of the *Networking – configuring logical networks* recipe of this chapter.

How it works...

By using Windows Server 2012/R2 virtual networking enhancement, VMM creates the necessary IP address mappings for the VMs.

You are required to set up the logical network first since VMM uses it to assign provider addresses (PA). It will then be visible to the physical network (for example, to hosts, physical switches, and gateways). However, it will not be visible to a virtual machine, which will have **customized addresses** assigned by VMM from an IP address pool associated with a virtual network (VM network).

In network virtualization, each virtual machine will be assigned two IP addresses:

- ▶ **Customer IP address (CA)**: This address is visible to the VM and is used to communicate with the virtual machine

- ▶ **Provider IP address (PA)**: This address is not visible to the VM and is only used by the Hyper-V server to communicate with the VM it hosts

The mechanism that can be used to virtualize the IP address of a VM is called **Network Virtualization with Generic Routing Encapsulation** (**NVGRE**), in which all of the VM's packets are encapsulated with a new header before they get transmitted on the physical network.

> Because the VMs on a specific host can share the same PA, IP encapsulation offers better scalability.

You can assign customer addresses through the DHCP server (it requires DHCPv4 Server Switch Extension), or by using static IP addresses. Then, when creating an IP address pool for a VM subnet, it will automatically provision IP addresses by either of the mechanisms.

Since VMM 2012 SP1, you can create a VM network through a gateway (VPN tunnel), if the gateway device has the required software provider.

There's more...

Check out this session for information on how to integrate gateways with VMM.

Adding a gateway device, a virtual switch extension, or network manager in VMM 2012 R2

Carry out the following steps to configure a gateway device to provide support for the VM network.

> It is required that you have previously installed the gateway provider on the VMM management server, and if the gateway requires a certificate, make sure it is imported.

1. In the **Settings** workspace, on the **Settings** pane, click on **Configuration Providers** and confirm that the gateway provider is installed.

2. Click on the **Fabric** workspace, and then in the **Home** tab, click on **Fabric Resources.**

3. In the **Fabric pane**, click to expand **Networking**; then, select **Network Services**, which include gateways, vSwitch extensions, **top-of-rack** (**TOR**) switches, and network managers.

4. In the **Add Gateway Wizard** window, type in the gateway name and description (optional) and click on **Next.**

5. On the **Manufacturer and Model** page, select the provider's manufacturer and model and click on **Next.**

6. On the **Credentials** page, provide the Run As account and click on **Next.**

[🔆 Alternatively, you can click on **Create Run As Account** to create a new Run As account.]

7. On the **Connection String** page, type in the gateway connection string in accordance with the vendor-predefined syntax (for example, `gateway.lab.local`) and click on **Next**.

8. In the **Certificates** page, if your gateway requires a certificate, select the checkbox to confirm that the certificate can be imported to the trusted certificate store and then click on **Next**.

9. On the **Provider** page, select the provider and click on **Next**.

[🔆 To carry out a simple validation check, click on **Test**.]

10. In the **Host Group** page, select the host groups that will have the gateway available to them.

11. In the **Summary** page, click on **Finish**.

12. If adding a gateway device, under **Network Services**, select the gateway, right-click on it, and select **Properties**. Click on **Connectivity** and do the following:

    ❑ Select **Enable front end connection**; then, select the network adapter of the gateway and the network site with external connectivity.

[🔆 If you need to allow VPN connectivity, make sure the network site has a route to/from the external network and a static IP address pool.]

    ❑ Select **Enable back end connection**; then, select the network adapter of the gateway and the network site with internal connectivity.

[🔆 Make sure **Hyper-V Network Virtualization** is enabled for the logical network and that the network site has a static IP address pool.]

See also

▸ The *Configuring VM Networks and Gateways in VMM* article at
  `http://technet.microsoft.com/en-us/library/jj721575.aspx`

▸ The *How to Use a Server Running Windows Server 2012 R2 as a Gateway with VMM*
  article at `http://technet.microsoft.com/en-us/library/dn249417.aspx`

▸ The *How to Add a Top-of-Rack Switch in VMM in System Center 2012 R2* article at
  `http://technet.microsoft.com/en-us/library/dn249414.aspx`

▸ The *Hyper-V Network Virtualization Overview* article at `http://go.microsoft.`
  `com/fwlink/p/?LinkId=243484`

▸ The *Hyper-V Network Virtualization technical details* article at
  `http://technet.microsoft.com/en-us/library/jj134174.aspx`

▸ The *Hyper-V Network Virtualization Gateway Architectural Guide* article at
  `http://technet.microsoft.com/en-us/library/jj618319.aspx`

Networking – configuring logical switches, port profiles, and port classifications

VMM 2012 SP1/R2 allows you to configure port profiles and logical switches. They work as containers for network adapter capabilities and settings, and by using them, you can apply the configuration to selected adapters instead of configuring those settings on each host network adapter.

How to do it...

Let's start by creating the port profiles, and then we will create the port classification, followed by the logical switch. Carry out the following steps to create port profiles for uplinks:

1. In the VMM console, click on **Port Profiles** in the **Fabric** workspace on the **Fabric** pane under **Networking**.

2. On the **Home** tab on the ribbon, click on **Create**, and then click on **Hyper-V Port Profile**.

3. In the **Create Hyper-V Port Profile Wizard** window, on the **General** page, type in the port profile and optionally a description.

4. Click on **Uplink port profile**, select the load-balancing algorithm and the team mode, and click on **Next**, as shown in the following screenshot:

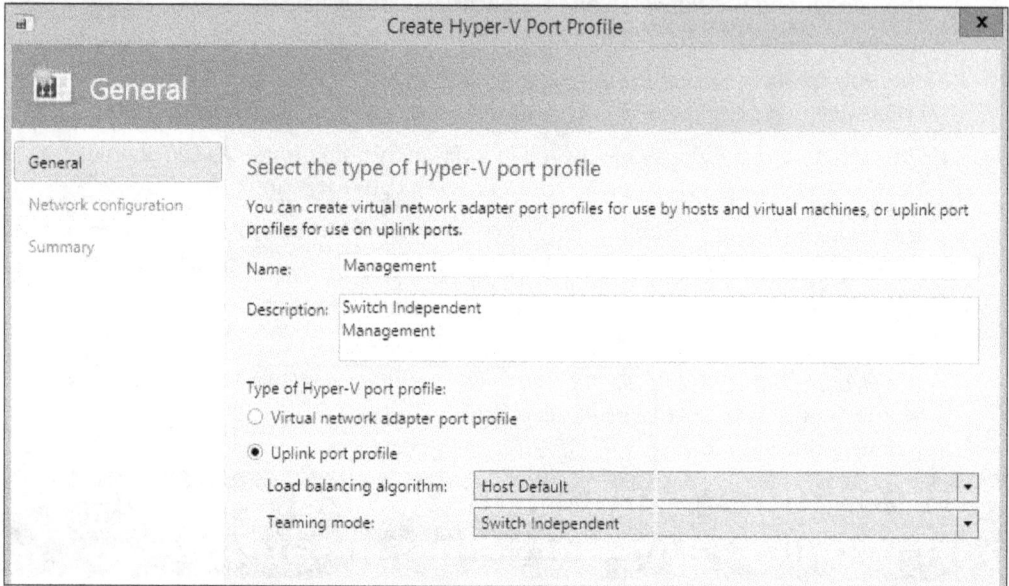

5. In the **Network configuration** page, select the network site (which could be more than one).

6. Optionally, to enable network virtualization support for it, click on **Enable Windows Network Virtualization**.

> This setting requires a logical network with the **Allow new VM networks created on this logical network to use network virtualization** setting checked.

7. Click on **Next**, and then on the **Summary** page, click on **Finish**.

How it works...

Profiles are useful features that can be used to apply settings or capabilities to an entire datacenter instead of configuring each adapter's settings.

After creating a Hyper-V port profile, the profile will need to be assigned to a logical switch. Make it available through the assigned logical switch, which can then be selected to be applied to a network adapter in a host. This will make the network consistent across the Hyper-V hosts.

There's more...

Since the VMM 2012 SP1 version, VMM supports port profiles, port classifications, and virtual switch extensions. Let's configure them.

Creating port profiles for VM adapters

VMM 2012 R2 makes use of virtual port profiles to define the configuration for the virtual NICs: offload settings, security settings, and bandwidth settings. There are already some preexisting configured virtual port profiles (for example, host management, cluster, live migration, iSCSI, and high bandwidth adapter), but you can create a customized one. Carry out the following steps to create native port profiles:

1. In the VMM console, click on **Port Profiles** in the **Fabric** workspace on the **Fabric** pane under **Networking**.

2. On the **Home** tab on the ribbon, click on **Create**, and then click on **Hyper-V Port Profile**.

3. In the **Create Hyper-V Port Profile Wizard** window, on the **General** page, type in the port profile and optionally a description.

4. Click on **Virtual network adapter port profile**, and then click on **Next**.

5. On the **Offload Settings** page, select the settings you want to enable (if any), such as virtual machine queue, IPsec task offloading, and Single-root I/O virtualization, and click on **Next**, as shown in the following screenshot:

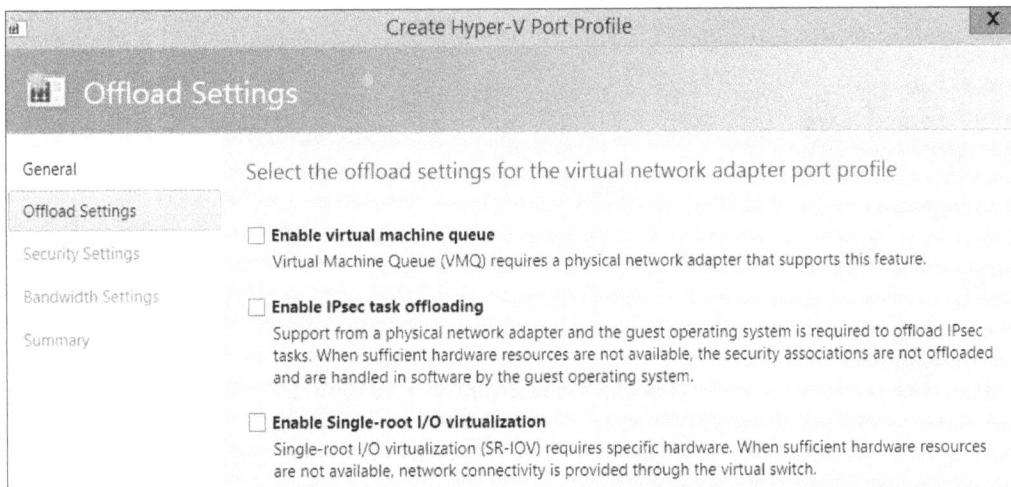

6. In the **Security Settings** page, select the settings you want to allow/enable (if any), such as **MAC spoofing**, **DHCP guard**, **router guard**, **guest teaming**, and **IEEE priority tagging**, and click on **Next**, as shown in the following screenshot:

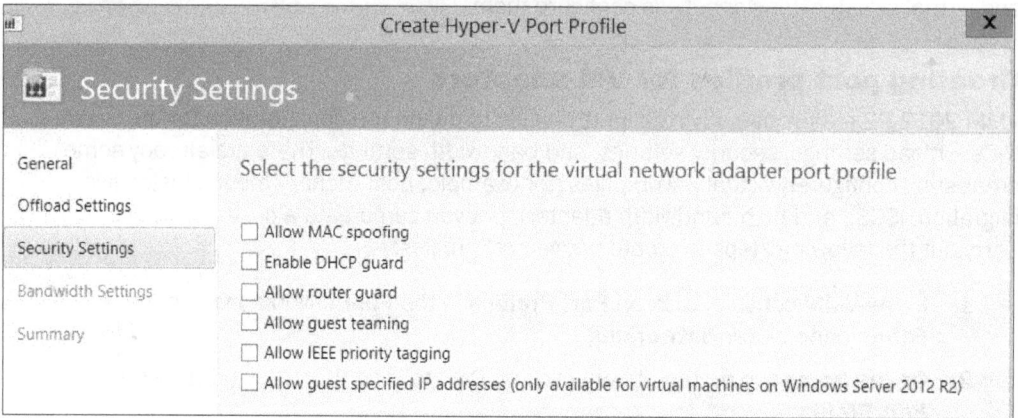

Create Hyper-V Port Profile	X

Security Settings

General
Offload Settings
Security Settings
Bandwidth Settings
Summary

Select the security settings for the virtual network adapter port profile

- [ ] Allow MAC spoofing
- [ ] Enable DHCP guard
- [ ] Allow router guard
- [ ] Allow guest teaming
- [ ] Allow IEEE priority tagging
- [ ] Allow guest specified IP addresses (only available for virtual machines on Windows Server 2012 R2)

7. On the **Bandwidth Settings** page, if SR-IOV is not enabled and you want to configure the bandwidth settings, specify **Minimum bandwidth (Mbps)**, **Minimum bandwidth weight**, and **Maximum bandwidth (Mbps)**, as shown in the following screenshot:

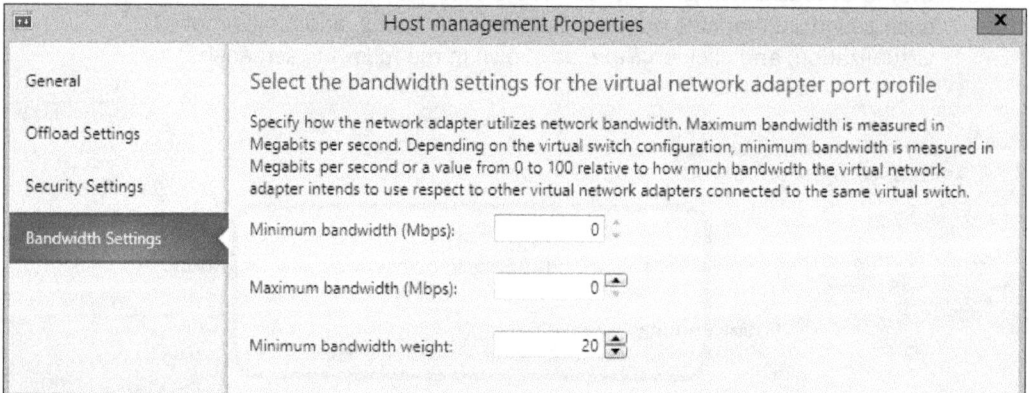

Host management Properties	X

General
Offload Settings
Security Settings
Bandwidth Settings

Select the bandwidth settings for the virtual network adapter port profile

Specify how the network adapter utilizes network bandwidth. Maximum bandwidth is measured in Megabits per second. Depending on the virtual switch configuration, minimum bandwidth is measured in Megabits per second or a value from 0 to 100 relative to how much bandwidth the virtual network adapter intends to use respect to other virtual network adapters connected to the same virtual switch.

Minimum bandwidth (Mbps): 0

Maximum bandwidth (Mbps): 0

Minimum bandwidth weight: 20

It is best practice to set up the weighted configuration. The total weight of all adapters and the virtual switch default should stream to 100. You can use the following PowerShell script to check the default bandwidth weight:

```
Get-SCVirtualNetworkAdapterNativePortProfile | ft name,
MinimumBandwidthWeight
```

8. On the **Summary** page, click on the **Finish** button.

Creating a port classification

Carry out the following steps to create port classifications:

1. In the VMM console, click on **Networking**, and then on **Port Classifications** on the **Fabric** pane in the **Fabric** workspace.

2. On the **Home** tab on the ribbon, click on **Create** and then on **Port Classification**.

3. In the **Create Port Classification Wizard** window, type in the port classification name and optional description and click on **OK**.

Adding a virtual switch extension manager

Carry out the following steps to add a virtual switch extension in VMM 2012 SP1. Note that it is required that you already have the provider installed on the VMM management server.

> Refer to the *Adding a gateway device, a virtual switch extension, or network manager in VMM 2012 R2* section of the *Networking – configuring VM networks and gateways* recipe for more details.

1. In the **Fabric** workspace, on the **Fabric** pane under **Networking**, click on **Switch Extension Managers**; then, on the **Home** tab, click on **Add resources**.

2. Click on **Virtual Switch Extension Manager**; then, in the **Add Virtual Switch Extension Manager Wizard** window, type in the gateway name and description (optional) and click on **Next**.

3. On the **Credentials** page, provide the Run As account and click on **Next**.

4. On the **Manufacturer and Model** page, select the provider's manufacturer and model and click on **Next**.

5. On the **Connection String** page, type in the connection string in accordance with the vendor-predefined syntax (for example, `vmswitch.lab.local`) and click on **Next**.

6. Select a Run As account by clicking on **Browse**, clicking on **OK**, and then on **OK** again to confirm the settings.

7. On the **Host Groups** page, select at least one host group that will have the virtual switch extension manager available and click on **Next**.

8. On the **Summary** page, click on **Finish**.

Creating a logical switch

Carry out the following steps to create logical switches:

1. In the VMM console, in the **Fabric** workspace on the **Fabric** pane, click on **Logical Switches**.

2. Right-click on it and then click on **Create Logical Switch**.

3. On the **Getting Started** page, click on **Next.**

4. In the **Create Logical Switch Wizard** window, type in the logical switch name and, optionally, a description.

5. If the network adapter has SR-IOV support and you want to enable it, click on **Enable Single Root I/O Virtualization (SR-IOV)**, as shown in the following screenshot:

☐ Enable single root I/O virtualization (SR-IOV)
SR-IOV allows a device, such as a network adapter, to gain direct access to physical networks adapters that support SR-IOV. Using SR-IOV, network performance can achieve nearly the same performance as in non virtualized environments.

ⓘ You can enable SR-IOV only when a logical switch is created. To change your SR-IOV usage in the future, you must create a different logical switch.

6. If you are using the virtual switch extensions, select the extensions on the **Extensions** page, making sure they are in the order they are to be processed in, and click on **Next**, as shown in the following screenshot:

Choose the extensions you want to use with this logical switch

Select the check box for each extension that you want installed and configured when an instance of the logical switch is created on a host. Only one forwarding extension can be selected.

Virtual switch extensions:

Name	Extension Type	Extension Manager	
☐ Microsoft NDIS Capture	Monitoring	N/A	Move Up
☑ Microsoft Windows Fil...	Filter	N/A	Move Down

> The Windows 2012/R2 Hyper-V extensible switch allows you to add extensions to the virtual switch that can capture, filter, or forward traffic.

7. On the **Uplink** page, select the uplink mode, **Team** or **No Uplink Team**, then click on **Add** to add port profiles that will be available, as shown in the following screenshot. Now, click on **Next**:

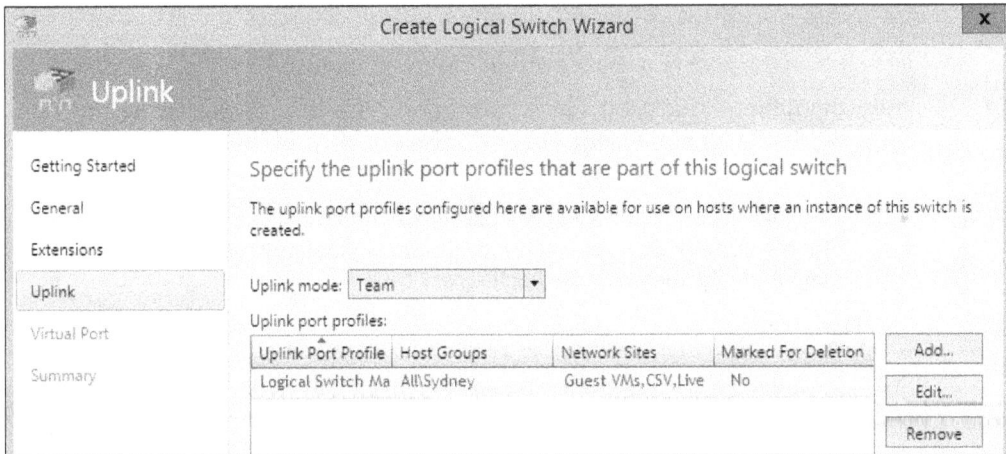

8. On the **Virtual Port** page, click on **Add** to add port classifications that are associated or not to a VM network adapter port profile, as shown in the following screenshot. Then, click on **Next**.

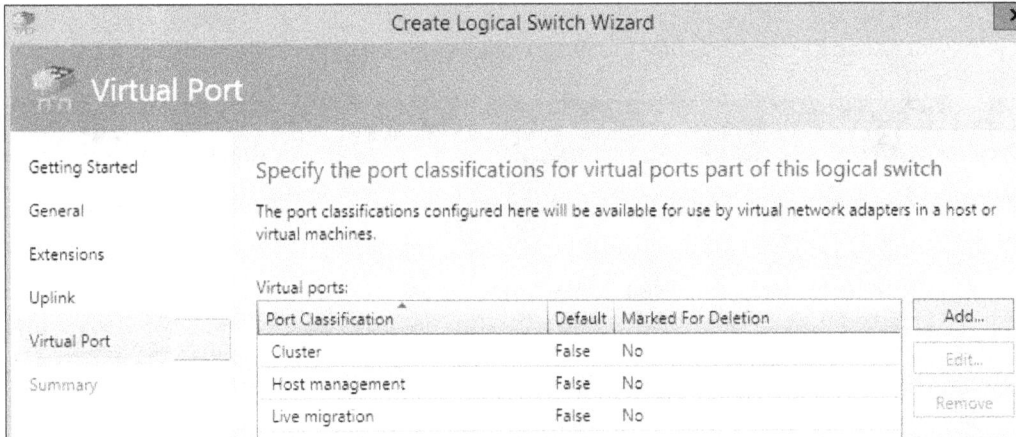

9. On the **Summary** page, click on **Finish**.

Configuring the network adapter for VMs and host management

Carry out the following steps to configure the network adapter:

1. In the **Fabric** workspace, on the **Fabric** pane, navigate to **Servers | All Hosts** and select a host group; then, select a host in the **Hosts** main pane.

2. Right-click on the host and click on **Properties**, and then click on the **Hardware** tab.

3. In **Network Adapters**, select the physical network adapter to be configured. For VMs, click on **Available for placement**. For management, click on **Used by management**.

> If a logical switch and an uplink port profile were previously configured for the network adapter, when you click on **Logical network connectivity**, the result connectivity will be displayed.

4. Do not change individual settings if you are planning to use a logical switch and uplink port profiles. Instead, apply the configuration to the virtual switch on the hosts.

5. Click on **OK** to finish.

See also

▸ The *Hyper-V Network Virtualization Overview* article at http://go.microsoft.com/fwlink/p/?LinkId=243484

▸ The *Network Virtualization technical details* article at http://technet.microsoft.com/en-us/library/jj134174.aspx

Integrating and configuring the storage

VMM 2012 supports block-level storage devices and file storage solutions. Their descriptions are given in the following list:

▸ **Block-level storage devices**: These expose logical unit numbers for storage, using fibre channel, iSCSI, and SAS connection mechanisms. You can integrate these arrays with VMM using a storage provider, meaning that you will be able to manage the arrays through the VMM console.

> From Windows 2012 onward, the Windows WMI-based Windows **Storage Management API** (**SMAPI**) replaces the **Virtual Disk Service API** (**VDS**). See http://blogs.msdn.com/b/san/archive/2012/06/26/an-introduction-to-storage-management-in-windows-server-2012.aspx for more information.

The supported storage providers in VMM 2012 are as follows:

- **SMI-S CIM-XML**: VMM 2012 SP1/R2 uses SMAPI to interconnect with SMI-S compliant servers. This in turn uses the Microsoft-Standards-based Storage Management Service to communicate with the SMI-S external storage.

> If your storage is SMI-S compatible, install the SMI-S provider on a server accessible by the VMM management server over the network by an IP address or a **fully qualified domain name** (**FQDN**). If using FQDN, confirm that the DNS is resolving.

- **SMP** (supported only by VMM 2012 SP1/R2): VMM uses SMAPI to directly connect with the SMP storage devices.

> For a complete list of supported storage providers, see `http://social. technet.microsoft.com/wiki/contents/articles/4583 scvmm-2012-storage-and-load-balancer-provider- downloads-en-us.aspx` and `http://go.microsoft.com/ fwlink/p/?LinkID=212013`.

- **File storage**: In VMM 2012 SP1/R2, you can use SMB 3.0 network shares for storage, which can reside on a Windows Server 2012 file server or on a vendor **Network Attached Storage** (**NAS**). For more information, refer to the *How to Add Windows File Server Shares in VMM* article available at `http://technet. microsoft.com/en-us/library/jj860437.aspx`, and the *How to Assign SMB 3.0 File Shares to Hyper-V Hosts and Clusters in VMM* article available at `http://technet.microsoft.com/en-us/library/jj614620.aspx`.

Getting ready

My first recommendation is to find out whether your storage is compatible with VMM 2012, or better, with VMM 2012 R2. If your storage is not supported by VMM 2012, it still recognizes the local storage and remote storage that is on the storage array. However, you will not be able to perform storage management operations such as logical unit creation or removal and assignment of storage through VMM to hosts/clusters. For the unsupported storage, you will need to perform these operations in the vendor storage console.

> Other than WMI, SMP providers from Dell EqualLogic and Nexsan storage providers must *not* be installed on the VMM management server, as they are not supported by Microsoft.

The following figure describes the workflow to automate Storage deployment in VMM 2012 R2:

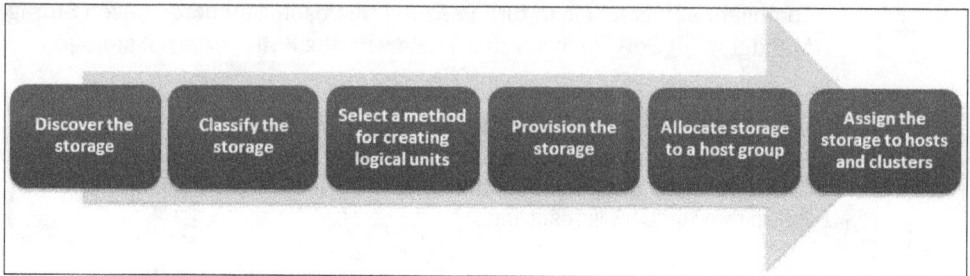

You need to create a Run As account with rights to access the SMI-S provider before configuring it.

In this recipe, I will assume that you have a Dell EqualLogic Storage array (iSCSI PS series) and that you have installed VMM 2012 R2. You will also need to have an account to download Dell EqualLogic Host Integration Tools 4.5.

For our deployment, I will be using the following local server *iSCSI network* configuration conventions:

Physical NIC	IP address
Intel(R) 82577LM Gigabit #3	192.168.1.10/24
Intel(R) 82577LM Gigabit #4	192.168.2.10/24

The following table shows the EqualLogic configuration:

Storage	IP	Group name	Log in as	Password
EqualLogic	192.168.1.1	grpAdmin	Administrator	Password1

How to do it...

Carry out the following steps to configure a VMM 2012 R2 with the Dell EqualLogic storage array:

1. Log in to the VMM management server, vmm-mgmt01.

2. Download and install Dell EqualLogic Host Integration Tools 4.5, and then restart the server. To download this, go to http://www.dellstorage.com/WorkArea/DownloadAsset.aspx?id=1229.

3. Start the VMM command shell with administrative rights (**Run as Administrator**). Import the EqualLogic PowerShell Tools module using the following command:

```
PS C:\> Import-Module -Name "C:\Program Files\EqualLogic\bin\
EQLPSTools.dll"
```

The following steps will help you add/discover the storage in VMM 2012 R2:

1. In the VMM console, in the **Fabric** workspace on the **Fabric** pane to the left, right-click on **Storage** and then click on **Add Storage Devices**.

2. In the **Add Storage Devices Wizard** window, on the **Select Provider Type** page, choose **SAN and NAS devices discovered and managed by a SMI-S provider** or **SAN devices managed by a native SMP provider**.

3. If you chose the SMI-S provider, in the **Specify Discovery Scope** page on the **Protocol** list, choose between **SMI-S CMXML** and **SMI-S WMI**. Then type the FQDN or IP of the storage provider and port number to connect to it, and then select a Run As account by clicking on **Browse**.

4. If you chose the SMP provider, click on **Import** to refresh the list. VMM will then discover and import the storage device information. If you are using SSL, check whether the certificate contains a CN value that matches the value used in VMM, or disable CN check by adding a DWORD value of 1 in the HKEY_LOCAL_MACHINE/SOFTWARE/Microsoft/Storage Management/DisableHttpsCommonNameCheck registry.

5. Click on **Next**, and then on the **Select Storage Devices** page, select the **Classification** column for each storage pool that requires classification and then click on **Next**.

6. On the **Summary** page, click on **Finish**.

How it works...

Storage automation through VMM 2012 is only supported for Hyper-V servers.

In VMM 2012 R2, there are three possible types of storage management: **SMI-S provider**, **SMP provider**, and **Windows-based file server storage**.

VMM 2012 makes use of the Microsoft Storage Management Service to enable the storage features and communicate with the storages through either SMI-S or SMP providers (VMM 2012 R2). It needs to be previously installed on a server other than the VMM management and Hyper-V hosts.

[Contact your storage vendor to obtain the storage provider and installation steps.]

By making use of the storage providers and automating the process, VMM allows you to assign and add storage to Hyper-V hosts and clusters, for example.

The following are the steps to automate the storage in VMM. To install the storage provider, discover and classify the storage, create the logical units (provision), assign the storage to host groups, and then as CSV, assign it to Hyper-V hosts/clusters.

Windows-based file server storage makes use of network shares for storage, and it does support SMB 3.0.

Install the **Multipath I/O (MPIO)** feature for iSCSI storage and set the **Microsoft iSCSI Initiator** service to start automatically.

For fibre channel storage support, each Hyper-V host must have an HBA zoned correctly.

In addition, if the storage pool does support thin provisioning in VMM 2012 R2 by creating a logical unit, you will be able to select the **Create thin storage logical unit with capacity committed on demand** option.

To view the added/discovered storage, click on **Arrays**. The following settings will be shown: array name, total and used capacity, managed storage pools, provider name, port, and status.

There's more...

After configuring the storage provider, you will be able to carry out tasks such as bringing storage pools and assigning classifications.

Creating an iSCSI session on a host

Carry out the following steps to create the iSCSI sessions on each Hyper-V server connected to the storage:

1. On each Hyper-V server (for example, **hyperv02**), confirm that **Microsoft iSCSI Initiator Service** is started and set to **Automatic**.

2. In the VMM console, in the **Fabric** workspace on the **Fabric** pane to the left, expand **Servers**, click on **All Hosts**, right-click on the Hyper-V server to configure, and then click on **Properties**.

3. In the **Properties** dialog box, click on the **Storage** tab, and if the storage is not listed, click on **Add** in **iSCSI Arrays** to add it.

4. In the **Create New iSCSI Session** dialog box, select the iSCSI storage in the array list and then click on **Create** if choosing the automatic setup. For manual/customized settings, click on **Use advanced settings** and select the target portal, target name, and the IP address of the initiator, and then click on **Create**. The array will appear under **iSCSI Arrays**.

> VMM creates the iSCSI session by matching the host initiator IP address subnets with the iSCSI target portal IP subnets.

Bringing the storage pools under management and assigning classifications

Carry out the following steps:

1. In the VMM 2012 R2 console, in the **Fabric** workspace on the **Fabric** pane to the left, expand **Storage**, click on **Arrays**, right-click on the array, and then click on **Properties**.

2. In the **Array Name Properties** dialog box, in the **Storage Pools** tab in the **Storage Pools** section, select the storage pool.

3. In the **Classification** section, select a previously created classification. You can create a new one by clicking on **Create classification** and typing in the classification name (for example, GOLD). Click on **OK** to confirm.

Configuring the allocation method for a storage array

To configure new logical units that will be allocated while rapidly provisioning VMs through the SAN copy technology, carry out the following steps:

1. In the VMM console, in the **Fabric** workspace on the **Fabric** pane to the left, expand **Storage**, click on **Arrays**, right-click on the array, and then click on **Properties**.

2. Click on the **Settings** tab, and then in the **Storage array settings** window, choose between **Use snapshots** (default) and **Clone logical units**.

Creating logical units (LUN)

Carry out the following steps:

1. In the VMM 2012 R2 console, in the **Fabric** workspace on the **Fabric** pane to the left, expand **Storage**, click on **Classifications and Pools**, and then select the storage pool.

2. On the **Home** tab, click on **Create Logical Unit** as shown in the following screenshot:

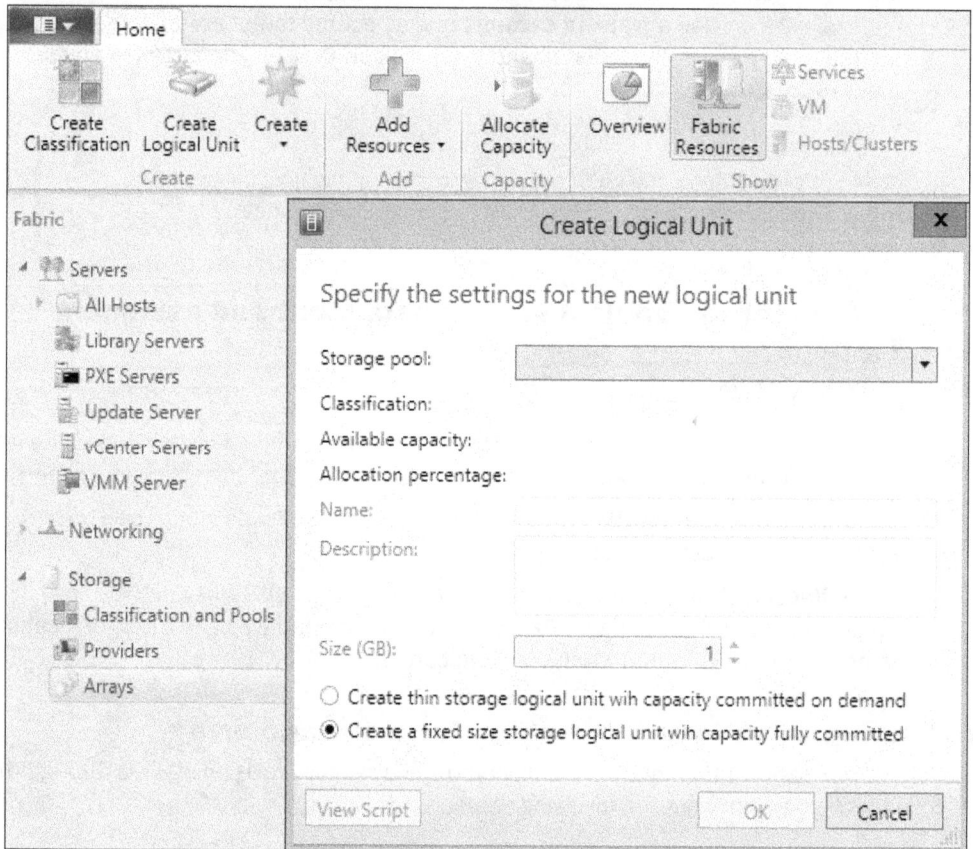

3. In the **Create Logical Unit** dialog box, type the logical name (for example, VMs), a description (optional), and the logical unit size.

> If the storage pool supports thin provisioning, you can click on **Create thin storage logical unit with capacity committed on demand**.

4. To format the disk, in **Format new disk**, click on **Format this volume as NTFS volume with the following settings**.

5. In the **Mount point** section, choose **Assign the following drive letter** and select the drive letter (**V**, for example), or choose **Mount in the following empty NTFS folder**, and then select an empty folder by clicking on **Browse**; or do not assign a drive letter or path.

6. Click on **OK** to confirm.

Allocating logical units and storage pools to a host group

Carry out the following steps:

1. In the **Fabric** workspace, on the **Fabric** pane, click on **Storage**; then, on the **Home** tab, click on **Allocate Capacity** and select the host group from the **Host groups** list.

> If you are logged on as a delegated administrator, right-click on the host group, click on **Properties**, and then click on the **Storage** tab.

2. Click on **Allocate Logical Units**, select each logical unit to be allocated to the host group, and click on **Add**.

> Optionally, select the **Display as available only storage arrays that are visible to any host in the host group** checkbox.

3. Click on **OK** to complete.

See also

▶ The *How to Allocate Storage Pools to a Host Group in VMM* article at
http://go.microsoft.com/fwlink/p/?LinkID=212429

▶ The *How to Configure Storage on a Hyper-V Host in VMM* article at
http://go.microsoft.com/fwlink/p/?LinkID=212536

Creating a physical computer profile (host profile)

A **host profile** or **physical computer profile** is the configuration setting that can be used to deploy a new physical server using Bare Metal deployment.

For the purpose of this section, we will be using the configuration established in the *Networking – configuring logical networks* recipe. The configuration is shown in the following figure:

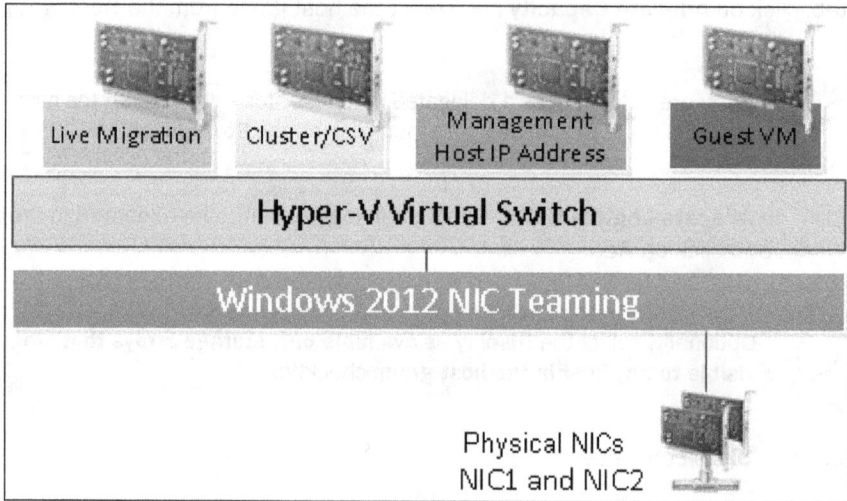

Getting ready

In order to create the host profile, make sure you have already configured the logical switches.

For this section, we will have two physical NICs allocated to a logical switch named `logical Switch Management`.

Although you are not required to use **Consistent Device Naming (CDN)**, if the physical server that is going to be provisioned does support CDN, you will have to first configure the CDN in the BIOS. This will allow the OS to read the information from the BIOS at deployment time and then, when configuring the network in the host profile, you will be able to provide the name in the configuration settings, which will then allocate the networking settings to the correct physical NIC. The following screenshot shows a BIOS that supports CDN:

```
ROM-Based Setup Utility, Version 3.00
Copyright 1982, 2012 Hewlett-Packard Development Company, L.P.

Sy MPS Table Mode                        ProLiant DL380p Gen8
Po ROM Selection                         : ............
PC NMI Debug Button                      duct ID: ..........
PC Virtual Install Disk                  BIOS P70 12/08/2012
St PCI Bus Padding Options        ons    kup Version 12/08/2012
Bo Power-On Logo                         tblock 03/11/2012
Da F11 Boot Menu Prompt                  er Management Controller - 3.1
Se Consistent Device Naming
Se Network Boot Retry Support            16384MB Memory Configured
BI Reset on Boot Device Not Found
Se H
Ad   CDN Support for LOMs Only           Proc 1:Intel 2.50GHz,15MB L3 Cache
Syst Disabled                            Proc 2:Not Installed
Util

    CDN Support for LOMs Only            Press <TAB> for More Information

<↑/↓> Changes Configuration Selection
<Enter> Saves Selection; <ESC> to Cancel
```

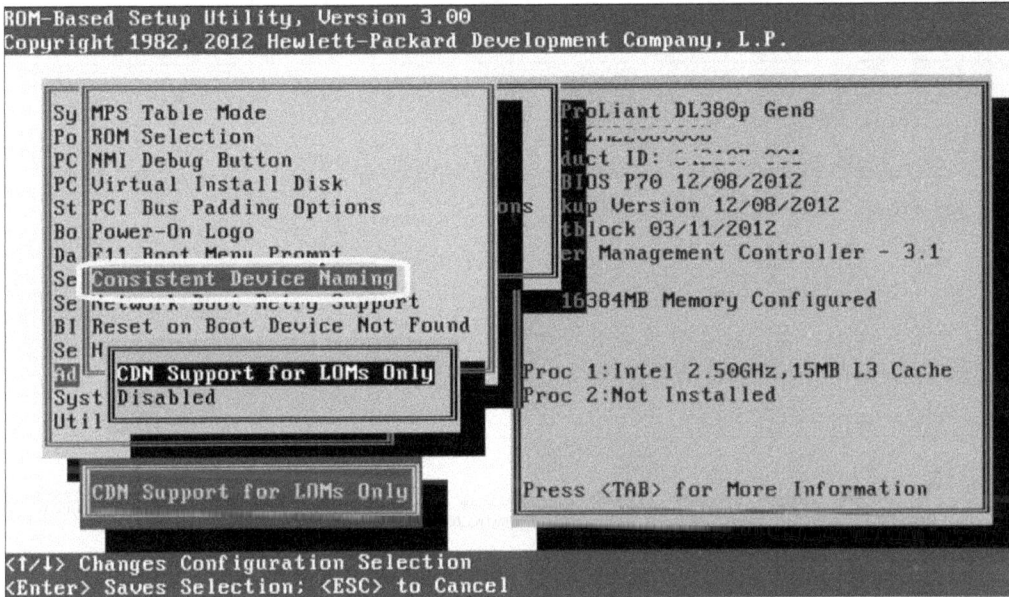

The following are the operating systems that can be used when using a VHD format:

▸ Windows Server 2012

▸ Windows Server 2008 R2 with SP1

▸ Windows Server 2008 R2

The following are the operating systems that can be used when a using a VHDx format (VMM 2012 SP1/R2):

▸ Windows Server 2012

▸ Windows Server 2012 R2

How to do it...

Carry out the following steps:

1. Connect to the VMM 2012 console by using the VMM admin account previously created (lab\vmm-admin); then, on the bottom-left pane, click on **Library**.

2. On the **Library** tab, click on **Create Physical Computer Profile**.

3. Type in a name (for example, Hyper-V) and an optional description.

4. Select **VM Host** as a role and click on **Next**, as shown in the following screenshot:

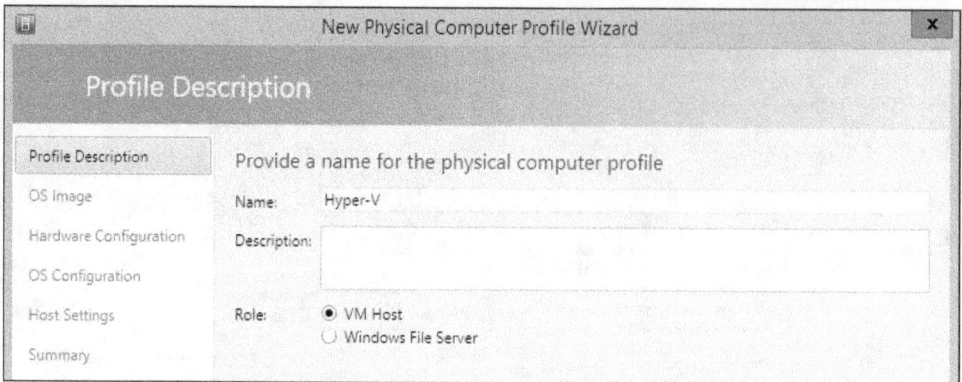

5. In the **OS Image** window, type in the path to the sysprepped virtual hard disk containing the operating system.

6. Now, you need to add the physical network adapters to the profile. In the **Hardware Configuration** window, click on the **+Add** button to add a physical network adapter.

> The number of physical NICs that you need to add depends on the physical server that will receive the profile. For this exercise, we will configure NIC1 and NIC2 as per the figure at the start of this section. The other two physical NICs (NIC3 and NIC4) will be used for storage communication. NIC1 and NIC2, in our example, should be assigned to a logical switch. In this case, it is called **Management**.

7. To add NIC1, click on **+Add** and select **Physical Network Adapter**.

8. Now, expand the **Physical NIC #1** and click on **Physical Properties**, as shown in the following screenshot:

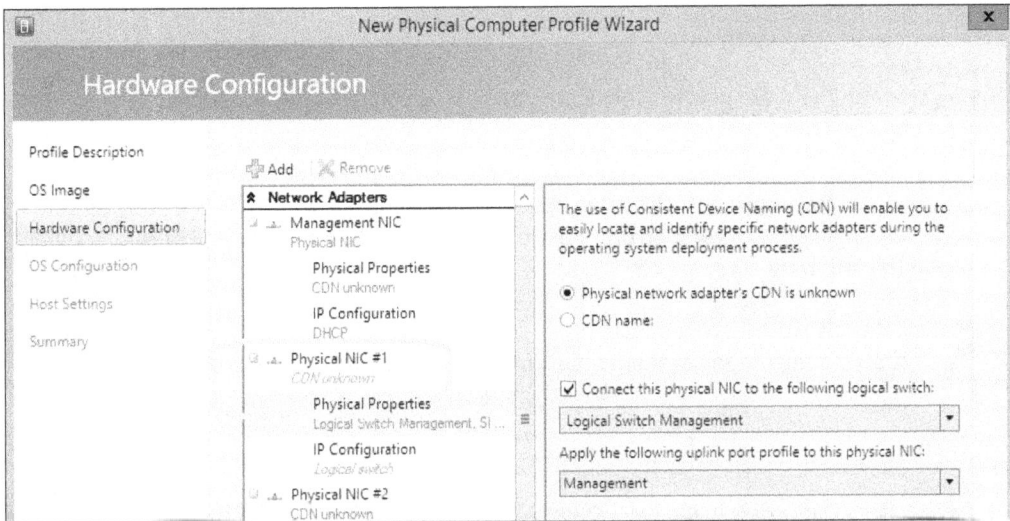

9. Although not required, you can provide the CDN if the physical server that is going to be provisioned does support it, or you can select **Physical network adapter's CDN is unknown**.

> The CDN should be enabled on the physical server BIOS beforehand.

10. Select **Connect this physical NIC to the following logical switch** and select a previously created logical switch (in our example, select **Logical Switch Management**).

11. Select the port profile for the **Apply the following uplink port profile to this physical NIC** option. This is the profile that we created for **Logical Switch Management** earlier in this chapter. In our example, **Management**.

12. Repeat steps 7 through 11 to add NIC2.

[There are now two teamed physical NICs configured with the same logical network management.]

13. Click on **Management NIC**. Now, based on the figure described at the start of this section, select **Create a virtual network adapter as the Management NIC**, as shown in the following screenshot:

[Configure the **Management NIC** adapter in order to have the physical host communicating with the VMM server.]

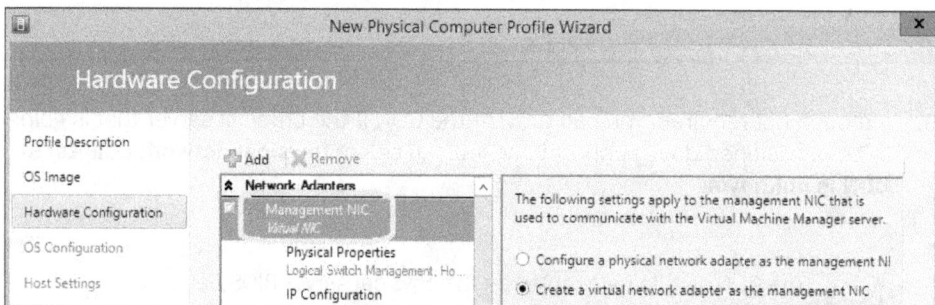

[This configuration will depend on your network design and the number of physical adapters. You can choose to have a dedicated NIC for host management or you can use a Virtual NIC. In our example, we will be using a virtual NIC, as shown in the figure in the introduction to this section. A vNIC will be the most common scenario (for more info on converged networks, see `http://technet.microsoft.com/en-us/library/hh831829.aspx`).]

14. Expand **Physical Properties** and select the **Host Management** port classification.

[This virtual NIC will be assigned to **Logical Switch Management** as there are no other options available. This is shown in the following screenshot. If there were more physical NICs assigned with other logical switches, you would have the option to select them.]

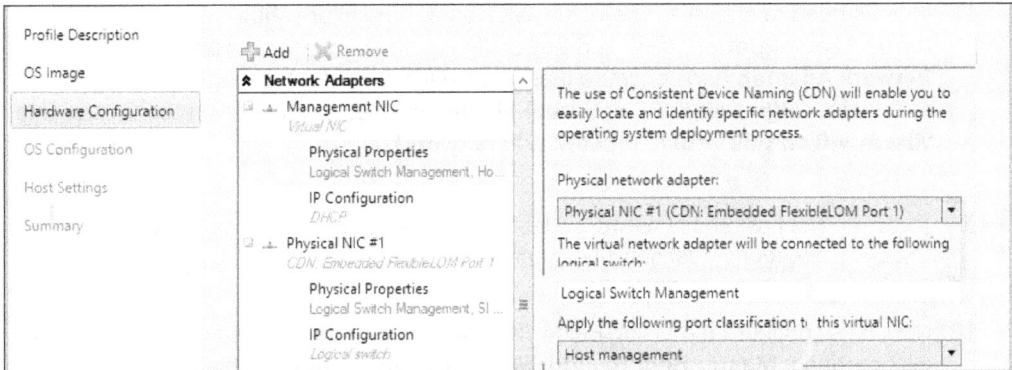

> On the **IP Configuration** window, you can select whether to acquire an IP address through a DHCP server or to assign a static IP address from the logical network that you specify.

15. Expand **IP Configuration** and select **Management** from **Create this virtual NIC on this virtual network (VM network)**, as shown in the following screenshot:

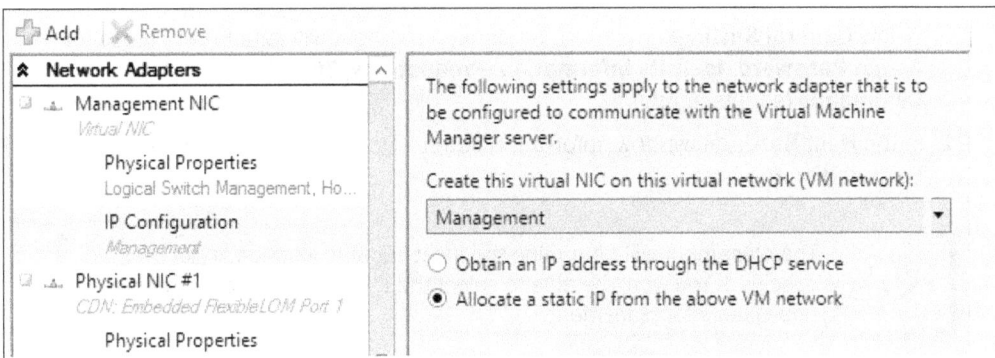

16. Select the **Allocate a static IP from the above VM network** option.

> This option will be disabled if this were a physical network adapter that you have connected to a logical switch.

17. You will need to create all the virtual NICs as per the figure shown at the start of this recipe: **Live Migration, CSV**, and **Guest VM**. To do so, click on **+Add**, select **Virtual Network Adapter**, and configure it as you did for the virtual management NIC, but select **Live Migration, CSV**, or **Virtual Machines** when applicable on the **Create this virtual NIC on this virtual network (VM network)** option.

> The host profile network adapter should now show two physical NICs and four virtual network adapters.

18. Now, let's configure the disks. Below **Disk and Partitions**, for the first disk, select the disk partition: **Master Boot Record (MBR)** or **GUID Partition Table (GPT)**.

> To add a new disk or a new partition, click on the **+Add** button and then choose **Disk** or **Partition**.

19. Below **Driver Options**, select the filter drivers that will be applied during host deployment: **Filter drivers with matching PnP IDs** or **Filter drivers with all matching tags specified below**.

20. Below **General Settings**, mention the domain the host will join. Enter values for **Admin Password, Identity Information, Product Key, Time Zone**, and **Commands** (scripts, if any).

21. In the **Host Settings** window, inform the path to store files related to the VMs that will be stored on the host.

> The placement will determine the most suitable location, if not specified. You won't be able to select the C drive because it remains unavailable for placement.

22. In the **Summary** window, click on **Finish**. The host profile is now complete.

How it works...

After making sure the network is configured (logical switches), we can start creating the host profile, which will contain a reference to a sysprepped virtual hard disk comprising the OS, the OS configuration settings, and the networking configuration.

To start creating the host profile, open the **VMM Library** tab and select **Create Physical Computer Profile**, provide the name, select **VM Host** as the server role, and provide the OS and network settings.

When configuring the settings, you can choose whether to convert the virtual hard disk type to fixed during deployment or not.

During the Bare Metal process, VMM will check for the availability of free space on the physical server, and it will fail with the VHD_BOOT_HOST_VOLUME_NOT_ENOUGH_SPACE error if the hard disk's free space is smaller than the sysprepped hard disk containing the operating system, as shown in the following screenshot:

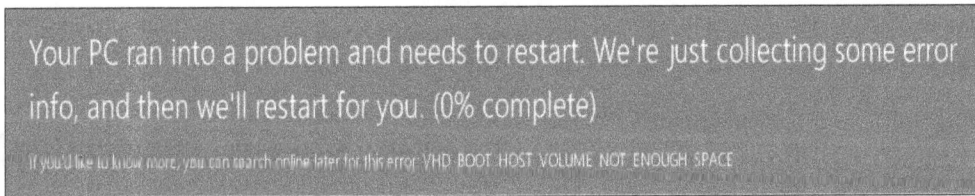

Your PC ran into a problem and needs to restart. We're just collecting some error info, and then we'll restart for you. (0% complete)

If you'd like to know more, you can search online later for this error VHD_BOOT_HOST_VOLUME_NOT_ENOUGH_SPACE

In the Bare Metal deployment process, there is a feature called **deep discovery** that will get the physical NIC information for the correct assignment.

Although not required, you can provide the CDN if the physical server that is going to be provisioned does support it, or you can select the **Physical network adapter's CDN is unknown** option.

> The CDN should be enabled on the physical server BIOS beforehand.

See also

- The *How to Create a Physical Computer Profile to Provision File Servers in VMM* article at http://technet.microsoft.com/en-us/library/dn466531.aspx
- The *How to Add Driver Files to the VMM Library* article at http://technet.microsoft.com/en-us/library/gg610589.aspx

Provisioning a physical computer as a Hyper-V host – Bare Metal host deployment

In this recipe, we will go through the steps to use VMM 2012 R2 to discover a physical computer, install an operating system, add the Hyper-V role, and then add the machine to a host group with streamlined procedures in a highly automated operation called **Bare Metal deployment**.

Getting ready

Before starting a Bare Metal deployment, a one-time configuration of the environment is required. When that is completed, you can start provisioning physical servers.

To deploy a Hyper-V server, you will need to run the **Add Resources** wizard, which will discover the physical computers preconfigured for PXE. You will then configure settings such as host group, physical computer profile, and custom settings, before starting to deploy the physical server.

Go through the following steps to prepare the infrastructure for a Bare Metal deployment:

1. **Deploying a PXE server**: Install a new server (for example, **w2012-wds01**) with **Windows Deployment Services** (**WDS**) to provide PXE services. Configure both the deployment server and transport server options.

   [You can use an existing PXE server if it is provided through Windows Deployment Services.]

2. **Configuring a PXE server in VMM 2012**: Add the PXE server to VMM 2012/R2 management using the VMM console. Refer to the *How to Add a PXE Server to VMM* article at http://technet.microsoft.com/en-au/library/gg610651.aspx.

3. **Configuring DHCP server**: The Hyper-V servers must be configured to start from the network by executing a PXE boot, which will also require a DHCP server.

4. **Adding a base image for the operating system installation**: Using the Windows Server 2012 R2 VHDX file, you can add a base image for the operating system installation to the VMM library and optional hardware driver files. See the *How to Add Driver Files to the VMM Library* article at http://technet.microsoft.com/en-au/library/gg610589.aspx.

> Only Windows Server 2012/R2 can boot from a .vhdx file format.

5. **Creating a Run As account**: You need to create a Run As account for the host add operation (for example, vmm-admin). We created that previously in the *Creating credentials for a Run As account's in VMM* recipe in *Chapter 3, Installing VMM 2012 R2*.

6. Create DNS entries and Active Directory computer accounts for the computer names that will be provisioned.

7. **Creating a host profile**: We can create a host profile as per the article, *How to Create a Host Profile in VMM*, which is available at http://go.microsoft.com/fwlink/p/?LinkID=212435 and can use a generalized Windows-Server-2012-based VHD/VHDX file.

8. Make sure the physical network infrastructure is configured.

> If you are using deep discovery during the search for the physical computers, VMM will show more detailed information about the computer.

How to do it...

First, we will perform the initial configuration of the physical server. Follow these steps:

1. Enable the virtualization technology and the **Execute Disable Bit** option on the physical server BIOS to support virtualization.

2. Enable booting from a network adapter for access to the PXE.

3. Upgrade the firmware and configure the BMC board by doing the following:

   □ Enabling the out-of-band management protocol that could be IPMI (Version 1.5 or 2.0), DCMI (Version 1.0), or SMASH (Version 1.0). For example, on a Dell PowerEdge server, enable IPMI over LAN.

   □ Configuring the network settings, which include **Host Name**, **Domain Name**, **IP Address**, and **Subnet** (you should be able to ping this IP from the VMM management and console).

   □ Enabling system services.

   □ Configuring login credentials to allow VMM 2012 R2 remote access.

4. Create DNS entries with the server's name that will be assigned to the hosts when they are deployed.

The next step is to discover the physical server and deploy it as a managed Hyper-V host in VMM 2012 R2. Perform the following steps to do so:

1. In the VMM console, in the **Fabric** workspace, click on **Servers** on the **Fabric** pane to the left.

2. Click on **Add Resources** on the **Home** tab, and then click on **Hyper-V Hosts and Clusters**.

3. On the **Resource location** page, select **Physical computer to be provisioned as virtual machine hosts** and click on **Next**, as shown in the following screenshot:

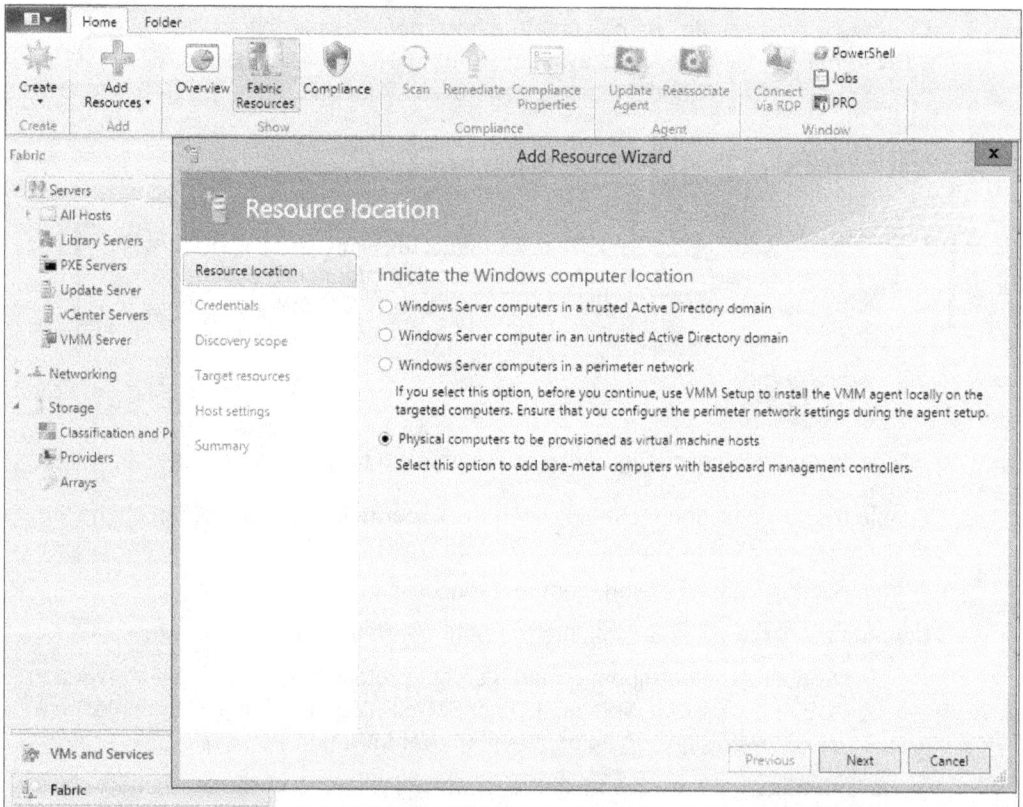

4. On the **Credentials and protocol** page, select the Run As account (with BMC access permissions) by clicking on **Browse** (for example, select **lab\host-admin**) and click on **OK**.

5. In the **Protocol** list, select the out-of-band management protocol previously configured (for example, **Intelligent Platform Management Interface (IPMI)**) and click on **Next**.

> Select **Intelligent Platform Management Interface (IPMI)** to use **Data Center Management Interface (DCMI)**.

6. In the **Discovery scope** page, type in the IP scope and click on **Next**.

7. By specifying an IP subnet or an IP address range, select the server(s) to be installed as Hyper-V host(s) in the **Target resources** page, and click on **Next**.

> Make sure you select the correct server(s) and document the IP addresses of the BMCs by creating a spreadsheet to track them, or use the IPAM server (recommended).

8. On the **Provisioning options** page, in the **Host group** list, select the target host group for the new Hyper-V host(s), for example, **Sydney\Standalone Hosts\Hyper-V**.

9. Configure the hosts in such a way that they receive the network settings from a DHCP server (the **Obtain IP addresses and other network settings through a DHCP service** option), or that the hosts will have static IP addresses from a VMM-managed IP address pool (the **Specify static IP addresses and customize deployment settings for each host** option).

> You need to select a host profile with these predefined settings in the **Host profile** list.

10. Select each server, and then, on the left-hand side, click and amend the settings accordingly if you want it to be different from the host profile; for example, specify any missing adapter's information or switches.

As previously mentioned in step 9, the following steps will specify the network settings through DHCP, that is, if you select **Obtain IP addresses and other network settings through a DHCP service**:

1. In the **Host profile** list, select the host profile (for example, **W2012R2 Host DHCP Profile**) and click on **Next**.

2. In the **Deployment customization** page, select a BMC IP address from the list.

3. Provide a unique computer name for each listed server (for example, `hyperv02.lab.local`), click on **Next**, and then click on **OK**.

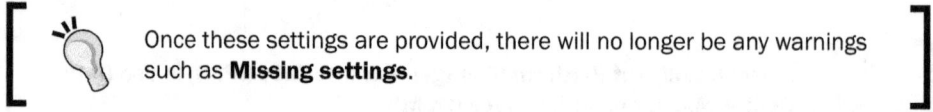

> Once these settings are provided, there will no longer be any warnings such as **Missing settings**.

The following steps will specify the network settings through static IP addresses, that is, if you chose **Specify static IP addresses and customize deployment settings for each host**:

1. In the **Host profile** list, select the host profile (for example, **W2012R2 Host Static Profile**) and click on **Next**.

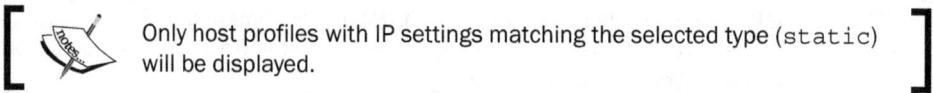

> Only host profiles with IP settings matching the selected type (`static`) will be displayed.

2. On the **Deployment customization** page, type in the server name (for example, `hyperv02.lab.local`).

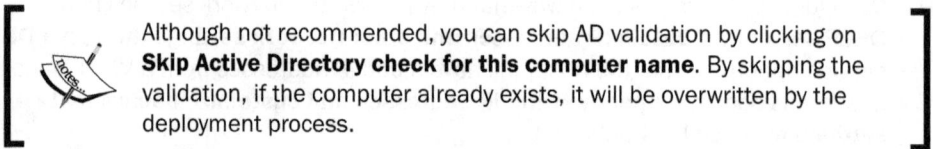

> Although not recommended, you can skip AD validation by clicking on **Skip Active Directory check for this computer name**. By skipping the validation, if the computer already exists, it will be overwritten by the deployment process.

3. Type in the **MAC address** of the Hyper-V management network adapter (for example, `10.1.2.10`).

4. Select the logical network from the **Logical Network** list (**Intranet**).

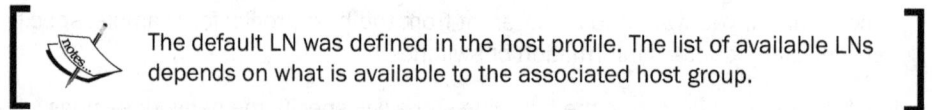

> The default LN was defined in the host profile. The list of available LNs depends on what is available to the associated host group.

5. Select the correct IP subnet that counterparts the network site location, or else the deployment will fail. You can assign an IP address as follows:

   - To automatically obtain it from a static IP address pool (first available), select **Obtain an IP address corresponding to the selected subnet**
   - To manually specify a specific IP address, select the IP address range and type an available IP address matching the subnet range

When all this is done, you can click on **Next** and then click on **OK** to continue. Lastly, on the **Summary** page, click on **Finish** to start the deployment.

How it works...

VMM can deploy a physical computer with Windows 2012 or Windows 2012 R2; add a Hyper-V role, and then add it to be managed by VMM.

To start, you need a PXE server (it can be an existing one) provided through Windows Deployment Services. Then, you need to add it to the VMM management server.

On each physical server, in the BIOS, configure virtualization support and boot from PXE and the BMC. This will require you to have a working DHCP server in place.

Then, create the DNS entries for each server; add the required resources to the VMM library. These resources include a generalized Windows Server VHD/VHDX file that will be used as the base image, and optional driver files to add to the operating system during installation.

The following are the possible operation systems when using a VHD format:

▶ Windows Server 2012

▶ Windows Server 2008 R2 with SP1

▶ Windows Server 2008 R2

The following are the possible operation systems when using a VHDx format (VMM 2012 SP1/R2):

▶ Windows Server 2012

▶ Windows Server 2012 R2

Create host profiles (which include image location, hardware, and OS settings) in the VMM library.

> **Consistent Device Naming (CDN)** can be configured in the host profiles and, if supported by the physical server (Hyper-V), it will identify and associate physical NICs to the correct logical switches.

Use VMM to discover (scan) the physical computers, to configure deployment and settings, and to start the deployment of the OS and Hyper-V role configuration. VMM will use BMC commands during this phase to power the servers off/on.

> If you decide to assign IP addresses from a VMM IP address pool to the Hyper-V hosts (on the management network), be prepared to manually enter the MAC address of the physical NIC that is used for PXE or use the VMM deep discovery feature to retrieve the information. CDN provides the physical NIC's name, but not the MAC addresses.

When the servers restart, the PXE server will respond to the boot request with a customized image (Windows PE). The Windows PE agent will then prepare the server by downloading and applying the OS image and specified driver files from the library and adding the Hyper-V server role; then, it restarts the server.

On the **Deployment customization** page, a small amount of wait time (minutes) for the deep discovery to complete is normal; when it is complete, VMM will show a success message.

After the host deployment, if a post-deployment task is required, right-click on the host and click on **Run Script Command** to run a script.

See also

▸   The *How to Add a PXE Server to VMM* article at `http://technet.microsoft.com/en-US/library/gg610651.aspx`

▸   The *Prepare the Physical Computers in VMM* article at `http://technet.microsoft.com/en-US/library/gg610690.aspx`

▸   The *How to Add Driver Files to the VMM Library* article at `http://technet.microsoft.com/en-US/library/gg610589.aspx`

▸   The *How to Create a Host or a Physical Computer Profile to Provision a Hyper-V Host in VMM* article at `http://technet.microsoft.com/en-US/library/gg610653.aspx`

▸   The *System Center VMM 2012 R2 Bare Metal Deployment with Converged Fabric and Network Virtualization* article at `http://www.hyper-v.nu/archives/mvaneijk/2013/08/system-center-vmm-2012-r2-bare-metal-deployment-with-converged-fabric-and-network-virtualization-part-1-intro/`

Adding and managing Hyper-V hosts and host clusters

This recipe will guide you through the steps involved in adding an existing Hyper-V host or a Hyper-V cluster by VMM.

In VMM 2012, you can add Hyper-V hosts/clusters running on the same domain as the VMM, on a trusted domain, or in a disjointed namespace. You can also add Hyper-V hosts (not clusters) running on an untrusted domain and a perimeter network (for example, DMZ).

In VMM 2012 R2, you can add Windows Server 2012 and Windows Server 2012 R2 as the OS for managed Hyper-V hosts. Using Bare Metal deployment as we described before, you can add physical computers with no OS, as well.

If you want to manage a standalone host that is in a workgroup, use the method to add a host in a perimeter network.

Getting ready

Make sure virtualization support is enabled in the BIOS. If the Hyper-V role is not installed, VMM will install it as part of the setup.

The following steps will guide you through how to add a Hyper-V host or Hyper-V cluster in a trusted Active Directory domain.

How to do it...

Carry out the following steps to add a trusted Hyper-V host or cluster:

1. In the VMM console, click on the **Fabric** workspace; then, on the **Fabric** pane, click on **Servers**.

2. On the **Home** tab, click on the **Add Resources** button on the ribbon, and then click on **Hyper-V Hosts and Clusters**.

3. On the **Resource location** page, click on **Windows Server computers in a trusted Active Directory domain**, and then on **Next**.

4. On the **Credentials** page, specify an existing Run As account, for example, **Hyper-V Host Administration Account** (created in *Chapter 3, Installing VMM 2012 R2*), or manually type in the user credentials, for example, `lab\vmm-admin`.

> To create a Run As account at this point, click on **Browse**, and in the **Select a Run As Account** dialog box, click on **Create Run As Account** and enter the requested information.

5. Click on **Next**, and in the **Discovery scope** page, select between the following options:

   - **Specify Windows Server computers by names**: Type in the IP or server name / cluster name (one per line). Click on **Next**.

> If you type just part of the name, the wizard will list the servers that match.

> ❑ **Specify an Active Directory query to search for Windows Server computers**: Type in an AD query or click on **Generate an AD query** to create it. Click on **Next**.

Both options are shown in the following screenshot:

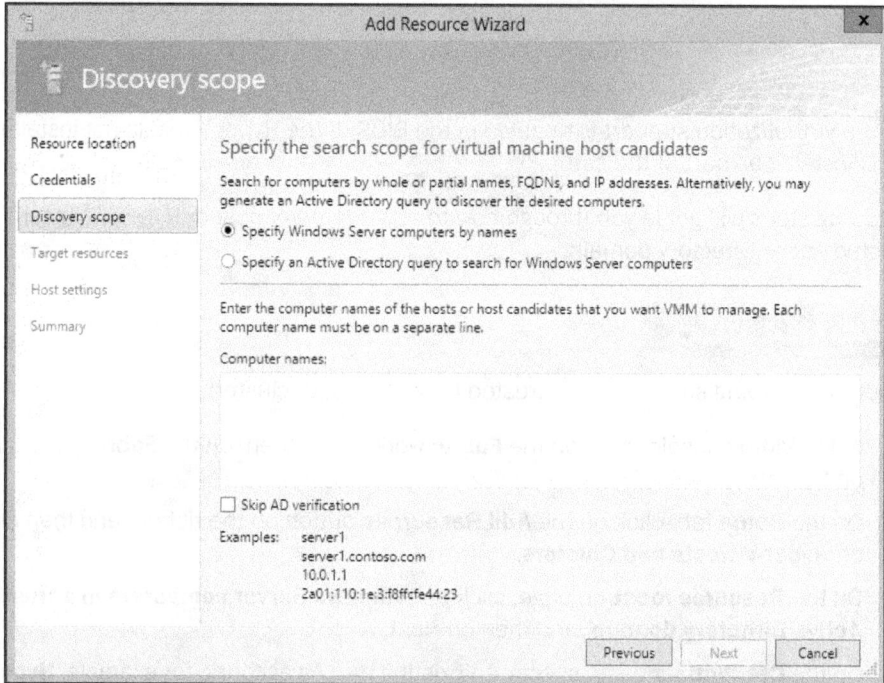

6. On the **Target resources** page, select the computer(s) or cluster name(s).

> If the Hyper-V role is not enabled, a message will be displayed stating that the role will be installed and the server will restart. Click on **OK**.

7. Click on **Next**, and on the **Host settings** page, select the host group from the **Host group** list.

> Click on **Reassociate this host with this VMM environment** if the host was associated with another VMM server.

8. When adding a standalone host, type in the local host path to store VM files (for example, D:\VMS), click on **Add**, click on **Next**, and then click on **Finish**.

How it works...

When adding a standalone server or cluster in a trusted domain environment, where the domain is not the same as VMM, make sure there is a two-way trust factor in place.

Use **Group Policy** (**GPO**) to configure WinRM, which is the only supported method for WinRM service settings, but also consider the following:

- ▶ The GPO settings that VMM supports are **Allow automatic configuration of listeners**, **Turn On Compatibility HTTP Listener**, and **Turn on Compatibility HTTPS Listener**, and this is only for hosts that are in a trusted domain

- ▶ WinRM Client settings through GPO are unsupported

- ▶ It may not be possible to install VMM Agent if you enable other WinRM settings by GPO

> The use of the VMM service account to add or remove Hypor V hosts is not recommended, as it could impose security risks.

When installing a standalone server, you will be required to provide a local VM path (if it does not exist, it will be created). If left empty, the default will be used (`%SystemDrive%\ProgramData\Microsoft\Windows\Hyper-V`). When installing a cluster, the path will be located on shared storage.

> Using the OS drive to store VM files is not recommended.

There's more...

You can also add Hyper-V hosts that are not on the same domain or that are on a perimeter network.

Adding Hyper-V hosts in a disjointed namespace

Carry out the same steps to add a trusted Hyper-V host or cluster, considering the following points:

- ▶ On the **Credentials** page, type in the domain account credentials (for example, `poc\vmm-admin`)

- ▶ On the **Discovery scope** page, type in the FQDN of the host (for example, `hyperv03.poc.local`) and check the **Skip AD verification** checkbox

You will be required to add the SPN manually if the account does not have permission.

> VMM checks the domain for the SPN. If it does not exist, and if the VMM service account has permission to perform `setspn`, it will be created.

At the command prompt, with administrator rights, type in the following command (in the format, `setspn -A HOST/<FQDN> <NetBIOSName>`):

```
setspn -A HOST/hyperv03.poc.local hyperv03
```

Adding Hyper-V hosts in a perimeter network

The next sections list the steps required to add a standalone Hyper-V server that is in a perimeter network (for example, DMZ) to be managed by VMM.

Let's start by creating the following spreadsheet for documentation purposes:

Hyper-V server (Hostname)	Encryption key*	Location folder	IP address

> Keep this spreadsheet in a secure place.

Installing the agent on the standalone server

Carry out the following steps to install the VMM agent on a standalone Hyper-V server:

1. Connect to the standalone server, and from there, browse to the VMM setup folder. Right-click on **setup**, and then click on **Run as administrator**.

2. On the **Setup** menu, click on **Local Agent**. Click on **Optional Installation** and click on **Next**. And then, on the **License** page, click on **Next**.

3. On the **Destination Folder** page, enter the installation path and then click on **Next**.

4. On the **Security File Folder** page, check the **This host is on a perimeter network** checkbox and type in and confirm a complex security key.

> Take note of the security key.

5. Specify the location for the storage key by clicking on **Change**, and then copy the security file to a folder on the VMM console.

6. If you require it, select **Use a CA signed certificate for encrypting communications with this host** and type in the thumbprints.

> To obtain the thumbprint, select **Computer account** in the **Certificates** snap-in. Double-click on the certificate and select and copy the `Thumbprint` field value on the **Details** tab.

7. Click on **Next**, and on the **Host network name** page, choose whether VMM will communicate with the host using a local computer name or IP address.

8. Click on **Next**, and if you chose **Use IP address**, select an IP address from the list.

9. In the **Configuration settings** page, confirm the port settings (5986 and 443) and click on **Next**; then, click on **Install**.

Adding perimeter hosts to VMM

Carry out the following steps to add a Hyper-V server on a DMZ to VMM:

1. In the VMM console, in the **Fabric** workspace on the **Fabric** pane, click on **Servers**.

2. On the **Home** tab, click on **Add Resources** in the ribbon, and then click on **Hyper-V Hosts and Clusters**.

3. On the **Resource location** page, click on **Windows Server computers in a perimeter network** and click on **Next**.

4. On the **Target resources** page, type in the hostname or the IP, encryption key, and path for `securityFile.txt`, for each host. Select the target host group and then click on **Add**.

5. Click on **Next**, and in the **Host settings** page, type in the local host path to store VM files (for example, `D:\VMS`), click on **Add**, and then click on **Next**.

6. On the **Summary** page, click on **Finish**.

> For a detailed host status view in VMM, right-click on the host, click on **Properties**, and check the status for overall health, host agent health, and Hyper-V role health. If you find an issue, click on **Repair all**.

See also

▸ The *How to Add Untrusted Hyper-V Hosts and Host Clusters in VMM* article at `http://technet.microsoft.com/en-us/library/gg610609.aspx`

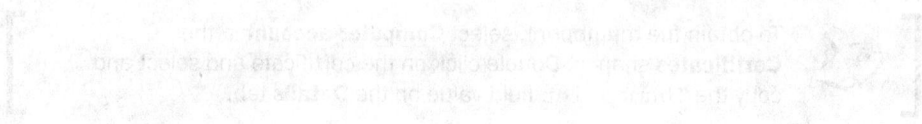

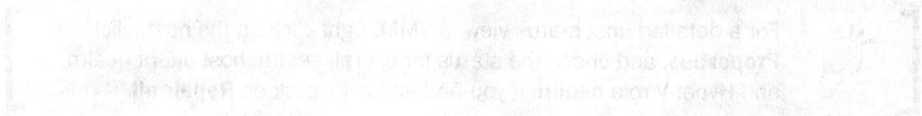

6
Deploying Virtual Machines and Services

In this chapter, we will cover the following:

- ► Creating private clouds
- ► Creating hardware, guest OSes, applications, and SQL profiles
- ► Creating user roles in VMM
- ► Creating and deploying virtual machines
- ► Creating virtual machine templates
- ► Creating and deploying service templates
- ► Rapidly provisioning a virtual machine using SAN Copy

Introduction

In VMM, a private cloud consists of a collection of resources (for example, host groups of servers running common or diverse hypervisors, storage, and networking) and settings that provide virtualization infrastructure for cloud users (for example, tenants and self-service users), and it is deployed within your organizational boundaries using your own hardware and software.

This chapter guides you through private cloud deployment and management, discusses VMs, and discusses the services in VMM 2012 R2, providing recipes to assist you to get the most out of the deployment.

Creating private clouds

This recipe provides guidance on how to create a private cloud from host groups that are running diverse hypervisors, such as Hyper-V, Citrix, VMware ESX hosts, or from a VMware resource pool in VMM 2012 R2.

Using VMM 2012 and by deploying a private cloud, you will be able to offer a unique experience for creating VMs and services, which will, in turn, lead towards the consumerization of IT.

A private cloud deployment allows resource pooling, where you can present a comprehensive set of fabric resources, but limit it by quotas that can be increased or decreased, providing fully optimized elasticity, without affecting the private cloud's overall user experience. In addition to this, you can also delegate the management to tenants and self-service users who have no knowledge of physical infrastructures such as clusters, storage, and networking.

A private cloud can be created using the following resources:

▶   Host groups that contain Hyper-V, VMware ESX, to Citrix XenServer hosts

▶   The VMware resource pool

Getting ready

First, start by configuring the fabric resources in VMM, as follows:

▶   **Network**: Refer to the recipes on networking in *Chapter 5, Configuring Fabric Resources in VMM*

▶   **Storage**: Refer to the *Integrating and configuring the storage* recipe in *Chapter 5, Configuring Fabric Resources in VMM*

▶   **Library servers and shares**: Refer to the *Setting up a VMM library* recipe in *Chapter 5, Configuring Fabric Resources in VMM*

▶   **Create the host groups**: Refer to the *Creating host groups* recipe in *Chapter 5, Configuring Fabric Resources in VMM*

▶   **Add the hosts**: Refer to the *Adding and managing Hyper-V hosts and host clusters* recipe in *Chapter 5, Configuring Fabric Resources in VMM,* and the *Adding VMware ESX hosts or host clusters to VMM* recipe in *Chapter 7, Managing VMware ESXi and Citrix® XenServer® Hosts*

In this recipe, we will create a private cloud, which we will name `My Cloud`. It will be created from the resources of previously configured host groups.

How to do it...

Carry out the following steps to create your own private cloud:

1. Connect to the VMM 2012 console using the VMM admin account that was previously created (for example, `lab\vmm-admin`), and then on the bottom-left pane, click on **VMs and Services** to open it on the **VMs and Services** workspace.

2. Under the **Home** tab on the ribbon, click on **Create Cloud**.

3. In the **Create Cloud Wizard** window, type the private cloud's name.

4. Type a description (optional) and then click on **Next**.

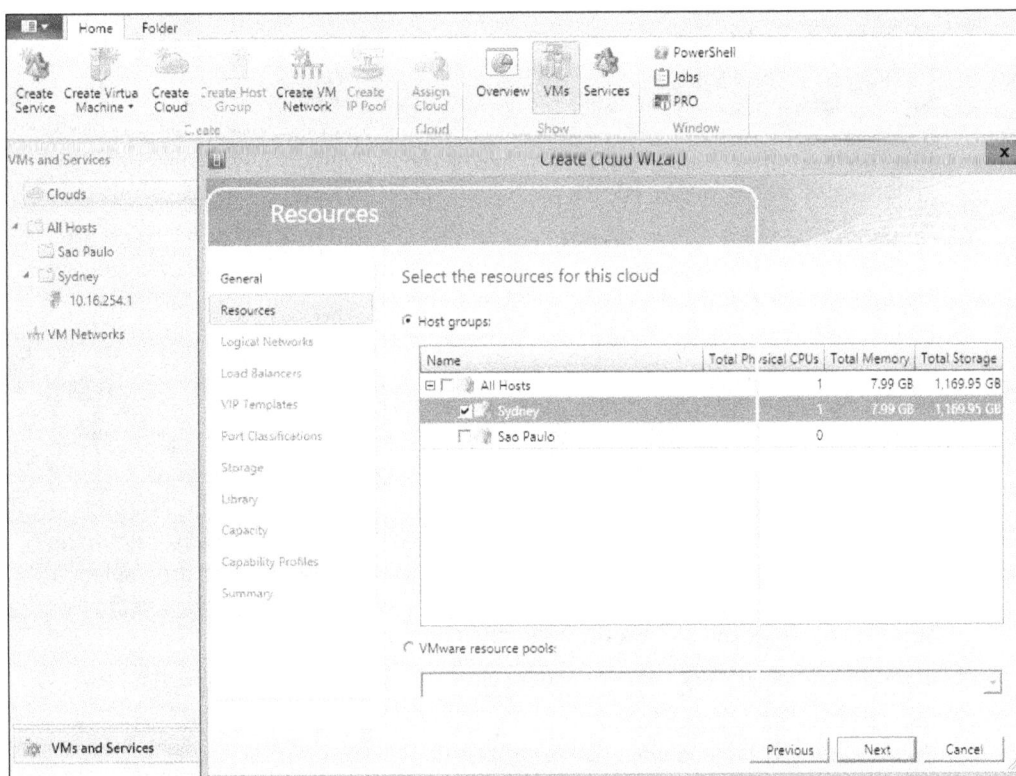

5. On the **Resources** page, select either of the following options:

   ❑ Select **Host groups**, then select the host group(s) that will be added to this private cloud (for example, **Sydney**), and then click on **Next**

   ❑ Select **VMware resources pools**, then select a VMware resource pool from the available options, and then click on **Next**

6. On the **Logical Networks** page, select the logical network(s) that will be made available to this private cloud (for example, **External Access**, which was created in the *Networking – configuring logical networks* recipe in *Chapter 5, Configuring Fabric Resources in VMM*) and then click on **Next**.

> Only logical networks that are associated with physical network adapters will be listed. Make sure you have configured the logical network and assigned it to the physical network beforehand.

7. On the **Load Balancers** page, if you have a load balancer deployed and integrated with VMM, select it and click on **Next**.

> Only associated load balancers will be displayed.

8. On the **VIP Profiles** page, select the VIP template(s), if any, that is available to this private cloud (for example, **HTTPS traffic**) and click on **Next**.

9. On the **Storage** page, if you do have a storage managed by VMM and if there are storage classifications for storage pools assigned to selected host groups, select the storage classification that will be available to this private cloud (for example, **GOLD**) and click on **Next**.

> For more information on storage classification, check the *Integrating and configuring the storage* recipe in *Chapter 5, Configuring Fabric Resources in VMM*.

10. On the **Library** page, provide the stored VM path by clicking on **Browse**, and in the **Select Destination Folder** dialog box, click on the library server and then select a library or a folder in the share to be used as the location for self-service users to store VMs in (for example, **StoredVMs**); then click on **OK**.

11. In the **Read-only library shares** section, click on **Add**, select the library share(s) for read-only resources, click on **OK** to confirm, and then click on **Next**.

12. On the **Capacity** page, configure the capacity limits and then click on **Next**. You can manually set quotas for the **Virtual CPUs**, **Memory (GB)**, **Storage (GB)**, **Custom quota (points)**, and **Virtual machines** dimensions as shown in the following screenshot:

To set up new quotas, unselect **Use Maximum**. Refer to the *Creating an application administrator (self-service user) role* subsection in the *Creating user roles in VMM* recipe of this chapter.

13. On the **Capability Profiles** page, select the VM capability profile(s) that matches the hypervisor running on the selected host group(s)—for example, **Hyper-V**—and click on **Next**.

Built-in capability profiles embody the minimum and maximum configured values for a VM for each hypervisor that is supported.

14. On the **Summary** page, click on **Finish**.

How it works...

Configure the fabric resources, such as the storage, network, library, host groups, and hosts, which will be available in the private cloud beforehand. Configure the library paths and set the capacity for the private cloud, which can be created from host groups that contain a unique mix of hypervisors—such as Microsoft Hyper-V, VMware ESXi, and/or Citrix XenServer hosts—and also from a VMware resource pool (which needs to be under VMM management).

> You cannot use VMM to manage/assign storage classifications for the storage of ESX hosts.

In the **Library** workspace, you can create custom capability profiles to limit the resources being used by the private cloud's VMs.

On the **Capacity** page, you can set the capacity limits manually by unselecting the option **Use Maximum**.

To verify whether the private cloud library was created, check if it is listed under **Cloud Libraries** in the **Library** workspace. If you configured read-only library shares, they will be listed together with a **Stored Virtual Machines and Services** node.

Self-service users require the store and redeploy permissions to save a VM on a library share; it must be located on a share different from the read-only resource location, which cannot be a child path of the user role data path. The self-service user role data path is configured when creating/modifying the user role.

> Since VMM 2012, the self-service user can log on to the VMM console directly.

When creating the private cloud, VMM creates the read-only library shares and stored VM path.

There's more...

After creating the private cloud, you need to assign users that will have access to manage it.

Assigning the private cloud to a user role

Now that you've created the private cloud, you can assign it to a user role(s). Carry out the following steps to do so:

1. In the VMM console on the bottom-left pane, click on the **VMs and Services** workspace and then expand **Clouds**.

2. Select the created private cloud (for example, **My Cloud**).

3. Under the **Home** tab on the ribbon, click on **Assign Cloud** and select the user role by choosing one of the following options:

    ❑   **Use an existing user role**: This option is enabled only if you had created any user roles previously

    ❑   **Create a user role and assign this cloud**: Click on **OK** to continue, and follow the steps to create and assign the user role to the private cloud

See also

▸   The *Creating hosts groups* recipe in *Chapter 5, Configuring Fabric Resources in VMM*

▸   The *Creating an application administrator (self-service user) role* subsection in the *Creating user roles in VMM* recipe in this chapter

Creating hardware, guest OSes, applications, and SQL profiles

Profiles are resources that are used to deploy VMs. For example, a SQL profile provides instructions for SQL Server instance deployment and customizations. An application profile provides instructions to install App-V applications.

Getting ready

You can create the following types of profiles in VMM to be used in a VM template:

Profile type	Purpose
Hardware	To configure hardware settings (for example, memory, network adapters, and DVD drives)
Guest OS	To configure common OS settings (for example, the computer name, domain name, product key, and time zone)
Application	To provide directives for Server App-V, Web Deploy, and SQL Server data-tier (DACs) applications, and to run scripts when deploying VMs as a service
SQL Server	To provide directives for a SQL customization when deploying a VM as a service

How to do it...

Carry out the following steps to create a hardware profile:

1. In the VMM console on the bottom-left pane, click on the **Library** workspace.

2. Expand **Profiles** on the left pane, click on **Hardware Profiles**, and then right-click and select **Create Hardware Profile**.

3. In the **New Hardware Profile** dialog box on the **General** page, type the hardware profile name, for example, **2 vCPU Server**.

4. Click on **Hardware Profile** on the left pane, configure the hardware settings, and click on **OK** to finish.

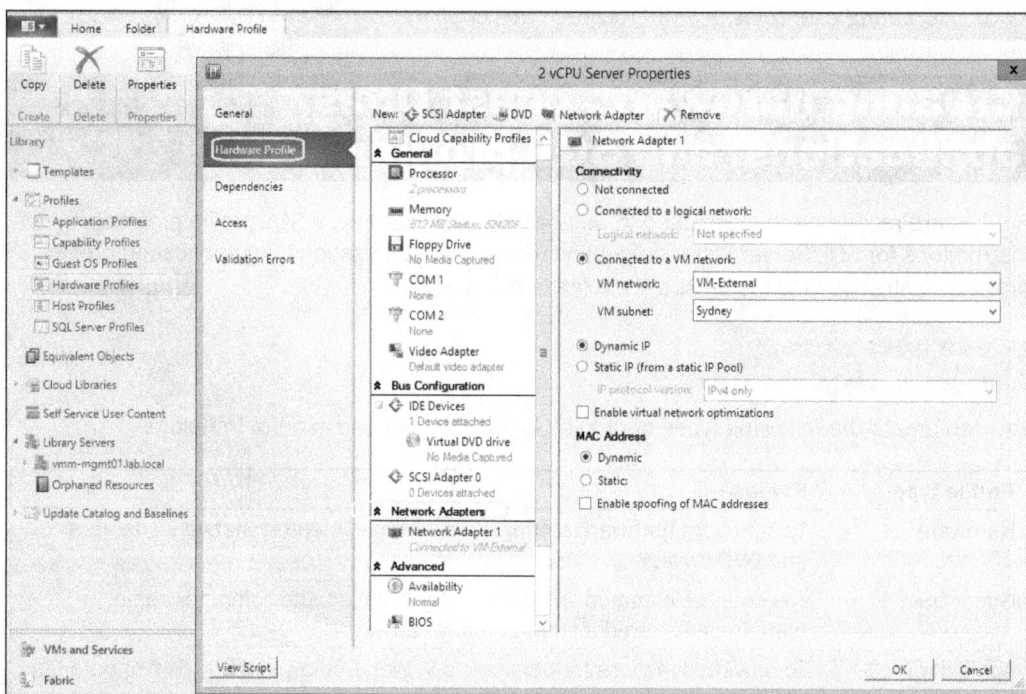

How it works...

Use this recipe to create the profiles that will contain the settings and specifications that VMM will use when deploying a VM. Start by creating a *profile*: expand **Profiles** in the **Library** workspace; click on **Create**, select the profile you want to create, and provide the settings to be used when deploying a VM. When deploying the VM to a private cloud, the capability profile must be supported by the private cloud.

When creating an application profile, you can add one or more application scripts, but only after adding and configuring an application with the appropriate settings. You can also create an application profile to deploy SQL Server DAC packages or scripts to an existing SQL Server in the **Compatibility** list by selecting **SQL Server Application Host**.

There's more...

The following sections will guide you through creating a guest OS, applications, and SQL Server profiles.

Creating a guest operating system profile

Carry out the following tasks to create a Guest OS Profile:

1. In the **Library** workspace, click on **Guest OS Profiles** by expanding **Profiles** on the left pane, and then right-click on **Guest OS Profiles** and select **Create Guest OS Profile**.

2. In the **New Guest OS Profile** dialog box, type the guest operating system profile name (for example, W2012 Standard).

3. Click on **Guest OS Profile** on the left pane and configure the settings, and click on **OK** to finish.

> You can provide a pattern for the computer names. For example, if you type W2012-SRV###, the computers will be named W2012-SRV001, W2012-SRV002, W2012-SRV003, W2012-SRV004, and so on.

Creating an application profile

Carry out the following steps to create an application profile:

1. In the **Library** workspace, click on **Application Profiles** and select **Create Application Profile**.

2. In the **Application Profile** dialog box, type the application profile name (for example, Marketing App).

3. Click on **Application Configuration** on the left pane and then on **OS Compatibility**, and then select the supported OS.

4. If an application package is available, click on **Add**, select the application type, and then provide the application package.

5. If a script is present, click on **Add** and then select the script to add to the application profile.

6. Click on **OK** to finish.

> An application package can contain settings that can be used for service deployment. The parameter in the **Value** field is in the format, @<Setting>@.

Creating a SQL Server profile

1. In the **Library** workspace, click on **SQL Server Profiles** and select **Create SQL Server Profile**.

2. In the **New SQL Server Profile** dialog box, type the SQL Server profile name (for example, SQL Production Marketing-Research).

3. Click on **SQL Server Configuration** and then on **Add: SQL Server Deployment**.

4. Select **SQL Server Deployment - Deployment 1** and type the SQL instance name and the account (the Run As account) to be used when installing it.

5. Select **Configuration** and provide information about the configuration (for example, the instance ID and the collation or authentication mode).

6. Select **Service Accounts** and provide the SQL Server service Run As accounts.

7. Click on **OK** to finish.

See also

▸ The *How to Create a SQL Server Profile in a Service Deployment* article at http://technet.microsoft.com/en-us/library/hh427294.aspx.

▸ The *How to Create a Host Profile* article at http://technet.microsoft.com/en-us/library/gg610653.aspx

Creating user roles in VMM

User roles in VMM 2012 are used to define the objects and management operations that specified users can create/manage/perform in VMM.

These user roles are as follows:

▸ **Administrator**: The members of this group can perform tasks/actions on all objects managed by VMM. In addition to this, only administrators can add XenServer hosts and clusters and WSUS servers to VMM.

▸ **Fabric (delegated) administrator**: The members of this group can perform tasks/ actions within their assigned scope (host groups, private clouds, and/or library servers). They can create delegated administrators with a subset of their scope.

▶ **Read-only administrator**: The members of this group are able to view the status and properties of objects or jobs within their assigned scope (host groups, private clouds, and/or library servers) and specify the Run As accounts that they can view.

▶ **Tenant administrator**: The members of this group can create/manage self-service users (specifying the tasks/actions they can execute on VMs and/or services), VM networks, and VM services.

▶ **Application administrator (self-service user)**: The members of this group can create, deploy, and manage their own VMs and services, such as specifying private clouds to have a VM or service deployed, granting access to logical and physical resources in the VMM library, and configuring quotas and PRO tip settings. Only administrators and delegated administrators (within their scope) have the rights to create application administrator roles, which can only view a simplified placement map (that contains only their VMs/services) on a VM or service deployment operation.

Getting ready

If the self-service user role has more than one private cloud within its scope, users will have to select the appropriate cloud before the placement is run.

When creating a self-service user role, you will be required to configure quotas that will only apply to the VMs deployed. They will not apply to the VMs in the library. The following table shows the supported quota types:

The quota types supported	A description of what can be consumed
Virtual CPUs	The maximum number of VM CPUs
Memory (MB)	The maximum amount of VM memory
Storage (GB)	The maximum amount of VM storage
Custom quota (points)	For backward compatibility, an arbitrary value that can be assigned to a VM template based on its anticipated "size"
Virtual machines	The number of VMs

> A quota is applied individually to each member of the user role.

How to do it...

Carry out the following steps to add a user to the built-in administrator user role:

1. In the VMM 2012 console in the bottom-left corner, click on **Settings** to open the **Settings** workspace and then expand **Security** on the left pane.

2. Click on **User Roles** and then click on the main pane; right-click on the **Administrator** user role and select **Properties**.

3. In the **Administrator Properties** dialog box, click on **Members** and then on **Add**.

4. In the **Select Users, Computers, or Groups** dialog box, type in an AD user account or group (for example, `lab\vmm-admin`).

5. Click on **OK** to continue, and then click on **OK** to save and finish.

> To delete a user, on the **Members** page, select the user or group and click on **Remove**.
>
> The preceding steps can also be used to add users to other user roles.

How it works...

The built-in administrator user role is created when you install VMM, and then the user account that you used to run the VMM setup and all the domain users in the local `Administrators` group are added to the built-in administrator user role.

To add users or groups to or remove them from roles, you can use this recipe; note that only administrators can add/remove users to/from the administrator user role.

You can also use this recipe to create the new tenant administrator role if you are an administrator or delegated administrator (with rights). Tenants can also have quotas on VMs and resources.

There's more...

There are more user roles that can be created.

Creating a delegated or read-only administrator user role

Carry out the following steps to create an optional delegated or read-only user role:

1. In the VMM 2012 console in the **Settings** workspace, click on **Create User Role** on the ribbon.

2. In the **Create User Role Wizard** window, type the name (for example, `vmm-delegated-admin`) and the optional description, and click on **Next** to continue.

3. To create a delegated or read-only administrator, on the **Profile** page, select either of the two options:

   ❏ **Fabric Administrator**: Select this to create and add a user as a delegated administrator

   ❏ **Read-Only Administrator**: Select this to create and add a user as a read-only administrator

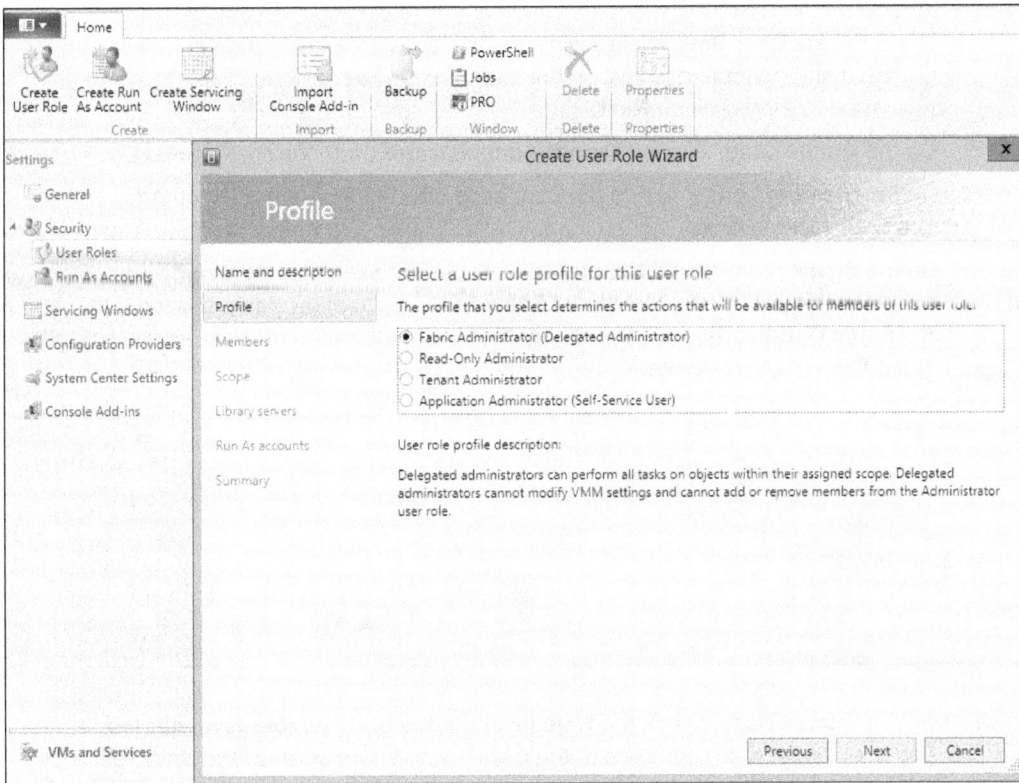

4. Click on **Next** and then on the **Members** page to add the user account(s) or group(s), then click on **Add**, and finally, click on **Next**.

5. On the **Scope** page, select the private cloud(s) or host group(s) (for example, **My Cloud**) that will have to be be managed by this role and then click on **Next**.

6. On the **Library servers** page, to select one or more library servers, click on **Add**, then click on **OK** after selecting a server, and then click on **Next**.

7. On the **Run As Accounts** page, click on **Add**, select the Run As account, and then click on **OK** to add the account. When you have finished adding the account, click on **Next** to continue.

8. Click on **Finish**.

Creating a tenant administrator role

The likely use for a scenario where you will need to create multiple tenant administrators, is in hosting environments with multiple customers, or in enterprise environments where you have multiple teams and each one of them wants to have and manage their own environment. Carry out the following steps to create the self-service user:

1. In the VMM 2012 R2 console in the **Settings** workspace, click on **Create User Role** on the ribbon.

2. In the **Create User Role Wizard** window, type the name (for example, `DevTeam-tadmin`) and optional description (for example, `Development Team Tenant Admin`), and then click on **Next**.

3. On the **Profile** page, click on **Tenant Administrator** and then click on **Next**.

4. On the **Members** page, to add the user account(s) or group(s), click on **Add** and then click on **Next**.

5. On the **Scope** page, select the private cloud(s)—for example, **My Cloud**—that can be managed by this role, select **Show PRO tips** to allow **Performance and Resource Optimization** (**PRO**) management, and then click on **Next** as shown in the following screenshot:

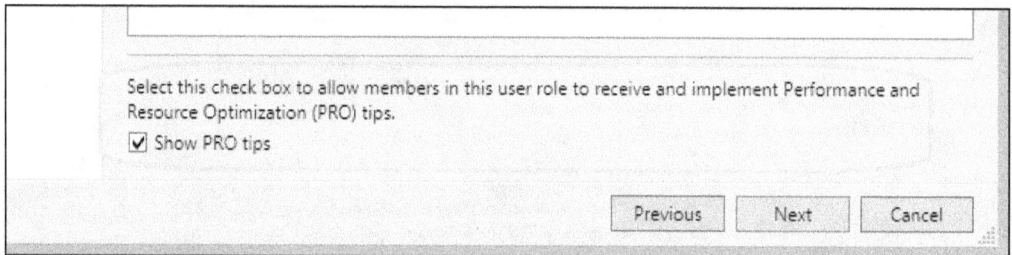

6. On the **Quotas** page, check the **Role level quotas** and **Member level quotas** sections. If you need members of the user role to share quotas, add an AD security group instead of a user account.

Role level quotas:
All members of this user role combined can use resources up to the specified limits.

Dimension	Available Capacity	Use Maximum	Assigned Quota
Virtual CPUs:	2	✓	2
Memory (MB):	2048	✓	2048
Storage (GB):	Unlimited	✓	Unlimited
Custom quota (points):	Unlimited	✓	Unlimited
Virtual machines:	Unlimited	✓	Unlimited

Member level quotas:
Each member of this user role combined can use resources up to the specified limits.

Dimension	Available Capacity	Use Maximum	Assigned Quota
Virtual CPUs:	2	✓	2
Memory (MB):	2048	✓	2048
Storage (GB):	Unlimited	✓	Unlimited
Custom quota (points):	Unlimited	✓	Unlimited
Virtual machines:	Unlimited	✓	Unlimited

7. On the **Networking** page, select the VM networks that can be used by this role and click on **Next**.

> Click on **Add** to add the VM networks.

8. On the **Resources** page, click on **Add** to select the resources and then click on **OK**; then, click on **Browse** and select the library upload data path.

9. Click on **Next**, and on the **Actions** page, select the allowed actions and click on **Next** again, as shown in the following screenshot:

10. On the **Summary** page, click on **Finish**.

> To change members, scope, quotas, resource, and/or actions, select the user role, right-click on it, and then select **Properties**.

Creating an application administrator (self-service user) role

Carry out the following steps to create an application administrator role:

1. In the VMM 2012 console in the **Settings** workspace, click **Create User Role** on the ribbon.

2. In the **Create User Role Wizard** window, type the name (for example, `DevTeam-AppAdmin`) and optional description (for example, `Development Team Application Admin`), and then click on **Next**.

3. On the **Profile** page, click on **Application Administrator** and then click on **Next**.

4. On the **Members** page, to add a user account(s) or group(s), click on **Add** and then on **Next**.

> To share a VM's ownership created by other members, use either an AD group for the user role or use the **Share** and **Receive** actions.

5. On the **Scope** page, select the private cloud(s)—for example, **My Cloud**—that can be managed by this role, select **Show PRO tips** to allow PRO management, and then click on **Next**.

6. On the **Quotas** page, enter the quota for each previously added private cloud(s) that is in the user's scope and click on **Next**.

> An individual page will show for each cloud if more than one private cloud is assigned to the user.

7. On the **Networking** page, select the VM networks that can be used by this role and click on **Next**.

> Click on **Add** to add the VM networks.

8. On the **Resources** page, click on **Add** to select the resources (for example, the hardware, OS, application and/or SQL profiles, VM templates, and/or service templates) and then click on **OK**; then, click on **Browse** and select the library upload data path.

9. On the **Actions** page, select the action(s) that the self-service users can perform and then click on **Next**, as shown in the following screenshot:

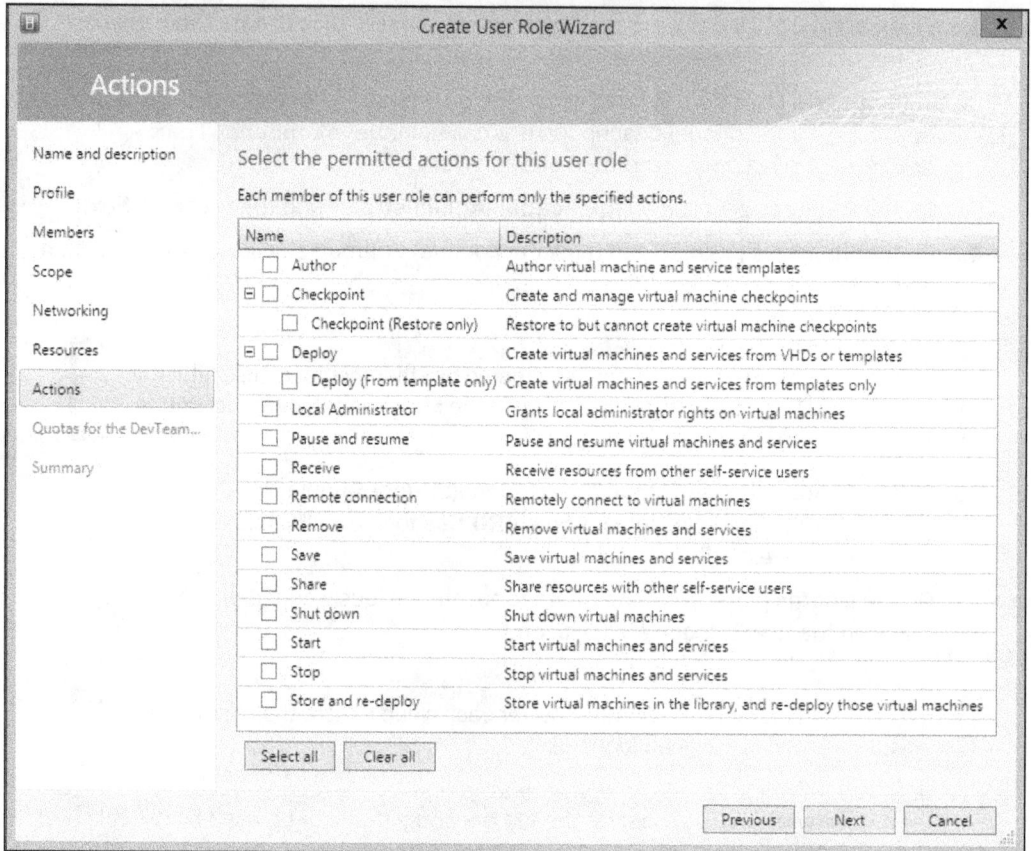

If you select **Author**, click on **Next** and select the Run As account that will be used to create the VMs and services, and then click on **Next**.

10. On the **Summary** page, click on **Finish**.

Configuring self-service user roles to share and receive resources

Carry out the following steps to enable the sharing and receiving of resources between role members:

1. In the VMM 2012 console in the **Settings** workspace, expand **Security** and click on **User Roles** on the left pane.

2. On the **User Roles** pane, select user role, right-click on it, and then select **Properties**.

3. Click on the **Actions** page, select **Share** and **Receive**, and then click on **OK**.

See also

▸   The *Configuring the Library to Support Self-Service Users* article at http://
    technet.microsoft.com/en-us/library/gg610608

▸   The *Available actions to Self-Service User Roles in VMM 2012* article at http://
    social.technet.microsoft.com/wiki/contents/articles/12554.
    actions-available-to-self-service-user-roles-in-vmm-2012.aspx

Creating and deploying virtual machines

In this recipe, we will create a virtual machine that will later be used as a template.

Getting ready

Creating a VM is straightforward. You can create a new virtual machine using an existing virtual hard disk, or you can create a machine with a blank virtual hard disk and then install the OS.

If you are creating a new VM from a blank VHD/VHDX disk, be prepared to link an ISO hosted in the VMM library or a CD/DVD drive with the OS media that is to be installed.

Windows 2012 R2 Hyper-V has recently introduced Virtual Machine (VM) generation 2, which provides new benefits such as the following:

▸   The PXE boot that uses the synthetic network, which means that you won't need to install the legacy network adapter anymore

▸   The boot from SCSI VDHx, which allows for the disk to be added/removed on the fly

▸   The Secure boot

▸   The boot from SCSI DVD

▸   UEFI firmware support

> [You can only create Gen 2 VMs if deploying Windows Server 2012/R2 or Windows 8/8.1. Check out the following article to understand the differences between Gen 1 and Gen 2 VMs at `http://technet.microsoft.com/en-us/library/dn440675.aspx`.]

How to do it...

Carry out the following steps to create a virtual machine:

1. In the VMM 2012 R2 console in the bottom-left corner, click on the **VMs and Services** workspace.

2. On the ribbon, click on **Create Virtual Machine** and then select **Create Virtual Machine**.

3. On the **Select Source** page, choose between the **Create the new virtual machine with a blank virtual hard disk** (the OS will have to be installed after the VM's creation) and **Use an existing virtual machine, VM template or virtual hard disk** options and then click on **Next**.

> [You won't be able to use a Gen 1 VM as a source to create a Gen 2 VM.]

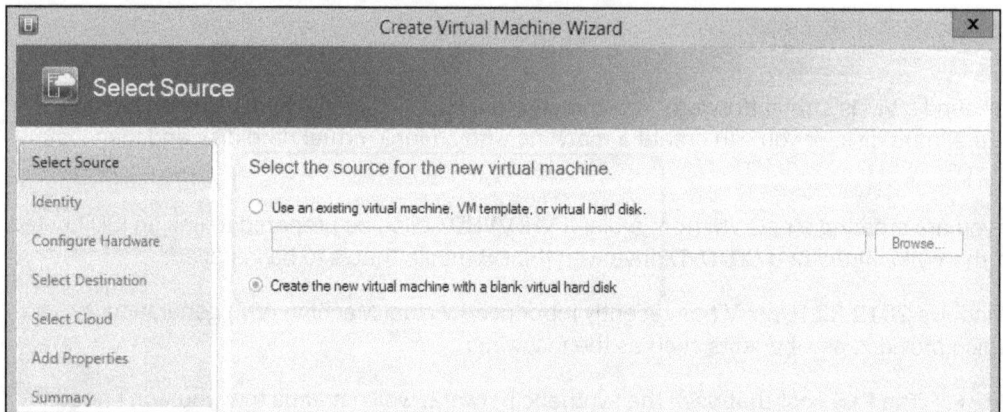

4. On the **Specify Virtual Machine Identity** page, type the virtual machine name (for example, `W2012-FS02`), type a description (optional), select the VM generation type (**1** or **2**) from the drop-down list, and then click on **Next**.

5. On the **Configure Hardware** page, provide the hardware settings or select a previously created hardware profile and then click on **Next**, as shown in the following screenshot:

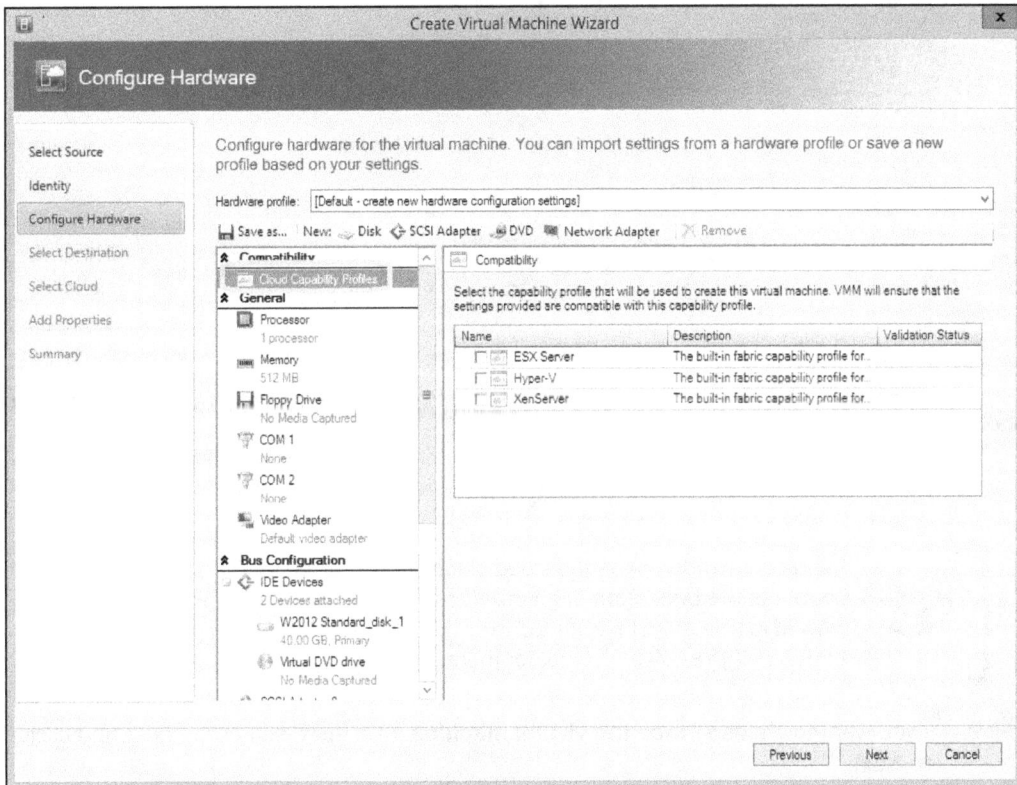

> For the VM generation 1 to be booted from the network (PXE boot), in order to install an OS in the **Network Adapters** section, add a legacy network adapter type.

6. If you are creating a new VM from a blank VHD/VHDX disk, click on the **Bus Configuration** section; then, click on **IDE Devices** for the generation 1 VM and **SCSI** for the generation 2 VM and the **Virtual DVD Drive** map within it, and select the ISO hosted in the VMM library or in a CD/DVD drive with the OS media to be installed.

> To make the VM highly available, select **Make this virtual machine highly available** in the **Availability** section under the **Advanced** section.

7. On the **Select Destination** page, choose whether you want to deploy or store the VM (as shown in the following screenshot) and click on **Next**.

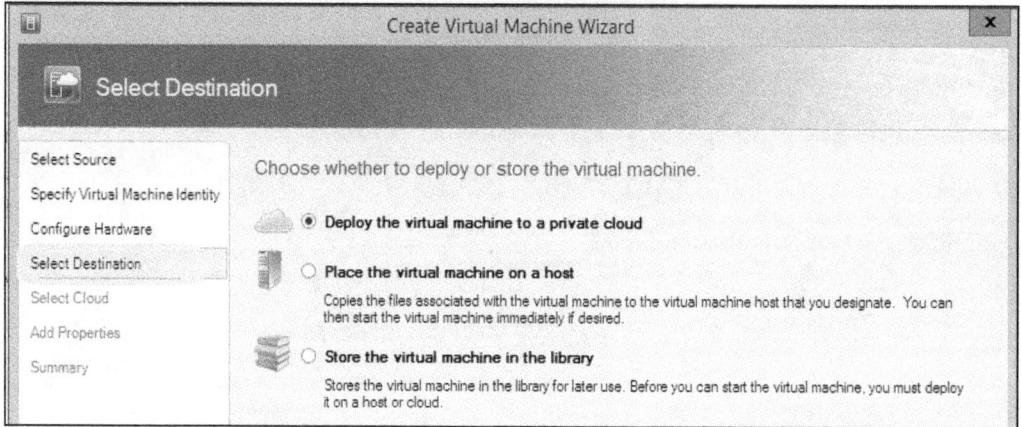

8. If you want to choose **Deploy the virtual machine to a private cloud**, select the cloud, confirm/modify the settings, and click on **Next**.

> The recommendation on the cloud placement is based on the star rating. Check out the *Understanding Virtual Machine Placement and Ratings in VMM* article at `http://technet.microsoft.com/en-us/library/jj860428.aspx` for more information.

9. If you want to choose **Place the virtual machine on a host**, select the host and click on **Next**.

10. On the **Configuration Settings** page, review/update the VM settings and click on **Next**.

11. If the **Select Networks** page appears, you can select the VM network, virtual switch, and/or VLAN to be used by this VM and then click on **Next**.

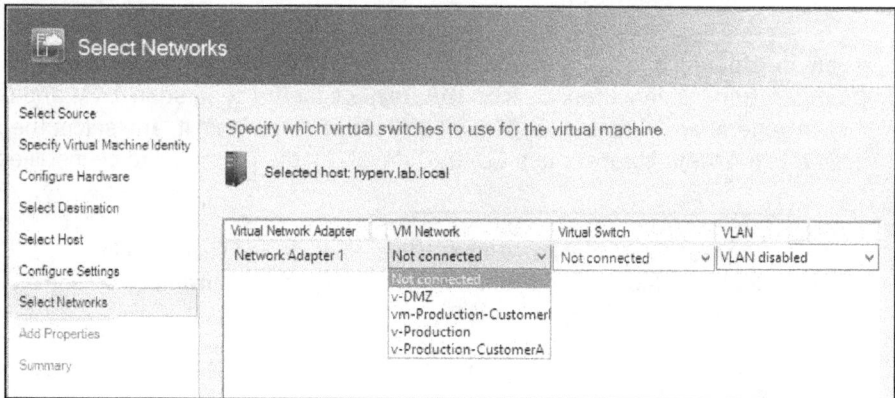

12. If you want to choose **Store the virtual machine in the library**, select the library server and click on **Next**. Then, click on **Browse** to select the share location path to deploy the VM and click on **Next**.

13. In the **Add Properties** page, select the automatic actions that need to be taken and the OS to be installed.

14. On the **Summary** page, click on **Create**.

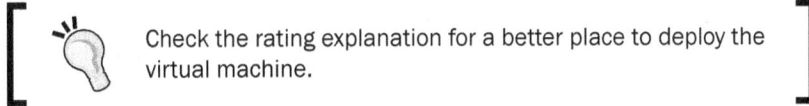

Check the rating explanation for a better place to deploy the virtual machine.

How it works...

This recipe guided you to create and deploy VMs to a private cloud or a specific host, or to store them in a VMM library. When **Create Virtual Machine Wizard** starts, select whether VMM will deploy the new VM to the private cloud, directly to a host, or to a library. Once VMM knows that the VM is to be deployed to a cloud or host, a list of hosts will be provided, and each one will be rated for how well it will be able to handle the VM (check the **Rate Explanation** tab).

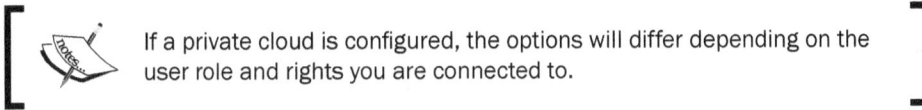

If a private cloud is configured, the options will differ depending on the user role and rights you are connected to.

VMM 2012 R2 has recently introduced generation 2 Virtual Machines (VM). When creating a VM, you have the option to select the VM generation.

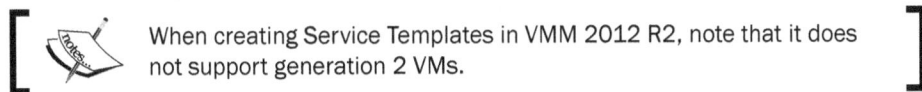

When creating Service Templates in VMM 2012 R2, note that it does not support generation 2 VMs.

VMM uses intelligent placement by analyzing the hosts' performance and rating them on a scale of one to five stars in order to weigh the better host/cloud available for deployment. The following table indicates how the ratings are calculated:

Rating	Formula
CPU	[1 – (CPU utilization / (100 – CPU reserve))] x CPU weight
Memory (RAM)	[1 – (RAM used / (total RAM – RAM reserve))] x RAM weight
Disk I/O capacity	[1 – (disk IOPS / max disk IOPS)] x disk weight
Network	[1 – (network utilization / (100 – network reserve))] x network weight

> For generation 1 VMs only, in **Configure Hardware**, take into account that the VMM adds a legacy network adapter by default. You should delete it and then add a synthetic network adapter to make use of it, and then connect it to a VM network or virtual switch.

For private cloud support, click on the **Cloud Compatibility Profile** menu option and select the capability profile (Hyper-V, VMware ESX, or Citrix XenServer). VMM uses capability profiles to define the virtual machine's limits. By specifying the capability profile, VMM will determine how much maximum RAM, disk space, and other resources can be assigned to a virtual machine.

> If you have standalone hosts running different processor versions in the same family (for example, Intel to Intel or AMD to AMD), to allow live migration between the hosts, select **Allow migration to a virtual machine host with a different processor version** in the **Processor** section.

You can use the **Save as...** option to save the hardware profile configuration.

If you stored the VM in the VMM library before deploying it to a host, you need to use one of the default blank virtual hard disks of the VMM library on the **Select Source** page.

You can also use this recipe to create a VM template by running through the **Create a New Virtual Machine** wizard and selecting **Store the virtual machine in the library**. Name the file appropriately, for example, W2012 Datacenter.

> VMM will generalize the VM while running the **Create Virtual Machine Template** wizard from a deployed VM, but if you are creating a VM from an existing VHD file, make sure it has been generalized using **Sysprep** (http://technet.microsoft.com/en-us/library/hh824816.aspx); otherwise, the VM will have the same ID as the source.

In VMM 2012 R2, the **Select Cloud** and **Select Host** pages in the **Deployment and Transfer Explanation** tab will show information regarding whether the *fast file copy*—a new VMM 2012 R2 feature that uses ODX—can be used. For more information on ODX, check out the *Windows Offloaded Data Transfers Overview* article at http://go.microsoft.com/fwlink/p/?LinkId=317143.

There's more...

If you are creating a VM from an existing VHD file, you need to generalize the guest OS.

Generalizing the guest OS using Sysprep

Carry on the following tasks to create a generalized OS:

1. Start the virtual machine.

2. Go through the steps to install the OS.

3. Once the OS has been installed, configure the server roles and features, if necessary.

4. Run the Sysprep process (for Windows 2008 R2 and higher, it can be found at `C:\Windows\System32\sysprep`).

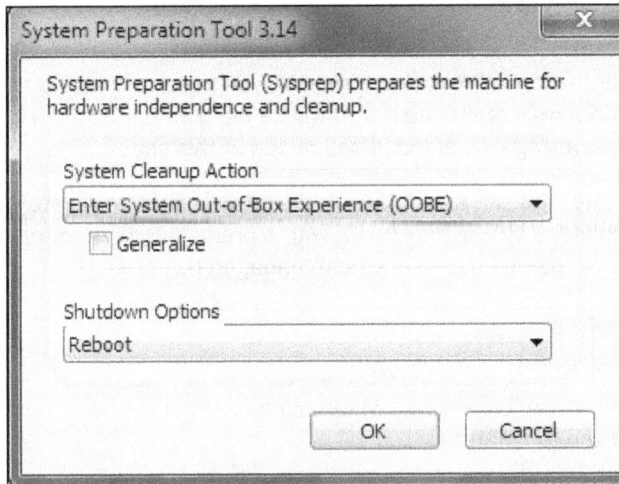

System Preparation Tool 3.14

System Preparation Tool (Sysprep) prepares the machine for hardware independence and cleanup.

System Cleanup Action

Enter System Out-of-Box Experience (OOBE)

☐ Generalize

Shutdown Options

Reboot

OK   Cancel

5. After the VM has shut down, copy `SYSPREP VHD/VHDX` file to the library share.

6. The VM is now ready to be used as a template.

See also

- ▸ The *Creating virtual machine templates* recipe
- ▸ The *How to Create and Deploy a Virtual Machine from an Existing Virtual Machine* article at `http://technet.microsoft.com/en-us/library/hh882400.aspx`
- ▸ The *How to Create and Deploy a Virtual Machine from an Existing Virtual Hard Disk* article at `http://technet.microsoft.com/en-us/library/hh882391.aspx`

Creating virtual machine templates

In this recipe, we will create virtual machine templates that use generalized images as the source.

VMM virtual machine templates are used to perform the automated installation and configuration of servers, dramatically reducing the time to release a server, and automate all these processes in a simple and uncomplicated deployment method.

Getting ready

Before you can create the virtual machine template, you need to create a new VM and install a vanilla OS (fresh Windows install) into it that will be used as the base for the template. Refer to the *Creating and deploying virtual machines* recipe of this chapter.

To create a VM template, you can select the source for which the template will be created from an existing template, a virtual disk (VHD) with a preinstalled operating system, or even a virtual machine that is being used in any host managed by VMM.

How to do it...

Carry out the following steps to create a VM template based on either an existing virtual hard disk or a virtual machine template:

1. In the VMM 2012 console, click on the **Library** workspace, then click on the ribbon, and then click on **Create VM Template**.

2. On the **Select Source** page, select **Use an existing VM template or a virtual hard disk stored in the library**.

3. Click on **Browse**, select a generalized Windows Server .vhdx file, then click on **OK**, and then click on **Next**.

4. Type the VM template name (for example, W2012 Standalone Template) and click on **Next**.

5. If the selected source is a VHDx disk, the VM Generation box will show up. Select between the **Gen 1** or **Gen 2** virtual machine format.

6. On the **Configure Hardware** page, provide the hardware settings or select a hardware profile, and then click on **Next**.

To make the template highly available, in the **Availability** section, which is present under the **Advanced** section, select **Make this virtual machine highly available**.

If the network adapter is configured to use static IP addresses, the MAC address also needs to be configured as static.

7. On the **Configure Operating System** page, select a guest OS profile or provide the settings for it, and then click on **Next** as shown in the following screenshot:

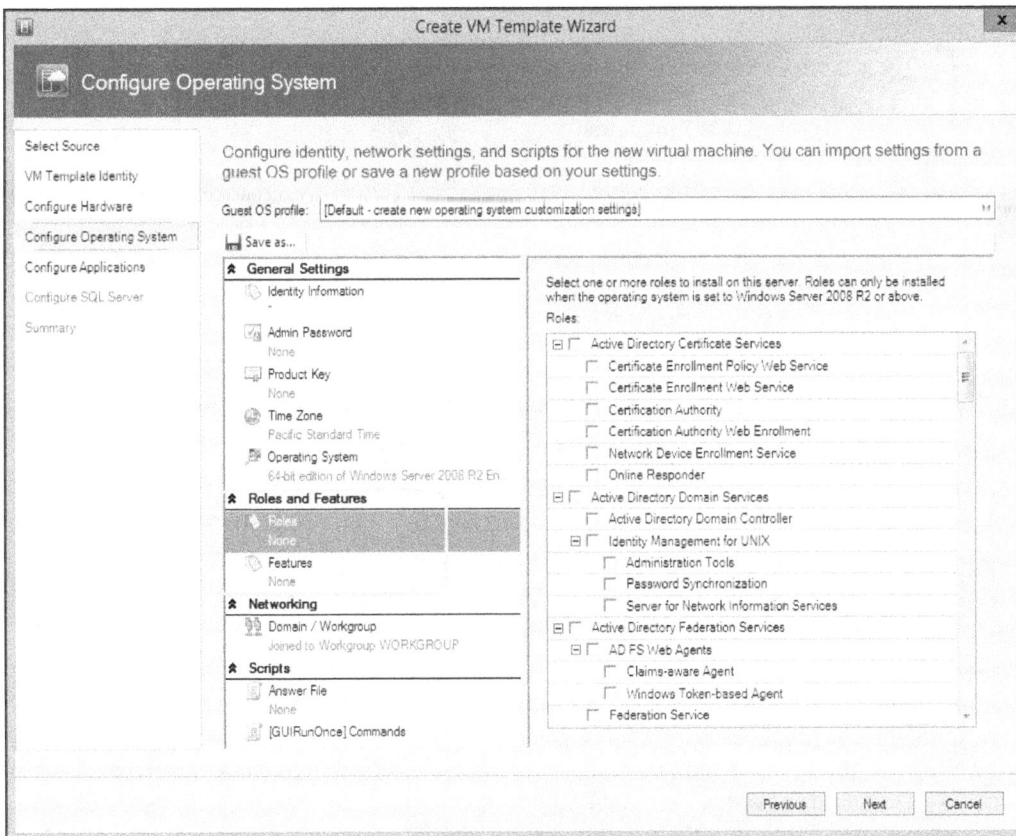

The **Roles and Features** settings can only be installed if the VM template is used in a service template and the source virtual hard disk has Windows Server 2008 R2 or higher installed.

8. On the **Configure Applications** page, configure the settings or select an application profile, if any, and then click on **Next**.

9. On the **Configure SQL Server** page, configure the settings or select a SQL Server profile, if any, and then click on **Next**.

> Application and SQL Server deployment settings do not apply if the template is designated for standalone VMs that are not part of a service.

10. On the **Summary** page, click on **Create**.

> To verify whether the template has been created, in the **Library** workspace, expand **Templates** on the left-hand pane and then click on **VM Templates**.

How it works...

Start by selecting the source that the template will be created for. You can use an existing template, a virtual disk (VHD/VHDX) with a preinstalled operating system, or even a virtual machine that is being used in any host managed by VMM.

On the **Configure Hardware** pane, specify the hardware configuration—such as a disk, the network, the memory, the processor—or select an existing hardware profile. For generation 1 VMs, VMM adds a legacy network adapter by default. You should delete it and then add a synthetic network adapter to make use of it, and then connect it to a logical network or virtual network.

Click on the **Cloud Compatibility Profile** menu option to select the capability profile to validate it against the hardware profile for private cloud support. You can also use the **Save as...** option to save the hardware profile configuration.

On the **Configure Operating System** pane, specify the information for the Windows automated installation, such as the computer name, product key, local administrator password, and operating system. Using the # symbol, the virtual machine will be named based on a numeric sequence. To create random names, use the * symbol. If the template used has Windows 2008 R2, 2012 or the new 2012/R2 operating system, you can use the new **Roles and Features** option, which makes it possible to select the server roles and/or features that will automatically be installed.

In the **Configure Applications** option, you can add and configure applications and scripts to automatically be installed after the OS installation.

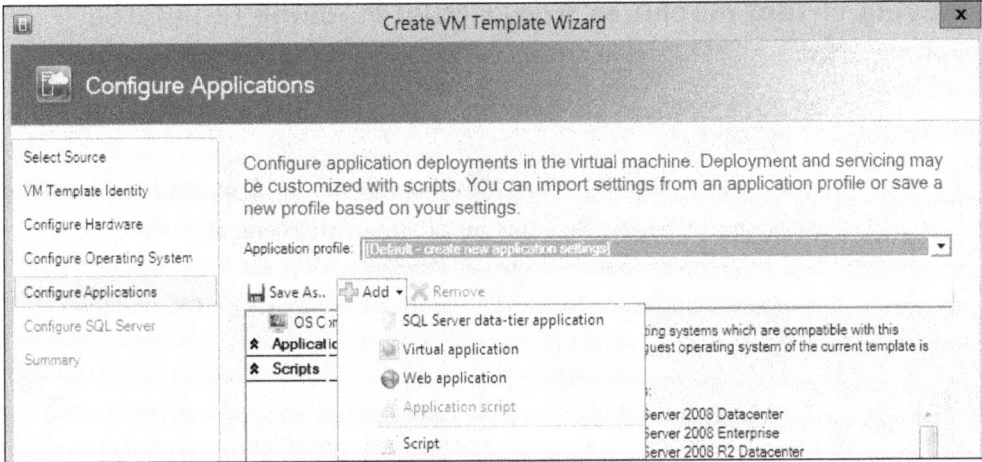

On the last screen in **Configure SQL Server**, you can also specify the information and configuration for the SQL installation.

> To use the same options provided to automate the creation of templates through PowerShell, click on **View Script**.

There's more...

Now that the VM template has been created, let's see how we can deploy it.

Enabling MAC spoofing

The **Enable spoofing of MAC address** setting is required if you plan to host the VM on a Windows 2008 R2 Hyper-V host with **Network Load Balancing** enabled.

> A known issue when selecting the **Enable spoofing of MAC addresses** checkbox is that it does not change the setting on the GUI.

The only way to enable MAC spoofing is by using the VMM command shell to configure this setting after you create the template. This is done in the following manner:

```
PS C:\> $VMTemp = Get-SCVMTemplate -Name "W2008R2 Enterprise"

PS C:\> $vNetAdapter = Get-SCVirtualNetworkAdapter -VMTemplate
$VMTemp

PS C:\> Set-SCVirtualNetworkAdapter -VirtualNetworkAdapter
$vNetAdapter -EnableMACAddressSpoofing $True
```

Deploying virtual machines from virtual machine templates

Carry out the following steps to create virtual machines from virtual machine templates:

1. In the VMM 2012 R2 console in the bottom-left corner, click on the **VMs and Services** workspace.

2. On the ribbon, click on **Create Virtual Machine**, then select **Create Virtual Machine**.

3. On the **Select Source** page, select **Use an existing virtual machine, VM template, or virtual hard disk** and click on **Browse**.

4. Select the template (for example, W2012 Standalone), click on **OK**, and then click on **Next**.

> A message displaying that the template settings will be ignored will appear if the template has roles or features configured or application or SQL deployment settings.

5. In the **Identify/Specify Virtual Machine Identity** section, type the VM name (for example, W2012-web01) and click on **Next**.

6. On the **Configure Hardware** page, adjust the settings for the new VM and click on **Next**.

> You need to select a capability profile that is supported by the cloud you previously created.
>
> If you set up the network to use a static IP, the MAC address should also be configured to static.
>
> If creating a VM to use the VMware .vmdk disk, you need to add a Legacy network adapter.

7. On the **Configure Operating System** page, provide the identity, network settings, and scripts (if any) for the new VM as shown in the following screenshot:

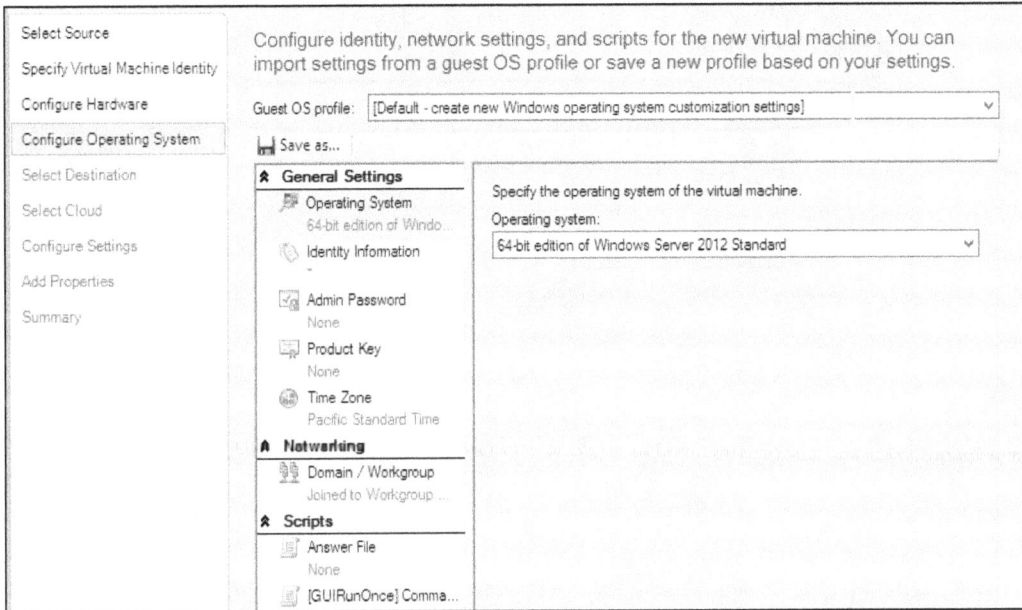

Select Source	Configure identity, network settings, and scripts for the new virtual machine. You can import settings from a guest OS profile or save a new profile based on your settings.
Specify Virtual Machine Identity	
Configure Hardware	Guest OS profile: [Default - create new Windows operating system customization settings] ▾
Configure Operating System	⊟ Save as...
Select Destination	☆ **General Settings**
Select Cloud	🗗 Operating System — Specify the operating system of the virtual machine.
	64-bit edition of Windo... Operating system:
Configure Settings	🗔 Identity Information — 64-bit edition of Windows Server 2012 Standard ▾
Add Properties	
Summary	🗝 Admin Password / None
	🗗 Product Key / None
	🕓 Time Zone / Pacific Standard Time
	☆ **Networking**
	📇 Domain / Workgroup / Joined to Workgroup...
	☆ **Scripts**
	📄 Answer File / None
	📄 [GUIRunOnce] Comma...

8. On the **Select Destination** page, choose whether to deploy the VM to a host or private cloud and click on **Next**.

9. If you choose **Deploy the virtual machine to private cloud**, select the cloud, and on the **Configuration settings** page, review/update the VM settings and click on **Next**.

10. If you choose **Place the virtual machine on a host**, select the host, click on **Next**, and on the **Configuration settings** page, review/update the VM settings and click on **Next**. On the **Select Networks** page, select the VM network, virtual switch, and/or VLAN to be used by this VM, and then click on **Next** as shown in the following screenshot:

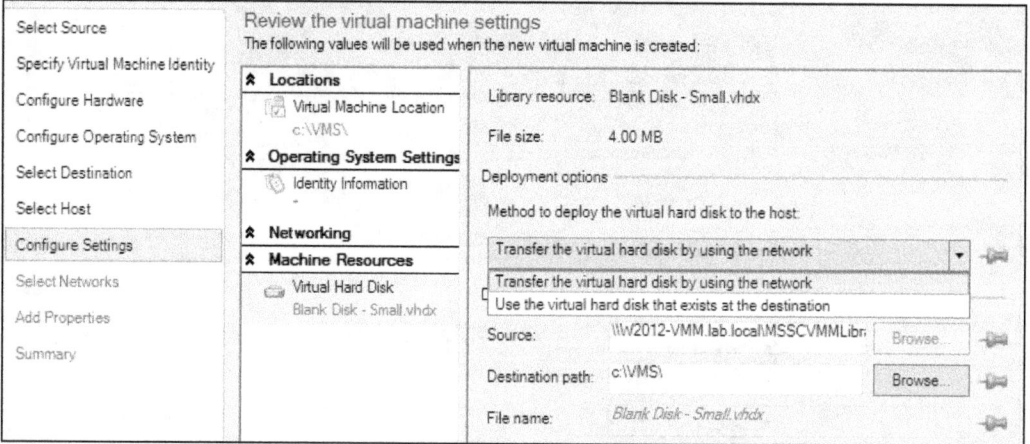

11. If you selected a cloud or a host, on the **Add properties** page, select the automatic actions that are to be undertaken.

12. On the **Summary** page, click on **Create**.

> If you placed the virtual machine on a host cluster, if you click on **Browse** in the **Select Destination Folder** dialog box, the file shares will be listed under the **File Shares** node.

See also

▶ The *How to Configure NLB for a Service Tier* article at http://technet. microsoft.com/en-us/library/hh335098

Creating and deploying service templates

In VMM 2012, a service is a set of VMs configured and deployed together and managed as a single entity. For example, it's like deploying a three-tier business application or a frontend web application with SQL Server running in the background.

A service template provides the capability to separate the OS configuration from the application installation, leaving you with fewer OS images.

Using service templates, you will be able to leverage variations in capacity, easily being able to add or remove VMs needed to support the application.

> It is the best practice to wrap even a single VM template into a service template as you scale it out, for example.

Getting ready

Ensure that the resources that you need in order to create the service are available. Review and document all the elements that the service needs to be up and running before starting. For example, identify the following:

- What servers need to be deployed to support the service
- Which existing VM template will be used
- What roles/features should be installed, and what applications or scripts need to be deployed
- Whether the needed VMM resources have been created and configured
- Which networking components are to be connected to
- Who will use the service

> The following are a few important things you need to keep in mind:
>
> To install applications beforehand, have the installation files, scripts, and configuration made available
>
> To use Server App-V, make sure to have sequenced the applications
>
> To deploy a SQL Server instance on a VM, make sure to have a VHD/VHDX file with a generalized SQL Server installation

How to do it...

Carry out the following steps to create the service template:

1. In the VMM 2012 console in the bottom-left corner, click on the **Library** workspace.

2. In the **Home** tab on the ribbon, click on **Create Service**, select **Create a service template**, and click on **OK**.

3. In the **New Service Template** dialog box, type the name for the service template (for example, `Marketing WebApp`).

4. Type the service template's release value for the version (for example, `1.0` or `CTP`) as a replacement of the value **new**.

> The release value is important for when you need to update the service. It helps identify the version of the service template.

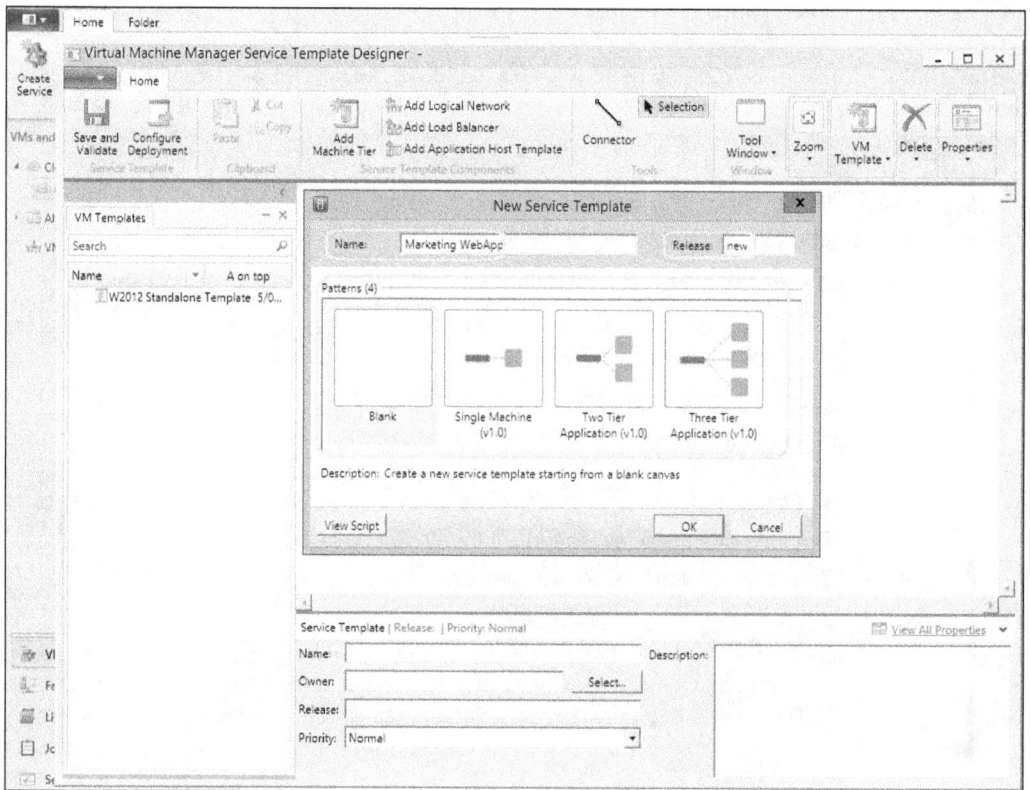

5. Select the number of tiers to be created in the service template (for example, **Two Tier Application**, which creates blocks that need to be configured as VMs) and click on **OK**. Wait for the service to be created.

6. Depending on the option selected, the design area could be empty or contain some default tiers.

> You can add a tier to a service template by dragging a VM template on to the canvas area or using the **Create Machine Tier Template** wizard.

7. In the **Virtual Machine Manager Service Template Designer** window, perform the following steps for each of the networking components:

    1. On the ribbon, click on **Add VM Network** (to add a box representing the logical network) and select the logical network box (for example, **NIC 1**).

    2. On the properties pane (bottom), select the network to be associated from the **Network** list.

    3. On the ribbon, click on **Connector** and drag the connector from the VM network box to the network adapter box.

> ![note icon] A connecting line that links both the boxes will appear, indicating that the logical network is connected to the network adapter.

8. On the ribbon, click on **Save and Validate** and then click on **Configure Deployment**.

    Type the name of the service template to be published and click on **OK**.

    An icon that warns of configuration issues will be displayed if there is a validation error, and an error icon that indicates which tier/element is causing the error will be displayed, as shown in the following screenshot:

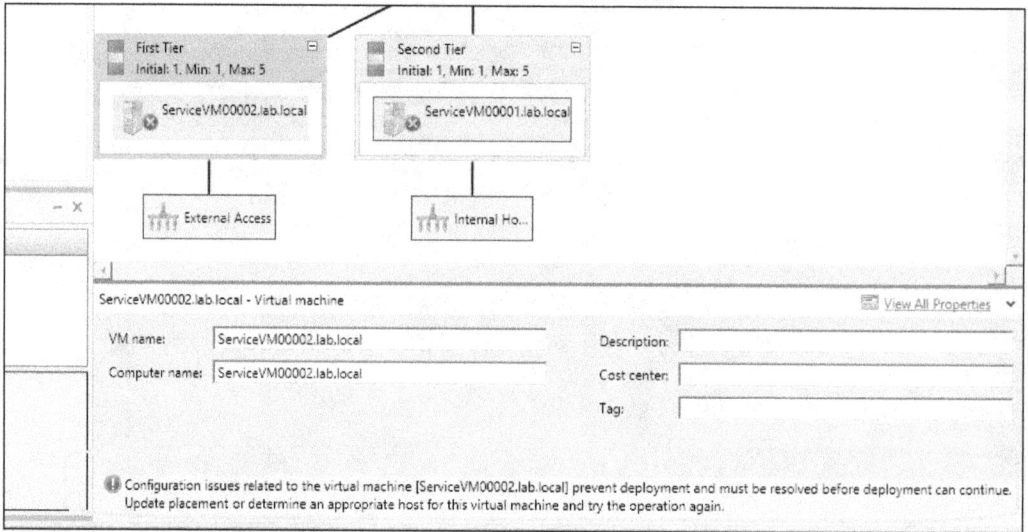

How it works...

A service template is a set of elements (for example, VMs, apps, networks) bonded together to define the services' configuration.

To create a service template in the VMM console, click on **Create a Service** to open the **Virtual Machine Manager Service Template Designer** window.

You can use an existing VM template on a service template, which includes the VMs (deployed as a service), applications to be installed, and network settings.

After the service template is created, you can add/remove elements (for example, VMs, networks, apps), deploy it to a private cloud/host, and/or deploy the updated service template to a deployed service to update that as well.

> If you are changing a service template that is in use by a deployed service, a new release value will be required before you save it.

After the service template has been saved, it will be located in the **Library** workspace on the service templates node. To open an existing one, click on the **Library** workspace, and then in the designer select the service template. On the ribbon, in the **Service Template** tab, click on **Open Designer**.

> For a great example on how to use service templates, check out the *VMM Service Template for SharePoint 2013 to your Microsoft private cloud* blog at `http://blogs.technet.com/b/privatecloud/archive/2013/04/03/application-management-example-deploying-a-service-to-your-private-cloud-part-1.aspx`.

There's more...

Now that we have created the service template, let's deploy it.

Deploying a service from the VMs and Services workspace

The **Deploy Service** window contains three panes. The left pane contains two tabs, namely, **Services Components**—which lists the service tiers that will be deployed—and **Settings**—which shows the configuration that will be used for application deployment.

The center pane shows the service design with all of the instances that will be deployed as a part of the service.

The right pane is a **Minimap**, which contains a map of the service. This is illustrated in the following screenshot:

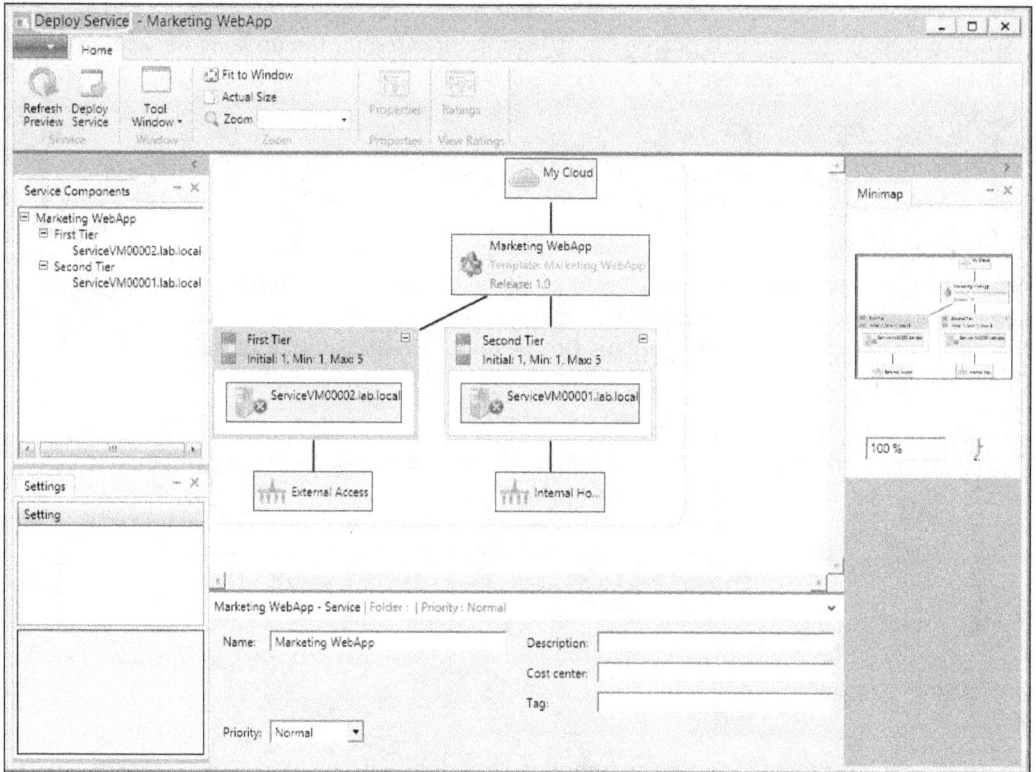

Carry out the following steps to deploy a service:

1. In the VMM 2012 R2 console in the bottom-left corner, click on the **VMs and Services** workspace.

2. Select the private cloud or host group to deploy the service.

3. Under the **Home** tab on the ribbon, click on **Create Service**.

4. In the **Create Service** dialog box, click on **Use an existing service template**, then click on **Browse**, then select the service template (for example, **Marketing WebApp**), and click on **OK**.

> Only VM generation 1 are supported for service templates.

5. Type the service name and enter the location in the **Destination** list.

6. Click on **OK**.

> VMM performs a placement check to determine the best location to deploy the service on and then opens the **Deploy Service** window. Follow the steps described to resolve any errors and warnings, and then deploy the service. For information on how to make changes, refer to *How to Configure Deployment Settings for a Service* available at `http://technet.microsoft.com/en-us/library/hh411278`.

Scaling out a service in VMM

The `scale out` feature in VMM is useful if you need to set up additional VMs on any tier of a deployed service. For example, during Australian Boxing Day, due to the increase in online sales and, hence, an increase in web traffic, your website may require additional servers (for example, IIS, app, or SQL Server) to handle the traffic. The scale out process creates a new VM that is identical to the other VMs in the tier, and deploys OS roles, features, and required applications.

> Scaling out a service in VMM does requires a load balancer and a VIP template in the service definition. Refer to *Configuring Load Balancing in VMM Overview* at `http://technet.microsoft.com/en-us/library/jj721573.aspx`.

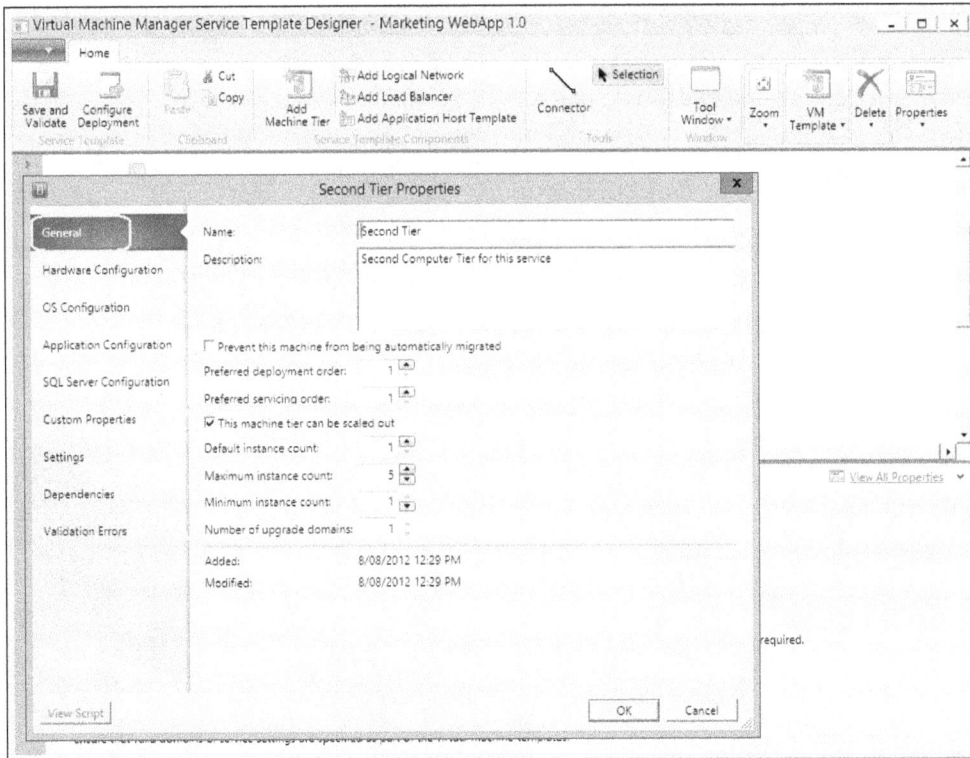

Updating a service in VMM

To allow an update on a deployed service based on a service template, VMM retains the trail of the service template that was used to deploy this service. (That is why you are required to increase the release version before saving the new version.) To update a deployed service you can use one of the following two methods:

▶ **Apply updates to existing virtual machines in-place**

▶ **Deploy new virtual machines with updated settings**

The following screenshot illustrates the use of these methods:

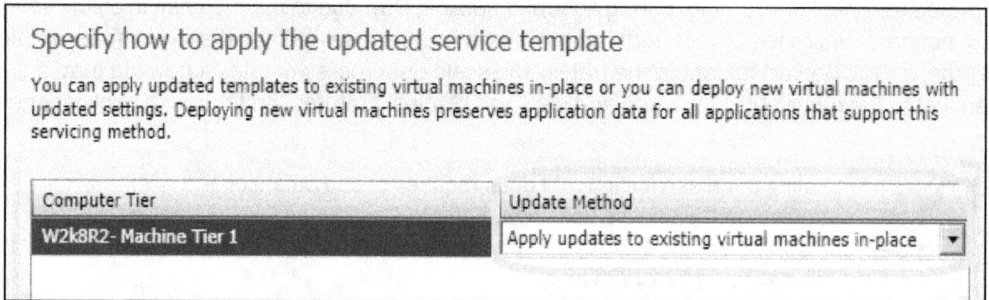

Specify how to apply the updated service template

You can apply updated templates to existing virtual machines in-place or you can deploy new virtual machines with updated settings. Deploying new virtual machines preserves application data for all applications that support this servicing method.

Computer Tier	Update Method
W2k8R2- Machine Tier 1	Apply updates to existing virtual machines in-place ▾

See also

▶ The *How to Configure the Properties of a Service Template* article at `http://technet.microsoft.com/en-us/library/hh410346`

▶ The *How to Add a Tier to a Service Template* article at `http://technet.microsoft.com/en-us/library/hh410345`

▶ The *How to Deploy a Service in VMM* article at `http://technet.microsoft.com/en-us/library/gg650471`

▶ The *How to Scale Out a Service in VMM* article at `http://technet.microsoft.com/en-us/library/gg675080.aspx`

▶ The *How to Create an Updated Service Template in VMM* article at `http://technet.microsoft.com/en-us/library/gg675120`

▶ The *How to Apply Updates to a Deployed Service in VMM* article at `http://technet.microsoft.com/en-us/library/gg675106`

Rapidly provisioning a virtual machine using SAN Copy

This recipe will guide you through the steps to rapidly provision a virtual machine using the **Storage Area Network (SAN)** Copy technology (for example, snapshots and cloning).

Using rapid provisioning, you can quickly create and deploy VMs, but if you want to use a template that is SAN Copy capable, the storage must support SAN Copy through cloning or snapshots.

> VMM 2012 R2 now supports ODX, which allows the provisioning of multiple VMs per LUN.

The template that is SAN Copy capable allows VMM, when deploying a new VM, to create a read/write copy of the LUN containing the VHD/VHDX file, which then places the VM files on the new LUN assigned to a destination host/cluster. For this operation, a storage transfer is used instead of a network transfer.

Getting ready

Make sure that the following prerequisites are met if you want to use the SAN Copy capability:

- Storage support should be provided for VMM storage management using the SMI-S or SMP provider.

- Storage support should be provided for cloning or snapshots.

- Storage providers should be installed, configured, and accessible from the Hyper-V servers and VMM management server.

- If you are planning rapid provisioning, VMM should be managing the storage pool, and it should be allocated to a host group. Also included are the following prerequisites:

  - The target Hyper-V hosts should be members of a host group and should use the same type of storage connectivity

  - The library server should be a member of the same host group and a Hyper-V host, if you are planning to create a template that is SAN Copy capable from an existing VM and want to create and assign the LUN from a library server

- The **Multipath I/O (MPIO)** feature should be added to each host that needs a fibre channel or iSCSI storage array.

> Using the **Microsoft Device Specific Module** (**DSM**), VMM automatically enables MPIO for supported storages.
>
> If you have already installed vendor-specific DSMs, they will be used to communicate with the storage instead.
>
> If before adding the MPIO feature, you add a Hyper-V host to a VMM management server, you will be required to configure the MPIO or install vendor-specific DSMs manually outside VMM.

▶ If you are using fibre channel storage, each host that will access the storage array should have a **host bus adapter** (**HBA**) installed and be zoned accordingly so that it can access the storage array.

▶ If you are using an iSCSI SAN, make sure that the iSCSI portals have been added, the iSCSI initiator is logged into the array, and **Microsoft iSCSI Initiator Service** on each host has been started and set to **Automatic**.

How to do it...

You need to create an NTFS-formatted LUN beforehand and assign a drive letter from the managed storage pool. Carry out the following steps to configure the storage for rapid provisioning in VMM:

1. In the VMM console in the bottom-left corner, click on the **Fabric** workspace.

2. Expand **Storage** and click on **Arrays**, select the storage, and **right-click** on it and then select **Properties**.

3. In the storage properties window, click on **Settings**, select the snapshot type for the SAN transfer, and click on **OK**.

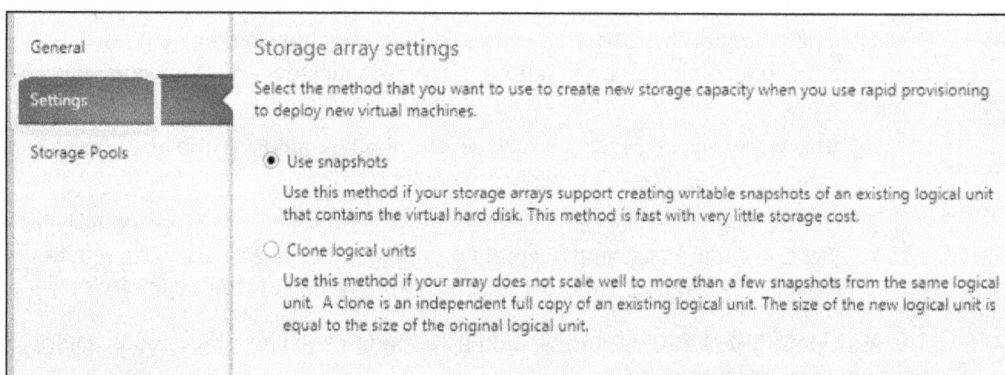

4. To create a logical unit, under the **Fabric** workspace, expand storage, click on **Arrays**, click on **Create Logical Unit**, and then type the LUN name (for example, lun-VMS).

5. To allocate the created LUN to a host group, on the **Fabric** workspace, click on **Servers**, select the host group (for example, Sydney), right-click, select **Properties**, and then click on **Storage** in the left menu.

6. Among the properties of the storage, click on **Allocate Logical Units**, assign the **Available Logical Units** to **Allocated Logical Units**, and click on **OK**.

7. In the **Fabric** workspace, click on **Servers**, select the VMM library host, right-click, select **Properties**, and then click on **Storage**.

8. In the **Storage properties** window, click on **Add** and select **Add Disk**.

9. For the logical unit, select the created LUN (`lun-VMS`) from the drop-down list.

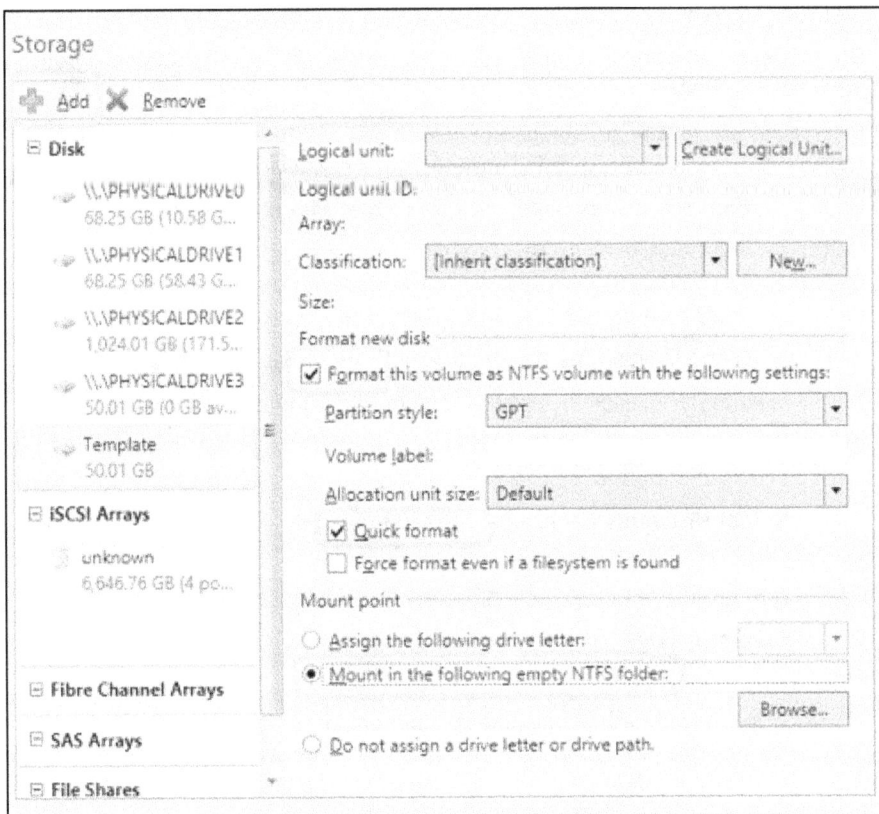

10. Select **Format this volume as NTFS volume with the following settings** to format it as the NTFS volume, type the volume name, and select **mount in the following empty NTFS folder**.

11. Select the `template` folder under the library share and click on **OK**.

12. In the **Library** workspace, expand **Library Servers**, select the **VMM library share**, right-click, and select **Refresh**.

Now, carry out the following steps to create `SAN Copy-capable VHD/VHDX` on a host:

1. In the VMM console in the bottom-left corner, click on the **VMs and Services** workspace.

2. Under the **Home** tab on the ribbon, click on and select **Create Virtual Machine**.

3. On the **Select Source** page, click on **Create the new virtual machine with a blank virtual hard disk** and then on **Next**.

4. On the **Specify Virtual Machine Identity** page, type the VM name (for example, `W2012-Datacenter`), an optional description, and click on **Next**.

5. On the **Configure Hardware** page, confirm/change the hardware settings and click on **Next**.

6. On the **Select Destination** page, select **Place the virtual machine on a host** and click on **Next**.

7. On the **Select Host** page, select a host with the assigned LUN and click on **Next**.

8. On the **Configure Settings** page, click on **Virtual Machine Location**.

9. On the **results** pane, click on **Browse**, verify the text that the **SAN (Migration Capable)** field displays after the drive information, and select the drive—for example, **(S:\) [199.2 GB free of 200 GB, SAN (Migration Capable)]**.

10. Click on **OK**, and in **Machine Resources**, click on **Virtual Hard Disk**.

11. On the **results** pane, click on **Browse**, select the same drive that was selected in step 9 (**S**), and click on **OK**.

12. Click on **Next** to continue.

13. On the **Select Networks** page, select the VM network, virtual switch, and/or VLAN setting.

14. On the **Add properties** page, select the automatic actions to be undertaken.

15. On the **Summary** page, click on **Create**.

> Once the new virtual machine is deployed, install and configure the guest OS, server roles, features, and applications. Generalize the image. Refer to the *Generalizing the guest OS using Sysprep* subsection in the *Creating and deploying virtual machines* recipe of this chapter.

How it works...

Rapid provisioning allows the deployment of VMs using storage capabilities. VMM won't need to copy the VM from the VMM library to the Hyper-V host, alleviating I/O loads on the storage and network.

There are two methods to rapidly provision a LUN in the VMM 2012 console: snapshot copies and clones. You can also use PowerShell commands if you need more granularities. Snapshot copies are provisioned almost immediately.

VMM 2012 R2 now supports ODX, which allows the provisioning of multiple VMs per LUN.

To use the SAN Copy capability, you must create and assign an empty storage LUN from a storage pool to the target host beforehand. You can use either VMM or the storage vendor management tools for this purpose.

The next step is to create a VM with a blank virtual hard disk file (VHD/VHDX) on that LUN.

Then, install and customize the guest OS and applications and generalize the image using Sysprep.

To finalize, using **New VM Template**, create a template that is SAN Copy capable from the created VM. VMM will then transfer the files in the LUN from the host to the VMM library through a SAN transfer.

> The library will index the new VHD/VHDX file during the next refresh.

There's more...

Now, let's create a template that is SAN Copy capable and then deploy it.

Creating a template that is SAN Copy capable

Carry out the following steps to create a template that is SAN Copy capable:

1. In the VMM 2012 console in the bottom-left corner, click on the **Library** workspace.
2. On the ribbon, click on **Create VM Template**.
3. On the **Select Source** page, click on **From an existing virtual machine that is deployed on a host**.
4. Click on **Browse**, select the VM (for example, **W2012-Datacenter**), click on **OK**, and then click on **Next**.

5. Then, click on **Yes**.

6. On the **VM Template Identity** page, type the VM template name (for example, `W2012 Datacenter Template - SAN Provision`) and click on **Next**.

7. On the **Configure Hardware** and **Configure Operating System** pages, click on **Next**.

8. On the **Select Library Server** page, select the VMM library after verifying whether the **Transfer Type** column indicates **SAN**, and click on **Next**.

9. On the **Select Path** page, click on **Browse**. Select the path to store the VM files, click on **OK**, and then click on **Next**.

10. On the **Summary** page, click on **Create**.

Deploying a virtual machine through rapid provisioning

Carry out the following steps to deploy a VM using rapid provisioning:

1. In the VMM console in the bottom-left corner, click on the **VMs and Services** workspace.

2. In the **Home** tab on the ribbon, click on and select **Create Virtual Machine**.

3. On the **Select Source** page, click on **Use an existing virtual machine, VM template or virtual hard disk** and then click on **Browse**.

4. In **Type: VM Template**, select the previously created template (for example, **W2012 Datacenter Template – SAN Provision**) and click on **OK**.

> Make sure that **SAN Copy Capable** is selected to **Yes**.

5. On the **Select Source** page, click on **Next**.

6. Complete the steps featured in the wizard to create and deploy the VM, while taking the following points into consideration:

    1. On the **Configure Hardware** page in the **Bus Configuration** section, select the storage classification that ties the LUN classification (or do not use classification at all—leave it empty)

    2. On the **Select Host** page or the **Select Cloud** page, verify that the **Transfer Type** field indicates **SAN**

See also

▶ The *How to Create a SAN Copy-Capable Template from an Existing Virtual Machine* article at `http://technet.microsoft.com/en-us/library/gg610597.aspx`

▶ The *How to Deploy a New Virtual Machine from the SAN Copy-Capable Template* article at `http://technet.microsoft.com/en-us/library/gg610618`

▶ The *Storage Automation in VMM 2012* article at `http://blogs.technet.com/b/scvmm/archive/2011/03/29/storage-automation-in-vmm-2012.aspx`

▶ The *How to Configure Storage on a Hyper-V Host in VMM* article at `http://go.microsoft.com/fwlink/p/?LinkID=212536`

▶ The *How to Provision Storage Logical Units in VMM* article at `http://go.microsoft.com/fwlink/p/?LinkID=213750`

7
Managing VMware ESXi and Citrix® XenServer® Hosts

In this chapter, we will cover the following:

- Adding VMware vCenter Server to VMM
- Adding VMware ESX hosts or host clusters to VMM
- Configuring network settings on a VMware ESX host
- Configuring host BMC settings
- Importing VMware templates
- Converting VMware virtual machines to Hyper-V
- Managing Citrix® XenServer® hosts and pools
- Converting Citrix® virtual machines to Hyper-V

Introduction

This chapter has recipes that will help administrators use VMM 2012 R2 to manage daily operations of VMware ESX and Citrix hosts and host clusters, such as the identification and management of hosts. In addition, it will provide you with the ability to create, manage, save, and deploy VMs on VMware ESX and Citrix hosts, all from the VMM console.

System Center 2012 has the concept of a fabric, which is made up of hosts, host groups, and library servers, as well as networking and storage configurations. This architecture abstracts the underlying infrastructure from the users but lets them deploy VMs, applications, and services irrespective of whether the infrastructure is running on the Microsoft hypervisor technology or hypervisors from VMware or Citrix.

As multiple hypervisors can be managed through a common console, we can deploy VMs and applications in a consistent manner and get the same capabilities from different hypervisors. We can choose to utilize a mix of hypervisors, aggregating one or more hypervisors' host groups into a private cloud without worrying about the underlying hypervisor's capabilities and limitations. Abstracting the hypervisor layer reduces complexity and makes it easier to perform common actions on heterogeneous environments.

Note that in order to fully monitor and manage VMware and Citrix environments, you will need the following System Center 2012 R2 family components:

- **Virtual Machine Manager**: This enables you to deploy and manage virtual machines and services across multiple hypervisor platforms, including Citrix, VMware ESX, and ESXi hosts.

- **Orchestrator (SCORH)**: This includes over 41 built-in workflow activities to perform a wide variety of tasks. You can expand its functionality by installing integration packs; for example, the integration pack for VMware vSphere helps you automate actions by enabling full management. For more information about Orchestrator Integration packs, go to http://technet.microsoft.com/en-us/library/hh295851.aspx.

- **Operations Manager (OpsMgr)**: This helps you monitor VMware environments by using third-party management packs such as those from Veeam (refer to the *Extending monitoring with management packs* recipe in *Chapter 9, Integration with System Center Operations Manager 2012*), which will enable all Operations Manager functionalities, such as alerts on the performance and events; integrated notifications, responses, and automation; and detailed reporting and auditing for all VMware components (ESXi hosts, vCenter, and so on). The following figure shows you an integration between VMM and OpsMgr using Veeam Management Pack to monitor VMware hosts:

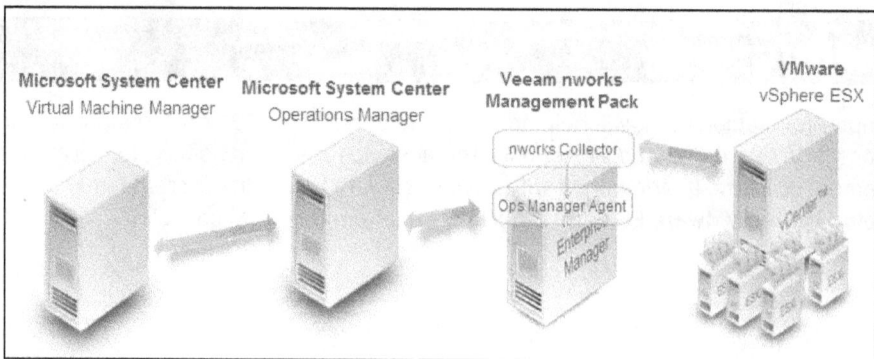

Adding VMware vCenter Server to VMM

In order to manage VMware hosts, you need to integrate VMM with any existing VMware vCenter Server. VMM supports the VMware vCenter Server virtualization management software for managing hosts.

The features that are supported when VMM manages ESX/ESXi hosts are as follows:

Functionalities supported by VMM	Notes
Private clouds	The ESX/ESXi host resources are available to a VMM private cloud when creating the private cloud from host groups with ESX/ESXi hosts or from a VMware resource pool.
	VMM does not support or integrate with VMware vCloud.
Dynamic Optimization	The new VMM Dynamic Optimization features can be used with ESX hosts.
Power Optimization	For this functionality, the Dynamic Optimization feature in VMM or VMware Distributed Resource Scheduler can be used.
Live migration	Live migration between hosts within the cluster is supported by VMM 2012 and uses VMware vMotion.
Live storage migration	Supported by VMM 2012 and uses VMware Storage vMotion.
Networking	VMM identifies and uses the existing (it does not automatically create one) VMware vSwitches and port groups for the VM deployment.
Storage	VMM supports and identifies **VMware Paravirtual SCSI** (**PVSCSI**) storage adapters and thin-provisioned virtual hard disks.
	VMware VMs with virtual hard disks that are connected to an **Integrated Drive Electronics** (**IDE**) bus are not supported by VMM. Also, note that the storage connection for the VMware ESX hosts should be configured outside VMM, as the new VMM storage automation features are not supported on the ESX hosts.

Functionalities supported by VMM	Notes
Library	You can organize and store VMware VMs, **VMware Virtual Machine Disk (VMDK) files**, and templates in the VMM library. You can create new VMs from templates or by converting stored VMware VMs to Hyper-V VMs.
	The VMware thin provision disk is converted to thick when migrated to the VMM library.
	VMM does not support older VMDK disk types. Supported disks are: VMFS and monolithicflat, vmfsPassthroughRawDeviceMap, and snapshots: vmfssparse.
The VMM command shell	VMM PowerShell commands are common across the supported hypervisors.
Services	You can deploy VMM services to ESX hosts, but keep in mind that VMM uses a different model than VMware vApp, and the two methods can coexist.
	VMM cannot be used to deploy vApps.

Getting ready

There are some prerequisites that need to be taken into account when integrating VMware vCenter with VMM 2012 R2. These requirements are as follows:

-   One of the following supported versions of VMware vCenter is running:
    -   VMware vCenter Server 4.1
    -   VMware vCenter Server 5.0
    -   VMware vCenter Server 5.1

> Due to release updates, always check for the updated supported version at the Microsoft official site at http://technet.microsoft.com/library/gg697603.aspx.

-   An SSL certificate is required for communication between the VMM management server and the VMware vCenter Server if encryption is being used in order to verify the identity of the vCenter Server.

-   You must create a Run As account that has administrative permissions on the vCenter Server. It is possible to use a local account or a recommended domain account (for example, lab\VMwareAdmin). Either way, the account needs local admin rights on the vCenter Server.

How to do it...

Carry out the following steps to integrate the vCenter Server with VMM.

> If a *self-signed certificate* is being used, you can use the steps given in the following section, or you can import the certificate during the *adding vCenter to VMM* task you will be prompted to.

Importing the VMware self-signed SSL certificate

For the integration to work, VMM needs to communicate with the vSphere infrastructure via vCenter over SSL. Carry out the following steps to import the self-signed SSL certificate:

1. Make sure you log on to the VMM server as a local administrator or with a domain account with local administrator rights (for example, `lab\vmm-admin`).

2. Open Internet Explorer and go to `https://vCenter.lab.local/`.

> If you have logged in using an account that doesn't have local administrator rights, hold down the *Shift* key and right-click on the Internet Explorer icon, and then click on **Run as administrator**.

3. Click on **Continue to this web site (not recommended)** when you get a warning that says that the SSL certificate is not trusted.

4. Click on **Certificate Error** in the Security Status bar, select **View Certificate**, and click on **Install Certificate**.

5. On the **Certificate Import Wizard** window, click on **Place all certificates in the following store** and then click on **Browse**.

6. On the **Select Certificate Store** window, select the checkbox for **Show physical stores**.

7. Expand **Trusted People**, select **Local Computer**, and click on **OK**.

> If you don't see the **Local Computer** option under **Trusted People**, it means that you are logged in with an account that does not have sufficient permissions.

8. Click on **Finish** to complete the process of importing the certificate.

9. Click on **OK** when a window that says the import was successful is displayed.

10. To verify the process, close Internet Explorer, and then reopen it. Next, browse to the location of the vCenter Server (for example, `https://vCenter.lab.local/`); if you do not receive a certificate error, it means the certificate was correctly imported and you can proceed to the next step.

Adding vCenter to VMM

Carry out the following steps to add VMware vCenter in VMM:

1. Open the VMM console, and in the **Fabric** workspace in the **Fabric Resources** pane, click on **Servers**, and then click on **vCenter Servers**, as shown in the following screenshot:

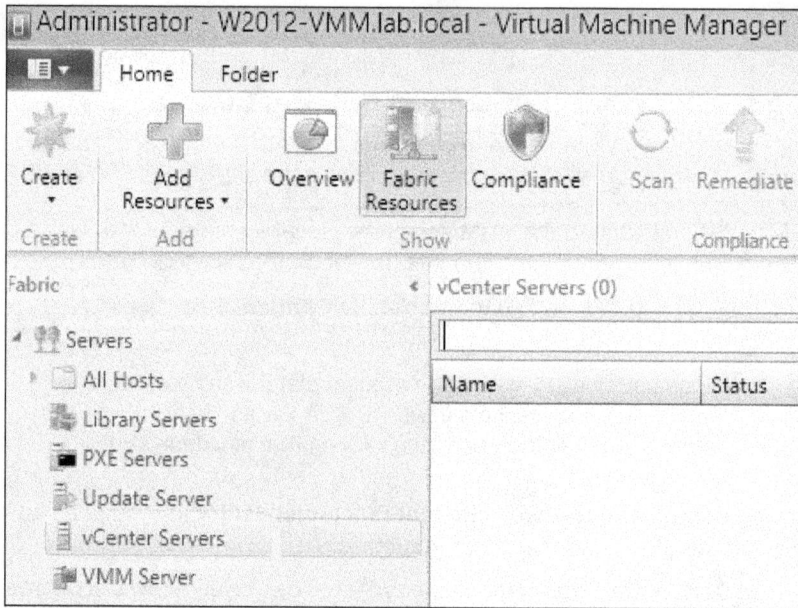

2. On the **Home** tab in the ribbon, click on **Add Resources**, and select **VMware vCenter Server**.

> You can also select **vCenter Servers** in the left-hand side pane, and then right-click on it and select **Add VMware vCenter Server**.

3. On the **Add VMware vCenter Server** dialog box in the **Computer name** field, type in the name of the vCenter Server (for example, `vcenter.lab.local`), that is, you can enter the NetBIOS name, FQDN, or the IP address.

4. On the **TCP/IP port** field, type in the port number that is required to connect to the vCenter Server (the default is `443`), or use the drop-down arrows.

5. For the **Run As account** field, click on **Browse**, and select a Run As account that has administrative rights on the vCenter Server; then, click on **OK**. The following screenshot shows the **Add VMware vCenter Server** dialog box:

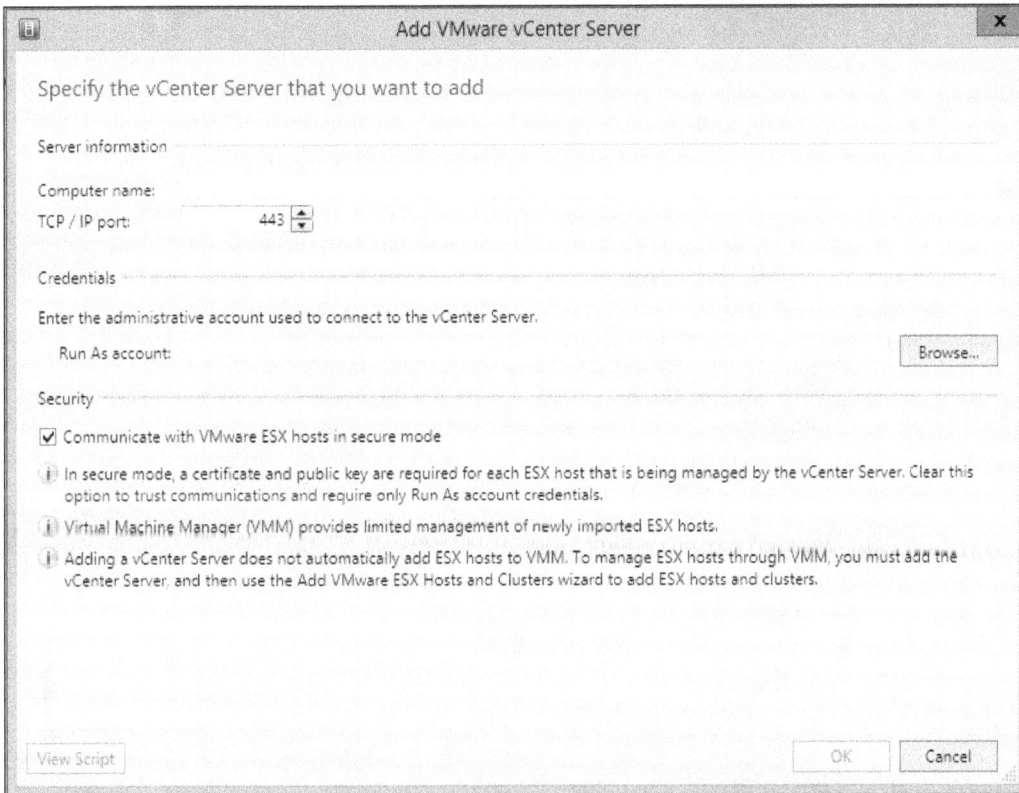

6. Under **Security**, select **Communicate with VMware ESX hosts in secure mode** to use the SSL encryption.

> When **Communicate with VMware ESX hosts in secure mode** is selected (the recommended approach), a certificate and public key will be required for each vCenter host.
>
> If this option is not selected, you will only need the Run As account credentials for communication between VMM and vCenter.

7. Click on **OK** to finish and then verify that the vCenter Server has the status of **Completed** in the **Jobs** dialog box.

8. If you are making use of a self-signed certificate for vCenter, make sure that you have first copied it into the **Trusted People certificate store** on the VMM management server. Otherwise, click on **Import** in the **Import Certificate** dialog box to have the certificate added to the Trusted People certificate store.

How it works...

VMM has an abstraction layer that lets you manage multiple hypervisor platforms, such as Hyper-V, Citrix XenServers, and VMware vSphere, making resources from these platforms available for datacenter and private cloud deployments by using a common user interface (the VMM console and PowerShell).

In order to manage VMware hosts, VMM requires integration with the VMware vCenter Server. You can then use the VMM console to manage VMware ESX/ESXi hosts and host clusters, such as the discovery of these hosts and the ability to create, manage, save, and deploy VMs on them.

Before integrating VMware vCenter with VMM, it is highly recommended that you create a Run As account with local administrative access rights on the vCenter Server.

In VMM 2012, in terms of adding/integrating a VMware vCenter Server, VMM no longer imports, merges, or synchronizes the VMware tree structure. You will need to manually select and add ESX servers and hosts to a VMM host group. Therefore, you will come across fewer issues during the synchronization.

> You don't need to enable SSH (the root secure shell) access on the ESX hosts. The VMM delegate is not supported since VMM 2008 R2 as VMM 2012 no longer supports SFTP for file transfers.

In order to ensure best practice, it is recommended that you use the secure mode communication to integrate VMM and VMware vCenter. To do so, you can import the self-signed SSL certificate from vCenter, or you can use a third-party certificate. You can choose to use the self-signed certificate in addition to the vCenter certificate; in this case, you will be required to resolve the ESX hosts' SSL certificates so that they are trusted, or you can choose to simply rely on the Run As account.

> If you choose to use a public third-party certificate, you are not required to import the SSL certificate into the Trusted People certificate store.

See also

▶ The *System Requirements: VMware ESX Hosts* article at `http://technet.microsoft.com/library/gg697603.aspx`

Adding VMware ESX hosts or host clusters to VMM

Now that you've integrated vCenter with VMM, you can start adding the ESX hosts that are to be managed by VMM.

Getting ready

The following is a list of some prerequisites and recommendations that need to be taken into account when adding VMware hosts to VMM 2012 R2:

▸ The VMware vCenter Server that manages the ESX hosts must already be configured and integrated into VMM

▸ The host must run a supported version of VMware vSphere. For more information, refer to *Chapter 1, VMM 2012 Architecture*

▸ If encryption is required for communication between VMM and the vSphere hosts, a certificate and public key for each managed ESX/ESXi host will be needed

▸ Although it is not a requirement, you can create a host group to organize the hosts (for example, VMware Hosts)

▸ As per best practices, create a Run As account with root credentials on the VMware ESX hosts

> Although it is possible to create the Run As account when adding the ESX hosts, as per VMM best practice, it is recommended that you create it before the addition of hosts.

How to do it...

Carry out the following steps to add VMware ESX hosts or clusters to VMM:

1. On the **Fabric** workspace in the VMM console, click on **Add Resources** in the **Home** tab; then, click on **VMware ESX Hosts and Clusters**, as shown in the following screenshot:

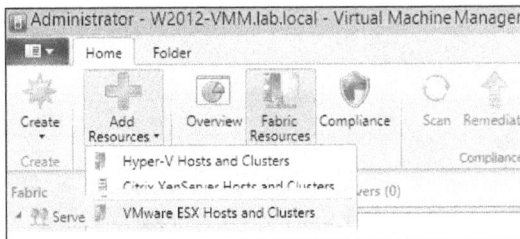

2. On the **Run As account** box in the **Credentials** page of the **Add Resource Wizard** window, click on **Browse** and select a Run As account with root credentials on the VMware ESX/ESXi host.

3. Click on **OK**, and then click on **Next**.

4. On the **VMware vCenter Server** list in the **Target resources** page, select the vCenter Server (for example, **vcenter**).

> The available ESX hosts and clusters will be listed for the selected vCenter Server.

5. Select the VMware ESX host(s) or host cluster to be added, as shown in the following screenshot:

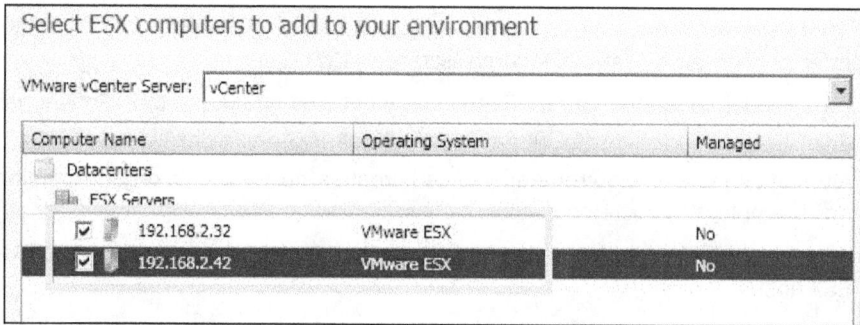

Select ESX computers to add to your environment

VMware vCenter Server: vCenter

Computer Name	Operating System	Managed
Datacenters		
ESX Servers		
☑ 192.168.2.32	VMware ESX	No
☑ 192.168.2.42	VMware ESX	No

6. Click on **Next**.

7. On the **Location** list in the **Host settings** page, select the host group to assign the hosts to, and click on **Next**.

> You can change the placement path for these hosts if you want to.

8. On the **Summary** page, click on **Finish**.

9. After verifying that the **Job Status** column displays **Completed**, close the dialog box.

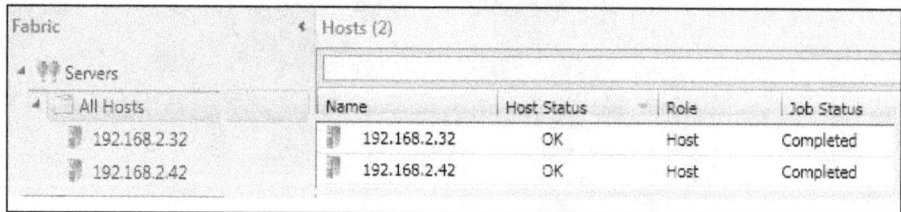

Fabric		Hosts (2)			
▲ Servers					
▲ All Hosts		Name	Host Status	Role	Job Status
192.168.2.32		192.168.2.32	OK	Host	Completed
192.168.2.42		192.168.2.42	OK	Host	Completed

How it works...

The steps to add VMware hosts or clusters are pretty straightforward. After integrating vCenter, select **VMware ESX Hosts and Clusters** on the **Add Resources** wizard, making sure that you have created a Run As account that has root credentials in the ESXi hosts. You can add one or more hosts, as well as VMware clusters.

If you require encryption, you can either use the self-signed certificate that was created when you installed the VMware ESX/ESXi hosts or a public, trusted certificate. Note that if you decide to use the self-signed certificate, you are required to import it from each ESX host to the VMM management server. You don't need to carry out this task if you are using an SSL certificate from a trusted certification authority.

There's more...

Carry out the following steps to verify that the ESX host or host cluster was added correctly:

1. On the **Fabric** workspace in the VMM console, expand **Servers**; go to **All Hosts**, and then expand and select the host group where you previously added the ESX host/cluster (for example, VMware Hosts).

2. Verify that each host in the **Hosts** pane has a status of either **OK** or **OK (Limited)**.

> If the status of the host shows **OK (Limited)**, it could indicate that the specified Run As account does not have the correct credentials (that is, it does not have the root credentials or does not have the requisite permissions) or that you have enabled the secure mode but have not imported an SSL certificate and public key.

3. If the host status is **OK (Limited)**, you should correct the credentials or remove the secure mode for that host to enable management through VMM.

Updating the host status to OK

To update the host status to **OK**, perform the following steps:

1. On the **Fabric** pane in the VMM console, expand **Servers**, and then expand **vCenter Servers**.

2. On the **vCenter Servers** pane, select and right-click on the vCenter Server; click on **Properties**, confirm the secure mode setting, and click on **OK** to close it.

3. For each VMware host that has the **OK (Limited)** status, right-click and click on **Properties**.

4. Select the **Management** tab, and confirm the Run As account.

5. Click on **Retrieve** to claim the host SSL certificate and public key, and then click on **View Details** to see the certificate.

6. Click on **Accept the certificate for this host** to confirm, and then click on **OK**.

7. If the credentials of the secure mode are correctly configured, the host status will display **OK** in the **Hosts** pane.

8. Repeat these tasks for each host with the **OK (Limited)** status.

See also

▸ The *Adding VMware vCenter Server to VMM* recipe

Configuring network settings on a VMware ESX host

This recipe will guide you through the configuration of a logical network on the VMware host and show you how to view compliance data for the physical network adapters on that host.

To make the host physical network adapters visible to the VMs that need external network access, you will need to assign them to logical networks.

Compliance data specifies whether or not IP subnets and/or VLANs allotted to a logical network are assigned to a host physical network adapter.

How to do it...

Carry out the following steps to associate logical networks with a physical network adapter:

1. On the **Fabric** pane in the VMM console, expand **Servers**, expand **All Hosts**, and then select the host group where the VMware ESX host resides (for example, VMware Hosts).

2. On the **Hosts** pane, select the VMware ESX host, and then click on **Properties** in the **Host** tab in the ribbon.

3. Select the **Hardware** tab, and select the physical network adapter to be configured in **Network Adapters**.

> Be careful when selecting the logical network, as all the logical networks for this host group will be listed and not just the available ones.

4. On the **Logical network connectivity** list, select the logical network(s) that are to be associated with the physical network adapter.

> In the previous VMM 2012 version, click on **Advanced** to configure the advanced settings.

Configuring the network settings for a host

Carry out the following steps to apply the logical network to a host:

1. In the **Fabric** pane, expand **Servers**, and then expand **All Hosts**.

2. Select the *host* you want to configure and on the **Hosts** pane, click on **Properties** in the ribbon.

3. When the dialog box appears, click on the **Virtual Switches** tab and select the previously created *logical switch* from the list.

> You can click on **New Virtual Switch**, and then click on **New Logical Switch** to create a new logical switch.

4. Select the *logical switch* from the list, and then select the physical adapter.

5. Select **Uplink Port Profile** from the list.

> If profile displays no port, review the logical switch configuration.

6. Click on **OK** to complete the configuration.

> To team two or more physical network adapters, make sure that the uplink mode setting is configured to team and then apply the same logical switch and uplink port profile.

How it works...

To assign VMM logical networks with a physical network adapter, select the VMware ESXi host in the **Fabric** workspace, and then select the physical network adapter under **Hardware**. Note that when selecting the logical network, *all logical networks* are listed.

For each selected logical network, the IPs and VLANs defined for a host group, or ones inherited through the parent host group, will be assigned to a physical network adapter by default.

If no IPs or VLANs show up in the **Available** or **Assigned** columns, it means that no network site exists for the selected logical network that is defined on or inherited by the host group.

If you're using VLANs, you will need to make use of VMware vCenter to configure the port groups with the VLAN for the corresponding network site.

There's more...

You can verify a VMware ESX host's network settings and compliance information in VMM. We'll see how to do this in the upcoming sections.

Verifying the settings for a virtual switch

Carry out the following steps to check the network settings for a virtual switch:

1. On the **Fabric** pane in the VMM console, expand **Servers**; under **Servers**, expand **All Hosts**, and select the host group where the VMware ESX host resides (for example, VMware Hosts).

2. On the **Hosts** pane, select the ESX host; then, on the **Host** tab in the ribbon, click on **Properties**, and click on the **Virtual Switches** tab.

3. On the **Virtual Switches** list, select the virtual network whose properties you'd like to view.

4. In the **Logical** network list, check whether the logical network is assigned to a physical network adapter.

Viewing the compliance information for a physical network adapter

Carry out the following steps to see the compliance information for a physical network adapter:

1. On the **Fabric** workspace in the VMM console, expand **Networking** on the **Fabric** pane; then, click on **Logical Networks**.

2. On the **Home** tab in the ribbon, click on **Hosts**.

3. On the **Logical Network Information for Hosts** pane, expand the host and select a physical network adapter. For this network adapter, the assigned IP subnets and VLANs will be displayed in the details pane.

4. In the **Compliance** column, the compliance status will show you one of the following values:

   - **Fully compliant**: This status confirms that all the IPs and VLANs that are included in the network site are allotted to a physical network adapter.

   - **Partially compliant**: This status indicates incomplete information. The IPs and/or VLANs in the network list and those assigned to a network adapter do not match.

> Check the reason for partial compliance in the **Compliance errors** section.

- **Non-compliant**: This status indicates there are no IPs and/or VLANs defined for the logical networks that are associated with a physical network adapter.

See also

▶ The *Adding VMware vCenter Server to VMM* recipe

Configuring host BMC settings

VMM 2012 supports Dynamic Optimization and Power Optimization on Hyper-V host clusters and on managed VMware ESX and Citrix XenServer host clusters that support live migration.

Power Optimization, an optional feature of Dynamic Optimization, is enabled only if a host group is configured for the live migration of VMs through Dynamic Optimization. In order to meet resource requirements and save energy, it shuts down hosts that are not needed by the cluster and turns them on only when they are needed.

There is a requirement that the servers must have a **Baseboard Management Controller** (**BMC**) that supports out-of-band management.

In order to configure the host BMC, the installed BMC controller must support one of the following BMC protocols:

▶ **System Management Architecture for Server Hardware** (**SMASH**) Version 1.0 over WS-Management (WS-Man)

▶ **Intelligent Platform Management Interface** (**IPMI**) Version 1.5 or 2.0

▶ **Data Center Management Interface** (**DCMI**) Version 1.0

How to do it...

Carry out the following steps to configure the BMC settings:

1. On the **Fabric** pane in the VMM console, expand **Servers**; under **Servers**, expand **All Hosts**; then, in the **Host** pane, select the host you want to configure.

2. On the **Host** tab in the ribbon, click on **Properties**.

3. Select the **Hardware** tab, and click on **BMC Setting**; then select **This physical machine is configured for OOB management with the following settings**.

4. Select the *BMC protocol* from the power management configuration provider list.

5. In the **BMC address** field, type in the IP address of the BMC.

> VMM will automatically fill in the port number for the selected BMC protocol.

6. For the Run As account field, click on **Browse**, select the Run As account with the BMC access rights, and click on **OK**.

How it works...

For Power Optimization to work, the servers must have a supported BMC controller. In order to benefit from Power Optimization, it is important to verify that your server has a supported BMC and that you have installed one of the supported protocols before carrying out the process to configure the BMC on each host.

By using a BMC, VMM can power the host on or off.

There's more...

Now that the BMC is configured, you can use it to turn the servers on or off.

Powering a computer on or off through VMM

Carry out the following steps to turn servers on or off through VMM:

1. On the **Fabric** pane in the VMM console, expand **Servers**; then, expand **All Hosts**, and select the host that is to be configured in the **Host** pane.

2. On the **Host** tab, select one of the following available options: **Power On**, **Power Off**, **Shutdown**, or **Reset**.

> To view the BMC log information, select the **Hardware** tab in the host properties, and in the **Advanced** section, click on **BMC Logs**.

See also

▶ The *Configuring Dynamic and Power Optimization in VMM* article at
  http://technet.microsoft.com/en-us/library/gg675109.aspx

Importing VMware templates

This recipe focuses on importing VMware templates to VMM.

In VMM 2012, the VMware virtual machine disk (.vmdk) file is not copied/moved to the VMM library while importing a VMware template. Now, VMM copies the metadata associated with the VMware template, and the VMDK file remains in the VMware datastore.

By employing this approach, VMM allows you to deploy VMs more efficiently and quickly when using templates. Moreover, VMM 2012 does not delete the source template.

> VMM 2012 is highly dependent on the VMware template that resides on the vCenter Server.

How to do it...

Carry out the following steps to configure the BMC settings:

1. On the **Library** workspace in the VMM console, click on **Import VMware Template** on the **Home** tab in the ribbon.

2. Select the VMware template(s) to be imported and click on **OK**.

3. To confirm that the template was added, expand **Templates**, and click on **VM Templates** in the **Library** pane.

How it works...

In VMM, only the metadata associated with a VMware template is copied to the VMM library. The virtual machine disk (.vmdk) file remains in the VMware datastore.

If the template is removed from vCenter Server, it will go into a missing state in VMM. On the other hand, if you convert it into a VM, make some changes, and then convert it back to a template, the ID will remain the same and VMM will set its state as OK instead of missing.

> When the VMware template is removed from the VMM library, it is not deleted from the VMware datastore.

See also

▶ The *Adding VMware ESX hosts or host clusters to VMM* recipe

Converting VMware virtual machines to Hyper-V

You can convert any virtual machine that runs on a VMware ESX host or is stored in the VMM library, but VMM does not support virtual-to-virtual (V2V) conversion of a VMware VM that has an IDE bus.

The following versions of VMware ESX are supported for V2V conversions by VMM 2012 R2:

- ESX/ESXi 3.5 Update 5
- ESX/ESXi 4.0
- ESX/ESXi 4.1
- ESX/ESXi 5.0
- ESXi 5.1

> Before you convert a VMware VM to a Hyper-V VM, you must uninstall VMware Tools on the source VM.

This recipe will guide you on how to convert a VMware VM to a Hyper-V VM through the V2V conversion process.

How to do it...

Carry out the following steps to convert VMs:

1. On the **VMs and Services** workspace in the VMM console on the **Home** tab in the ribbon, click on **Create Virtual Machine** and then on **Convert Virtual Machine**, as shown in the following screenshot:

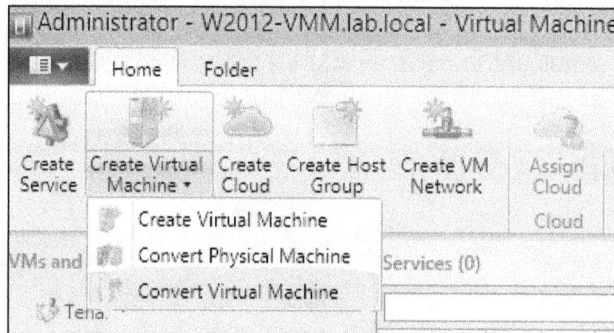

2. On the **Select Source** page in **Convert Virtual Machine Wizard**, click on **Browse...**, and select the VMware VM that is to be converted, as shown in the following screenshot:

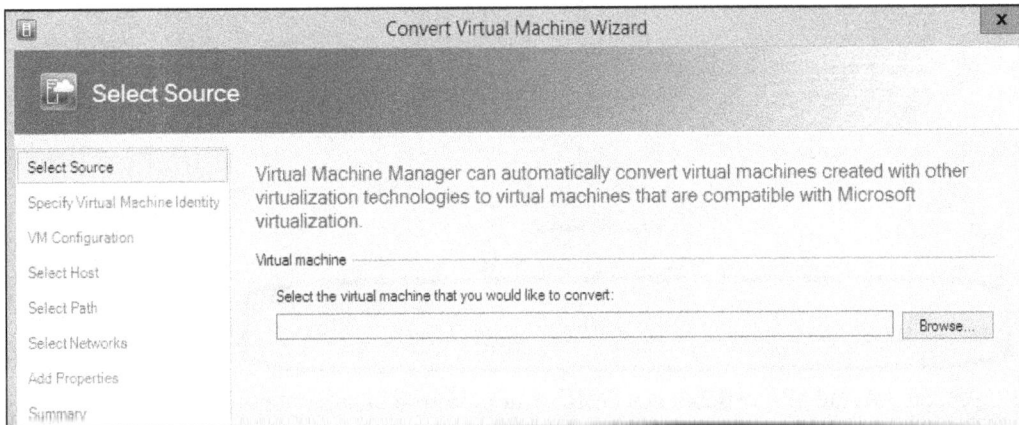

3. Click on **OK**; then, on the **Select Source** page, click on **Next**.

4. On the **Specify Virtual Machine Identity** page, confirm the VM name (you can change it if you want), type in a description (optional), and click on **Next**.

> The VM name does not have to match the computer name (the NetBIOS name), but as a best practice, it is recommended that you keep both names the same.

5. On the **Virtual Machine Configuration** page, set the number of processor(s) and the memory, and click on **Next**.

6. On the **Select Host** page, select the target Hyper-V host, and click on **Next**.

7. On the **Select Path** page, specify the VM file's storage location.

> The default VM paths on the target host will be displayed now. You can select a different path. Click on **Browse**, select the path/folder, and click on **OK**. Then, you can click on **Add this path to the list of default storage locations on the host** if you want this path to be a part of the default VM's path.

8. On the **Select Networks** page, select the VM network, logical network, and VLAN (if applicable) and click on **Next**.

Specify which virtual switches to use for the virtual machine.

Selected host: hyperv.lab.local

Virtual Network Adapter	VM Network	Virtual Switch	VLAN
Network Adapter 1	Not connected ⌄	Not connected ⌄	VLAN disabled ⌄
	Not connected		
	v-DMZ		
	vm-Production-Customer		
	v-Production		
	v-Production-CustomerA		

9. On the **Add properties** page, select your preferred actions from the **Automatic actions** list.

10. On the **Summary** page, click on **Start the virtual machine after deploying it**; then, click on **Create**.

11. Verify that the job status shows **Completed**, and then close the dialog box.

12. To verify that the virtual machine was converted, select the Hyper-V host that you chose earlier in this task in the **VMs and Services** workspace.

13. On the **Home** tab, click on **VMs**; then, in the **VMs** pane, verify that the VM appears.

How it works...

If you are running a supported version of a VMware VM, start by confirming that the source VM does not have an IDE bus, as VMM does not support it.

Then, open the VMM console and click on **Convert Virtual Machine** on the ribbon. Carry out the steps given in the previous section by first selecting the VM that you want to convert.

You can change the VM name when prompted for the VM identity, and optionally, you can type in a description for it. The VM name does not necessarily have to match the computer name (the NetBIOS name), but as a best practice, it is recommended that you keep them the same.

On the VM's configuration page, you can change the number of allocated processors and the memory assigned while keeping the source configuration or changing it for the target VM.

By default, the VM paths on the target host will be displayed when selecting the path for the VM, but you can specify a different one (if required) and make it the default path, as well.

Select the network you want the VM to be assigned to, and configure the desired settings on the **Add Properties** page. Confirm all the settings on the summary page, and click on **Create** to start the virtual-to-virtual machine conversion process.

See also

▶   The *Adding VMware ESX hosts or host clusters to VMM* recipe

Managing Citrix® XenServer® hosts and pools

Using VMM, you can deploy and manage Citrix XenServer hosts and pools (clusters). VMM manages XenServer hosts directly.

You can perform functions such as discovery, creation, management, storage, and deployment of VMs and services on XenServer hosts and pools.

You can also make XenServer resources available to private cloud deployments using the VMM console or PowerShell.

The following Xen features are supported by VMM:

▶   Standalone XenServer hosts and pools (clusters).

▶   VM placement based on host ratings when creating, deploying, and migrating XenServer VMs.

▶   The deployment of VMM services to XenServer hosts.

▶   XenServer resources, which can be made available to a private cloud when creating it from host groups that have XenServer hosts.

▶   You can configure quotas for private clouds and application (self service) roles assigned to private clouds.

▶   The VMM Dynamic Optimization feature for XenServer hosts and clusters.

▶   The live migration between XenServer hosts in a cluster (pool); it is only supported through Citrix XenMotion.

▶   The LAN migration between a host and the library through BITS.

▶   A XenServer host that can be placed in the maintenance mode using the VMM console if it is managed by VMM.

▶   You can store XenServer VMs, VHD files, and VMM templates in the VMM library. VMM supports the creation of new VMs from these templates.

▶   Although you cannot use XenServer templates with VMM, you can use XenCenter to create a VM and then create a VMM template from this VM.

▸ VMM networking management features are supported on XenServer hosts, but you are required to create external virtual switches through XenCenter. VMM will recognize and use existing external networks for the VM deployment.

▸ All virtual disk storage repositories that are supported by XenServer.

▸ Converting a XenServer VM that runs a supported guest OS to a Hyper-V VM is supported using the (physical-to-virtual) P2V machine conversion.

> The VMM 2012 R2 version does not have the P2V feature. You can use the VMM 2012 SP1, and when doing so, it is not required to remove Citrix Tools before the P2V process.

▸ VMM can also support **Paravirtual** (**PV**) and hardware-assisted virtualization (HVM) VMs, but with restrictions.

▸ Monitoring and alerting for XenServer hosts through VMM, when it is integrated with SC Operations Manager and PRO.

The following Xen features are not supported by VMM:

▸ The LAN migration (host-to-host migration of VMs that have been stopped) between XenServer and other hosts

▸ Updating management through VMM (you cannot use WSUS to update XenServer hosts)

▸ Conversion of a Bare Metal computer to a XenServer host and cluster creation

This recipe will take you through the process of integrating Citrix XenServer with VMM.

Getting ready

Make sure you install and configure XenServer before adding the hosts to the VMM management.

> If you want to add a XenServer pool (multiple XenServer host installations that are bound together as a single-managed entity), you will first need to create and configure it in Citrix XenCenter.

Also, you must have a DHCP server to assign the IP addresses automatically; it needs to be accessible from the management network for Citrix Transfer VMs; these are templates for virtual machines that support Paravirtualization, which are created and deleted on the XenServer host during operations in XenServer.

Also, check whether the following conditions are met:

▸ Whether the Citrix Host(s) meets the requirements. Refer to the *System Requirements: Citrix XenServer Hosts* article at `http://go.microsoft.com/fwlink/p/?LinkID=217487`

▸ Whether you've already created a Run As account with root credentials on the Citrix hosts that you want to add

How to do it...

Carry out the procedures discussed in the upcoming sections to integrate Citrix with VMM.

Creating a pool on Citrix® XenCenter®

Carry out the following steps to create a pool in XenCenter:

1. Open XenCenter, and on the toolbar, click on the **New Pool** button, as shown in the following screenshot:

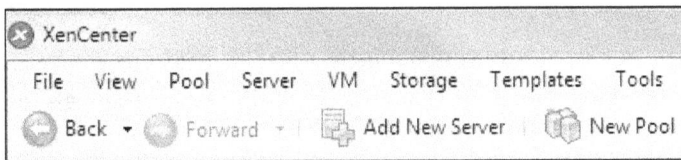

2. Type in a name and optional description for the new pool (for example, `XS Pool1`).

3. Nominate the pool master by selecting a host from the **Master** list; then, select the second host to be placed in the new pool from the **Additional members** list.

4. Click on **Create Pool** and confirm that the new pool shows in the **Resources** pane, as shown in the following screenshot:

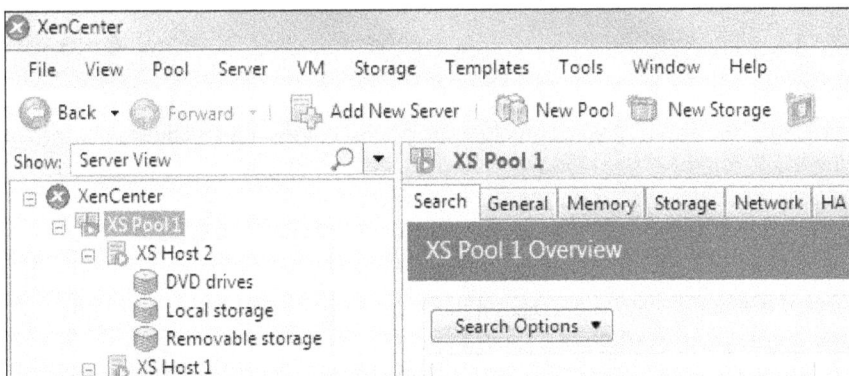

Adding Citrix® XenServer® hosts to VMM

Carry out the following tasks to add the XenServer host to VMM:

1. On the **Fabric** pane in the VMM console, expand **Servers**; on the **Home** tab in the ribbon, click on **Add Resources**.

2. Click on **Citrix XenServer Hosts and Cluster**; in the **Add Resource Wizard** window, go to the **Server Settings** page, and type in the name of the XenServer host in the **Computer name** field.

> You can type in the FQDN, the NetBIOS, or the IP address. To add a XenServer pool, you can type in the IP address or the name of any XenServer host in the pool.

3. On **TCP port**, specify the XenServer host port.

> The default XenServer host port is TCP 5989.

4. Select **Use certificates to communicate with this host**.

5. Click on **Browse** to select the Run As account with root credentials (or equivalent) on the XenServer host(s), click on **OK**, and then click on **Next**.

6. On the **Host group** list, select the target host group (for example, **Citrix Servers**), and click on **Add**.

7. Each XenServer host that is listed should match the name of the issued certificate. Confirm that the certificate for each host is valid, select **These certificates have been reviewed and can be imported to the trusted certificate store**, and click on **Next**.

8. On the **Summary** page, click on **Finish**.

9. Verify that the job has the status of **Completed**, and then close the dialog box.

How it works...

You can add Citrix XenServer hosts and clusters (pools) using **Add Resources** in the **Fabric** pane on the VMM console. When adding a Xen pool (cluster), you don't need to specify the master host, as you can select it during the operation.

You can specify an IP address or name, but it needs to be resolved by your DNS servers.

VMM discovers the XenServer(s) and lists it in the lower pane. When you add a pool, it will be listed along with each XenServer host in the pool.

During the addition process, you need to verify whether each listed XenServer matches the name of the issued certificate by clicking on a host and then clicking on **View certificate**. If you find XenServer with a certificate that is not valid, click on **Remove** to delete it from the list.

If all XenServer hosts have a valid certificate, you can select **These certificates have been reviewed and can be imported to the trusted certificate store**.

Confirm the settings and click on **Finish** to add the XenServer(s) to the VMM management.

There's more...

If you have issues adding a XenServer host, check whether the DNS name is getting resolved and whether you can ping the host.

Troubleshooting a failed job when adding XenServer® hosts

Carry out the following steps to troubleshoot a failed job when adding XenServer hosts:

1. Using the following command, check whether it is possible to ping the host by the name or IP address:

   ```
   C:\> ping 192.168.4.21
   ```

2. Check whether the server/computer name is getting resolved by the DNS server using the following commands:

   ```
   C:\>nslookup  xen-host1
   C:\>ping   -a xen-host1
   ```

3. Verify that the supplemental pack is correctly installed on each XenServer host, as follows:

   ```
   C:\>winrm enum http://schemas.citrix.com/wbem/wscim/1/cim-
   schema/2/Xen_HostComputerSystem -r:https://<XenHost>:5989 -
   encoding:utf-8 -a:basic -u:<USER> -p:<PASSWD> -skipcacheck -
   skipcncheck
   ```

   Here, <XenHost> is the XenServer host, <USER> is the XenServer root user, and <PASSWD> is the password of the root user.

   > If the command does not return information about the host computer, it could indicate that the supplemental pack is not installed or is malfunctioning. In such a case, reinstall it.

4. Verify whether the host was added successfully; in the **Fabric** pane on the VMM console, expand **Servers**; then, expand the host group (for example, **Citrix Hosts**), and select the XenServer host. In the **Hosts** pane, confirm that the XenServer host status shows **OK**.

See also

▶ The *System Requirements: Citrix XenServer Hosts* article at
`http://go.microsoft.com/fwlink/p/?LinkID=217487`

▶ The *How to Configure Network Settings on a Citrix XenServer Host* article at
`http://technet.microsoft.com/en-us/library/gg610697.aspx`

▶ The *Citrix XenServer® 5.6 Feature Pack 1 Quick Start Guide* document at
`http://support.citrix.com/servlet/KbServlet/`
`download/25588-102-666369/QuickStartGuide_BasicVersion.pdf`

Converting Citrix® virtual machines to Hyper-V

Converting a Citrix XenServer VM to a Hyper-V VM is supported, and it is done using the P2V process. The procedure described in this recipe is exactly the same as the one used to convert physical servers to Hyper-V VMs.

> VMM 2012 R2 no longer has the P2V feature, and now it is not possible to use VMM 2012 R2 to convert a XenServer VM to a Hyper-V VM or perform other P2V conversions.

The steps described in this section are valid for the VMM 2012 SP1 version. An alternative is to use the Disk2VHD tool, for which the P2V process is described at `http://social.technet.microsoft.com/wiki/contents/articles/9790.hyper-v-p2v-with-disk2vhd.aspx`. You can also use third-party tools such as 5nine Migrator, which offers P2V, V2V Migration, and Capacity Planning, and can be found at `http://www.5nine.com/p2v-migration.aspx`.

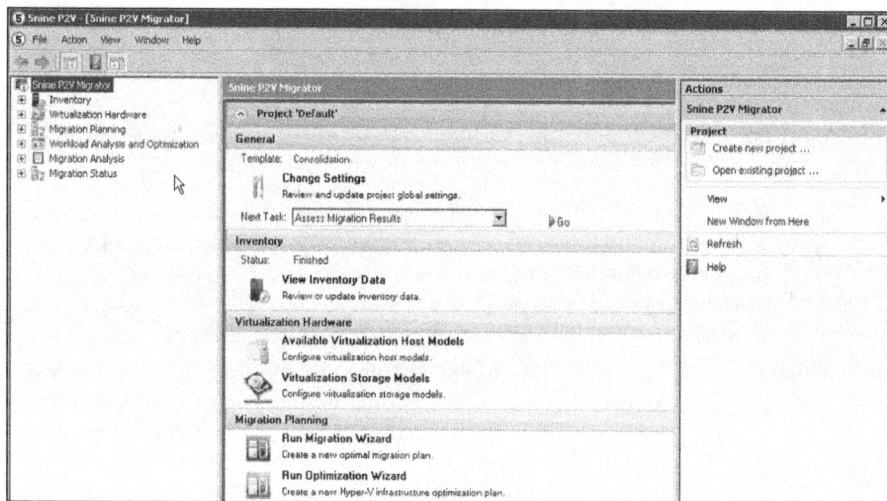

However, note that only running VMs are supported for the conversion in VMM 2012 SP1. The source VM must also be running a supported Windows guest OS. You can check the supported operating systems at `http://technet.microsoft.com/en-us/library/hh427293.aspx`.

Additionally, the source machine needs to meet the following requirements:

- A minimum RAM of 512 MB
- Cannot have a volume larger than 2 TB
- Must have an **Advanced Configuration and Power Interface** (**ACPI**) BIOS
- Must be accessible to the VMM management server and host
- Should not have encrypted volumes

How to do it...

Carry out the following steps with VMM 2012 SP1 to convert a Citrix VM to a Hyper-V VM:

1. On the **Home** tab in the ribbon in the **VMs and Services** workspace on the VMM console, click on **Create Virtual Machine** and then select **Convert Physical Machine**.

2. Inside the **Convert Physical Server (P2V) Wizard** window, in the **Computer name or IP address** field in the **Select Source** section, type in the name or IP address of the XenServer virtual machine to be converted. The following screenshot shows you the **Select Source** section:

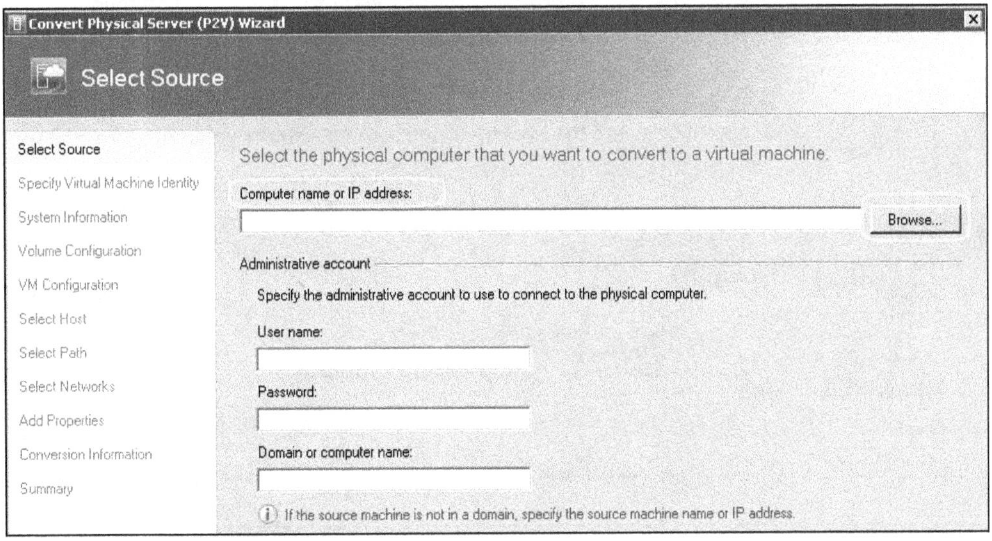

3. In the **Administrative account** section, specify the administrator credentials: **User name**, **Password**, and **Domain or computer name** (if applicable) to connect to the VM; then, click on **Next**.

4. On the **Specify Virtual Machine Identity** page, type in the VM's name and description (optional), and click on **Next**.

5. On the **System Information** page, click on **Scan System** to collect information about the VM as shown in the following screenshot, and then click on **Next** to continue:

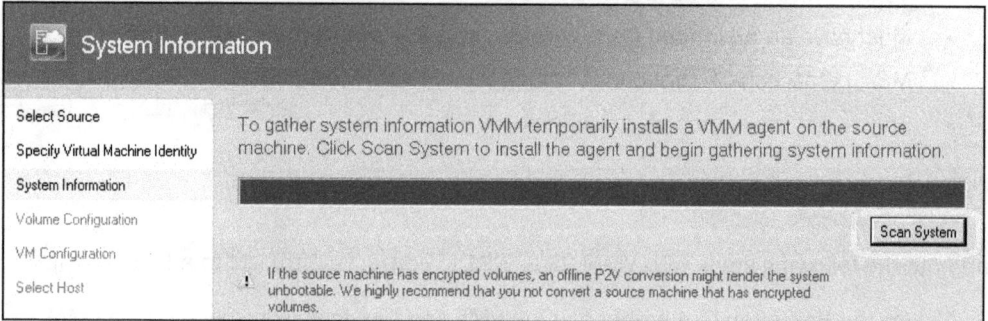

> VMM will install a VMM agent on the XenServer virtual machine to gather the system information.

6. In the **Volume Configuration** section, select the volumes to convert or clear the checkbox next to a particular volume if you don't want to convert it. The following screenshot shows you the **Volume Configuration** section:

> You cannot deselect the system or the system reserve volume.

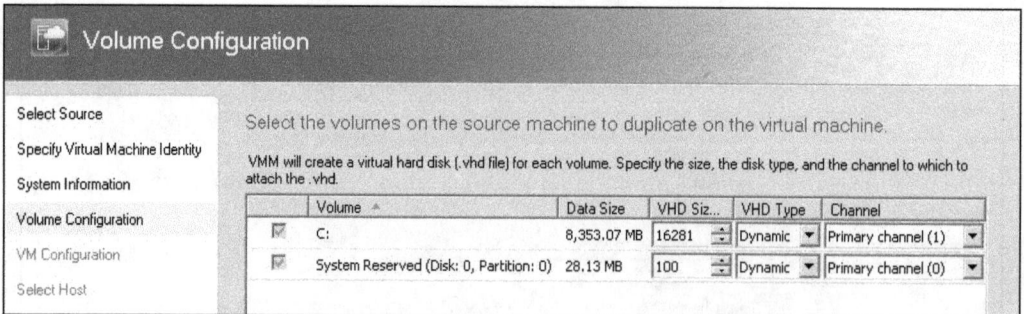

7. Confirm or modify the **VHD Size (MB)**, **VHD Type**, and **Channel** settings.

8. Click on **Conversion Options**; in the **Conversion Options** section, select **Online conversion** or **Offline conversion**, and click on **Next**.

> Optionally, click on **Turn off source computer after conversion**.

9. In the **Offline Conversion Options** section, if you select **Offline conversion**, you can either choose to use DHCP to automatically obtain an IP address, or you can choose a specific IP address. In the latter case, you will need to provide the IP address manually and click on **Next** to continue.

10. On the **VM Configuration** page, set the number of processors and the amount of memory for the new VM; then, click on **Next**.

11. On the **Select Host** page, review the host placement ratings, select a host (for example, **Hyperv01**), and click on **Next**.

12. On the **Select Path** page, specify the host storage location for the VM files, and then click on **Next**.

13. On the **Select Networks** page, configure the **VM Network, Logical Network**, and **VLAN** (if applicable) settings for each virtual network adapter, as shown in the following screenshot, and then click on **Next**:

Specify which virtual switches to use for the virtual machine.

Selected host: hyperv.lab.local

Virtual Network Adapter	VM Network	Virtual Switch	VLAN
Network Adapter 1	Not connected	Not connected	VLAN disabled
	Not connected		
	v-DMZ		
	vm-Production-Customer1		
	v-Production		
	v-Production-CustomerA		

14. On the **Add properties** page, select your preferred actions from the **Automatic actions** list.

15. If issues (for example, the guest OS is not supported or there are encrypted volumes) show up on the **Conversion Information** page, select the issue to view the error and see the suggested resolution. You should resolve the issues before continuing to the next step.

16. If no issues are detected, click on **Next**.

17. On the **Summary** page, click on **Start the virtual machine after deploying it**, and then click on **Create**.

18. Check the job status and then close the dialog box.

How it works...

To start, go to the VMM 2012 SP1 console, and then go to the **Home** tab in the **VMs and Services** workspace; then, click on **Convert Physical Machine** under the **Create Virtual Machine** button on the ribbon.

> The P2V feature was removed from VMM 2012 R2.

Specify the IP address or machine name, followed by the domain and login credentials. Keep in mind that you need administrative rights on the physical server that should be accessible from the VMM server.

It is possible to select the volume(s) that will be included in the conversion, but you cannot remove the system volume or system reserve volume. By default, VMM creates a VHD file for each volume.

If you choose to manually enter an IP address, after typing the address, you can select the network adapter that the IP address will be bound to.

After you click on the **Create** button to start the P2V process, it will take some time to process the VM conversion, as it depends on network speed and data size.

Make sure to turn off the XenServer VM if it has not been selected in the steps; otherwise, there will be a conflict between the two servers because the newly converted VM is a clone of the XenServer VM.

See also

▸ The list of supported operating systems in the *P2V Prerequisites in VMM* article at http://technet.microsoft.com/en-us/library/hh427293.aspx

▸ The *How to Convert Physical Computers to Virtual Machines* article at http://technet.microsoft.com/en-us/library/hh427286.aspx

8

Managing Hybrid Clouds, Fabric Updates, Resources, Clusters, and the New Features of R2

In this chapter, we will cover the following:

- ▶ Creating Hyper-V clusters
- ▶ Managing fabric updates
- ▶ Configuring Dynamic Optimization and Power Optimization
- ▶ Live migrating virtual machines
- ▶ Managing Linux virtual machines
- ▶ Configuring availability options and virtual NUMA for VMs
- ▶ Configuring resource throttling
- ▶ Integrating with the IPAM server for IP management
- ▶ Deploying SC App Controller 2012 R2 for hybrid cloud management
- ▶ Configuring Synthetic Fibre Channel

Introduction

In this chapter, we'll take a closer look at the additional management and features provided by VMM 2012 R2. We will also cover SC App Controller (which is the replacement for VMM Self-Service Portal), which will allow you to integrate with Windows Azure and manage your hybrid cloud.

In this chapter, we will continue to learn more about VMM management capabilities such as live migration, availability options, resource throttling, and virtual **Non-Uniform Memory Access** (**NUMA**).

Creating Hyper-V clusters

This recipe will guide you to create a Hyper-V cluster using VMM. Using the steps provided here, you will be able to select Hyper-V servers and join them to a cluster, configuring networking and storage resources in the process.

Getting ready

Before you start creating a Hyper-V cluster, there are some requirements that you need to look at. These are discussed in the next sections.

Prerequisites for cluster creation using VMM 2012

Make sure that the following prerequisites are met before creating a cluster:

- You need at least two standalone Hyper-V servers, and they need to be under VMM management already (see the *Adding and managing Hyper-V hosts and host clusters* recipe in *Chapter 5*, *Configuring Fabric Resources in VMM*).

- The hosts should meet the requirements for a Failover Clustering and should be running one of the following operating systems:

  - **For VMM 2012**: Windows Server 2008 R2 Enterprise Edition (SP1 or higher) or Windows Server 2008 R2 Datacenter Edition (SP1 or higher)

  - **For VMM 2012 SP1**: Windows Server 2008 R2 (Enterprise or Datacenter Edition) or Windows Server 2012 (any edition)

  - **For VMM 2012 R2**: Windows Server 2012 or Windows Server 2012 R2

> The roles and features are the same for all Windows 2012 editions (Standard or Datacenter).

▸ The OS is updated and the required hotfixes are applied.

> For clusters that have three or more nodes running Windows Server 2008 R2 SP1, refer to the Microsoft Knowledge Base (KB) article at `http://go.microsoft.com/fwlink/p?LinkId=225883`.

▸ The Hyper-V hosts must all be part of the same domain to be added as cluster nodes.

▸ The VMM management server must either be in the same domain as the hosts or on a trusted domain.

▸ If the Hyper-V hosts are configured with static IP addresses, make sure these IP addresses are in the same subnet.

▸ The Hyper-V hosts that are going to be added as cluster nodes need to be in the same host group.

▸ Each Hyper-V host must have access to the storage array.

▸ The **Multipath I/O** (**MPIO**) driver must be installed on each host that will access Fibre Channel or the iSCSI storage array.

> If the MPIO driver is already installed (before the host is added to VMM), VMM will enable it for the supported storage arrays using the Microsoft-provided **Device Specific Module** (**DSM**).
>
> If you installed vendor-specific DSMs for your supported storage arrays and then added the host to VMM, the vendor-specific MPIO settings will be used to connect to the storage arrays.
>
> If you added a host to VMM before installing the MPIO feature, you will need to manually install and configure the MPIO driver or vendor-specific DSMs to have the device hardware IDs added.

Prerequisites for fabric configuration

Make sure that the fabric configuration meets the following prerequisites:

▸ For VMM-managed shared storage, ensure the following:

  ❏ The storage is added, configured, and classified in the Fabric workspace

  ❏ The logical units are created and allocated to the target host group or parent host group and not provisioned to any host

▶ For unmanaged shared storage, ensure the following:

❑ Disks are made available to all the nodes in the new cluster

❑ One or more of the logical units are provisioned to the hosts

❑ The cluster disk is mounted and formatted on one of the hosts

> When working with asymmetric storage in VMM, you must configure each node of the cluster as a possible owner of the cluster disk. *VMM is agnostic regarding the use of asymmetric storage.*

When using a Fibre Channel **storage area network (SAN)**, each node must have a **host bus adapter (HBA)** installed, with its ports correctly zoned.

When using an iSCSI SAN, make sure the iSCSI portals have been added and the iSCSI initiator is logged in to the storage array. Likewise, make sure **Microsoft iSCSI Initiator Service** on each host is configured to start automatically and is already started.

Prerequisites for networking

Make sure the following prerequisites for networking are met:

▶ The Hyper-V hosts should be configured in the Fabric workspace, with at least one, common logical network; if it has associated network sites, a network site should be defined for the target host group

▶ In addition, on each Hyper-V host, the logical networks should be linked with physical network adapters

▶ External virtual switches don't need to be created beforehand; if you did create them, make sure the names of the external switches and associated logical networks are exactly the same on all Hyper-V hosts

> After creating the cluster in VMM, you can create and configure the external switches (virtual networks) on all of the nodes of the cluster. You can also configure the virtual network settings for the cluster after it has been created.

Check whether you have configured the fabric resources and deployed the Hyper-V servers (see *Chapter 5, Configuring Fabric Resources in VMM*) and whether the prerequisites have been met.

How to do it...

Carry out the following steps to deploy a cluster in VMM:

1. Go to the **Fabric** pane in the **Fabric** workspace on the VMM console, and click on **Servers**.

2. On the **Home** tab on the ribbon, click on **Create**, and then click on **Hyper-V Cluster** as shown in the following screenshot:

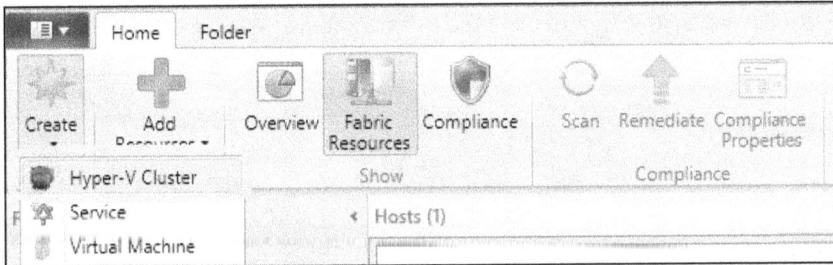

3. On the **Create Cluster Wizard** window in the **Cluster name** box on the **General** tab, type in a cluster name (for example, ProdHyperClust.lab.local).

4. Specify a Run As account (recommended), or type in the credentials for an account with local admin rights on all of the servers that will be added to the cluster in the format domain\username (for example, lab\host-admin).

> The domain for the account must be the same for the servers being added. Additionally, the account needs the permissions **Create Computer objects** and **Read All Properties** in the container that is used for the server computer accounts in AD.

5. Click on **Next**.

6. In the **Host group** list on the **Nodes** page, click to select the host group that contains the hosts that are to be clustered (for example, Sydney\HypervHosts).

> The Hyper-V hosts that are to be clustered must all be in the same host group. In addition, they must meet the OS prerequisites in order to be displayed under **Available hosts**.

7. In the **Available hosts** list, select a Hyper-V host that you want to add to the cluster and click on **Add**; you will see the hosts that you added move to the **Hosts to cluster** column.

> You can press and hold down the *Ctrl* key and click on each host to select various hosts together; or, you can press and hold down the *Shift* key, click on the first host, and then click on the last host to select a series.

The following screenshot depicts the **Create Cluster Wizard** dialog:

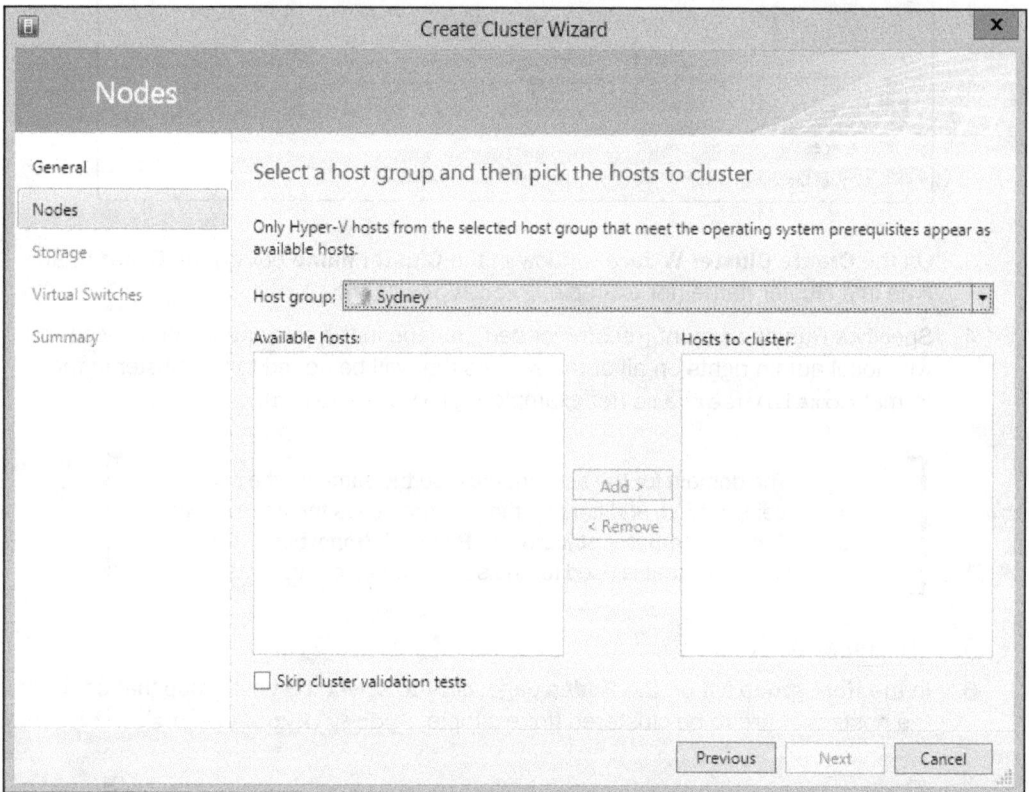

Create Cluster Wizard			X
Nodes			

General	Select a host group and then pick the hosts to cluster
Nodes	
Storage	Only Hyper-V hosts from the selected host group that meet the operating system prerequisites appear as available hosts.
Virtual Switches	
Summary	Host group: Sydney ▼

Available hosts: Hosts to cluster:

Add >

< Remove

☐ Skip cluster validation tests

Previous   Next   Cancel

> If you select **Skip cluster validation tests** (not recommended), the cluster will have no support from Microsoft as there will be no guarantee that the servers meet the cluster requirements.

8. Click on **Next**.

9. The **IP Address** page of the wizard will be displayed if, among all the hosts, at least one physical network adapter is configured with a static IPv4 address and there is a physical network adapter on all other hosts that are assigned to the same subnet.

> VMM will display the list of associated networks for that static IPv4 subnet.

10. In the **Network** column, select the network(s) that you want to allocate a static cluster IPv4 address to, and then do either of the following:

    ❑   When no static IPv4 address pools are associated with the subnet, type in the IP address of the selected network in the IP **Address** column.

    ❑   When static IPv4 address pools are associated with the subnet, choose one of the following options:

    In the **Static IP Pool** column, select an IPv4 address pool for VMM to automatically assign a static IPv4 from that pool.

    In the **IP Address** column, type in an available IPv4 address within the same subnet, and make sure not to select an IP pool in the **Static IP Pool** column. VMM will detect if you type an IPv4 address that is in the range of the IPv4 address pool and not assign that to another host.

> If any host has a physical network adapter configured with DHCP that falls in the same subnet, you don't need to set up a static IPv4.

11. Click on **Next**.

12. On the **Storage** page, select the disk(s) to be added to the cluster and then configure these options: **Classification**, **Partition Style**, **File System**, **Volume Label**, **Quick Format**, and **CSV**.

> The list of available disks characterizes the logical units associated with the nominated host group.
>
> When assigning storage as out-of-band storage, as the disks are not managed by VMM, all of the disks will be selected and shown as available. You will not be able to change the selection.
>
> Additionally, do not select clustered filesystem disks for the cluster when using a third-party CFS; if you do this, the cluster creation will be unsuccessful.
>
> If the number of selected hosts is even, the smallest disk (>500MB) will automatically be chosen as the witness disk and become unavailable for selection.

13. On the **Virtual Networks** page, select a logical network that is to automatically be associated with the external virtual network when VMM creates it on each cluster node.

> The logical network associated with a physical network adapter (including associated VLAN IDs) must be identical on all nodes.
>
> The logical networks already assigned to external virtual networks will not be displayed.

14. Type in a name and description (optional) for the external virtual network.

15. If you want to allow the management of hosts through this network, select **Allow hosts to access VMs through this virtual network**.

> It is recommended that you have a dedicated physical network card for host management instead of sharing it with VM traffic.

16. If you need to communicate with the hosts over a VLAN, select the **Hosts can access the VLAN ID** checkbox and then select the VLAN (defined as part of the logical network).

17. Click on **Next**, verify the settings on the **Summary** page, and then click on **Finish**.

How it works...

During the cluster creation process, VMM verifies whether the hosts meet the prerequisites, such as the required operating system versions and the domain. For each host, VMM enables the Failover Clustering feature, unmasks the logical units of the selected storage, and creates the external switches (virtual networks).

The setup continues; VMM runs the cluster-validation process, and then it creates the cluster with the quorum and enables CSV for each logical unit designated as a **Cluster Shared Volume** (**CSV**). When managing a logical unit's assignment, VMM creates one storage group per host node by default. In a cluster configuration, it creates one storage group per cluster node.

> In VMM, a storage group binds host initiators, target ports, and logical units (which are exposed to the host initiators through the target ports) together.
>
> A storage group can have multiple host initiator IDs; that is, it can have an **iSCSI Qualified Name** (**IQN**) or a **World Wide Name** (**WWN**).

For some types of storage, it is ideal to use one storage group for the entire cluster, where host initiators of all nodes will be restricted to a unique storage group. For this configuration, use VMM PowerShell to set the `CreateStorageGroupsPerCluster` property to `$true`, as follows:

```
$StorageName = @(Get-SCStorageArray)[0]
Set-SCStorageArray -StorageArray $StorageName –
CreateStorageGroupsPerCluster $true
```

You can force the storage format using **Force Format**; on the **Storage** page, right-click on the column header and then click on **Force Format**.

> Use the **Force Format** option with extreme caution as the current disk data will be overwritten during cluster creation.

When the cluster creation job is finished, verify the cluster status by clicking on the created host cluster and confirming that the host status for each node (in the **Host Status** column in the **Hosts** pane) is set to **OK**.

To view the detailed status information for the created host cluster (including the cluster validation test report), select the host and right-click on it, click on **Properties**, and then click on the **Status** tab.

There's more...

Now, let's talk about some other options.

Adding a Hyper-V host as a cluster node

Carry out the following steps to add a Hyper-V server to an existing cluster:

1. In the **Fabric** workspace on the VMM console, in the **Fabric** pane, expand **Servers**, expand **All Hosts**, and then select the host to add and drag it to the host cluster name.

2. In the **Add Node to Cluster** dialog, type in the credentials (for example, `lab\host-admin`) for an account with administrative rights on the host or specify a Run As account.

3. Click on **OK**. VMM will then add the node to the cluster. In the **Jobs** workspace, check the job status.

> You can verify that the cluster node was added by going to the **Fabric** pane, expanding **Servers**, expanding **All Hosts**, and then locating and clicking on the host cluster. In the **Hosts** pane, confirm that the new node is displayed in the host cluster with a host status of **OK**.

See also

▸ The *Failover Clustering Hardware Requirements and Storage Options* article at `http://technet.microsoft.com/en-us/library/jj612869.aspx`

▸ The *Failover Cluster Step-by-Step Guide: Configuring Accounts in Active Directory* article at `http://go.microsoft.com/fwlink/p/?LinkId=213267`

Managing fabric updates

A VMM-managed fabric server comprises the following workloads: Hyper-V hosts and host clusters, VMM library servers, **Pre-boot eXecution Environment** (**PXE**), the **Windows Server Update Management** (**WSUS**) server, and the VMM management server; refer to the following diagram:

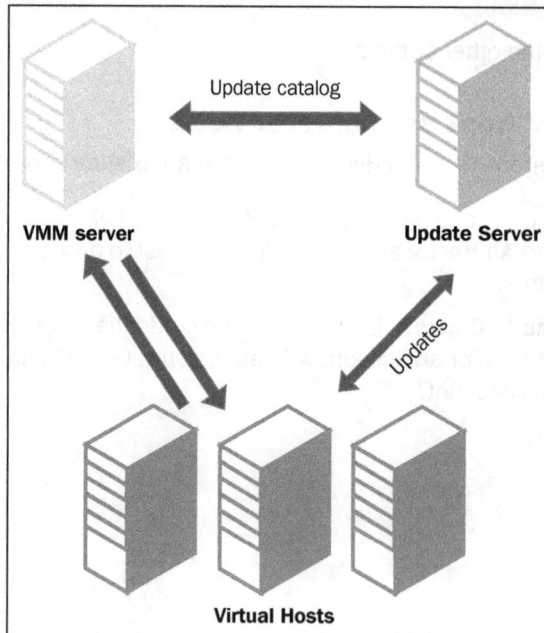

You can monitor the update status of the servers, scan for compliance, and update all or a set of the servers' resources as well as exempt resources from the installation of an update.

You can also orchestrate an update remediation on Hyper-V host clusters, where VMM will place one node of the cluster at a time in maintenance mode and install the updates. If the cluster supports live migration, the Intelligent Placement feature will be used to live-migrate the VMs off the node; otherwise, VMM will save the state for the VMs, and the host will start the VM after updating it.

> After integrating the WSUS server with VMM, it is recommended that you manage it only through the VMM console (unless you have SC Configuration Manager sharing the same WSUS server). Do not use the WSUS administration console to manage the integrated WSUS server.

Getting ready

In order to use VMM to manage the updates, it is recommended that you install a dedicated WSUS server, but you can use an existing one or install it on the VMM server if it is a small deployment.

As a prerequisite, install the WSUS administration console on the VMM management server before integrating WSUS with VMM (if the WSUS server is not installed on the VMM management server) and then restart the VMM service.

> It is neither a recommended approach nor the best practice to install the WSUS server on the VMM management server, unless it is a lab, POC, or a small deployment.

How to do it...

The following sections detail the procedures to configure a WSUS integration with VMM.

Installing WSUS for VMM 2012

Carry out the following steps to install WSUS for VMM:

1. Install a WSUS role (which was covered in *Chapter 1, VMM 2012 Architecture*). Use the following PowerShell commands:

   ```
   PS c:\> Install-WindowsFeature -Name UpdateServices,
   UpdateServices-Ui
   ```

The output is shown in the following screenshot:

```
Administrator: Windows PowerShell                              — □ X
Windows PowerShell
Copyright (C) 2012 Microsoft Corporation. All rights reserved.

PS C:\Windows\system32> Install-WindowsFeature -Name UpdateServices, UpdateServices-Ui

Success Restart Needed Exit Code      Feature Result
------- -------------- ---------      --------------
True    No             Success        {Windows Server Update Services, WSUS Serv...
WARNING: Additional configuration may be required. Review the article Managing WSUS Using PowerShell at TechNet Library
  (http://go.microsoft.com/fwlink/?LinkId=235499) for more information on the recommended steps to perform WSUS
installation using PowerShell.
```

The next screenshot shows the output of the following commands:

```
## Assuming D:\WSUS is the update content folder
PS c:\Program Files\Update Services\Tools> WsusUtil.exe
PostInstall CONTENT_DIR=D:\WSUS
```

```
PS C:\Program Files\Update Services\Tools> .\WsusUtil.exe PostInstall CONTENT_DIR=c:\WSUS
Log file is located at C:\Users\vmm-admin.lab\AppData\Local\Temp\tmpD7BB.tmp
Post install is starting
Post install has successfully completed
PS C:\Program Files\Update Services\Tools> _
```

2. In the Windows Start menu, launch **Windows Server Update Services** and configure the following in the **Configuration Wizard** dialog (refer to the next screenshot):

   ❑ Microsoft Report Viewer 2008 (not required if you installed the WSUS server on the VMM server)

   ❑ Upstream Server

   ❑ Languages

   ❑ Proxy Server

   ❑ Products (at least Windows OS, SQL, IIS, and System Center)

   ❑ Classifications (at least critical and security updates)

   ❑ Sync Schedule (manual)

> If you installed the WSUS server on a server other than the VMM management server (recommended), install the WSUS administration console on the VMM management server and restart the VMM service.

Windows Server Update Services Configuration Wizard:W2012-VMM

Before You Begin

Things you should do before starting this wizard

Before You Begin
Microsoft Update Improvement Program
Choose Upstream Server
Specify Proxy Server
Choose Languages
Choose Products
Choose Classifications
Configure Sync Schedule
Finished
What's Next

Before you begin:

1. Is the server firewall configured to allow clients to access the server?
2. Can this computer connect to the upstream server (such as Microsoft Update)?
3. Do you have user credentials for the proxy server, if needed?

To run this wizard again, launch the WSUS Administration Snap-in and go to Options

< Back   Next >   Finish   Cancel

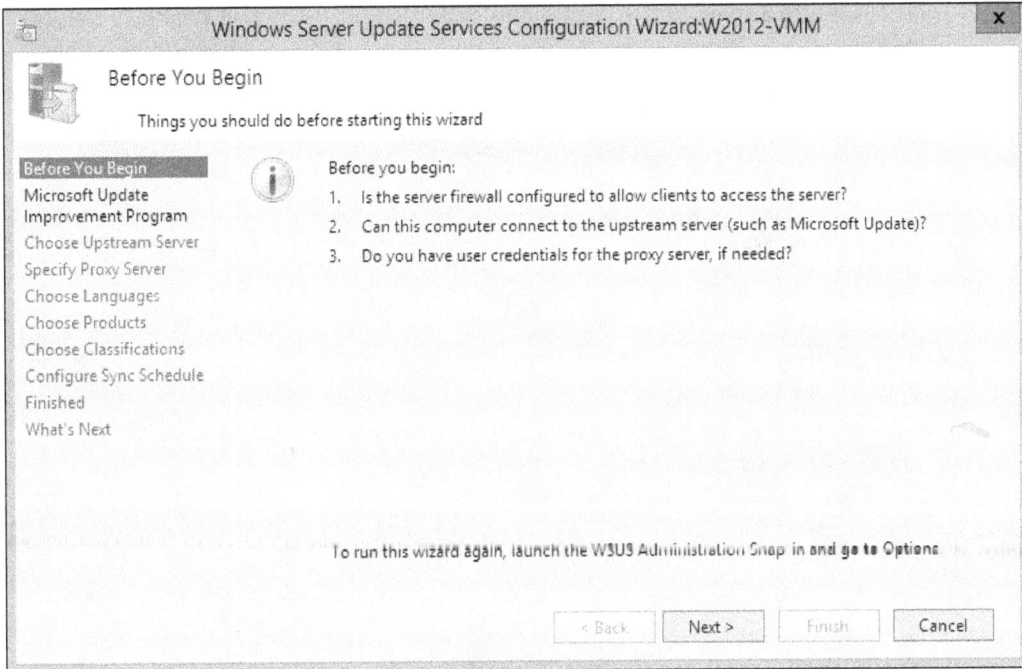

3. Click on **Finish**, and then click on **Synchronizations** on the navigation pane to confirm that the initial sync succeeded.

Integrating WSUS with VMM

Carry out the following steps to add WSUS to VMM:

> It is not recommended that you install WSUS on the same machine that you are installing VMM on. I would recommend a remote-dedicated WSUS.

1. In the **Fabric** workspace on the VMM console, click on **Add Resources** on the **Home** tab on the ribbon.

2. Select **Update Server**, and in the **Computer name** field in the **Add Windows Server Update Services Server** dialog, type in the FQDN of the WSUS server (for example, `w2012-wsus.lab.local`), as shown in the following screenshot:

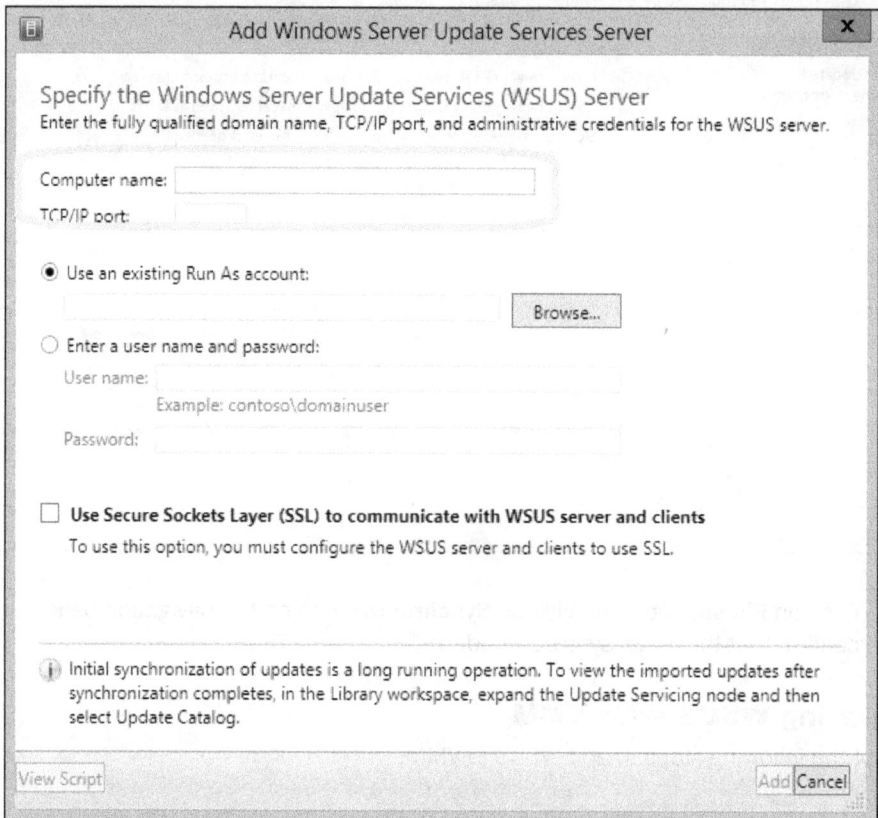

3. Specify the WSUS TCP/IP port (the default is `8530`).

4. Click on **Use an existing Run As account** and then click on **Browse** to select the Run As account; or, click on **Enter a user name and password** and then type in the user credentials (in the format `domain\username`, for example, `lab\wsus-admin`) for an account with administrative rights on the WSUS server, to connect to the WSUS server.

5. If required, select the **Use Secure Socket Layer (SSL) to communicate with the WSUS server and clients** checkbox and click on **Add**.

These steps will add the WSUS server to VMM, followed by an initial synchronization of a collection of updates. This operation could take a long time, as it depends on a number of factors, such as the network, updates, bandwidth, and so on.

> If you get an *error 444: your_vmm_server is a VMM management server. A VMM management server cannot be associated with another VMM management server*, check if you have deployed WSUS to a clustered VMM. Deploy WSUS to a dedicated remote VM and then integrate it with VMM using the previous steps.

How it works...

VMM uses WSUS to send updates to managed computers, but in a different way from Configuration Manager. VMM provides two, inbuilt update baselines that can be used to apply security and other critical updates to the servers in your VMM environment, but you must assign these baselines to host groups, clusters, or individually managed computers before you start using them.

You can install WSUS on the same server that you installed the VMM management server on. Note that this is only recommended in small scenarios.

> The WSUS administration console is required on each VMM management server.

To check whether the WSUS server was successfully integrated into VMM, in the **Fabric** workspace, expand **Servers** and click on **Update Server**. On the **Results** pane, you should be able to see the configured WSUS server.

In the **Library** workspace, expand **Update Catalog and Baselines** and click on **Update Catalog** to see which updates were downloaded through the WSUS synchronization.

Subsequently, you should configure the proxy server for synchronization by clicking on **Update Server**, clicking on **Properties** in the **Update Server** tab on the ribbon, and adjusting the update categories, products, and supported languages that will be synchronized by WSUS.

There's more...

You can assign computers to a baseline. To do this, carry out the following steps:

1. On the **Library** workspace on the VMM console, on the **Library** pane, expand **Update Catalog and Baselines** and click on **Update Baselines**.

2. On the **Baselines** pane, select the baseline (for example, **Sample Baseline for Critical Updates**).

3. On the **Home** page, click on **Properties** on the ribbon and then click on **Updates** on the baseline dialog box.

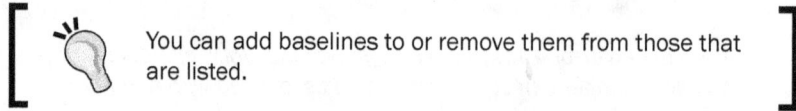

> You can add baselines to or remove them from those that are listed.

4. Click on **Assignment Scope** and then select the hosts, host groups, and/or clusters that are to be added to the baseline.

5. Select the computers symbolized by the roles they perform in VMM, or click on **All Hosts** to apply the baseline to all computers. Note that all of the roles that the computer performs will be selected.

6. To confirm, click on **OK**. This will save the changes.

Scanning servers for compliance

You can scan computers to check their compliance status for a particular baseline. You will be required to scan the servers again if the server was moved from one host group to another, if an update was added to / removed from a baseline assigned to that server, or if it was just added to the scope of a baseline. To perform the scan, carry out the following steps:

1. In the **Fabric** workspace, go to the **Fabric** pane and click on **Servers**.

2. On the **Home** tab, click on **Compliance** and then check the compliance status in the **Results** pane.

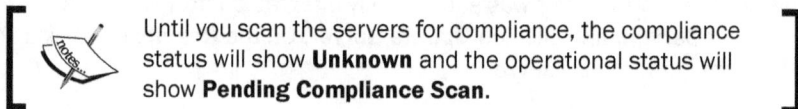

> Until you scan the servers for compliance, the compliance status will show **Unknown** and the operational status will show **Pending Compliance Scan**.

3. In the **Compliance** view, select the servers to scan.

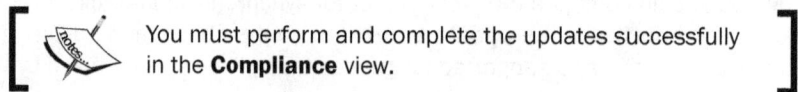

> You must perform and complete the updates successfully in the **Compliance** view.

4. In the **Home** tab, click on **Scan**.

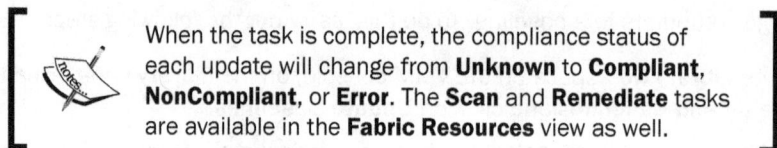

> When the task is complete, the compliance status of each update will change from **Unknown** to **Compliant**, **NonCompliant**, or **Error**. The **Scan** and **Remediate** tasks are available in the **Fabric Resources** view as well.

Remediating updates for a standalone server in VMM

To make noncompliant standalone servers compliant, carry out the following steps in VMM:

1. In the **Compliance** view, select the servers to remediate as shown in the following screenshot:

> Click on a specific server to display the baselines checked for it.

2. Select an update baseline or a single update within a baseline that is **NonCompliant**, then right-click and click on **Remediate** or click on **Remediate** in the **Home** tab, as shown in the following screenshot:

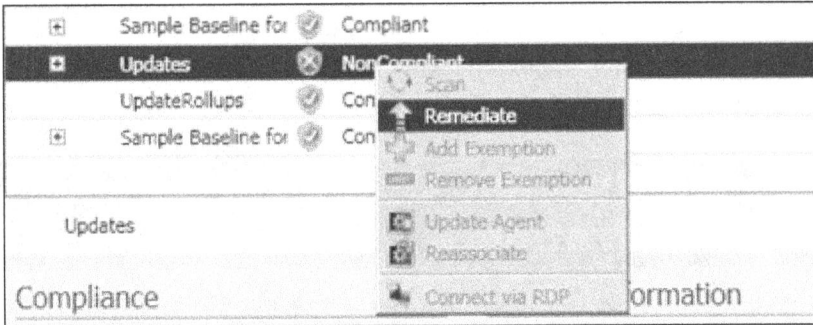

3. In the **Update Remediation** dialog, optionally select or clear the update baselines or specific updates to limit which updates are applied.

4. If the update requires a restart, select the **Do not restart the servers after remediation** checkbox to manually restart the server after the update is applied.

5. Click on **Remediate** to begin the remediation process.

Remediating updates for a Hyper-V cluster in VMM

To make the noncompliant servers in a Hyper-V cluster compliant, carry out the following steps in VMM:

1. In the **Compliance** view, click on **Remediate**.

2. In the resource list in the **Update Remediation** dialog, select the cluster to remediate.

3. If the update requires a restart, select the **Do not restart the servers after remediation** checkbox to manually restart the server after the update is applied.

4. Select **Allow remediation of clusters with nodes already in maintenance mode** to bypass maintenance mode for a particular node (which happens by default).

5. Select **Live migration** to move the VMs before starting the process, or **Save State** to shut down the VMs and then proceed with the updates.

6. Click on **Remediate** to begin the remediation process.

See also

▸ The *How to Integrate Fabric Updates with Configuration Manager* article at `http://technet.microsoft.com/en-us/library/hh341476.aspx`

▸ The *How to Update WSUS Settings in VMM* article at `http://technet.microsoft.com/en-us/library/gg710534.aspx`

▸ The *How to Create and Remove Update Exemptions for Resources in VMM* article at `http://technet.microsoft.com/en-us/library/gg710535.aspx`

Configuring Dynamic Optimization and Power Optimization

Dynamic Optimization (**DO**) is a new VMM feature that initiates the live migration of VMs that are on a cluster to improve load balancing among cluster nodes and correct any placement constraint violations.

It can be configured with a specific frequency and aggressiveness on a host group, which determines the amount of load discrepancy required to trigger a live migration.

Dynamic Optimization settings can be configured for the CPU, memory, disk I/O, and network I/O.

By default, VMs are migrated every 10 minutes with medium aggressiveness. You must take into consideration the resource cost (for example, the network) of extra migrations against the advantages of load balancing among cluster nodes when setting the frequency and aggressiveness for Dynamic Optimization.

> By default, a host group inherits DO settings from its parent host group.

Power Optimization, an optional feature of Dynamic Optimization, is enabled only if a host group is configured for the live migration of VMs through Dynamic Optimization. It helps meet resource requirements and saves energy by shutting down hosts that are not needed by the cluster, and turns them back on only when they are needed.

Power Optimization settings comprise CPU, memory, disk space, disk I/O, and network I/O settings.

> For Power Optimization, the servers are required to have a **baseboard management controller** (**BMC**) that supports out-of-band management. See the *Configuring host BMC settings* recipe in *Chapter 7, Managing VMware ESXi and Citrix® XenServer® Hosts*.

The rules of thumb for Power Optimization are as follows:

▶ For clusters that are created outside VMM and then added to VMM, the following can be done:

    ❑ One node can be shut down on a cluster with five to six nodes.

    ❑ Two nodes can be shut down on a cluster with seven to eight nodes.

    ❑ Three nodes can be shut down on a cluster with nine to ten nodes.

▶ For VMM-created clusters, the following can be done:

    ❑ One node can be shut down on a cluster with four to five nodes.

    ❑ Two nodes can be shut down on a cluster with six to seven nodes.

    ❑ Three nodes can be shut down on a cluster with eight to nine nodes.

Then, for each extra one to two nodes on a cluster, one more node can be shut down.

Getting ready

To enable Dynamic Optimization and Power Optimization, the VM needs to be running on a cluster.

Additionally, for Power Optimization, confirm the BMC-supported protocol. See the *Configuring host BMC settings* recipe in *Chapter 7, Managing VMware ESXi and Citrix® XenServer® Hosts*.

How to do it...

We will carry out the steps in the next sections to configure the settings for Dynamic Optimization and Power Optimization.

Configuring settings for Dynamic Optimization (DO)

Carry out the following tasks to configure DO:

1. In the **Fabric** workspace on the VMM console, expand **Servers**, expand **All Hosts** under **Servers**, and then select the host group to configure.

2. Click on **Properties** on the **Folder** tab on the ribbon, and then click on **Dynamic Optimization**.

3. If you don't want to inherit the parent host group settings, on the **Dynamic Optimization** page, deselect **Use dynamic optimization settings from the parent host group** as shown in the following screenshot:

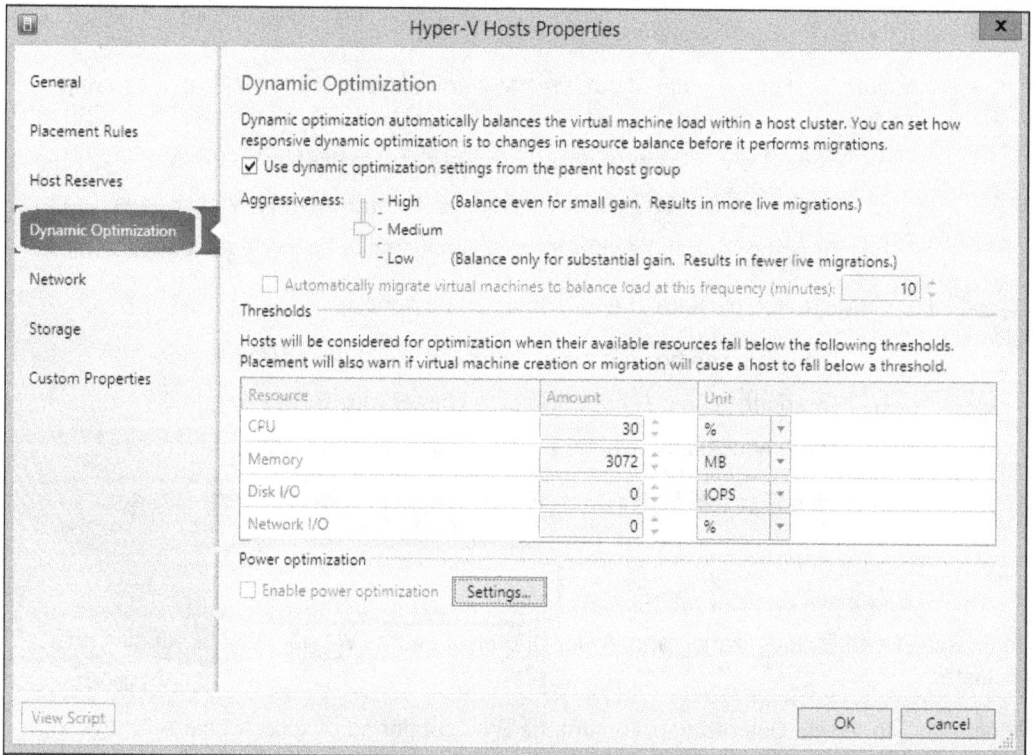

4. To set the **Aggressiveness** level, select either **High, Medium, Low**, or any value in between.

> If you select a higher level of aggressiveness, the result will be more live migrations; on the other hand, if you lower the aggressiveness level, the end result will be less live migrations. The default value is **Medium**. Live migrations will happen based on the ratings determined by Intelligent Placement.

5. To run Dynamic Optimization from time to time, select the **Automatically migrate virtual machines to balance load at this frequency (minutes)** checkbox and type in a value to specify how often it will run.

> You can type in any value between 10 (default) and 1440 minutes (24 hours).

6. Click on **OK** to save the changes.

Configuring settings for Power Optimization

Carry out the following steps to configure the settings for Power Optimization:

1. In the **Fabric** workspace on the VMM console, expand **Servers**, expand **All Hosts** under **Servers**, and then select a host group to configure (for example, **Sydney**).

2. Click on **Properties** on the **Folder** tab on the ribbon, and then click on **Dynamic Optimization**.

3. Select **Enable power optimization** to enable Power Optimization for the selected host group and click on **Settings**.

4. In the **Customize Power Optimization Schedule** dialog, configure the **CPU**, **Memory**, **Disk I/O**, and **Network I/O** resources settings, or leave the default values as they are, as shown in the following screenshot:

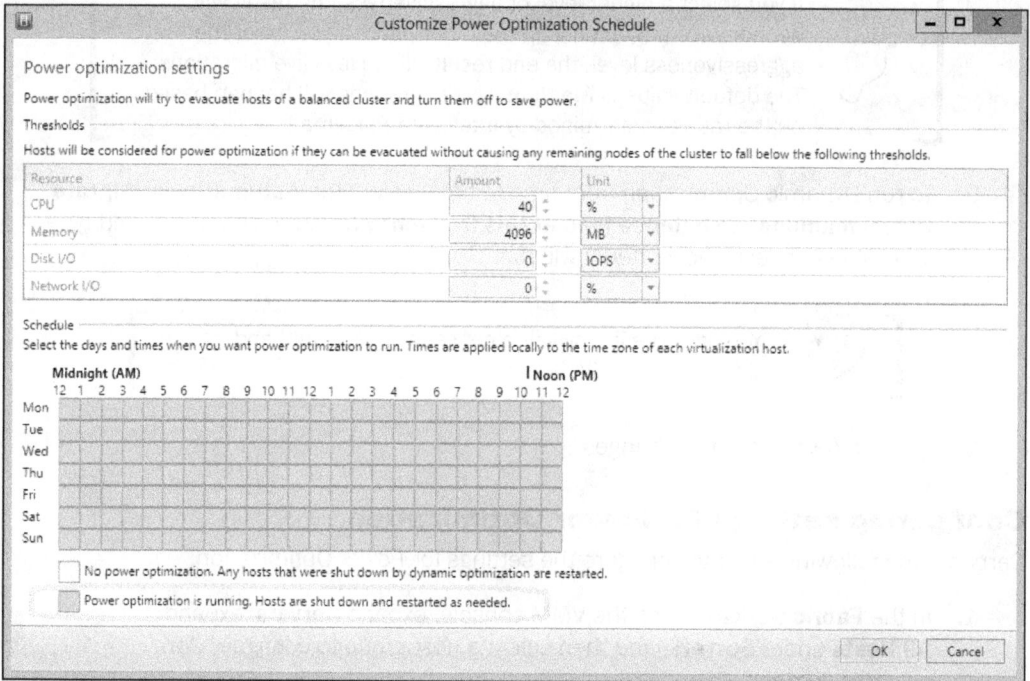

5. In the **Schedule** section, select the days and set the time at which you want Power Optimization to be performed.

6. Click on **OK** to save the changes and again on **OK** to close the **Properties** window.

> Power Optimization will be scheduled according to the time zone of each node in the cluster.

How it works...

Dynamic Optimization can be enabled only for clusters with two or more nodes and will only be performed on the clusters that support live migration, have shared storage, and are not in maintenance mode.

> If a host group comprises standalone hosts or clusters that do not support live migration, Dynamic Optimization will not be performed on those hosts/clusters.
>
> Also, VMs that are not highly available are not migrated during Dynamic Optimization.

Dynamic Optimization is also available for host clusters on demand, without the need to configure DO on the host groups, which can be done using the **Optimize Hosts** task in the **VMs and Services** workspace. When DO is requested for a host cluster, VMM lists all VMs that will be migrated and then requests for the administrator's approval.

In the **Dynamic Optimization** settings, you can set the level of aggressiveness, which is a measure of how responsive Dynamic Optimization is to changes in resource balance before it starts migrating VMs. Be cautious when balancing the resource cost of extra migrations against the benefits of load balancing among the nodes on a cluster, and always check the effectiveness of Dynamic Optimization in your environment for a certain period of time before increasing or decreasing the values.

When manually optimizing the hosts for load balancing (using the **Optimize Hosts** option), VMM will suggest VMs for migration, with the current and target hosts indicated.

> The list excludes any hosts that are in maintenance mode and VMs that are not highly available.

By configuring Power Optimization for the host group to meet resource requirements, VMM will shut down the hosts not needed by the cluster (migrating all VMs to other hosts in the cluster) and turn them on again when they are needed. VMM will perform the Dynamic Optimization process to live-migrate VMs and balance load within the cluster.

> Power Optimization is only available when VMs are being live-migrated automatically to balance load and the physical host has BMC settings configured.

Power Optimization settings specify the resource capabilities that must be kept when VMM shuts down a node cluster. These settings make a buffer of resources available to guarantee that oscillations in resource usage in the course of usual operations do not end in VMM powering the nodes of the cluster on and off unnecessarily.

It is possible to schedule the time (in hours and days) at which Power Optimization can be performed according to the time zone of each host.

> By default, Power Optimization will be run continuously if the feature is enabled.

There's more...

Now that we have enabled DO, let's take a look at how it is performed on a cluster.

Performing Dynamic Optimization (DO) on the host cluster

Carry out the following steps to perform a DO on a cluster:

1. In the **Fabric** workspace on the VMM console, expand **Servers**, expand **All Hosts** under **Servers**, and then select a host group.

2. On the **Folder** tab on the ribbon, click on **Optimize Hosts**. Click on **Migrate** to start the Dynamic Optimization process within the cluster.

> VMM will perform a Dynamic Optimization assessment to decide whether a VM should be live-migrated to improve load balancing in the cluster.

See also

*   The *Dynamic Optimization of the Private Cloud Infrastructure* article at `http://blogs.technet.com/b/server-cloud/archive/2012/02/08/dynamic-optimization-of-the-private-cloud-infrastructure.aspx`

Live migrating virtual machines

Live migration (**LM**) is a feature that saw a huge improvement back in the VMM 2012 SP1 version due to the following Windows Server 2012/R2 capabilities:

*   Live migration between two isolated Hyper-V servers (with no shared storage).
*   Live migration within cluster nodes.
*   Live migration between the nodes of two different clusters.
*   Live storage migration, where you can migrate the VM files (for example, VHD/VHDX, ISO, and VFD files) to update the physical storage or address bottlenecks in storage performance. Storage can be added to either an isolated Hyper-V host or a Hyper-V cluster, and then, the VMs can be live-migrated (moved) to the new storage.

▸ Live VSM, where you can use live system migration (VSM) to migrate both the VM and the storage in a single action.

▸ Concurrent live migration, where you can perform the multiple concurrent live migrations of virtual machines and storage. The limit of concurrent live migrations can be manually configured; the live migrations will be queued if the number of live migrations exceeds the specified limit.

> Note that the network usage for live migration might create a bottleneck.

Getting ready

The appropriated LM performance options, **TCP/IP**, **Compression**, or **SMB**, should be configured based on your environment and requirements as this will reduce the overhead on the network and CPU usage as well as reduce the amount of time for an LM operation.

Before you start performing live migrations, there are some requirements that you need to look at. These are discussed in the next sections.

Requirements for live migration

The following are the requirements that need to be met before a live migration can be performed:

▸ Two or more Hyper-V servers with processors from identical manufacturers (either all Intel or all AMD). This is because it is not possible to live-migrate from AMD to Intel processors and vice versa.

▸ Windows Server 2012/ or Windows Server 2012 R2.

> The live migration between hosts running Windows Server 2008 R2 SP1 or earlier and Windows Server 2012 is not supported.

- VMs should be configured to use Virtual Hard Disks (VHD/VHDs) or Virtual Fibre Channel disks. **Pass-through disks** are not supported by LM.

> Virtual Fibre Channel is now supported by VMM 2012 R2. It is supported by VMM 2012 R2, but you can configure it using **Virtual San Manager** under the **Actions** menu under **Hyper-V Manager**, and it will work perfectly as it is supported by Hyper-V as well, as shown in the following screenshot:

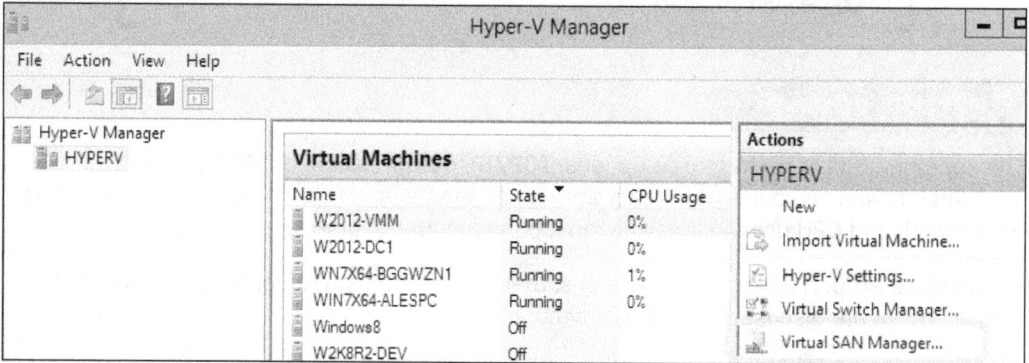

- A dedicated private network for live migration network traffic (recommended).
- Source and destination Hyper-V servers on the same domain or on trusted domains.
- If the source or destination VM VHD has a base disk, it should be in a share available to the target host as well, as live migration does not usually migrate the base disk.
- Live migration among clusters is only supported for hosts running Windows Server 2012/R2 with the Failover Cluster service and the CSV feature installed and enabled.
- If the source and destination Hyper-V hosts use shared storage, all VM files (for example, VHD/VHDX, snapshots, and configuration) must be stored on an SMB share with permissions to grant access on the share to both source and target computer accounts.

Requirements for live storage migration

The following are the requirements for a live storage migration:

- Live storage migration moves VM images (VHD, VFD, and ISO files), snapshot configurations, and data (saved state files)
- Storage migration is for virtual machines
- Storage migration does not migrate parent (base) disks, except for snapshot disks

Requirements for live system migration

The following are the requirements for a live system migration:

- The VM must exist in a location that is not visible to the destination host

- For individual Hyper-V Windows 2012/R2 hosts, the migration can happen among local disks or SMB 3.0 file shares

- For Hyper-V Windows 2012/R2 clusters, the VM can be migrated (moved) to either a CSV or SMB 3.0 file share on the target (destination) cluster

How to do it...

Carry out the following steps to perform the live migration of a VM between two standalone Hyper-V servers:

1. In the **VMs and Services** workspace on the VMM console, on the **VMs and Services** pane, expand **All Hosts**.

2. On the **VMs** pane, select the VM to migrate (for example, **W2012-FS01**).

> As this is a live migration, the virtual machine is running.

3. On the **Virtual Machine** tab, click on **Migrate Virtual Machine** to open the **Migrate VM Wizard** window as shown in the following screenshot:

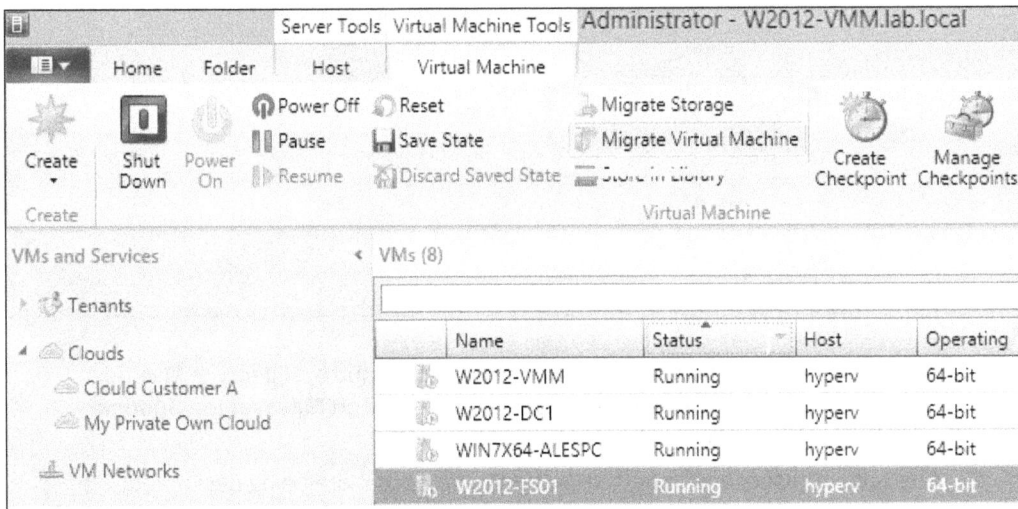

4. In the **Select Host** section, a list of possible destination hosts and their associated transfer types will be displayed as shown in the next screenshot:

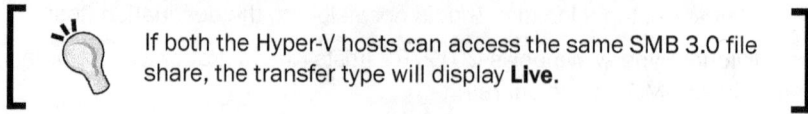

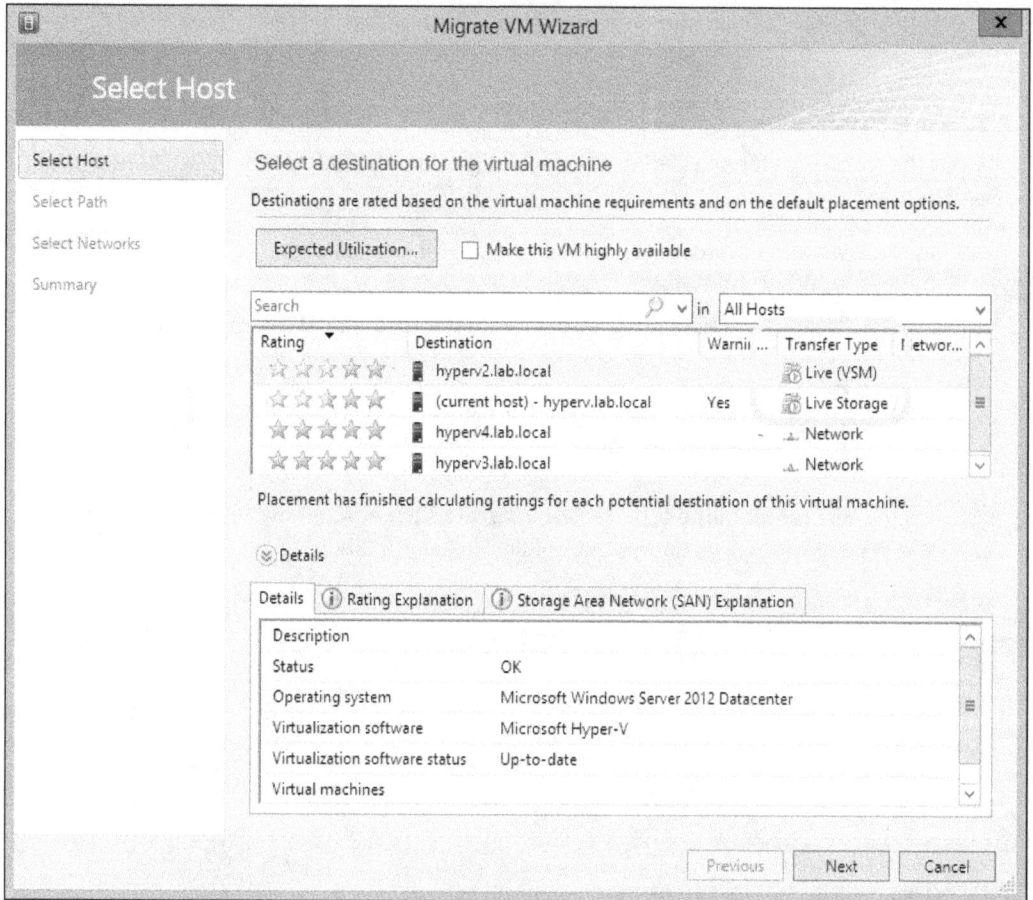

> If both the Hyper-V hosts can access the same SMB 3.0 file share, the transfer type will display **Live**.

5. Select a destination host that shows a better rating and transfer type **Live** (for example, **hyperv2.lab.local**), and click on **Next**. Click on **Move** on the **Summary** page to start the migration process.

6. The **Jobs** workspace will open, showing the tasks that are being performed.

How it works...

There are a number of ways in which live migration can be used. You can live-migrate a virtual machine from one Hyper-V host to another, keeping the VM files (VHD/VHDX, ISO, and VFD files) and configuration files in the same shared location (a CSV storage, an SMB share, and so on); move the VM files and the virtual machine together (live VSM); or move only the storage (live storage migration).

VMM reviews and validates the configuration settings of the target Hyper-V host before initiating the migration.

If the VM is running, the storage migration option enables you to live-migrate the storage from one location to another without stopping/breaking the workload of the VM. Storage migration can also be used when you need to move, provision, maintain, or upgrade storage resources, or to move a standalone or cluster VM to another location.

The live migration of a VM does not necessarily move the VM files (VHD/VHDX, ISO, and VFD files); keeping that in mind, you can perform the following actions:

▶ Configure the VM files to run on a file share that has access from both the source and target Hyper-V hosts, and then run a live migration.

▶ Run a live VSM, which is a combination of live migration and storage migration, but in a single action.

▶ Run a separate live storage migration.

There's more...

As we have seen before, there are many types of live migrations available, especially with the SC 2012 R2 version. Let's see how we can perform each one of them.

Performing live migration of a VM between hosts in two clusters

Carry out the following steps to perform the live migration of VMs between hosts in two different clusters:

1. In the **VMs and Services** workspace on the VMM console, on the **VMs and Services** pane, expand **All Hosts**.

2. On the **VMs** pane, select a highly available VM to migrate (for example, **W2012-FS02**).

3. On the **Virtual Machine** tab, click on **Migrate Virtual Machine** to initiate the **Migrate VM Wizard** window.

4. In the **Select Host** section, review and select a destination cluster node that shows a better rating and the transfer type **Live** (for example, **ClustHyperv2**), and then click on **Next**.

> To see the detailed rating, click on the **Rating Explanation** tab in the **Details** section.

5. Click on **Next**, and then click on **Move** in the **Summary** section.
6. To track the job status, open the **Jobs** workspace.
7. To check the migration status, on the **VMs and Services** pane in the **VMs and Services** workspace, select the destination host; on the **VMs** pane, you should see the VM status, **Running**.

Performing live storage migration between standalone hosts

The following steps will help you perform live storage migration between standalone hosts:

1. In the **VMs and Services** workspace on the VMM console, on the **VMs and Services** pane, expand **All Hosts**.
2. On the **VMs** pane, select the VM that you want to perform storage migration for (for example, **W2012-FS01**).
3. On the **Virtual Machine** tab on the ribbon, click on **Migrate Storage** to open the **Migrate VM Wizard** window as shown in the following screenshot:

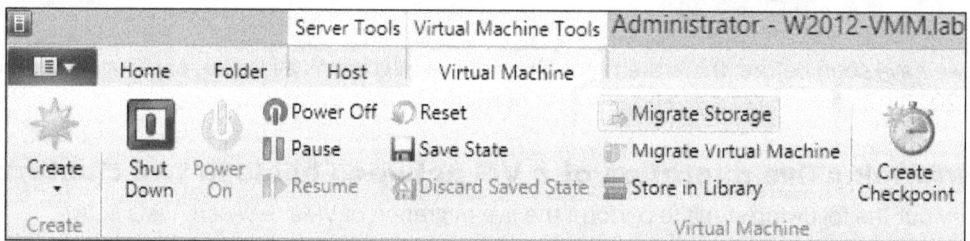

4. In the **Storage location for VM configuration** field in the **Select Path** section, select the default storage location or click on **Browse** to select the storage destination, and then click on **OK**.
5. Select the **Add this path to the list of default storage locations on the host** checkbox if you would like to make this the default path for the VM storage.

> Make sure to specify the FQDN of the destination file server in the share path if you specified an SMB 3.0 file share in the storage location field (for example, \\w2012-fs02.lab.local\vms).

The **Migrate VM Wizard** dialog is shown in the following screenshot:

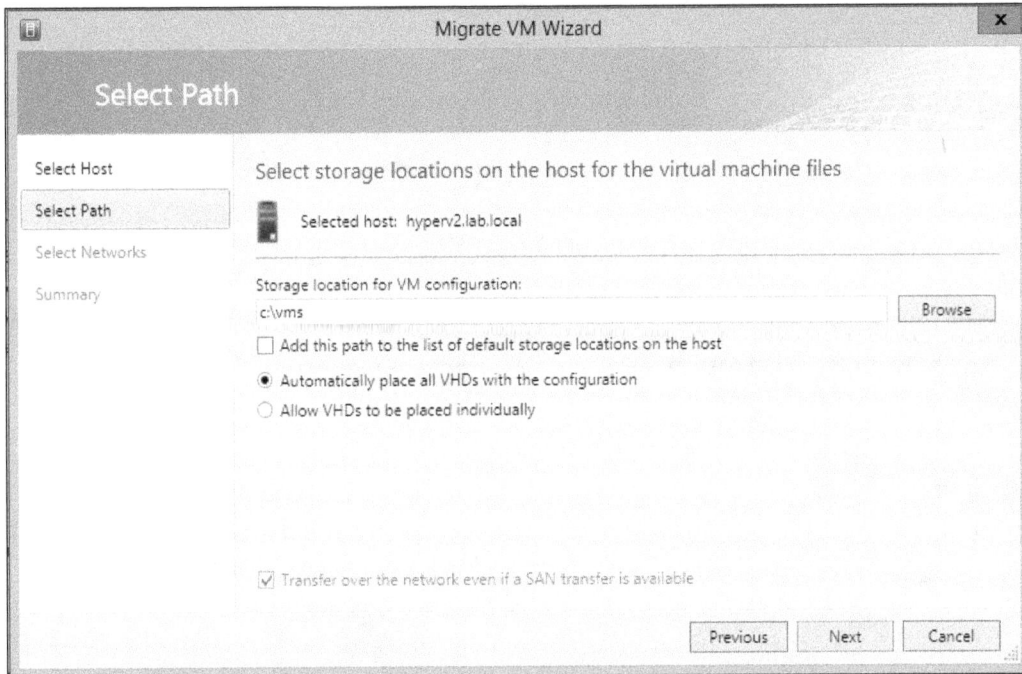

6. Click on **Next**, and then click on **Move** in the **Summary** section.
7. Check the job status in the **Jobs** workspace.

Performing concurrent live migrations

When you perform more than one live migration per host at a time, VMM runs it concurrently. On the VMM console, it is not possible to select multiple VMs at the same time for the live migration wizard; instead, you will need to start the multiple live migrations one by one.

> VMM considers live VSM as one live migration and one storage migration.

Carry out the following steps to view the concurrent migration settings:

1. In the **Fabric** workspace on the VMM console, select the Hyper-V host.
2. Right-click and select **Properties**, and then click on **Migration Settings** as shown in the following screenshot:

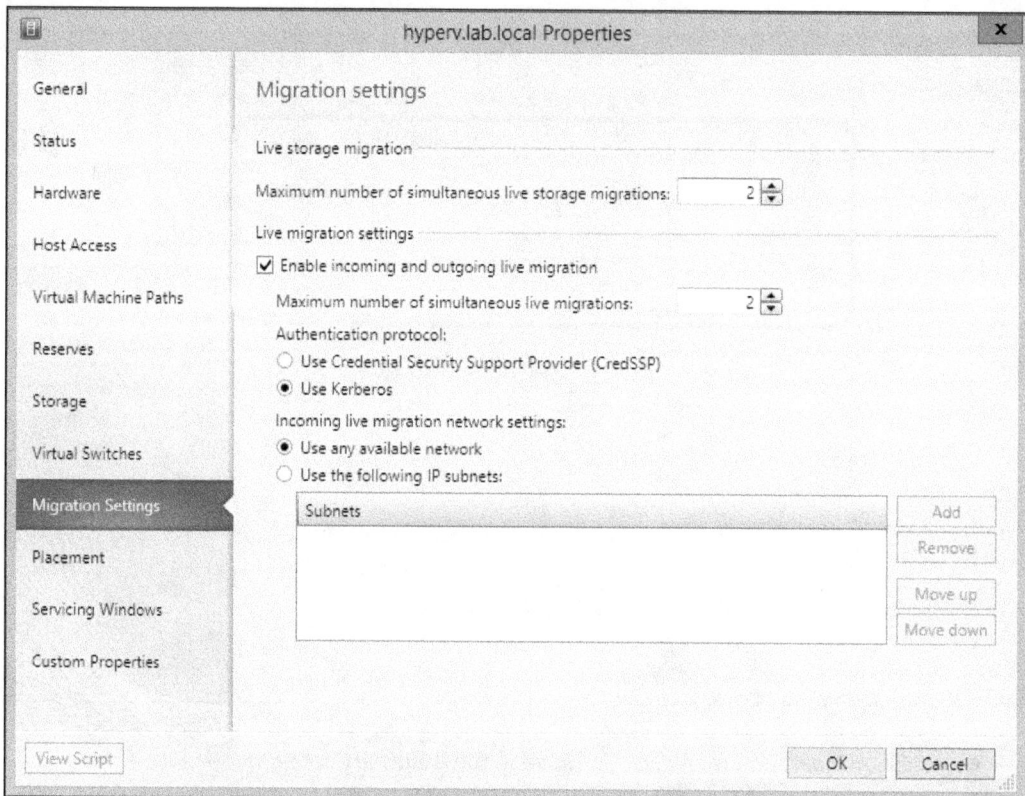

hyperv.lab.local Properties	
General	**Migration settings**
Status	Live storage migration
Hardware	Maximum number of simultaneous live storage migrations: 2
Host Access	Live migration settings
Virtual Machine Paths	☑ Enable incoming and outgoing live migration
Reserves	Maximum number of simultaneous live migrations: 2
	Authentication protocol:
Storage	○ Use Credential Security Support Provider (CredSSP)
	⦿ Use Kerberos
Virtual Switches	Incoming live migration network settings:
	⦿ Use any available network
Migration Settings	○ Use the following IP subnets:
Placement	Subnets — Add
Servicing Windows	Remove
Custom Properties	Move up
	Move down
View Script	OK Cancel

3. Change the concurrent live migration settings accordingly.
4. Click on **OK** to save.

> You need to perform this operation for every Hyper-V host.

See also

▶ The *Virtual Machine Live Migration Overview* article at `http://technet.microsoft.com/library/hh831435.aspx`

Managing Linux virtual machines

Linux-based VMs are now fully supported by VMM 2012 SP1 when hosted on a Hyper-V Server. This gives you the ability to add Linux-specific settings, such as OS specialization, when creating a Linux VM template, and additionally, the ability to add that template to a service template that deploys a multitier application or service.

Getting ready

Before deploying Linux VMs, check whether **Linux Integration Services** (**LIS**) is installed on the VMs. VMM does not check whether a VM meets the LIS requirements. However, if these requirements are not met, the VM will fail to deploy.

> Some Linux distributions include LIS by default. However, if LIS is not included, you will need to install it manually.

How to do it...

Carry out the following steps to install the VMM agent for Linux on a Linux VM:

1. Log in to the VMM management server with administrative rights.
2. Click on the Windows key (ÿ) and type cmd. Right-click on **cmd** and select **Run as administrator**.
3. Type in the following command in the command prompt:

   ```
   C:\>cd "\Program Files\Microsoft System Center 2012\Virtual
   Machine Manager\agents\Linux"
   ```

   The output is shown in the following screenshot:

4. Copy the agent installation files to a new folder on the Linux VM, and then open it on the Linux VM.

5. If your Linux VM is a 32-bit version, run the following command:

   ```
   #./install scvmmguestagent.1.0.0.544.x86.tar
   ```

6. If your Linux VM is a 64-bit version, run the following command:

   ```
   #./install scvmmguestagent.1.0.0.544.x64.tar
   ```

How it works...

When creating a VM with Linux as the guest operating system, if the Linux distribution does not already have LIS, you must install it; after the machine starts, you will need to install the VMM agent for Linux as well.

The following will be created on the virtual hard disk when installing the VMM agent for Linux:

- A configuration file (`scvmm.conf`) that contains the location of the logfile

- An installation logfile (`scvmm-install.log`)

- The logfile (`scvmm.log`) that will be generated at the next VM boot when the program starts automatically

- A default log folder (`/var/opt/microsoft/scvmmagent/log`)

- A default installation folder (`/opt/microsoft/scvmmagent/`)

See also

- The *About Virtual Machines and Guest Operating Systems* article at `http://go.microsoft.com/fwlink/p/?LinkId=271219`

- Installing LIS for Hyper-V on Windows Server 2012 on the *Hyper-V Overview* page at `http://go.microsoft.com/fwlink/p/?LinkId=271220`

- The *How to Install the VMM Agent for Linux* article at `http://technet.microsoft.com/en-us/library/jj860429.aspx`

Configuring availability options and virtual NUMA for VMs

Since VMM 2012 SP1, you can configure availability options for VMs that are deployed on Hyper-V host clusters, which include the following:

▸ **VM priority**: By configuring these settings, the host clusters will be instructed to start or place high-priority VMs before medium- or low-priority VMs, ensuring that the high-priority VMs are allocated memory and other resources first (for better performance).

▸ **Preferred and possible owners of VMs**: These settings influence the placement of VMs on the host cluster nodes. By default, there is no preferred owner, which means that the possible owners include all cluster nodes.

▸ **Availability sets**: By placing VMs in an availability set (to improve continuity of service), VMM will attempt to keep these VMs on separate hosts whenever possible.

You can also configure NUMA, which is a memory architecture that is used in multiprocessor systems. NUMA tries to reduce the gap between the speed of the CPU and memory usage; its benefits include the fact that slow processor performance can be avoided that is caused when various processors attempt to access shared memory blocks. A NUMA node is identified as a group of CPUs for each block of dedicated memory. For more NUMA concepts, refer to `http://msdn.microsoft.com/en-us/library/ms178144(v=sql.105).aspx`.

How to do it...

Carry out the following steps to configure priority for a VM or VM template on a host cluster:

1. Open the VMM console and execute one of the following options:

   ❑ To configure a deployed VM, on the **VMs** pane in the **VMs and Services** workspace, select the VM, right-click on it, and click on **Properties**.

   ❑ To configure a VM stored in the VMM library, in the **Library** workspace, select the stored VM, right-click on it, and click on **Properties**.

   ❑ To configure a VM at the time of creation, click on the **Configure Hardware** section.

   ❑ To configure a VM template, in the **Library** workspace, expand **Templates** on the left-hand pane, click on **VM Templates**, right-click on the VM template in the **Templates** pane, and click on **Properties**.

2. In the **Hardware Configuration** (or **Configure Hardware**) section, select **Advanced** (you will probably have to scroll down to see this option) and then click on **Availability**, as shown in the following screenshot:

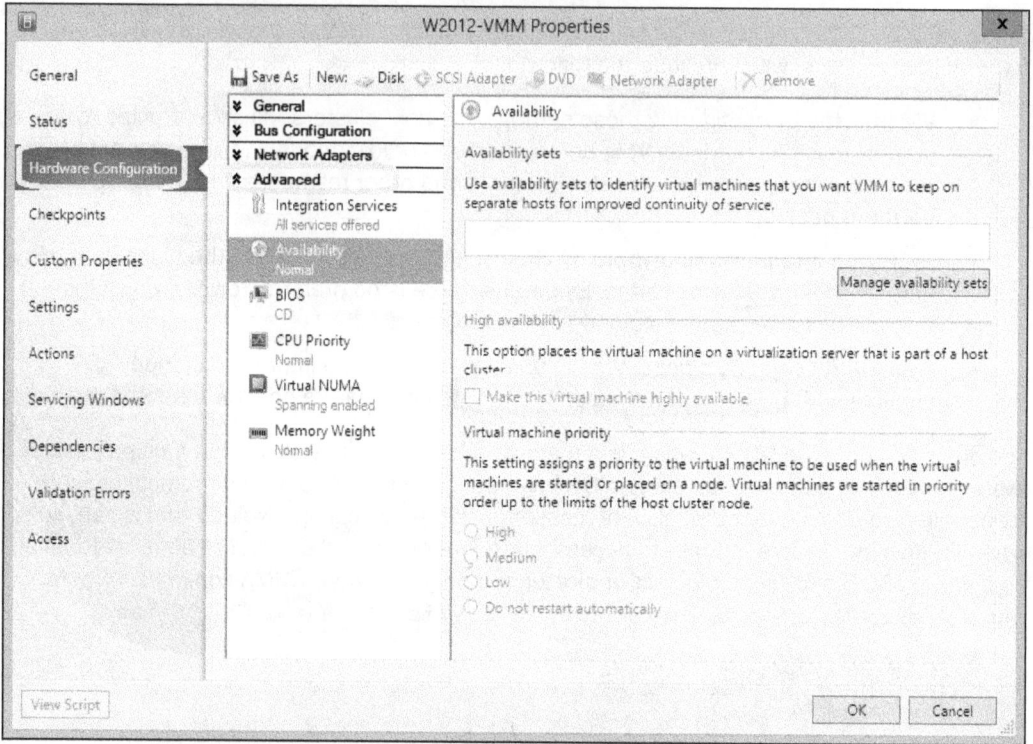

3. Select **Make this virtual machine highly available**.

This setting cannot be selected on a deployed VM as it depends on whether the VM is running on a host cluster or not.

4. In the **Virtual machine priority** section, select the VM priority as either **High**, **Medium**, or **Low**. However, if you want the VM to always start manually and never preempt other VMs, select **Do not restart automatically**.

5. Click on **OK** to save the settings.

How it works...

Availability options allow you to configure VM priority, the preferred and possible owners of VMs, and availability sets. These options are configured by the VM and will allow you to refine the VM high-availability settings by prioritizing resources, such as CPU and memory, as well as by influencing the placement of VMs in cluster nodes, all to improve performance and the continuity of service.

In case of a node failure, if high priority VMs (the VMs for which you selected the priority level as **High**) do not have the necessary resources to start, lower priority VMs will be taken offline to free up necessary resources. The preempted VMs will later be restarted in order of priority.

You can also use PowerShell for Failover Clustering to configure the **Availability sets** setting (**AntiAffinityClassNames**).

There's more...

Let's a have a look at more configuration options.

Configuring availability sets for a VM running on a host cluster

On the VMM console, perform the following steps:

1. For a deployed VM, in the **VMs and Services** workspace on the **VMs and Services** pane, expand **All Hosts** and then select the VM on the **VMs** pane.

2. For a stored VM, in the **Library** workspace, in the library server where the VM is stored, select the VM.

3. Right-click on the selected VM and then click on **Properties**.

4. On the **Hardware Configuration** tab, click on **Availability**.

5. Make sure to select **Make this virtual machine highly available**.

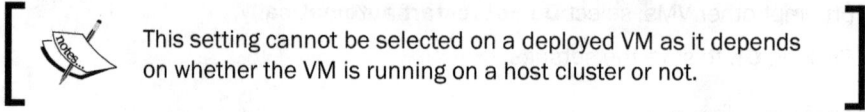

> This setting cannot be selected on a deployed VM as it depends on whether the VM is running on a host cluster or not.

6. In the **Availability sets** section, click on **Manage availability sets** as shown in the following screenshot:

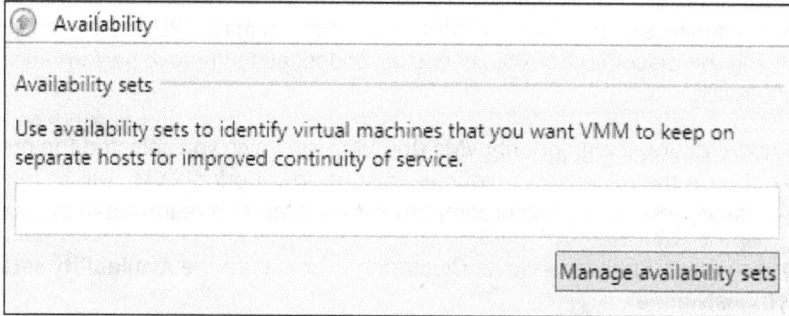

> Availability
>
> Availability sets
>
> Use availability sets to identify virtual machines that you want VMM to keep on separate hosts for improved continuity of service.
>
> Manage availability sets

7. Click on an availability set, and then click on either **Add** or **Remove**.

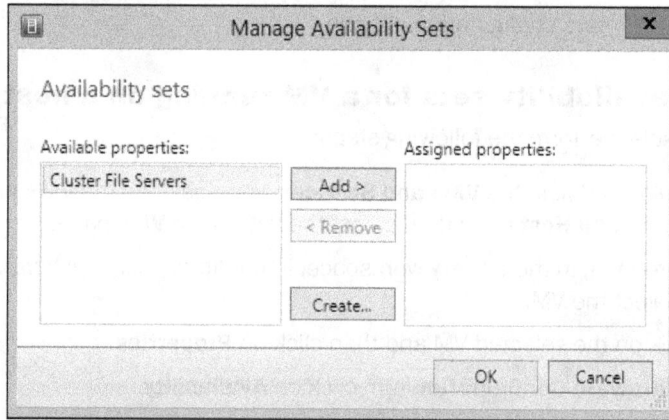

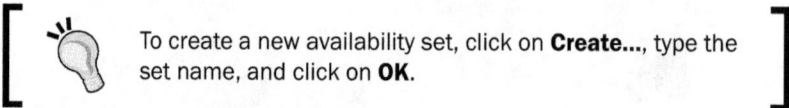

> Manage Availability Sets
>
> Availability sets
>
> Available properties:
> Cluster File Servers
>
> Add >
> < Remove
> Create...
>
> Assigned properties:
>
> OK   Cancel

> To create a new availability set, click on **Create...**, type the set name, and click on **OK**.

8. In the **Manage Availability Sets** dialog, click on **OK** to confirm.

9. In the VM properties sheet, click on **OK**.

Configuring preferred and possible owners for a VM

Carry out the following steps to configure the preferred owner for a virtual machine:

1. In the **VMs and Services** workspace on the VMM console, on the **VMs and Services** pane, expand **All Hosts** and then select the VM on the **VMs** pane.

2. Right-click on the selected VM and click on **Properties**.

3. Click on the **Settings** tab and perform the following:

   ❑ Configure the preferred owners list if you want to control which nodes in the cluster will own the VM regularly.

   ❑ Configure the possible owners list and do not include the nodes that you don't want as owners of the VM, if you need to prevent a VM from being owned by a specific node.

4. Click on **OK** to confirm.

Configuring virtual NUMA in VMM 2012 R2

Virtual NUMA projects the NUMA topology onto a virtual machine, which allows guest operating systems and applications to make intelligent NUMA decisions, aligning the guest NUMA nodes with host resources. Carry out the following steps to configure a virtual NUMA:

1. In the **Advanced** section of the VM properties, click on **Virtual NUMA** as shown in the following screenshot:

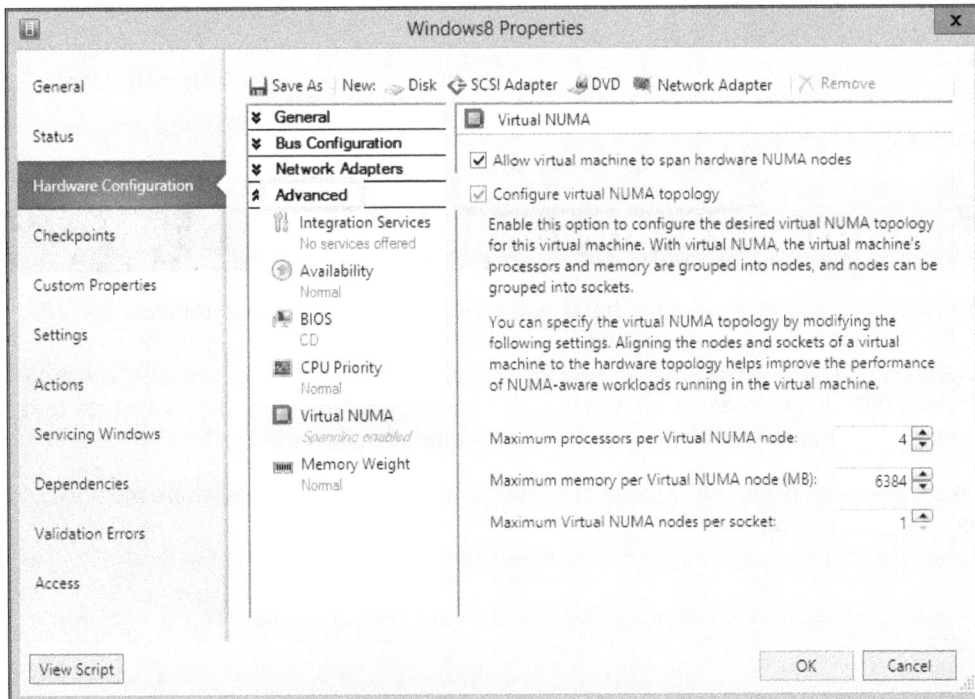

2. In the **Maximum processors per Virtual NUMA node** field, specify the maximum number of VPs on the same VM that can be used simultaneously on a virtual NUMA node. The value should be between 1 and 32.

3. In the **Maximum memory per Virtual NUMA node (MB)** field, specify the maximum amount of memory that can be assigned to a single virtual NUMA node. The value should be between 8 MB and 256 GB.

4. In the **Maximum Virtual NUMA nodes per socket** field, specify the maximum number of virtual NUMA nodes that are allowed on a single socket. The value should be between 1 and 64.

> To enable maximum bandwidth, configure different NUMA VMs to use different NUMA nodes.

5. To enable spanning, select the **Allow virtual machine to span hardware NUMA nodes** checkbox. Deselect the checkbox to disable NUMA spanning.

> Even if NUMA spanning is not enabled, based on the physical host topology, virtual nodes can still allocate memory from the same or different host NUMA nodes.

See also

▶ The *NUMA Concepts* section on the *Understanding Non-uniform Memory Access* article at `http://msdn.microsoft.com/en-us/library/ms178144(v=sql.105).aspx`

Configuring resource throttling

The additional features provided with the resource throttling feature in VMM 2012 SP1/R2 include enhanced CPU (processor) and memory throttling capabilities, which ensure that CPU and memory resources are allocated and used effectively. The ability to set the **virtual processor (VP)** weight to provide it with larger or smaller shares of CPU cycles ensures that VMs can be ranked when CPU resources are overcommitted.

Memory throttling helps rank access to memory resources in situations where memory resources are constrained.

How to do it...

Carry out the following steps in order to configure processor throttling:

1. On the VMM console, execute one of the following:

   ❑ To configure a deployed VM, on the **VMs** pane in the **VMs and Services** workspace, select the VM, right-click on it, and click on **Properties**

   ❑ To configure a VM stored in the VMM library, in the **Library** workspace, select the stored VM, right-click on it, and click on **Properties**

   ❑ To configure a VM at the time of creation, click on the **Configure Hardware** section

   ❑ To configure a VM template, in the **Library** workspace, expand **Templates** on the left-hand pane, click on **VM Templates**, right-click on the VM template in the **Templates** pane, and click on **Properties**

2. In the **Hardware Configuration** section, select **Advanced** (you will probably have to scroll down to see this option) and click on **CPU Priority** as shown in the following screenshot:

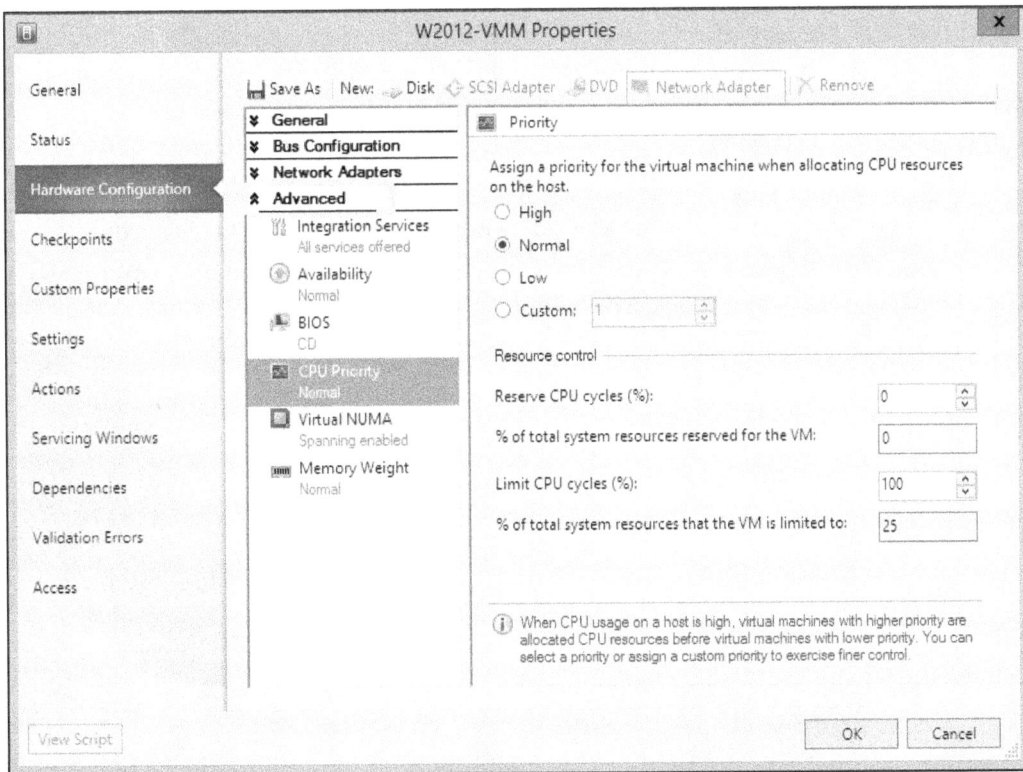

3. Select the VM priority, which specifies how the CPU resources will be balanced between VMs.

VM priority	Relative weight value in Hyper-V
High	200
Normal	100
Low	50
Custom	between 1 and 10000

4. In the **Reserve CPU cycles (%)** field, type in the percentage of the CPU resources in one logical processor that will be reserved for a VM.

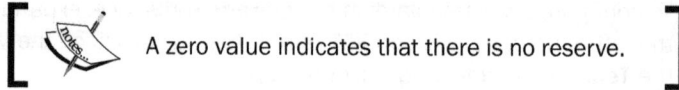

> A zero value indicates that there is no reserve.

5. In the **Limit CPU cycles (%)** field, type in the maximum percentage of the CPU resources in one logical processor that the VM will consume.

How it works...

In the **Advanced** section of the **CPU Priority** settings of the virtual machine, you can configure the weight of a virtual processor (VP) to make a share of CPU cycles available to it. You can configure the following settings:

- **High**, **Normal**, **Low**, or **Custom**: This defines how the CPU is shared when contention occurs, with the VMs that are defined as **High** being allocated CPU resources first

- **Reserve CPU cycles (%)**: This defines the percentage of CPU resources associated with one logical processor that should be reserved for the virtual machine; it is useful for CPU-intensive applications

▸ **Limit CPU cycles (%)**: This defines the maximum percentage of resources on one logical processor that the VM can consume

> The options to reserve CPU cycles and limit CPU cycles are only supported in Windows Server 2012 Hyper-V hosts.
>
> For highly intensive workloads, you can add more VPs, particularly when a physical CPU is near its limit.

There's more...

You can also configure the memory throttling feature; this will help rank access to memory resources in situations where they are constrained, which means that VMs that have the priority set to **High** will be given memory resources before VMs with lower priority.

Note that defining a VM as having a priority of **Low** might prevent it from starting when the available memory is low.

The memory priority settings and thresholds can be set to **Static**, in which you can assign a fixed amount of memory to a VM. They can also be set to **Dynamic**, in which you can define the following settings:

▸ **Start-up memory**: This is the memory that is allocated to the VM when it starts up. The value will be adjusted, as required, by **Dynamic Memory** (**DM**).

▸ **Minimum memory**: This refers to the minimum memory required by the VM. It allows a VM to scale back the memory consumption below the startup memory requirement (in case the VM is idle). The unbound memory can then be used by additional VMs.

▸ **Maximum memory**: This is the memory limit allocated to a VM.

▸ **Memory Buffer Percentage**: This defines the percentage of spare memory that will be assigned to the VM based on the amount of memory required by the applications and services running on the VM. The amount of memory buffer is calculated as the *amount of memory needed by the VM/(memory buffer value/100)*.

Configuring memory throttling

Carry out the following steps to configure memory throttling:

1. In the properties of the VM, in the **Hardware Configuration** section, select **General** and then click on **Memory** as shown in the following screenshot:

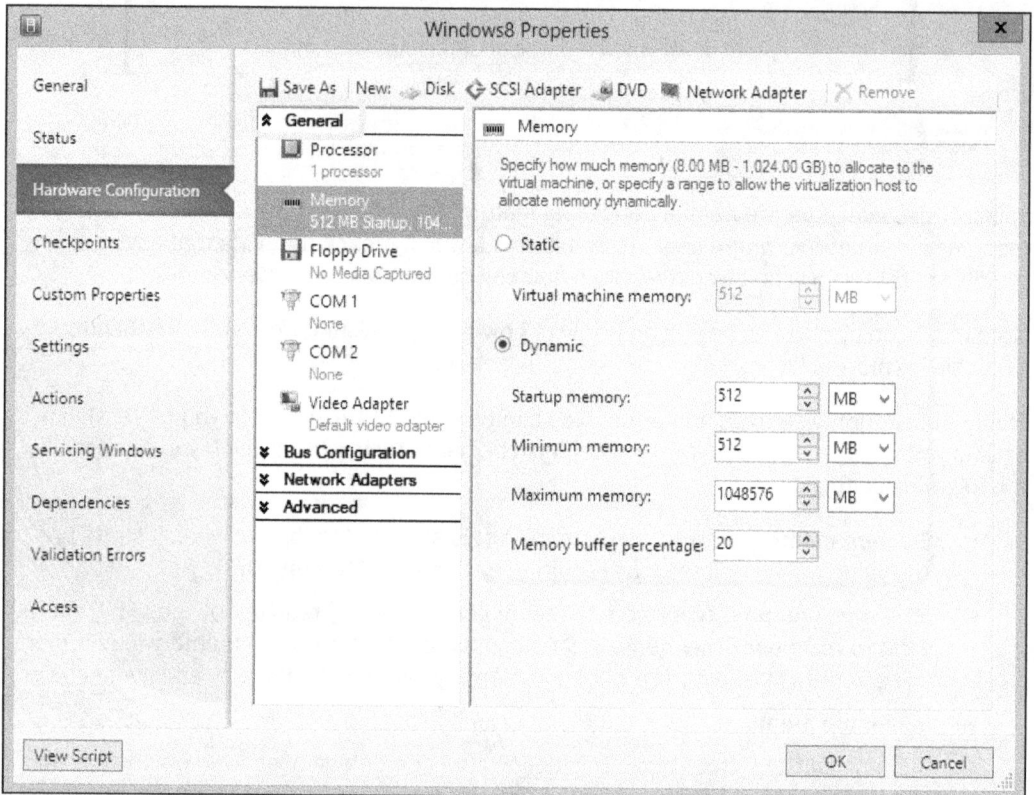

2. Click on **Static** to define the fixed memory that should be allocated to the VM.

3. Click on **Dynamic** and then do the following:

   1. In the **Startup memory** field, specify the memory for the VM for when it starts up.

   2. In the **Minimum memory** field, specify the minimum memory that the VM can run on.

   3. In the **Maximum memory** field, specify the maximum memory that can be allocated to the VM. For Windows Server 2012/R2, the default value is **1TB**.

   4. In the **Memory buffer percentage** field, specify the available memory that will be assigned to the VM (if it is needed).

Configuring memory weight

You can give priority to a VM when memory resources reach the limit. Configuring the VM with **High** will give it higher priority when allocating memory resources. On the other hand, if you set the VM priority to **Low**, the VM will not be able to start if the memory resources are reaching their limit.

To configure the memory weight for a VM, in the properties of the VM in the **Hardware Configuration** section, click on **Advanced** and then click on **Memory Weight** and configure the priority, as shown in the following screenshot:

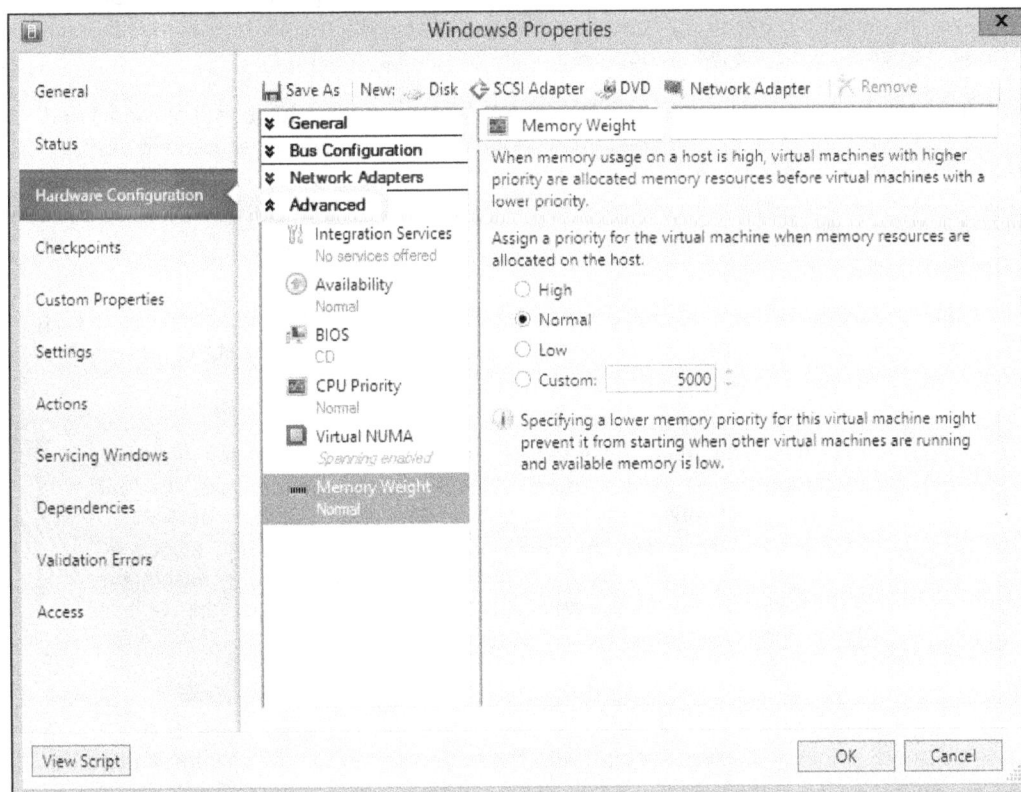

See also

▶ The *Configuring availability options and virtual NUMA for VMs* recipe of this chapter

Integrating with the IPAM server for IP management

New in VMM 2012 R2 is **IP Address Management** (**IPAM**) server integration, which allows the consolidated management of the IP address space on a corporate network and on Microsoft-powered cloud networks that run Windows Server 2012 R2.

After VMM has been integrated with IPAM, the IP address configuration associated with the logical networks and VM networks created in VMM will be synced with the IPAM server, which can detect and prevent IP address conflicts, duplication, and overlaps across multiple instances of VMM 2012 R2 (when deployed on large-scale datacenters).

As a VMM administrator, you can use IPAM GUI to configure and monitor logical networks and their associated network sites and IP address pools. VMM tenants, however, need to use the VMM server, not the IPAM server GUI, to configure VM networks that use network virtualization.

Getting ready

This chapter does not cover the installation of the IPAM server, which must be installed on a Windows 2012 R2 domain member server and meet the requirements that are described at `http://technet.microsoft.com/library/jj878315.aspx`.

> You can use the IPAM server to delete a logical network, keeping the VMM synchronization in place, by deleting the IP address subnets associated with that logical network and not deleting the name associated with the VMM **Logical Network** field on the IPAM server. By deleting the name associated with the VMM Logical Network on the IPAM server, in the VMM console, the correspondent network site and logical network must be deleted as well, for the deletion process to be completed.

Also, make sure of the following before you start:

- ▶ Create a domain service account with the password set to never expire, and make sure to add it to IPAM ASM Administrators and Remote Management Users on the IPAM server

- ▶ Confirm time synchrony on the IPAM server and VMM

How to do it...

Carry out the following steps to configure IPAM integration in the VMM management server:

1. In the **Fabric** workspace on the VMM console, click on **Fabric Resources** and then on the **Fabric** pane.

2. On the **Home** tab, click on **Add Resources** and then select **Network Service**.

3. In the **Add Network Service Wizard Name** window, type the network service name (for example, **IPAM**) and an optional description.

4. Click on **Next**.

5. In the **Manufacturer and Model** window, select **Microsoft** as **Manufacturer**, select **Microsoft Windows Server IP Address Management** as **Model**, and click on **Next**, as shown in the following screenshot:

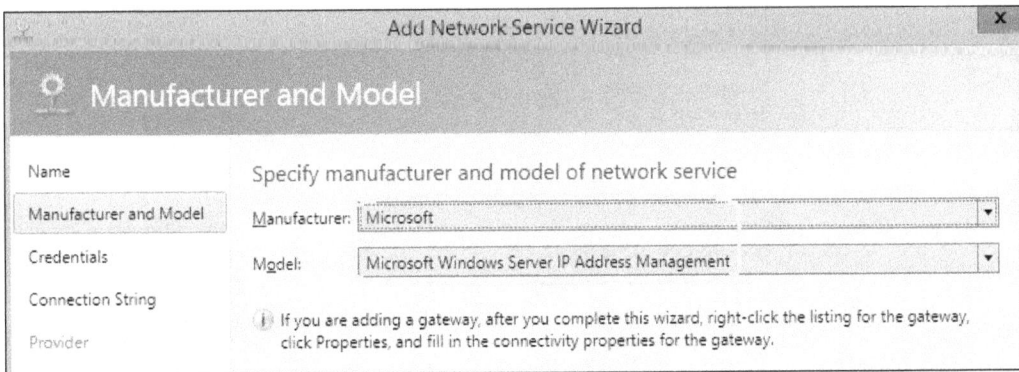

6. In the **Credentials** window, select **Service Account** by clicking on **Browse**; then, in the **Select a Run As Account** dialog box, click on **Next**.

> You can click on **Create Run As Account** to create a new Run As account with the required permissions.

7. In the **Connection String** window, type the connection string, which is the fully qualified domain name (FQDN) of your IPAM server (for example, `ipam.lab.local`), and then click on **Next**.

> If the IPAM server is using a port other than the default port (`48885`), you should specify the FQDN, followed by a colon and the port number (for example, `ipam.lab.local:48620`).

8. In the **Provider** window, select **Microsoft IP Address Management Provider** from the **Configuration provider** list as shown in the following screenshot:

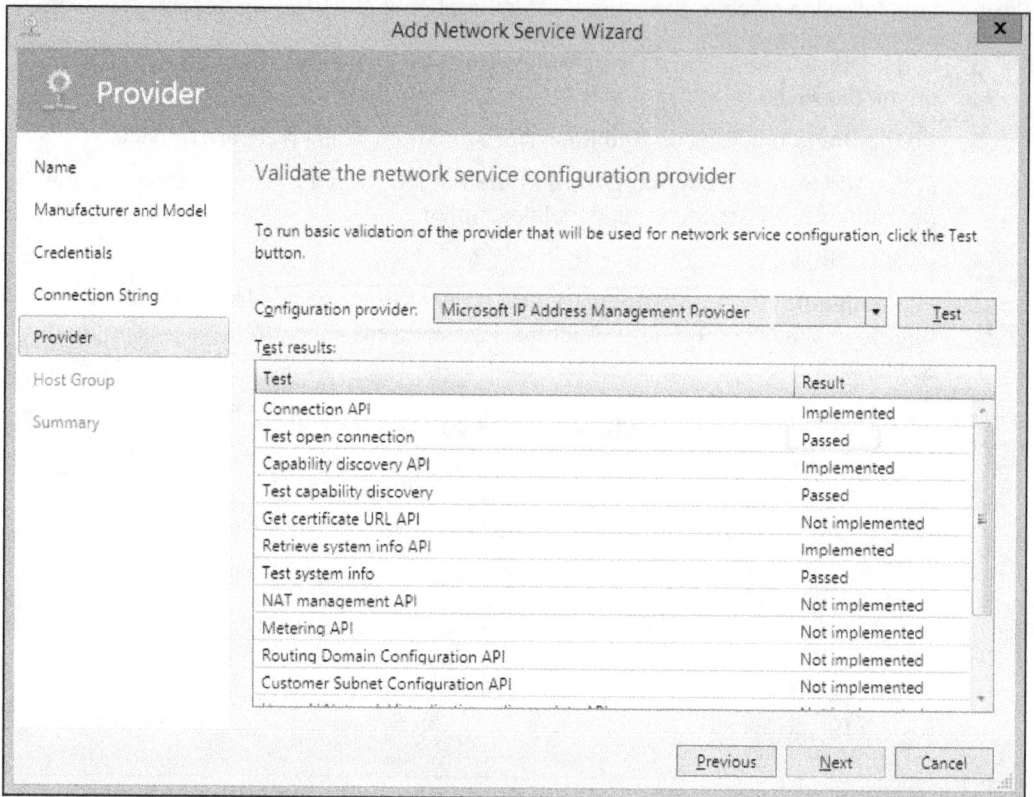

9. Click on the **Test** button.

> The results should show **Passed**, indicating that the provider works as expected with the IPAM server. A **Failed** result could be caused by insufficient permissions. Check the **Service Account/Run As account** option. The **Implemented** and **Not Implemented** reports indicate whether the selected provider supports the referred API and are informational only.

10. Click on **Next.**

11. In the **Host Group** window, select the host group(s) that will support the IPAM integration.

12. In the **Summary** window, confirm the configuration.

13. Click on **Finish** and confirm whether the IPAM server is listed under **Network Services**.

> To update the latest configuration to/from the IPAM server, right-click on the IPAM server and then click on **Refresh**.

How it works...

Deploying the Windows 2012 R2 IPAM server means that you don't need to rely on Excel spreadsheets to keep track of the server's IP anymore, as the IPAM service will take care of that for you. IPAM integrates with Directory Services (Active Directory), DNS, and DHCP as well with System Center 2012 R2 Virtual Machine Manager to keep its database up to date.

IP addresses are not monitored, especially in test/lab/stage environments and production environments where scalability is a must have, and when providing Infrastructure as a Service. IPAM can be the solution to automate the process to keep track of the IP address assignments.

Although, back in VMM 2012 SP1, we had the option to feed information into IPAM running on Windows 2012, in VMM 2012 R2 and Windows Server 2012 R2, Microsoft enhanced the integration between VMM and the IPAM server to provide full IP address management.

There's more...

Now that you integrated IPAM with VMM, there some other things to consider; they will be discussed in the next sections.

The IPAM and VMM time synchrony

To make sure of the time synchrony of the IPAM server and the VMM server is a requirement for the integration. If such tasks cannot be performed, the permissions on the IPAM server must be added/updated for the VMM provider to query the current time setting on the IPAM server.

Carry out the following tasks to update the permissions on the IPAM server console:

1. Right-click on the Windows Start button on the desktop and click on **Run**, as shown in the following screenshot:

2. Type `wmimgmt.msc` to open the **WMI Control (Local)** and right-click on **WMI Control (Local)**.

3. Select **Properties**, and on the **Security** tab, navigate to **Root\CIMV2** and then click on the **Security** button.

4. Click on **Add** to add the service account created previously.

5. Click on **Remote Enable** on the **Permissions for Authenticated Users** pane and select **Allow**, as shown in the following screenshot:

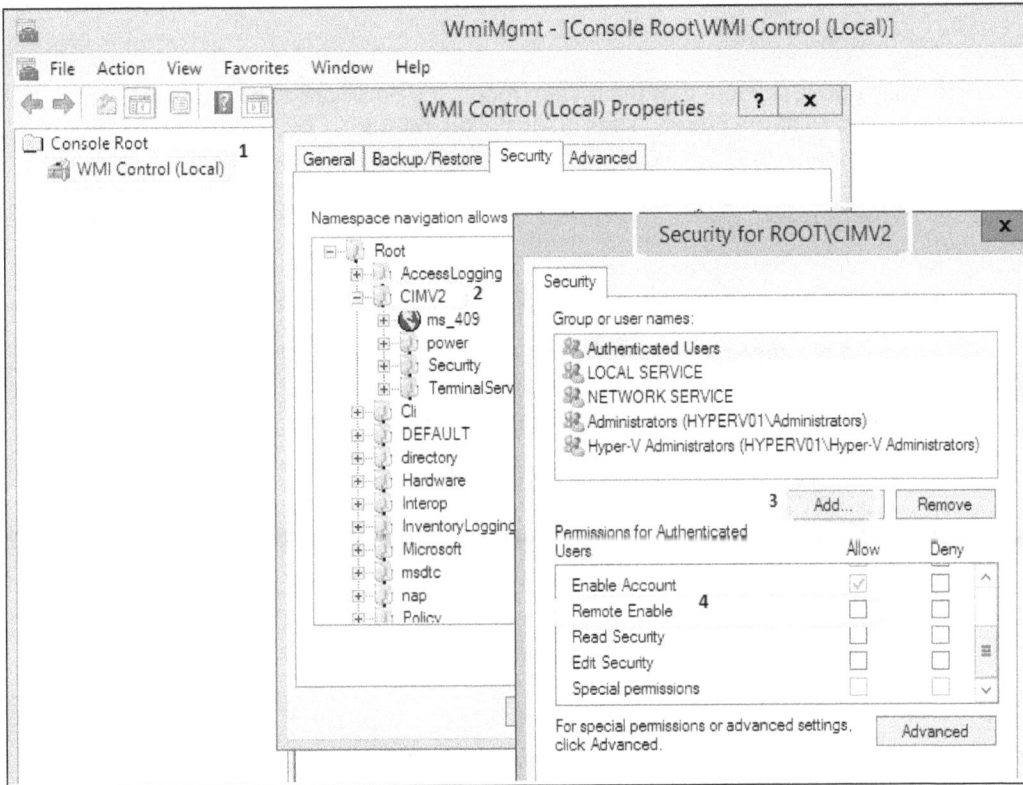

Deploying SC App Controller 2012 R2 for hybrid cloud management

System Center App Controller (**SCAC**) is a replacement for VMM Self-Service Portal. However, it is far from being just a replacement. It enables the integration and management of the VMM 2012 and Windows Azure services, which means that it enables you to manage private and public clouds all together in a single console. You can, for example, upload Windows Azure configuration files, package files, and virtual hard drives from on-premises Hyper-V machines to Windows Azure.

> Check the Service terms of use and privacy statement for the Windows Azure service at `http://azure.microsoft.com/en-us/support/legal/services-terms/`.

Getting ready

Before installing SCAC, ensure that the system meets the hardware and software requirements and all of the prerequisites are installed; refer to `http://technet.microsoft.com/en-us/library/gg696060.aspx` for more information.

How to do it...

Carry out the following steps to deploy System Center App Controller 2012 R2:

1. Log on to the server, if you plan to install SCAC 2012 R2, with local administrative rights, browse to the SCAC installation folder, double-click on the setup file, and click on **Install**, as illustrated in the following screenshot:

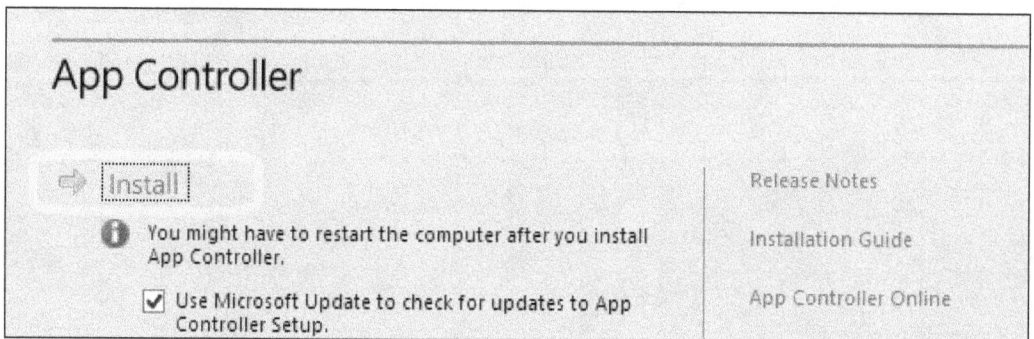

2. On the **Product registration information** page, type in the product key and then click on **Next**.

3. Select **I have read, understood, and agree with the terms of the license agreement** and click on **Next**.

4. The server will be checked to see whether the prerequisites have been met; if they are, you will have to type in the installation path in **Select the installation location** and click on **Next**. A screen will appear, as shown in the following screenshot:

Configure the services

Select an account under which to run App Controller services. You can use the Network Service account or a domain account.

○ Network Service account

◉ Domain account

   Domain and user name:
   lab\svc-scac

   Password:
   ••••••••|

   ⓘ The specified account will only be used for App Controller services that can be configured to use Domain Accounts.

Specify a port for App Controller to use for its internal communication

Port:
18622

5. On the **Configure the services** page, type in the user credentials (for example, `lab\svc-scac`, which is specifically designated for the App Controller services) and either accept the default (`18622`) or type in a new port, which will be used for communication between the App Controller services.

> You can enter the credentials for either of these two accounts: **Network Service account** or **Domain account**.

6. On the **Configure the website** page, type in or select an IP address from the list of IP addresses that users can use to access the application.

7. In the **Port** field, type the port on which `HTTP.sys` must listen for requests made to this website (for example, `443` for **HTTPS**), as shown in the following screenshot:

Configure the website

Specify the binding settings you want to use for the App Controller website.

Type: IP address: Port:
HTTPS All unassigned ▼   443

◉ Generate self-signed certificate

○ Use existing certificate:

                       ▼   View...   Refresh

> This assigned port cannot be changed without reinstalling App Controller.

8. Select whether to generate a self-signed certificate (which needs to be added to the Trusted Root Certification Authorities store of all of the computers that will access the App Controller website) or a previously imported SSL certificate and then click on **Next**.

9. On the **Configure the database** page, type in the values for the **SQL Server** name field and the **Port**, **Instance name**, and **Database Name** fields and click on **Next**.

> You can only have one SCAC database per SQL Server instance.

10. If you're using an existing App Controller database, like a highly available deployment of SCAC, on the **Configure encryption key** page, select the previously exported encryption key, type in the password, and click on **Next**.

> Use the `Export-SCACAesKey` PowerShell command to export the encryption key.

11. On the **Help improve App Controller for SC 2012** page, you can choose to opt for the **Customer Experience Improvement Program** (**CEIP**) and use or not use Microsoft Update, and then click on **Next**.

12. Click on **Install** to confirm, and then click on **Finish**.

How it works...

Before you begin the installation of the App Controller server, ensure that you have checked all the prerequisites as per the page at `http://technet.microsoft.com/en-us/library/gg696060.aspx`.

To install the App Controller server, you must be logged in as a domain user with local administrative rights. Also, the account must have a DB owner on SQL Server.

During the process, you will be required to provide the database connection, and if the SCAC database already exists on the SQL Server, you can provide the exported encryption key. This process is required when deploying an HA SCAC.

Be careful when selecting the SCAC website port as the assigned port cannot be changed without reinstalling App Controller.

At the end of the installation process, you have the option to start the SCAC website. Note that Silverlight is required to open it.

[If you are facing issues while installing SCAC, you can check the logfiles located in the `%LOCALAPPDATA%\AppController\Logs` folder.]

There's more...

To connect to SC App Controller, open the SCAC URL (for example, `https://w2012-vmm.lab.local`) on a web browser. Provide suitable credentials and click on **Sign in**. If single sign-on is enabled, you will not be prompted for credentials.

Connecting to private clouds – integrating with VMM 2012

Open the SCAC website and carry out the following steps to connect SCAC to SVMM:

1. On the **Overview** page, click on **Connect a Virtual Machine...** under **Private Clouds** (or click on **Clouds** and then on **VMM Server** on the ribbon) as shown in the following screenshot:

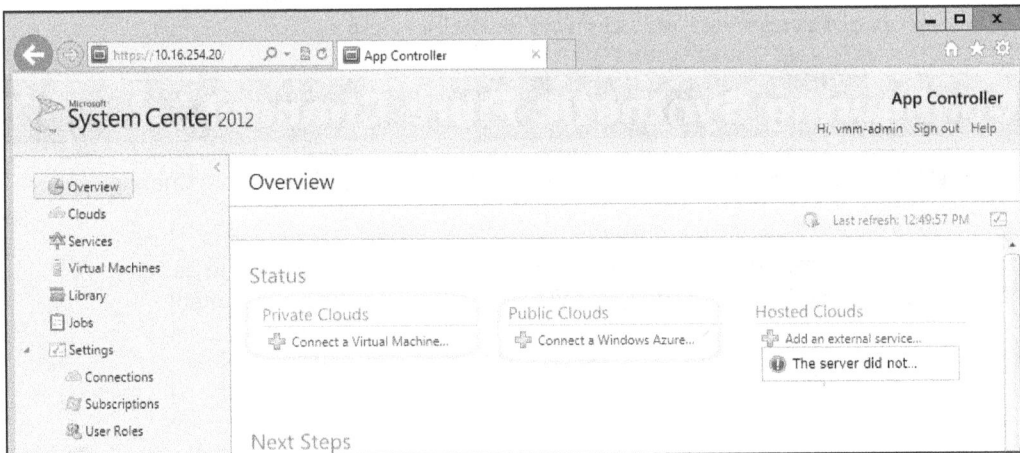

2. In the **Connect** dialog, type in the **Connection name**, an optional description, and the FQDN and port of the VMM management server.

3. Select **Automatically import SSL certificates** to allow files and templates to be copied to and from the VMM cloud libraries, and then click on **OK** to create the VMM connection.

Connecting to public clouds

Open the SCAC website (for example, `https://w2012-vmm.lab.local`) and carry out the following steps to connect SCAC to a Windows Azure subscription:

1. On the **Overview** page, click on **Connect a Windows Azure...** under **Public Clouds** (or click on **Clouds**, then on **Connect**, and then on **Windows Azure Subscription** on the ribbon).

2. In the **Connect** dialog, type in the name, an optional description, and the subscription ID that can be found on the Windows Azure Management Portal.

3. Click on **Browse** to import the management certificates, and then click on **OK** to create the Azure connection.

See also

▶   The *How to Connect to a Hosting Provider in System Center 2012 SP1* article at `http://technet.microsoft.com/en-us/library/jj605416.aspx`

▶   The *Managing Windows Azure Subscription Settings* article at `http://technet.microsoft.com/en-us/library/hh221354.aspx`

▶   The *How to Delegate Users* (to public or private clouds) article at `http://technet.microsoft.com/en-us/library/hh221343.aspx`

Configuring Synthetic Fibre Channel

New in VMM 2012 R2, Synthetic Fibre Channel adds support for Guest Fibre Channel in Hyper-V.

The new VMM feature, which makes use of the SMI-S provider, allows you to assign a Virtual Fibre Channel Adapter in the guest VM with cut down zone management.

Virtual Fibre Channel supports single/multiple storage arrays connected to single/multiple fabrics.

> Multiple storage arrays connected to multiple fabrics would provide dual-redundant paths to storage arrays.

Getting ready

To be able to use Virtual Fibre Channel, confirm that the following are in place:

- ▸ The SAN, Fibre Channel switches and HBA NIC firmware, and drivers are up to date
- ▸ The SAN is configured to present logical units
- ▸ The SAN SMI-S provider is installed and configured
- ▸ NPIV is configured and enabled on the Fibre Channel switches and HBAs
- ▸ The Hyper-V servers are running Windows Server 2012 or higher
- ▸ You are logged in with an account that is a member of the VMM Administrator or Delegated Administrator user role in the VMM console
- ▸ You have created a Run As account with permissions to access the SAN SMI-S provider

How to do it...

After confirming all of the mentioned prerequisites, carry out the following tasks to configure a guest VM direct access to the SAN (discover and add the Fibre Channel fabric and assign classifications to it):

1. In the VMM console, go to the **Fabric** pane in the **Fabric** workspace and click on **Storage**.

2. Click on **Add Resources** on the **Home** tab and then select **Storage Devices**.

3. On the **Select Provider Type** page, select **Fibre Channel fabric discovered and managed by a SMI-S provider** and click on **Next** as shown in the following screenshot:

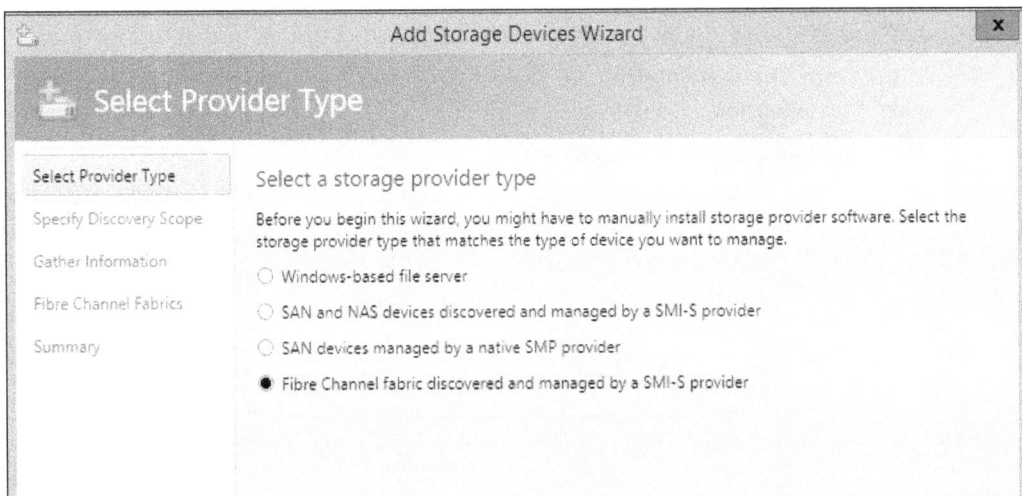

4. On the **Specify Discovery Scope** page, enter the following information:

   ❑ The IP address or FQDN of the storage provider

   ❑ The port number used to connect to the storage provider

   > If required, select **Use Secure Sockets Layer (SSL) connection** to enable HTTPS to communicate with the storage provider.

   ❑ The Run As account that has access to the storage provider

5. On the **Gather Information** page, VMM will automatically discover and import the Fibre Channel fabric information.

   > If the process is successful, the fabric name, switches, and **World Wide Node Names** (**WWNNs**) will be displayed on this page. To retry the discovery process for an unsuccessful attempt, click on **Scan Provider**.

6. Click on **Next** to continue.

   > If you selected the SSL connection, during discovery, the **Import Certificate** dialog box will be displayed. Review the certificate and click on **Import**.
   >
   > Also, during the import process, a verification of the common name (CN) will happen, and this may cause an issue if the certificate does not have a CN value or if it does not match the NetBIOS name, FQDN, or IP address that VMM uses.

7. On the **Fibre Channel Fabrics** page, select the Fibre Channel in the **Storage** column, select **Classification**, and then click on **Next**.

8. On the **Summary** page, click on **Finish**.

How it works...

A **virtual storage area network (vSAN)** is a collection of physical Fibre Channel **host bus adapter (HBA)** ports on a physical Hyper-V server that a virtual machine connects to in order to access Fibre Channel storages.

> One or more vSANs can be created for each physical server, but vSAN's can only have HBAs from the same fabric.

Virtual Host Bus Adapters (vHBAs) symbolize the virtualization of the Fibre Channel HBAs, which are then used by virtual machines to connect to a vSAN.

> The following VMM PowerShell scripts can be used to get and list the virtual machines with the assigned vHBA:
>
> `$VMsWithHBA = Get-VM | Where HasVirtualFibreChannelAdapters`
>
> `$VMsWithHBA | ft Name, Status`

Each vHBA has its own unique WWNN. The Windows 2012/R2 Hyper-V NPIV capability allows a physical HBA to have many associated vHBAs. You can add or remove HBA ports assigned to a vSAN as required.

> As a recommended best practice when working with Virtual Fibre Channel, make sure you update the firmware and drivers throughout the stack: servers, switches, storage, HBAs, and the OS. Also, confirm that each Hyper-V host has been configured identically. Template or Bare Metal host provisioning can help you with that. Alternatively, if you're PowerShell ready, there is DSC in 4.0.

There's more...

After discovering, adding, and classifying, you will be able to perform storage operations, as discussed in the next sections.

Creating virtual SANs

Carry out the following steps to create a vSAN:

1. In the **Fabric** workspace on the **Fabric** pane, select the Hyper-V server, right-click on it, and then click on **Properties**.

2. Click on the **Hardware** tab, then click on **New Virtual SAN**, and provide a name and description for the vSAN, as shown in the following screenshot:

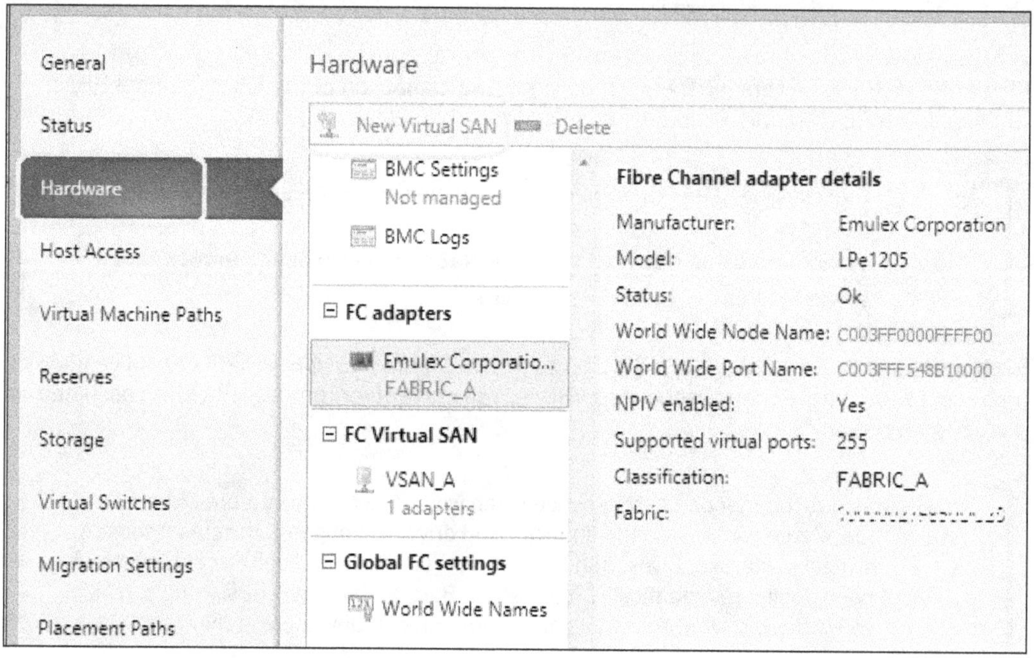

3. Below **Fibre Channel adapters**, select the HBAs that will be assigned to the vSAN and click on **OK**.

4. Create the zones and activate or inactive zone sets.

> Zones tie each server or virtual machine vHBA to a storage array.

5. In the **VMs and Services** workspace, select the virtual machine from the **Services** pane, right-click on it, and then click on **Properties**.

6. Click on the **Storage** tab, then click on **Add**, and then select **Add Fibre Channel Array**.

7. In the **Create New Zone** window, provide a value for **Zone Name**, select the storage array, switch, and the relevant WWPM port(s), and then click on **Create**.

> You can view the available zone aliases by clicking on **Show aliases**.
>
> To change an existing vHBA port configuration or to apply a new setting, you will need to recreate the port by removing it and adding it again.

8. Now, create the storage LUNs and register them for the Hyper-V servers, VMs, or service tiers, as required. For more information, see the *Configuring the allocation method for a storage array* section in *Chapter 5, Configuring Fabric Resources in VMM*.

9. Create a VM template, and for each Virtual Fibre Channel Adapter (vHBA) that is created, specify dynamic or static WWN assignments and select the fabric classification. The fabric classification is used to connect a vHBA to a storage fabric. For more information, see the *Creating a VM or a VM template with Virtual Fibre Channel* section.

10. Create a VM, select the destination host to deploy the VM to, zone a Fibre Channel array to the VM, add a disk to the VM, create a LUN, and then register (unmask) the LUN to the VM. For more information, see the *Creating a VM or a VM template with Virtual Fibre Channel* section.

11. Create a service template, add VM templates to it, and for each Virtual Fibre Channel Adapter (vHBA) that is created, specify dynamic or static WWN assignments and select the fabric classification. For more information about creating Services templates, see the *Creating and deploying service templates* recipe in *Chapter 6, Deploying Virtual Machines and Services*.

12. Create and deploy the service tier, zone a Fibre Channel array to it, add a disk to it, create a LUN, and finally register (unmask) the LUN to the service tier. For more information, see the *Creating a Service Tier for Virtual Fibre Channel* page at `http://technet.microsoft.com/en-us/library/dn458367.aspx`.

Creating a VM or a VM template with Virtual Fibre Channel

The next step is to create a VM or VM template with a vHBA. Follow the steps described in the *Configuring the allocation method for a storage array* section in *Chapter 5, Configuring Fabric Resources in VMM*, and then perform the ensuing steps:

1. On the **Configure Hardware** page, add a new Fibre Channel adapter.

2. Assign **Dynamic** or **Static** WWPN and choose a fabric classification for every created vHBA.

> When placing and deploying the VM on a Hyper-V host, make sure it contains a vSAN that ties it with the storage. For more information, see *Chapter 6, Deploying Virtual Machines and Services*.
>
> After the virtual machine is deployed to a Hyper-V host, the HBA can be zoned to that VM, and a LUN can be created for the array and registered to the VM.

Editing vSAN port assignments

Carry out the following steps to modify the Hyper-V HBA ports assigned to a vSAN:

1. On the **Fabric** pane of the **Fabric** workspace, select the Hyper-V host, right-click on it, and select **Properties**.

2. Click on the **Hardware** tab, and then below **FC Virtual SAN**, check/uncheck the listed HBA ports.

Removing a vSAN

Carry out the following steps to remove a vSAN:

1. On the **Fabric** pane of the **Fabric** workspace, select the Hyper-V host, right-click on it, and select **Properties**.

2. Click on the **Hardware** tab, and then below **FC Virtual SAN**, select the vSAN, click on **Delete**, and then click on **OK**.

Adding a new vHBA

Use the following procedure to add a Virtual Fibre Channel Adapter (vHBA) and assign it to a vSAN:

1. Open the **Fabric** workspace.

2. On the **Fabric** pane, right-click on the applicable host and then click on **Properties**.

3. On the **Properties** page, click on the **Hardware Configuration** tab, click on **New**, then click on **Fibre Channel Adapter**, and then perform the following:

   1. In the **Virtual SAN name** box, select a vSAN from the drop-down list to assign to the vHBA.

   2. If you want to dynamically assign the range of port settings for the vHBA, click on **Dynamically assign World Wide Names**.

   3. If you want to statically assign port settings for the vHBA, click on **Statically assign World Wide Names** and then enter primary and secondary WWNN and WWPN port settings for the vHBA.

   4. When completed, click on **OK**.

Editing vHBA WWNN and WWPN dynamic settings

Carry out the following steps to modify the port settings that can be assigned to a vHBA:

1. On the **Fabric** pane of the **Fabric** workspace, select the Hyper-V host, right-click on it, and select **Properties**.

2. Click on the **Hardware** tab, and then below **Global FC settings**, provide the **World Wide Node Name** and the lowest and highest WWPN port settings, and then click on **OK**.

See also

▸ The *Managing Virtual Fibre Channel in VMM* article at `http://technet.microsoft.com/en-us/library/dn458365.aspx`

9
Integration with System Center Operations Manager 2012 R2

In this chapter, we will cover the following:

- ▶ Installing System Center Operations Manager 2012 R2
- ▶ Installing management packs
- ▶ Managing Discovery and Agents
- ▶ Configuring the integration between Operations Manager 2012 and VMM 2012
- ▶ Enabling reporting in VMM
- ▶ Extending monitoring with management packs

Introduction

This chapter provides tips and techniques to allow administrators to integrate Operations Manager 2012 R2 with Virtual Machine Manager 2012 R2 to monitor the health and performance of virtual machine hosts and their virtual machines, as well as to use the Operations Manager reporting functionality.

In a hybrid hypervisor environment (for example, Hyper-V and VMware), using Operations Manager **management packs** (**MPs**) (for example, Veeam MP), you can monitor the Hyper-V hosts and the VMware hosts, which allow you to use only the System Center console to manage and monitor the hybrid hypervisor environment.

You can also monitor the health and availability of the VMM infrastructure, management, database, and library servers. The following screenshot will show you the diagram views of the virtualized environment through the Operations Manager:

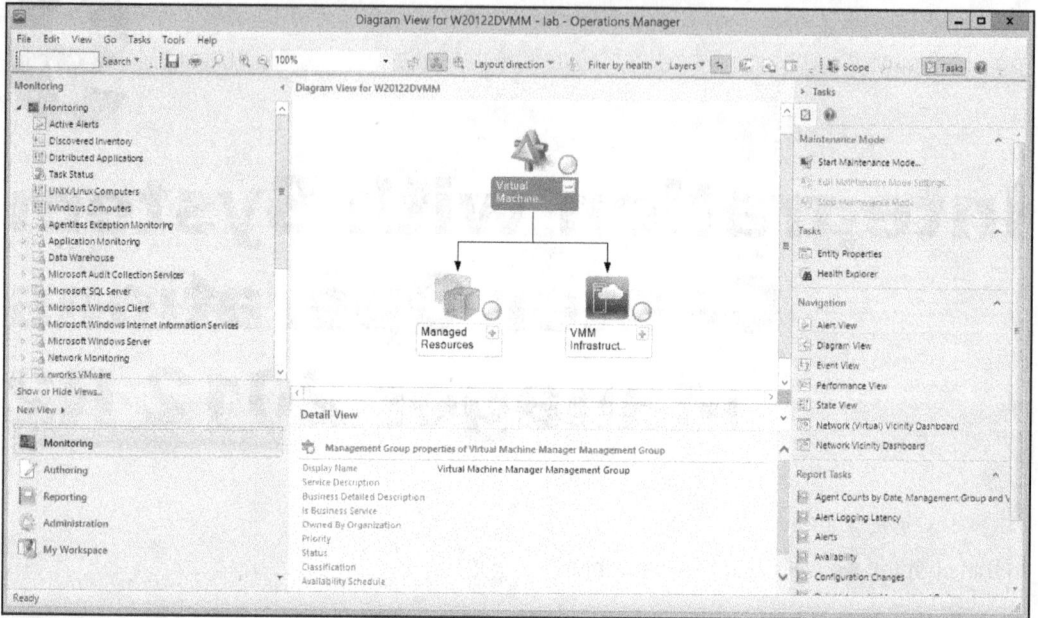

Installing System Center Operations Manager 2012 R2

This recipe will guide you through the process of installing System Center Operations Manager for the integration with VMM.

Operations Manager has integrated product and company knowledge for proactive tuning. It also allows the user to compute the OS, applications, services, and out-of-the-box network monitoring, reporting, and many more features' extensibility through management packs, thus providing cross-platform visibility.

The deployment used in this recipe assumes a small environment with all components installed on the same server. For datacenters and enterprise deployments, it is recommended to distribute the features and services across multiple servers to allow for scalability. For a complete design reference and complex implementation of SCOM 2012 R2, follow the Microsoft Operations Manager deployment guide, available at http://go.microsoft.com/fwlink/?LinkId=246682.

When planning, use *Operations Guide for System Center 2012 – Operations Manager* (`http://go.microsoft.com/fwlink/p/?LinkID=207751`) to determine the hardware requirements.

Getting ready

Before starting, check out the system requirements and design planning for System Center Operations Manager 2012 R2 at `http://technet.microsoft.com/en-us/library/jj656654.aspx`.

My recommendation is to deploy System Center Operations Manager 2012 R2 on Windows Server 2012 R2 and the SQL Server 2012 SP1 version.

How to do it...

Carry out the following steps to install Operations Manager 2012 R2:

1. Browse to the SCOM installation folder and click on **Setup**.
2. Click on **Install**.
3. On the **Select the features to install** page, select the components that apply to your environment, and then click on **Next**, as shown in the following screenshot:

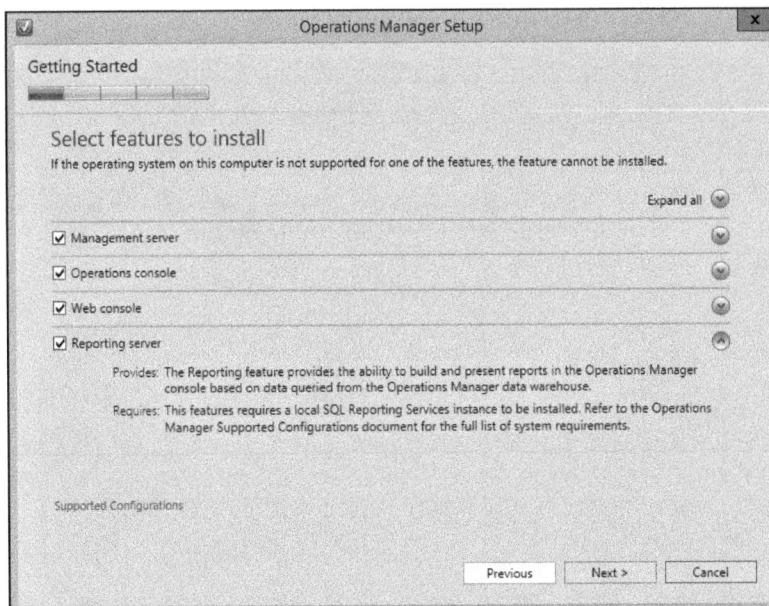

> The recommendation is to have a dedicated server, but it all depends on the size of the deployment. You can select all of the components to be installed on the same server for a small deployment.
>
> Note, though, that you cannot install Operations Manager in the same server that you installed or plan to install System Center Data Protection Manager on, as it is not supported by Microsoft.

4. Type in the location where you'd install Operations Manager 2012 R2, or accept the default location and click on **Next**.

5. The installation will check if your system has passed all of the requirements. A screen showing the issues will be displayed if any of the requirements are not met, and you will be asked to fix and verify it again before continuing with the installation, as shown in the following screenshot:

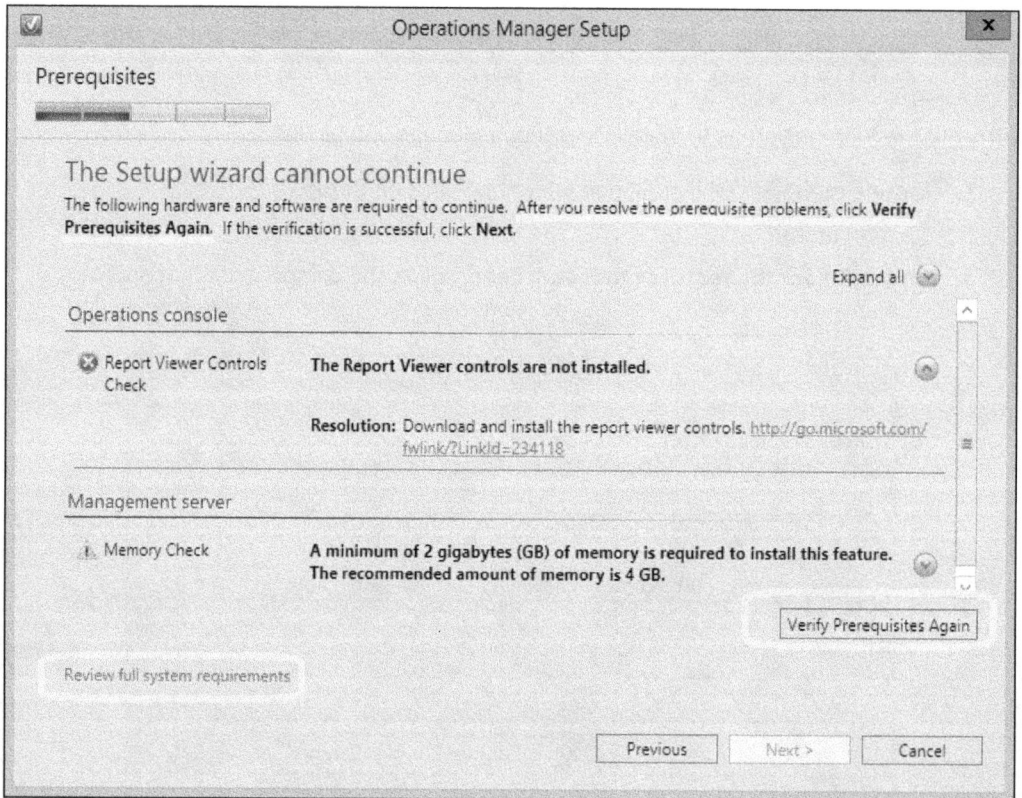

6. Once all of the prerequisites are met, click on **Next** to proceed with the setup.

7. On the **Specify an installation option** page, if this is the first Operations Manager, select the **Create the first Management server in a new management group** option and provide a value in the **Management group name** field. Otherwise, select the **Add a Management server to an existing management group** option, as shown in the following screenshot:

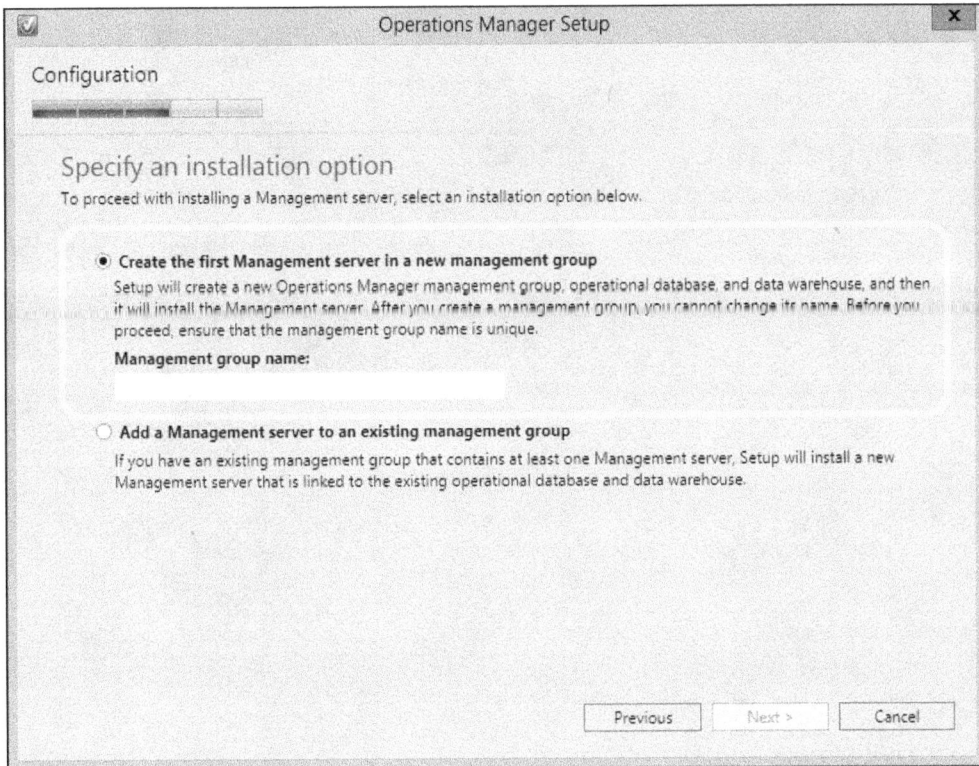

8. Click on **Next** to continue, accept the EULA, and click on **Next**.

9. On the **Configure the operational database** page, provide the SQL Database server and instance names, SQL Server port number, database name, database size, and database location, as shown in the following screenshot.

> It is recommended to keep the default value for **Database name**.

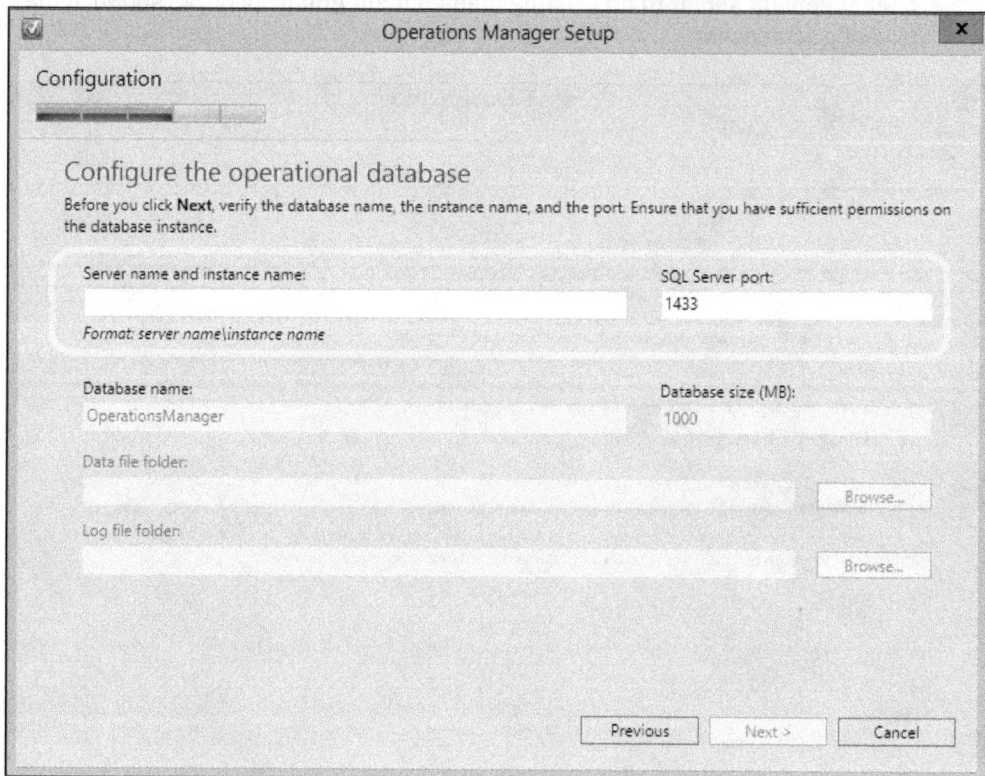

Operations Manager Setup   X

Configuration

Configure the operational database

Before you click **Next**, verify the database name, the instance name, and the port. Ensure that you have sufficient permissions on the database instance.

Server name and instance name:

SQL Server port:

1433

Format: server name\instance name

Database name:

OperationsManager

Database size (MB):

1000

Data file folder:

Browse...

Log file folder:

Browse...

Previous   Next >   Cancel

---

10. Click on **Next**.

> The installation account needs DB owner rights on the database.

11. On the **Configure the data warehouse database** page, provide the SQL Database server for the dataware and instance and provide the SQL Database server and instance name, SQL Server port number, database name, database size, and database location, as shown in the following screenshot:

12. On the **Specify a Website** page, leave the **Default Web Site** option selected and optionally select **Enable SSL**; then click on **Next**.

13. Select an authentication mode for use with the web console and click on **Next**.

> For *intranet* scenarios, select mixed mode authentication.

14. On the **SQL Server instance for Reporting Services** page, select the instance where you want to host the **Reporting Services (SSRS)**.

> Make sure SQL Server has the SQL Server Full-Text Search and Analysis server components installed.

15. On the **Configure Operations Manager accounts** page, provide the domain account credentials (for example, `lab\svc-scom`) for the Operations Manager services as shown in the following screenshot:

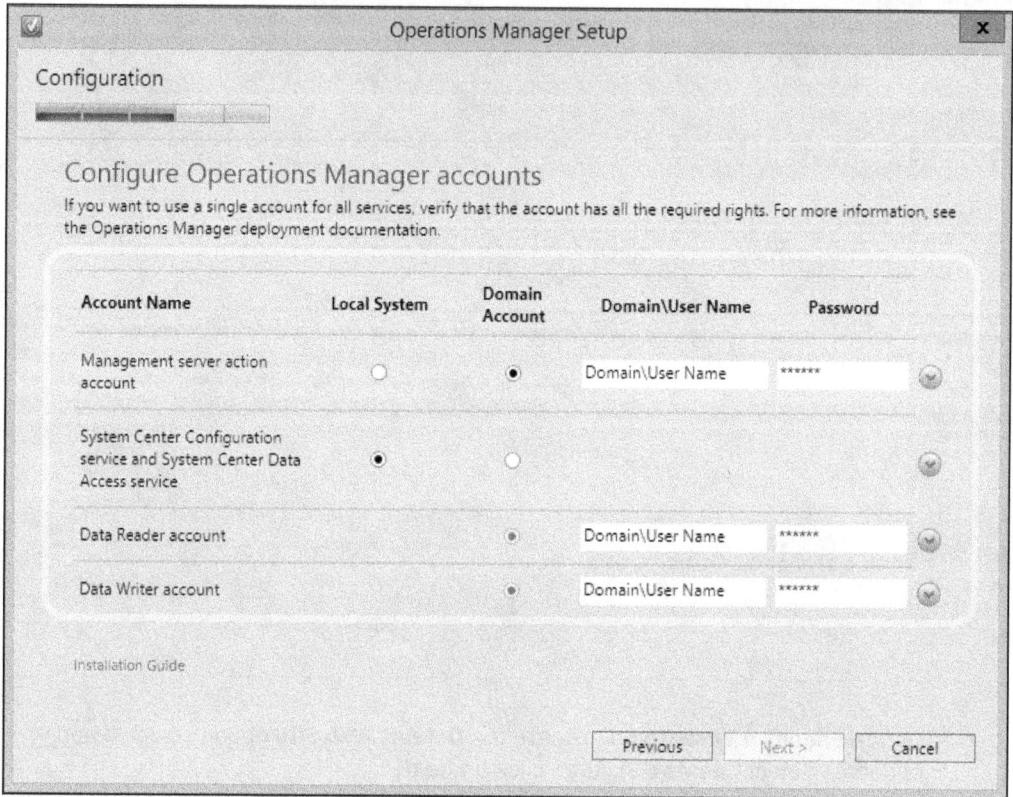

You can use a single domain account. For account requirements, refer to the Microsoft Operations Manager deployment guide at `http://go.microsoft.com/fwlink/?LinkId=246682`.

16. On the **Installation Summary** page, review the options and click on **Install**, and then on **Close**. The Operations Manager console will open.

How it works...

When deploying Operations Manager 2012 R2, it is important to consider the placement of the components. Work on the Operations Manager design before implementing it. Refer to the *OpsMgr 2012 Design Guide*, available at `http://blogs.technet.com/b/momteam/archive/2012/04/13/opsmgr-2012-design-guide.aspx`.

On the **Configure Operational Database** page, if you are installing the first management server, a new operational database will be created. If you are installing additional management servers, an existing database will be used.

On the **SQL Server instance for Reporting Services** page, make sure you have configured the Reporting Services at SQL setup previously using the Reporting Services Configuration Manager tool, and that the SQL Server Agent is running.

> I would recommend deploying the Reporting Server to another server when deploying Operations Manager on a production environment.

During the OpsMgr setup, you will be required to provide the **Management Server Action Account** credentials and the **System Center Configuration service and System Center Data Access service** account credentials too. The recommendation is to use a domain account so that you can use the same account for both the services.

> The setup will automatically assign the local computer's `Administrators` group to the Operations Manager administrator's role.

The single-server scenario combines all roles into a single instance and supports these services: monitoring and alerting, reporting, audit collection, agentless-exception management, and data.

> If you are planning to monitor the network, it is recommended to move the SQL Server `tempdb` database to a separate disk that has multiple spindles.

There's more...

To confirm the health of the management server, carry out the following steps:

1. In the OpsMgr console, click on the **Administration** workspace.

2. In **Device Management**, select **Management Servers** to confirm that the installed server has a green check mark in the **Health State** column.

See also

▶ The *Deploying System Center 2012 – Operations Manager* article, available at http://technet.microsoft.com/en-us/library/hh278852.aspx

Installing management packs

After installing Operations Manager, you need to install some management packs and agents on the Hyper-V servers and on the VMM server.

This recipe will guide you through the installation of management packs, but first make sure you have installed the Operations Manager Operations console on the VMM management server.

You need to import the following management packs for the VMM 2012 R2 integration:

▶ Windows Server Operating System

▶ Windows Server 2008 Operating System (Discovery)

▶ Internet Information Services 2003

▶ Internet Information Services 7

▶ Internet Information Services library

▶ SQL Server Core Library

Getting ready

Before you begin, make sure the correct version of PowerShell is installed, that is, PowerShell v2 for SC 2012 and PowerShell v3 for SC2012 R2.

Open the PowerShell command and type in the following:

```
PS \> $PSVersionTable
```

[💡 Alternatively, you can type Get-Host.]

How to do it...

Carry out the following steps to install the required MPs in order to integrate with VMM 2012 R2:

1. In the OpsMgr console, click on the **Administration** workspace on the bottom-left pane.

2. On the left-hand side pane, right-click on **Management Packs** and click on **Import Management Packs**.

3. In the **Import Management Packs** wizard, click on **Add**, and then click on **Add from catalog**.

4. In the **Select Management Packs from Catalog** dialog box, for each of the following management packs, repeat steps 5 to 7:

    ❏ Windows Server Operating System Library

    ❏ Windows Server 2008 Operating System (Discovery)

    ❏ Windows Server Internet Information Services 2003

    ❏ Windows Server 2008 Internet Information Services 7

    ❏ Windows Server Internet Information Services library

    ❏ SQL Server Core Library

[💡 The Windows Server 2008 and IIS 2003/7 MPs are required by VMM 2012 even though you are installing it on a Windows 2012 / 2012 R2 server.

There are numerous management packs for Operations Manager. You can use this recipe to install other OpsMgr MPs from the catalog web service. You can also download the MPs from Microsoft System Center Marketplace, which contains the MPs and documentation from Microsoft and some non-Microsoft companies. Save them to a shared folder and then import. Refer to http://systemcenter.pinpoint.microsoft.com/en-US/home.]

5. In the **Find** field, type in the management pack to search for in the online catalog and click on **Search**.

6. The **Management packs in the catalog** list will show all of the packs that match the search criterion. To import, select the management pack, click on **Select**, and then click on **Add** as shown in the following screenshot:

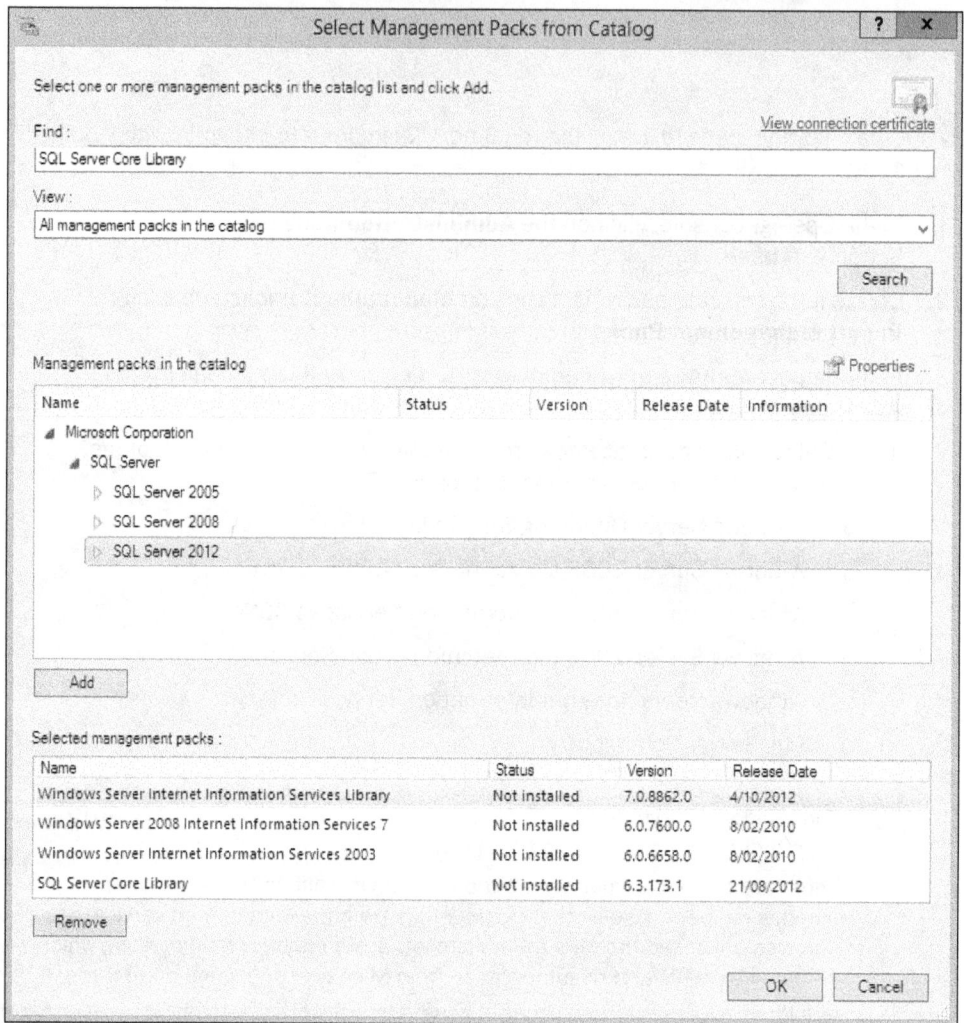

Select Management Packs from Catalog   [?] [X]

Select one or more management packs in the catalog list and click Add.

View connection certificate

Find :

```
SQL Server Core Library
```

View :

```
All management packs in the catalog                                          ⌄
```

[Search]

Management packs in the catalog   📄 Properties ...

Name	Status	Version	Release Date	Information
◢ Microsoft Corporation				
◢ SQL Server				
▷ SQL Server 2005				
▷ SQL Server 2008				
▷ SQL Server 2012				

[Add]

Selected management packs :

Name	Status	Version	Release Date
Windows Server Internet Information Services Library	Not installed	7.0.8862.0	4/10/2012
Windows Server 2008 Internet Information Services 7	Not installed	6.0.7600.0	8/02/2010
Windows Server Internet Information Services 2003	Not installed	6.0.6658.0	8/02/2010
SQL Server Core Library	Not installed	6.3.173.1	21/08/2012

[Remove]

[OK]   [Cancel]

> In the **View** section, you can refine the search by selecting, for example, to show only those management packs released within the last three months. The default view lists all of the management packs in the catalog.

7. Click on **OK** after adding the required management packs.

8. On the **Select Management Packs** page, the MPs will be listed with either a green icon, a yellow icon, or a red icon. The green icon indicates that the MP can be imported. The yellow information icon means that it is dependent on other MPs that are available in the catalog, and you can fix the dependency by clicking on **Resolve**. The red error icon indicates that it is dependent on other MPs, but the dependent MPs are not available in the catalog.

9. Click on **Import** if all management packs have their icon statuses as green.

10. On the **Import Management Packs** page, the progress for each management pack will be displayed. Click on **Close** when the process is finished.

How it works...

You can import the management packs available for Operations Manager using the following methods:

- ▶ **The OpsMgr console**: You can perform the following actions in the **Management Packs** menu of the **Administration** workspace:

  - ❑ Import directly from Microsoft's online catalog

  - ❑ Import from disk/share

  - ❑ Download the management pack from the online catalog to import at a later time

- ▶ **The Internet browser**: You can download the management pack from the online catalog to import at a later time, or to install on an OpsMgr that is not connected to the Internet

While using the OpsMgr console, verify that all management packs show a green status. Any MP displaying the yellow information icon or the red error icon in the import list will not be imported.

If there is no Internet connection on the OpsMgr, use an Internet browser to locate and download the management pack to a folder/share. Then copy the management pack to the OpsMgr server and use the option to import from disk/share.

See also

- ▶ The *Installing System Center Operations Manager 2012 R2* recipe

- ▶ Visit Microsoft System Center Marketplace at `http://go.microsoft.com/fwlink/?LinkId=82105` or `http://systemcenter.pinpoint.microsoft.com/en-US/home`

Managing Discovery and Agents

After installing the Operations Manager, you need to deploy the agents and start monitoring servers, network devices, services, and applications.

We also need to install the agents on the VMM management server and on all Hyper-V servers. This is required in order to integrate VMM with Operations Manager.

How to do it...

Carry out the following steps to install the OpsMgr agent on a Windows OS by using the **Discovery Wizard** tool:

1. On the OpsMgr console, click on **Administration** on the left-hand side, and then on **Discovery Wizard...** as shown in the following screenshot:

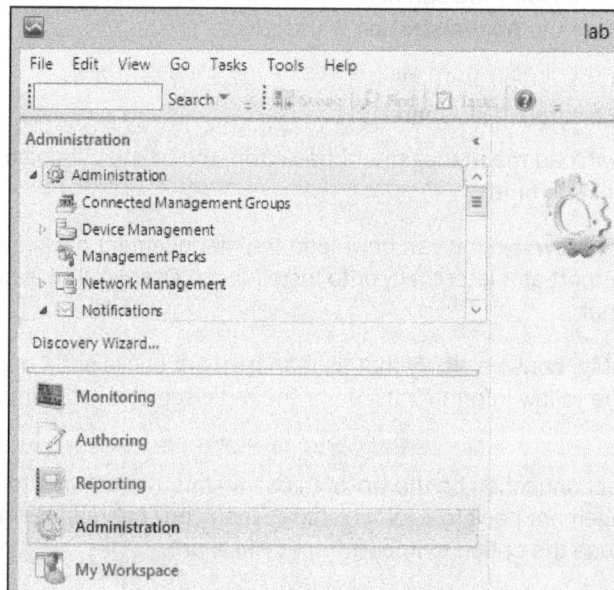

2. On the **What would you like to manage?** page (shown on clicking the **Discovery Type** tab), click on **Windows computers** and then on **Next**.

3. On the **Auto or Advanced?** page, select either **Automatic computer discovery** (to scan all of the Windows computers on the domain) or **Advanced discover**.

4. If you have selected **Advanced discovery**, perform the following steps:

   ❑ From the **Computer and Device Classes** drop-down list, select either **Servers and Clients**, **Servers Only**, or **Clients Only**

❑ From the **Management Server** drop-down list, select the OpsMgr management server or the gateway server

This is shown in the following screenshot:

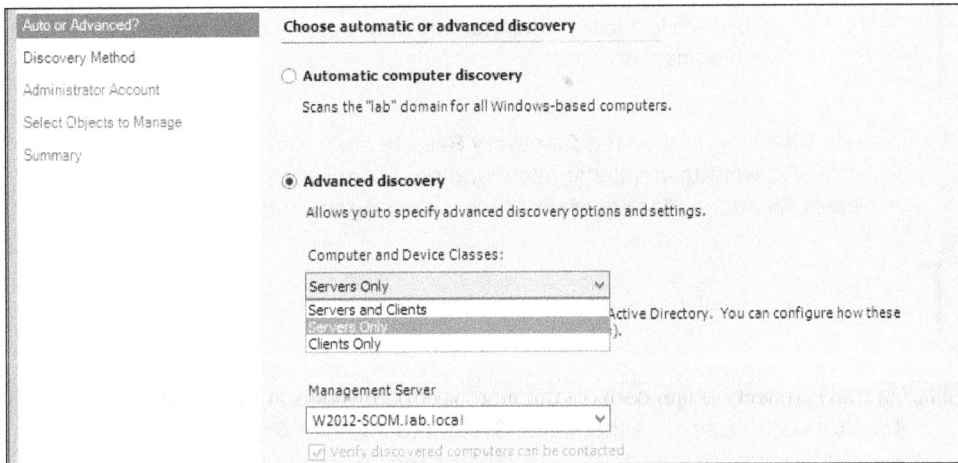

5. Click on **Next** to discover.

6. On the **Discovery Method** page (shown in the next screenshot), select **Scan Active Directory** or **Browse for, or type-in computer names**.

7. If you have selected **Scan Active Directory**, click on **Configure....** In the **Find Computers** dialog box, in the **Computers** tab or in the **Advanced** tab, provide the information of the search criteria and click on **OK**. Then select the domain from the **Domain** list.

8. If you selected **Browse for, or type-in computer names**, click on **Browse**, provide the computer names separated by a semicolon, comma, or a new line character (for example, **Hyperv01, w2012-vmm**), and then click on **OK**.

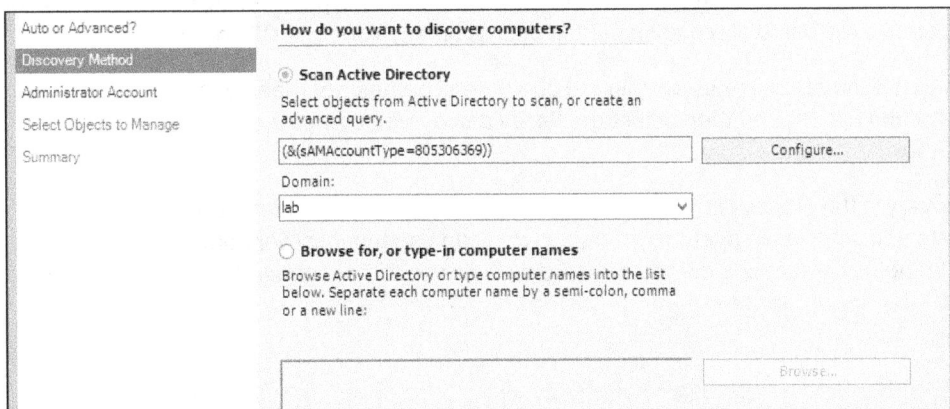

9. Click on **Next** and then on the **Administrator Account** page. Select **Use selected Management Server Action Account** or **Other user account** and provide the **User name** value, **Password**, and the **Domain** value (from the drop-down list).

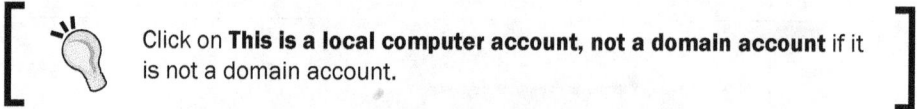

> Click on **This is a local computer account, not a domain account** if it is not a domain account.

10. Click on **Discover**, and on the **Discovery Results** page, select the computers on which you want to install the agent and be monitored by OpsMgr. Or click on **Select All** and in **Management Mode**, select **Agent** and then click on **Next**.

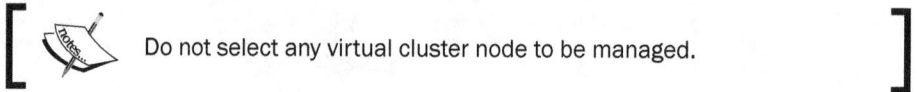

> Do not select any virtual cluster node to be managed.

11. On the **Summary** page, confirm the installation path and in the **Agent Action Account** section, select either **Local System** (default) or **Other**. In either case, you will need to provide the values in the **User name**, **Password**, and **Domain** fields.

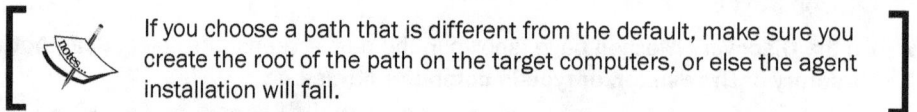

> If you choose a path that is different from the default, make sure you create the root of the path on the target computers, or else the agent installation will fail.

12. Click on **Finish**, and in the **Agent Management Task Status** dialog box, you will see the agent **Status** column changing from **Queued** to **Success**. This indicates that the computers are ready to be managed. Lastly, click on **Close**.

How it works...

In this recipe, as we are targeting the VMM server and the Hyper-V hosts, select **Servers Only**. You can use the same steps to install the agents on any Windows OS computer.

Note that if the AD does not contain the computers' names, you need to select the **Servers and Clients** option, and then select the **Verify discovered computers can be contacted** checkbox.

Discovery is the process in which OpsMgr searches the environment for all manageable objects and deploys an agent to monitor it. You can use the discovery process at any time to add the newly installed computers or roles/features to be managed.

For the OpsMgr agent to be installed, the account used to run the process requires local administrator rights on the target computer.

You can manually install the agents, or you can embed the agent in the host image of the monitored computer.

See also

▸ For information on port requirements for OpsMgr agents, refer to the link `http://go.microsoft.com/fwlink/p/?LinkId=230474`

▸ The *Install Agent on UNIX and Linux Using the Discovery Wizard* article available at `http://technet.microsoft.com/en-us/library/hh230722.aspx`

▸ The *Install Agent Using the MOMAgent.msi Setup Wizard* article available at `http://technet.microsoft.com/en-us/library/hh212915.aspx`

▸ The *Configuring Agents* article available at `http://technet.microsoft.com/en-us/library/hh212883.aspx`

Configuring the integration between Operations Manager 2012 and VMM 2012

This recipe will guide you through the process of configuring the connectivity between VMM and System Center Operations Manager 2012 / SP1 / R2.

By integrating VMM with Operations Manager (OpsMgr), you can use the OpsMgr console to monitor the health and availability of the VMs and Hyper-V servers, VMM management and database servers, library servers, and diagram views of the virtualized environment.

In order to establish a connection with VMM, you need to configure the Operations Manager servers to work with VMM. This configuration is done on the VMM console.

Getting ready

Before starting, make sure you do the following:

▸ Install the Operations Manager console on the VMM management server, as it is required for the integration between VMM and Operations Manager

▸ Install the required OpsMgr management packs as discussed in the *Installing management packs* recipe in this chapter

How to do it...

Carry out the following steps to set up the integration between Operations Manager 2012 and VMM 2012:

1. If you installed the Operations Manager on a separate server (recommended), install the Operations Manager agent on the VMM management server.

2. In the VMM console, in the **Settings** workspace to the left-hand side of the window, click on **System Center Settings**, and then right-click on **Operations Manager Server** and then select **Properties**:

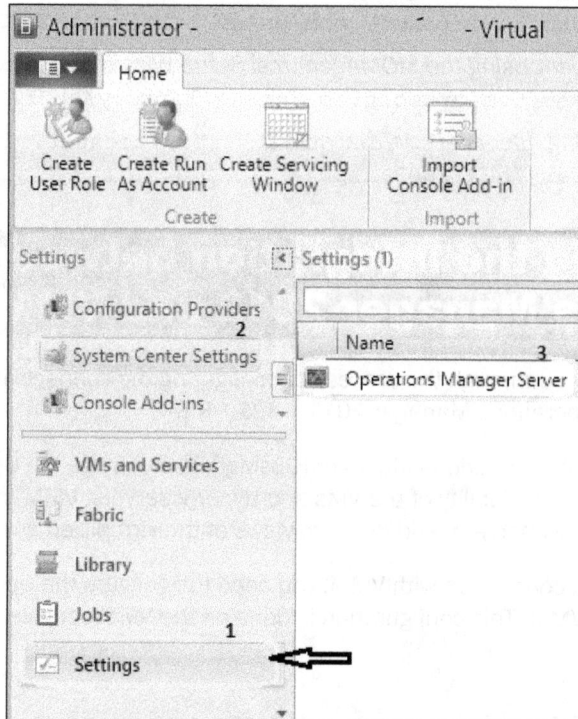

3. On the **Introduction** page, click on **Next**.

4. On the **Configure connection from VMM to Operations Manager** page, in the **Server name** field, type in the OpsMgr management server name (for example, w2012-scom).

5. Select the account that is going to be used to connect to for the purpose of integration. You can use the VMM server service account or specify a Run As account as shown in the following screenshot:

Add Operations Manager   x

Connection to Operations Manager

Introduction

Connection to...

Connection to VMM

Summary

Configure connection from VMM to Operations Manager

Specify the management server to use, and enter the administrative credentials for the management group to which you want VMM to connect.

Server name:

⦿ **Use the VMM server service account**

  Service account:

○ **Use a Run As account**

                                                              Browse...

☐ **Enable Performance and Resource Optimization (PRO)**

  You must separately enable PRO for each host group, host cluster, service, or cloud with which you want to use PRO.

☐ **Enable maintenance mode integration with Operations Manager**

  When Hosts are put in maintenance mode in VMM, attempt to also set them in maintenance mode in Operations Manager.

                              Previous   Next   Cancel

> Do not select **Enable Performance and Resource Optimization (PRO)** and **Enable maintenance mode integration with Operations Manager** at this point, or the operation will not succeed and will show the following error: **Operations Manager discovery failed with error: "Exception of type 'Microsoft.VirtualManager.EnterpriseManagement.Common. DiscoveryDataInvalidRelationshipSourceExceptionOM10' was thrown."**.

6. Click on **Next**; then type in the account credentials for Operations Manager to connect with the VMM management server (for example, `lab\svc-scom`). Now click on **Next**.

7. On the **Summary** page, click on **Finish**.

> This account will be added to the administrator user role in VMM.

How it works...

The process consists of registering the Operations Manager on the VMM management server using the VMM console.

During the connection process, the account informed to connect Operations Manager to VMM will be added to the administrator user role in VMM.

To verify that the VMM to OpsMgr integration was completed, open OpsMgr and select the **Monitoring** workspace. In the navigation pane, confirm that you see the following:

  ▸ **Virtual Machine Manager**: This includes the health and performance information for virtual machines, hosts, and VMM servers

  ▸ **Virtual Machine Manager View**: This displays diagrams for the managed systems

Note that the OpsMgr diagrams will not be displayed right after the connection is established. It may require many hours to get updated.

Do not enable the PRO or maintenance mode at the integration setup. Enable both later, after the connection is completed.

There's more...

Now that you have enabled the integration with Operations Manager, let's see what more we can do.

Enabling PRO tips and maintenance mode integration in VMM 2012

Performance and Resource Optimization (**PRO**) is a feature supported since VMM 2012 version when integrated with Operations Manager. Carry out the following steps to enable the PRO tips in VMM:

1. In the VMM console, in the bottom-left pane, open the **Settings** workspace.

2. Click on **System Center Settings** and select and right-click on **Operations Manager Server**.

3. On the **Details** page, select **Enable Performance and Resource Optimization (PRO)**.

4. Select **Enable maintenance mode integration with Operations Manager** and then click on **OK**.

> When in maintenance mode, the OpsMgr's agent suppresses alerts, notifications, rules, monitors, automatic responses, state changes, and new alerts. It also automatically places VMs in the maintenance mode when they are moved to the VMM library.

5. On the **Properties** window, click on **Test PRO**.

> Allow some time for the task to complete before clicking on **Test PRO** and after setting up PRO.

6. Confirm the results either in the VMM console (the **Jobs** workspace) or in the Operations console in Operations Manager.

> Note that Dynamic Optimization is now performed and configured in VMM in place of the host load balancing that was performed by PRO in VMM 2008 R2. VMM does include PRO monitors to monitor a VM's **dynamic memory** (**DM**) allocation and maximum VM memory aggregations on Hyper-V hosts.

See also

- ▸ The *Configuring Dynamic Optimization and Power Optimization* recipe in *Chapter 8, Managing Hybrid Clouds, Fabric Updates, Resources, Clusters, and the New Features of R2*
- ▸ The *Installing System Center Operations Manager 2012 R2* recipe

Enabling reporting in VMM

After integrating VMM with Operations Manager for monitoring, you can also enable the integration to provide reporting, which will give you the ability to create and view reports related to Hyper-V servers, VMs, and VMM-related components (for example, the management and library servers).

> Operations Manager only supports SQL Server Reporting Services in the native mode.

Getting ready

In order to enable reporting, you will need to have **SQL Server Analysis Service (SSAS)** preinstalled on the Operations Manager Reporting server (for example, `lab\w2012-scom`).

You also need to install **Analysis Management Objects (AMO)** on all of the VMM management servers for the SQL Server version you have installed. For SQL 2012 SP1, refer to `http://www.microsoft.com/en-us/download/details.aspx?id=35580`.

How to do it...

Carry out the following steps to configure the SQL Server Analysis Services in VMM:

1. Open the VMM console. On the bottom-left pane, click to open the **Settings** workspace, and then in the **Settings** pane to the left-hand side of the window, click on **System Center Settings**.

2. Select and then right-click on **Operations Manager Server**.

3. In the **Operations Manager Settings** dialog box (shown in the following screenshot), click on the **SQL Server Analysis Services** tab on the left pane.

4. Select **Enable SSAS**.

	Operations Manager Settings	✕
Details	**Configure connection to SQL Server Analysis Service (SSAS)**	
Management Packs	In order for the VMM server to use SSAS for forecasting analysis, specify the server and instance name of the SSAS instance server.	
SQL Server Analysis Services	☐ Enable SSAS	
	SSAS server:	
	SSAS instance:	
	Port: [0] ⌄	
	┌ Provide credentials with administrative rights on the SSAS instance ────────────	
	◉ Use an existing Run As account:	
	Browse...	
	○ Enter a user name and password:	
	User name:	
	Example: contoso\domainuser	
	Password:	
	View Script	OK	Cancel

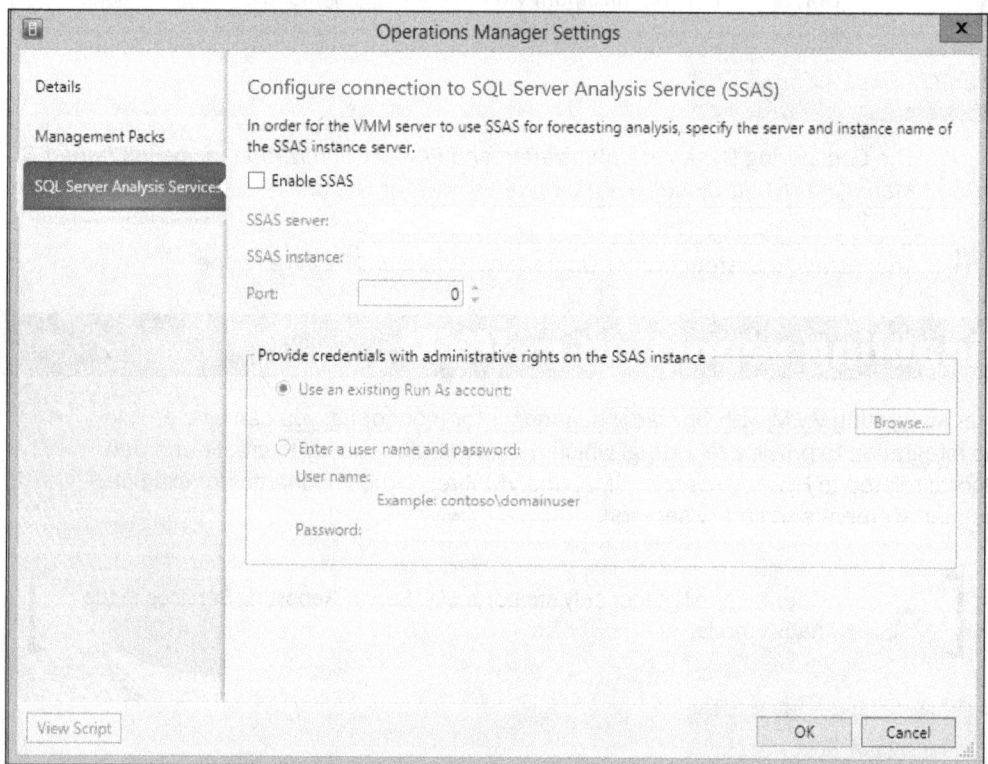

5. Type in the value in the **SSAS server**, **SSAS instance**, and **Port** fields.

6. On the **Provide credentials with administrative rights on the SSAS instance** page, select **Use an existing Run As account**, click on **Browse**, and provide the Run As account, or select **Enter a user name and password** and provide the username (for example, `lab\svc-scom`) and password.

7. Click on **OK** to confirm.

How it works...

The process to set up the SQL Server Analysis Services integration with VMM requires a VMM administrator user role. The account must belong to the **Operations Manager Report Security Administrator** profile.

On the setup wizard, provide the SSAS instance name, which must be the same as that of the SQL Server Reporting Services. You need to type the instance name even if it is already the default instance: **MSSQLSERVER**. The default port is 0 (zero).

Also, make sure that SQL Server Reporting Services allows report access by using the default HTTP port 80.

There's more...

You can view reports in the Operations Manager console's **Reporting** workspace by browsing through the OpsMgr report server (for example, **https://W2012-reports.lab.local/reports**).

You can choose from the following predefined reports or create your own:

▶ **Capacity Utilization report**: This specifies the detailed usage for hosts and other objects

▶ **Chargeback report**: This specifies the chargeback information to cost centers for virtual machines, as shown in the following screenshot:

- **Host Group Forecasting report**: This calculates host activity based on history

- **Host Utilization report**: This shows the number of VMs running, plus their usage (CPU / memory / disk)

- **Host Utilization Growth report**: This shows the percentage change in resource usage and the number of virtual machines that are running on selected hosts during a specified time period

- **Power Savings report**: This shows the summary / detailed information about the power saved for each host in a host group

- **SAN Usage Forecasting report**: This calculates the SAN usage based on history

- **Virtual Machine Allocation report**: This shows information about a VM's allocation

- **Virtual Machine Utilization report**: This shows information about resource utilization by VMs

- **Virtualization Candidates report**: This helps identify the physical computers that are good candidates for conversion to VMs

See also

- The *Using Reporting in VMM* article available at `http://technet.microsoft.com/en-us/library/hh882401.aspx`

Extending monitoring with management packs

With management packs, you can extend Operations Manager (OpsMgr) and its possibilities.

On a hybrid hypervisor environment, where there is a mix of Hyper-V and VMware ESXi servers, the Veeam MP extends the OpsMgr for monitoring, alerting, and for undertaking remedial actions on VMware vSphere.

Veeam MP for VMware uses the vSphere API to gather information to allow monitoring and reporting against all layers of the VMware stack, which include layers from the underlying hardware through network, storage, hosts, clusters, datacenters, and up to vCenter. Examples of the key metrics for the VMware admins include latency, CPU ready, disk, and memory pressure against a host.

> At the time of this writing, Veeam released a management pack for System Center, adding support to Microsoft Hyper-V. Now, with one MP, you have visibility of critical virtual systems, risk mitigation, and proactive monitoring of Hyper-V and vSphere from the Microsoft System Center console. For more information, refer to `http://go.veeam.com/mp-v7?ad=pr`.

Getting ready

For this recipe, Veeam Management Pack for VMware (SCOM) is required. You can download a trial version from `http://www.veeam.com/downloads/`.

Veeam recommends a dedicated server for the collector server. However, for a small deployment, you can install it on the OpsMgr management server. Such a scenario is what I will describe in this recipe, a single-server install.

You also need a service account (with local administrator rights on the collector server) and the user account (used to connect to VMware vCenter, which requires at least the read-only privilege), depending on which MP tasks you allow over the entire vSphere hierarchy and not only to specific objects.

New in Version 6.5, if you are also deploying Veeam Backup & Replication, the Veeam MP will provide monitoring, reporting, and capacity planning for backup.

For a complete list of system requirements, go to `http://www.veeam.com/vmware-microsoft-esx-monitoring-resources.html`.

The following screenshot illustrates how Veeam MP works integrated with Operations Manager:

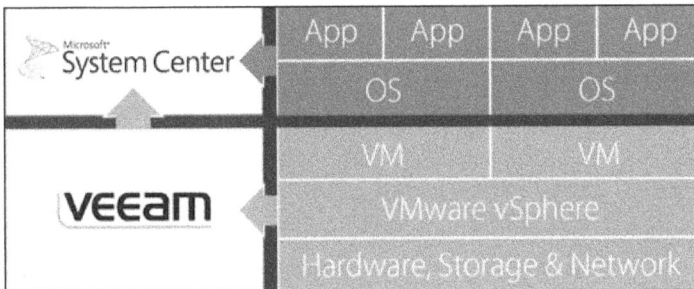

How to do it...

Carry out the following steps to install Veeam MP to monitor VMware:

1. Install the OpsMgr agent on the VMware vCenter Server as described in the *Managing Discovery and Agents* recipe.

2. On the **VMware vCenter** page, assign CIM interaction to the created user role (for example, `lab\scAdmin`) by editing the role settings. Navigate to **User Role | All Privileges | Host** and then click on **CIM** to enable **CIM interaction**, as shown in the following screenshot.

> This step is necessary only if you require hardware information, such as the temperature and power utilization to be collected from the VMware hosts.

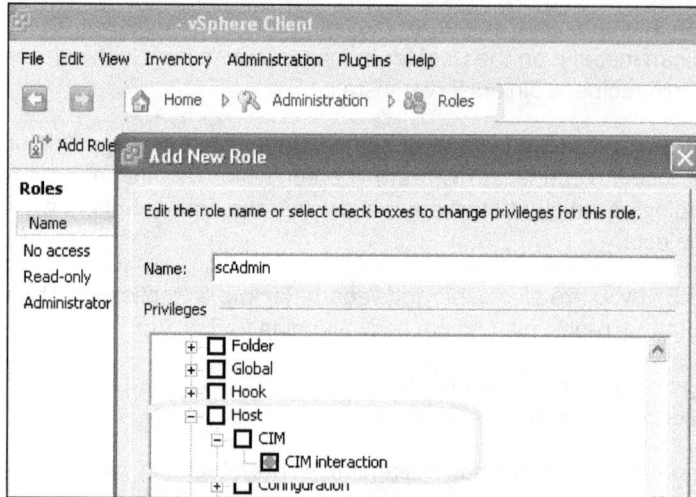

3. Download Veeam Management Pack and extract it to a local disk folder (for example, `C:\VeeamMP`).

> If you are installing it on a dedicated server, you need to install an OpsMgr agent.

4. Browse to `C:\VeeamMP`, right-click on **setup**, and click on **Run as Administrator**. Then click on **Veeam VE Suite**.

5. Click on **Next** to start the installation, accept the EULA, and then click on **Next**.

6. On the **Program Features** page, (shown in the following screenshot) confirm that all components will be installed on a local drive and click on **Next**.

> If you desire, change the installation directory.

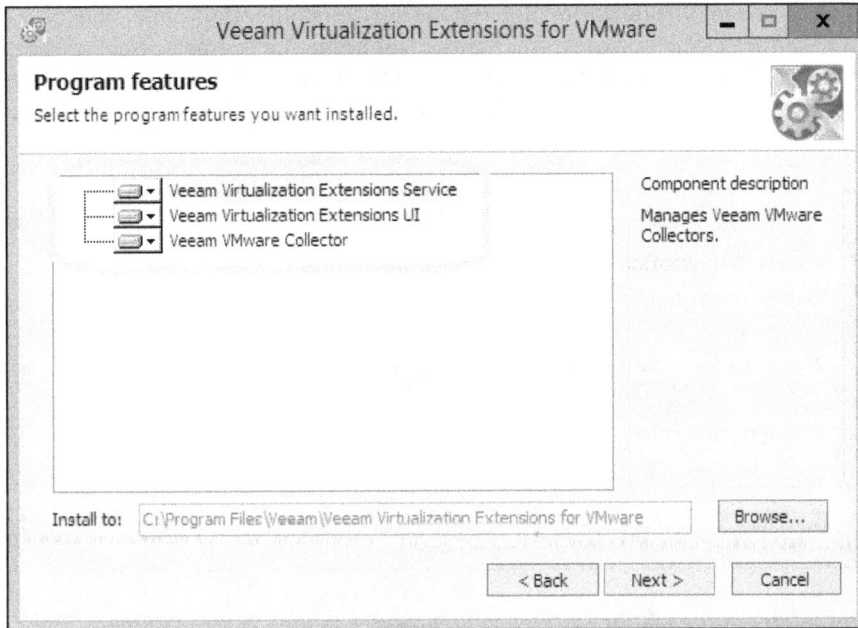

7. Click on **OK** to confirm that for Internet Explorer v11, the Veeam UI website must be manually added to the trusted sites list.

8. On the **Provide License** page, click on **Browse** to locate the required license file and then click on **Next**.

> You must have a Veeam account previously created to request a license file.

9. On the **System Configuration Check** page, the installer will perform a system configuration check. If all of the prerequisites are met, click on **Next** to continue. Otherwise, click on **Install** to install the missing components.

10. On the **Ports Selection** page, confirm the ports, click on **Next**, and then click on **Finish**.

11. On the **Veeam Virtualization Extensions service credentials** page, provide a domain account with local administrator rights: **User name** (for example, lab\scAdmin) and **Password**. Select **Use the same account for Veeam VMware Collector service** if you are using the same account for the collector service (as shown in the following screenshot), and click on **Next**:

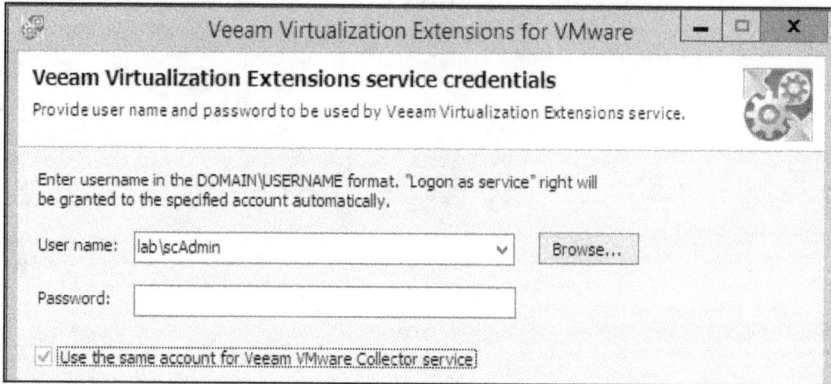

12. On the **Ready to Install** page, click on **Install** and then click on **Finish**.

13. To complete the installation, click on **Yes, to logoff/logon**.

14. Carry out the steps provided in the *Installing management packs* recipe in this chapter, but select the **Add from disk** option as shown in the following screenshot. Then browse to the installation folder (for example, C:\VeeamMP\SCOM 2012 MP), select all of the management packs and the Veeam.Virt.Extensions. RequiredOverrides.xml file, and click on **Import**.

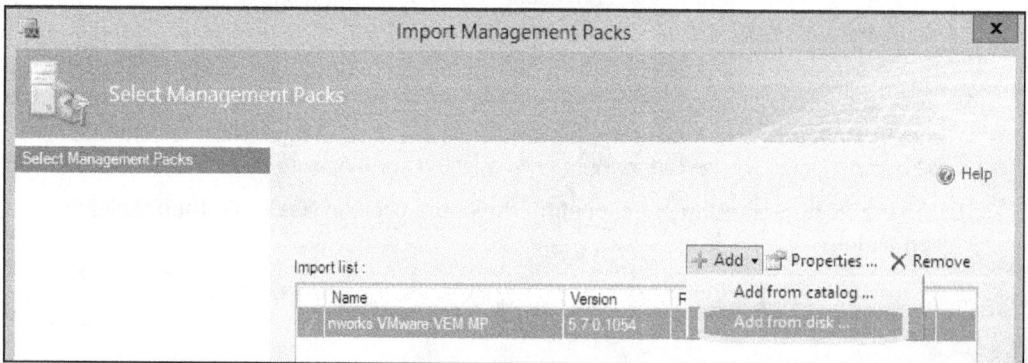

15. Click on **Install** to confirm the installation, and then click on **Close**.

16. Open Internet Explorer and type in http://localhost:4430/ to access the **Veeam Virtualization Extensions for VMware** page.

> If using IE11, add this site to trusted sites first.

17. On the **VMware Servers** tab, on the right-hand side panel, click on **Add VMware Server...** and then on the **Add VMware server** wizard, type in the VMware server connection settings as shown in the following screenshot, click on **Next**, and then click on **Finish**:

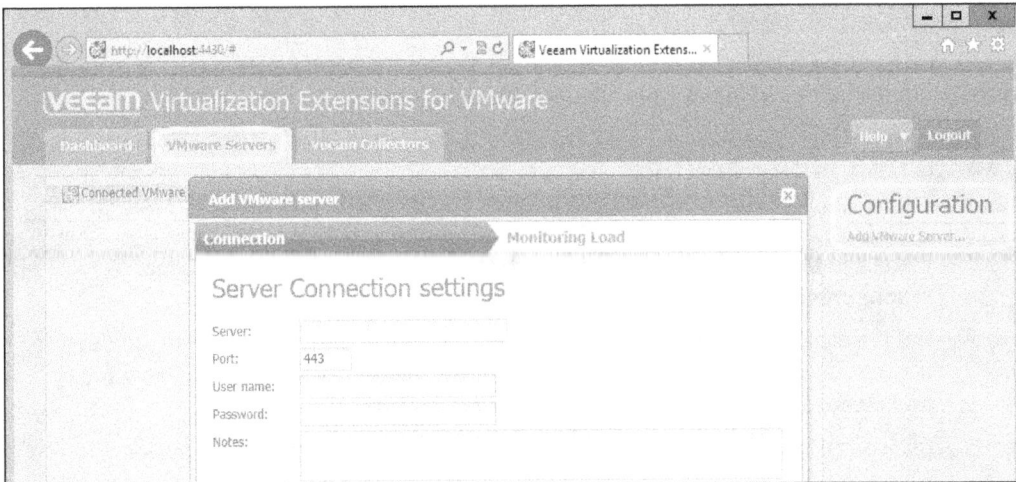

You should now be able to see information appearing in the **Veeam for VMware** node in the **Monitoring** tab.

How it works...

Create a domain account that can be used as a service account for MP and to access the VMware infrastructure.

During the single-server installation, the application setup will register the Veeam collector component with **Veeam Virtualization Extensions Service**. It will then be visible in the Veeam web console and two new application logs will be created, namely Veeam Collector and Veeam VMware.

When the install finishes and the Veeam collector service starts, there will be no monitoring jobs assigned (it will show as Inactive) until you add the VMware servers. After adding the ESXi hosts, the Veeam collector server will collect all of the information from the VMware ESX hosts servers, and then show the information on the OpsMgr's monitoring workspace. It is possible to install this role on the dedicated monitored servers or even on the OpsMgr management servers.

> Installation of Veeam components is not supported on the VMware vCenter Server.

Note that the collection server requires an OpsMgr agent installed, unless you install it on the OpsMgr management server. Either way, you also need to enable the agent proxy settings for each collector server.

There's more...

After installing Veeam MP, importing MPs, and adding the VMware servers, you also need to configure the proxy settings and configure the OpsMgr tasks.

Configuring proxy settings for an agent

Carry out the following steps for each Veeam collector server if the OpsMgr agent is installed:

1. In the OpsMgr console, in the **Administration** workspace, expand **Device Management** and then **Agent Managed**.

2. Double-click on the collector server on the right-hand side pane, and in the **Security** tab of the **Agent Properties** dialog box, select **Allow this agent to act as a proxy and discover managed objects on other computers**.

3. Click on **OK** and allow time for the settings to propagate through the system.

Configuring proxy settings for a management server

If you have installed the Veeam collector server on the OpsMgr management server, you also need to enable the proxy. To do this, carry out the following steps:

1. In the OpsMgr console, in the **Administration** workspace, expand **Device Management** and then **Management Servers**.

2. On the right-hand side pane, double-click on the management server, and in the **Management Server Properties** dialog box, in the **Security** tab, select **Allow this server to act as a proxy and discover managed objects on other computers**.

3. Click on **OK** and allow time for the settings to propagate through the system.

Configuring the OpsMgr Agent task to adjust the registry settings

Carry out the following steps *for each collector system* to configure an OpsMgr Agent task, which is included in the Veeam MP to automatically adjust the registry settings to maximize efficiency when processing large data volumes for the OpsMgr Health Service:

1. In the OpsMgr console, click in the **Monitoring** workspace.

2. Navigate to **Veeam for Vmware | Veeam Collectors | Veeam Collectors view**.

3. Select the collector system you want to configure.

4. On the **Actions** pane, click on **Veeam VMware Collector Service Tasks** and then select **Configure Health Service**.

> This task will cause the System Center Health Service to restart. For more information, refer to http://www.veeam.com/kb1026.

See also

► Check out the Veeam Deployment Planning Calculator at http://www.veeam.com/support/nworks_deployment.html

10

Scripting in Virtual Machine Manager

In this chapter, we will cover the following:

- ▶ Introducing VMM PowerShell
- ▶ Finding the command to automate tasks in VMM
- ▶ Creating a script from VMM wizards
- ▶ Storing and running scripts in VMM
- ▶ Using VMM sample scripts

Introduction

In this chapter, you will get an insight into the useful VMM command shell, which allows administrators to perform all the VMM administrative functions using commands or scripts (such as the configuration and management of the virtualization host, networking resources, and storage resources in order to create and deploy VMs and services).

The VMM command shell includes all the standard Windows PowerShell **cmdlets** and a comprehensive set of cmdlets that are designed specifically for VMM, which can be used to create scripts to automate complex tasks.

> Each cmdlet noun is now preceded by SC, which includes cmdlets that were included in the previous versions of VMM, for example, Get-SCVMHost.

Introducing VMM PowerShell

Windows PowerShell is based on object-oriented programming and the Microsoft .NET Framework Class Library. An object contains the following types of data:

- ▶ Object type
- ▶ Methods
- ▶ Properties

VMM objects can be used to manipulate data and take specific actions. Properties contain information about the state of an object. Methods are actions that you can perform on the item that an object represents. Methods can return data.

Getting ready

To be able to use the VMM PowerShell module, you must first ensure that it is already installed.

Installing the VMM PowerShell module

In order to install VMM Windows PowerShell, you need to install the VMM console. If you have already installed the VMM console, you don't need to install it again. For more information on installing the VMM console, refer to the *Installing the VMM console* recipe in *Chapter 3, Installing VMM 2012 R2*.

How to do it...

Let's see how to start VMM PowerShell.

Starting VMM PowerShell

When you start the VMM command shell, a Windows PowerShell session opens, automatically imports the VMM module, and establishes a connection to a VMM management server.

To open the VMM command shell window, carry out the following steps:

1. On the VMM console, click on **PowerShell** on the **Home** tab in the ribbon.

2. On a computer powered by either Windows 8 or Windows Server 2012 (with the VMM console installed), do the following:

   1. Press the Windows key on the keyboard.

   2. Right-click on **Virtual Machine Manager Command Shell**.

   3. On the taskbar, click on **Run as administrator**.

> In Windows 8.1 Update 1 and in Windows Server 2012 R2 Update, you will now see the right-click menu.

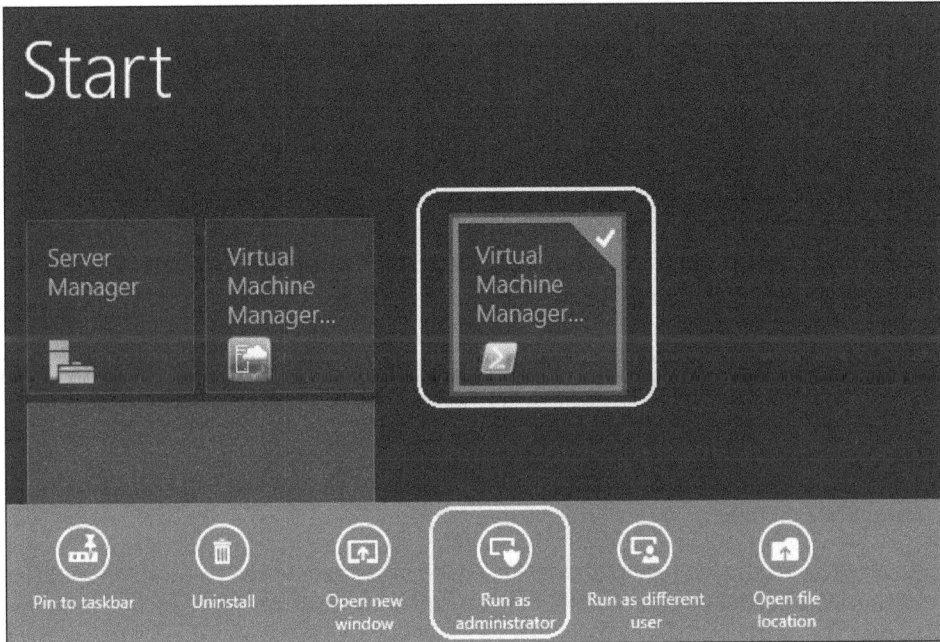

3. On a computer powered by either Windows 7 or Windows 2008 R2 Server (with the VMM console installed), do the following:

    1. Click on **Microsoft System Center 2012 R2**.

    2. Click on **Virtual Machine Manager**.

    3. Click on **Virtual Machine Manager Command Shell**.

4. Import the VMM PowerShell module into an existing Windows PowerShell session on a computer with the VMM console installed by performing the following steps:

    1. Run the PowerShell command prompt with administrator rights.

    2. Set the Windows PowerShell execution policy to allow the running of scripts using SET-ExecutionPolicy. For example, to allow scripts to run without restrictions, type in the following line:

        ```
        PS C:>Set-ExecutionPolicy Unrestricted
        ```

3. For help with setting the execution policy, type in Get-Help Set-ExecutionPolicy, as shown in the next line:

```
PS C:>Get-Help Set-ExecutionPolicy
```

4. To import the VMM module, type in the following line in the command prompt window:

```
PS C:\>Import-Module -Name virtualmachinemanager
```

How it works...

The default security settings built into Windows PowerShell prevent the execution of PowerShell scripts. The execution policy determines how (or if) PowerShell runs scripts. In Windows 2012, PowerShell's execution policy is set to **Restricted** by default, which means the scripts will not be executed.

> In Windows 2012 R2, **RemoteSigned** is the default policy.

You can verify the execution policy settings on the server by typing in Get-ExecutionPolicy in the PowerShell prompt.

The Set-ExecutionPolicy cmdlet enables you to determine which Windows PowerShell scripts (if any) will be allowed to run; you can use one of the following execution policies for this purpose:

- Restricted: No scripts can be run. PowerShell can be used only in interactive mode.
- AllSigned: Only the scripts signed by a trusted publisher can run.
- RemoteSigned: Downloaded scripts must be signed by a trusted publisher before they can run.
- Unrestricted: There are no restrictions; all Windows PowerShell scripts can be run. For example, the following command sets the execution policy to Unrestricted:

```
PS c:\> Set-ExecutionPolicy Unrestricted
```

There's more...

Let's learn more about PowerShell cmdlets.

Understanding PowerShell properties

To get the available properties of an object, use the Get-Member cmdlet and set the MemberType parameter to property.

For example, to get the properties for a logical network, get the logical network object and then use the pipeline operator (|) to send the object to Get-Member:

```
PS C:\> Get-SCLogicalNetwork -Name "Intranet" | Get-Member -MemberType
property
```

The result of the previous command line will be the following:

```
Intranet
```

To get the value of a property, use the dot (.) method. Perform the following two steps to use the dot method:

1. Get a reference to the object (for example, a variable that contains the object) or type in a command that gets the object.
2. Then, type in a dot (.), followed by the property name.

The following example stores the value of the Name property of a logical network object in a variable called $LogicalNet:

```
PS C:\> $LogicalNet = Get-SCLogicalNetwork -Name "Intranet"
```

You can check the value stored in this variable by typing in the following line in the command shell:

```
PS C:\> $LogicalNet.Name
```

The result is the following:

```
Intranet
```

Methods

You can get the available methods for an object using the Get-Member cmdlet and by setting the MemberType parameter to method.

The following example shows how to get the methods for a logical network:

```
PS C:\> Get-SCLogicalNetwork -Name "Intranet" | Get-Member -MemberType
method
```

The result of the previous command line will be the following:

```
Intranet
```

To invoke a method, type in a reference to the object and then specify the method name, separating the object reference and the method with a dot (.).

> To pass arguments to the method, enclose the arguments in parentheses, followed by the method name.
>
> An empty set of parentheses indicates that the method requires no arguments.

The following example shows how to use the `GetType` method to return the base type of a logical network (using our previously created `$LogicalNet` variable):

```
PS C:\> $LogicalNet.GetType()
```

The result of the previous command line will be the following:

```
Intranet
```

Object synchronization

VMM synchronizes its objects, which means that if you create two or more variables and then change the property of an object that is stored in either variable, VMM will synchronize the object property in both the variables.

The following example demonstrates how two variables get synchronized:

1. We first use `Get-SCLogicalNetwork` to get a value and store it in the variable `$LogicalNet`, as follows:

   ```
   PS C:\> $LogicalNet = Get-SCLogicalNetwork -Name "Intranet"
   ```

2. Then, we use `Get-SCLogicalNetwork` to get a value and store it in a second variable called `$Intranet`, as follows:

   ```
   PS C:\> $Intranet = Get-SCLogicalNetwork -Name "Intranet"
   ```

3. We then change the name of the logical network object using `$Intranet`, as follows:

   ```
   PS C:\> Set-SCLogicalNetwork -LogicalNetwork $Intranet -Name "VMInternalTraffic"
   ```

4. When we look at the name of the logical network stored in both the variables, `$Intranet` and `$LogicalNet`, the results are identical. When we type in the command, `$Intranet.Name`, the result is the following:

   ```
   VMInternalTraffic
   ```

5. On typing in the following line, the result is the same, that is, `VMInternalTraffic`:

   ```
   PS C:\> $LogicalNet.Name
   ```

See also

▸ The *Windows PowerShell Basics* article at `http://go.microsoft.com/fwlink/?LinkId=242715`

▸ The *Getting Started Windows PowerShell* guide at `http://go.microsoft.com/fwlink/?LinkId=242708`

▸ To learn more about signing scripts, type the command, `Get-Help About_Signing`, in the PowerShell prompt

▸ Information on VMM 2012's backward compatibility for cmdlets at `http://technet.microsoft.com/library/hh801915.aspx`

Finding the command to automate tasks in VMM

This recipe will show you how to find the VMM PowerShell command to automate tasks in VMM. The `Get-Help` cmdlet not only displays information about the cmdlet, but it also displays references, examples of usage, and notes.

Getting ready

Start the VMM PowerShell command with administrator rights. For more information, refer to the *Introducing VMM PowerShell* recipe in this chapter.

How to do it...

Help topics have been provided for each VMM PowerShell cmdlet, including general examples.

To display a list of all the VMM cmdlets, start the VMM PowerShell and use the `Get-Command` cmdlet:

```
PS c:\>Get-Command -CommandType Cmdlet
```

You can also use `Get-Command` to view all VMM cmdlets that contain specific nouns or verbs, for example, all related `SCCloud` commands:

```
PS C:\>Get-Command -Noun SCCloud
```

The result of this command is shown in the following screenshot:

```
Administrator: C:\ProgramData\Microsoft\Windows\Start Menu\Programs\Microsoft Syste...   _  □  x
PS C:\Windows\system32> Get-Command -Noun SCCloud

CommandType       Name                                              ModuleName

Cmdlet            Get-SCCloud                                       virtualmachinemanager
Cmdlet            New-SCCloud                                       virtualmachinemanager
Cmdlet            Remove-SCCloud                                    virtualmachinemanager
Cmdlet            Set-SCCloud                                       virtualmachinemanager


PS C:\Windows\system32> _
```

Using the Get-Help cmdlet

To get more specific help, you can use the Get-Help cmdlet. For example, to view a help topic for the New-SCCloud cmdlet, type in the following line in the command prompt window:

```
PS C:\>Get-help New-SCCloud
```

On running the preceding command, the results will be displayed as follows:

```
Administrator: C:\ProgramData\Microsoft\Windows\Start Menu\Programs\Microsoft System Center 2012...  _  □  x
PS C:\Windows\system32> get-help New-SCCloud

NAME
    New-SCCloud

SYNOPSIS
    Creates a private cloud.

SYNTAX
    New-SCCloud [-Name] <String> [-Description <String>] [-JobGroup <Guid>] [-JobVariable
    <String>] [-PROTipID <Guid>] [-RunAsynchronously <SwitchParameter>] [-VMHostGroup
    <HostGroup[]>] [-VMMServer <String ServerConnection>] [<CommonParameters>]

    New-SCCloud [-Name] <String> [-Description <String>] [-JobGroup <Guid>] [-JobVariable
    <String>] [-PROTipID <Guid>] [-RunAsynchronously <SwitchParameter>] [-VMMServer <String
    ServerConnection>] [-VMwareResourcePool <VMwareResourcePool>] [<CommonParameters>]

DESCRIPTION
    The New-SCCloud cmdlet creates a private cloud in System Center Virtual Machine Manager (VMM).
    A private cloud is a cloud that is provisioned and managed on-premise by an organization. The
    private cloud is deployed using an organization's own hardware to leverage the advantages of
    the private cloud model. Through VMM, an organization can manage the private cloud definition,
    access to the private cloud, and the underlying physical resources.

    You can create a private cloud from the following resources:

    - Host groups that contain resources from Hyper-V hosts, Citrix
      XenServer hosts, and VMware ESX hosts

    - A VMware resource pool

    For more information about private clouds, see "Creating a Private Cloud Overview" in the
    TechNet library at http://go.microsoft.com/fwlink/?LinkID=212407.

    For information about private cloud capacity, type: "Get-Help Set-SCCloudCapacity -detailed."

    For more information about New-SCCloud, type: "Get-Help New-SCCloud -online".
```

How it works...

The Get-Help command displays a help topic about a cmdlet. The default output that is returned contains basic information about the cmdlet.

To change the information that is shown when using the Get-Help cmdlet, you can use some of the following parameters associated with Get-Help:

- ▶ -full: This shows all the available help for the cmdlet
- ▶ -detailed: This shows the synopsis, syntax, detailed description, parameter descriptions, and examples
- ▶ -examples: This shows only the synopsis and examples
- ▶ -online: This opens the online version of the help topic in your default browser

The following screenshot shows the result of the Get-Help command for the Get-SCCloud cmdlet using the -examples parameter:

```
Administrator: C:\ProgramData\Microsoft\Windows\Start Menu\Programs\Microsoft System
PS C:\Windows\system32> get-help Get-SCCloud -examples

NAME
    Get-SCCloud

SYNOPSIS
    Gets a private cloud object.

    1: Get a specified private cloud.

    PS C:\> Get-SCCloud -VMMServer "VMMServer01.Contoso.com" -Name "Cloud01"

    This command gets the private cloud object named Cloud01 on VMMServer01.

PS C:\Windows\system32> _
```

There's more...

This section is about getting more help on PowerShell cmdlets.

Displaying About topics

To display the available About help topics for VMM, use the following command line:

```
PS C:\>Get-Help about_VMM*
```

To display an individual About help topic, type in the following line in the command prompt:

```
PS C:>Get-Help about_VMM_2012_Virtual_Networking
```

See also

- ▸ Help topics and About topics for VMM PowerShell cmdlets in the TechNet Library
- ▸ The online reference of the VMM cmdlet at `http://technet.microsoft.com/en-us/library/jj654428(v=sc.20).asp`
- ▸ VMM About topics at `http://go.microsoft.com/fwlink/?LinkId=242616`

Creating a script from VMM wizards

You can use the VMM console to help you with the PowerShell script to automate tasks.

Getting the script from a previous task that was executed in the VMM console will save you time when working with scripts. Save the script, then personalize it to make it generic. Every task that is created in VMM can be scripted.

How to do it...

You can create a script from one of the VMM wizards. In this recipe, we will create a script based on how a hardware profile is created. Carry out the following steps in order to do so:

1. Connect to the VMM 2012 R2 console using the VMM admin account that was created previously (`lab\vmm-admin`).

2. On the left-bottom pane, click on the **Library** workspace, expand **Profiles** on the left-hand side pane, and then click on **Hardware Profiles**.

3. Select and right-click on **Create Hardware Profile**.

4. In the **New Hardware Profile** dialog box, on the **General** page, type in the hardware profile name, for example, `1 vCPU Server`.

5. Click on **Hardware Profile** on the left-hand side pane and configure the hardware settings.

6. On the left-bottom pane, click on **View Script**.

7. A window will open, displaying the script (as shown in the following screenshot). Copy and paste this to Notepad or any PowerShell editor and save it with a `.ps1` extension.

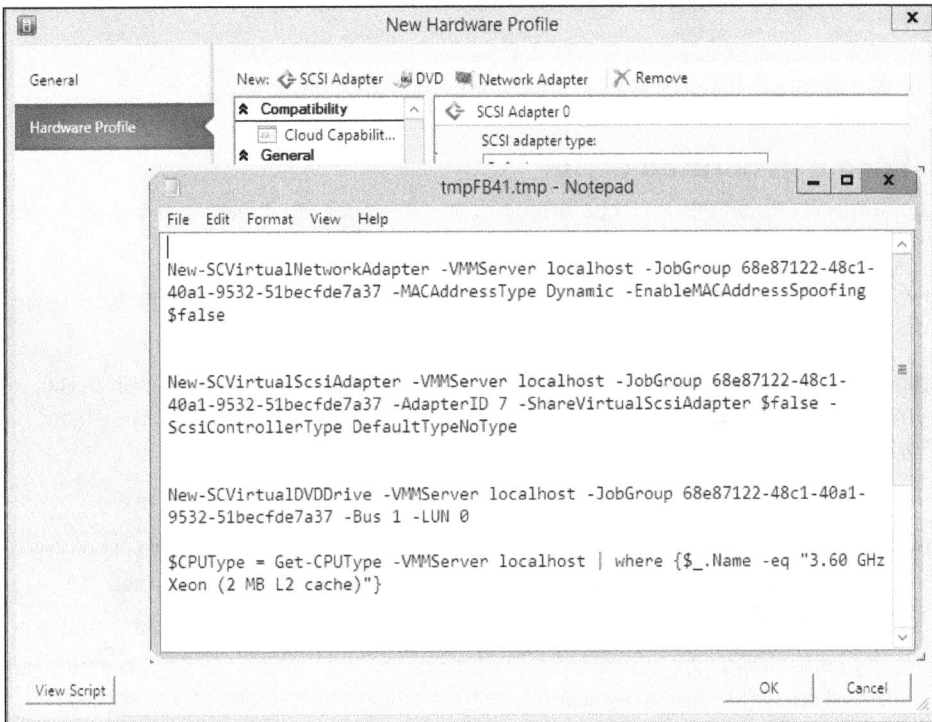

8. Click on **OK** to finish and save the hardware profile, or click on **Cancel** if you wish to abort the operation.

> 💡 You can also click on **Cancel** and then execute it after saving the script in order to see the hardware profile that was created using the command shell.

How it works...

To help get you started with writing scripts, you can try generating a script by running any wizard or updating the properties in the VMM console.

Use the **View Script** button on the **Summary** page of a wizard in the VMM console or the **Properties** page to view the set of cmdlets that will be run. Save the script as a file with the `.ps1` extension and then modify the commands as necessary.

There's more...

After creating a script, you can modify it according to your requirements.

Modifying a generated script

Most generated scripts have an ID parameter to identify specific objects that they will take actions on.

As we want to allow the script to take parameters, we can use a `Get` cmdlet to get an object that will make our script available for use with other objects.

The following is a generated script created after changing the private cloud's name. By changing a property value, the generated script uses the ID parameter to get the object to change, as follows:

```
$cloud = Get-SCCloud -ID "1f6a5a0a-83ed-46fd-a369-d45ee4ec6492"


Set-SCCloud -Cloud $cloud -Name "My Cloud-Renamed" -Description "" -
RunAsynchronously
```

As we want to start building a script library for future use, we replace the ID parameter with something that we can use as a standard. The following sample shows how to retrieve all those private clouds that have names beginning with `My Cloud` and place them in an array:

```
$Clouds = @( Get-SCCloud | where { $_.Name -like "My Cloud-Renamed*"
})
```

We place the first private cloud in the array and then update its name to **New Private Cloud** with the following command:

```
Set-SCCloud -Cloud $Clouds[0] -Name "MyCompany Private Cloud" -
RunAsynchronously
```

Adding parameters to a generated script

Another way to make a generated script more accessible is by defining parameters in the script. Script parameters work like function parameters. The parameter values are available to all the commands in the script. While running the script, users type in the parameters after the script name.

To add parameters to a script, use the `Param` statement. Modify the previous script to accept parameters. Save the following script as `ChangeCloudName.ps1`:

```
Param(
    [parameter(Mandatory=$true)]
    [String] $OldName = $(throw "Provide an existing Cloud."),
```

```
[parameter(Mandatory=$true)]

[String] $NewName = $(throw "Provide a new name."))
```

```
Get-SCCloud -Name $OldName | Set-SCCloud -Cloud $_ -Name $NewName -
RunAsynchronously
```

When we run the script, we need to provide the name of an existing logical network and give a new name to the logical network:

```
.\ChangeCloudName.ps1 -OldName "MyCompany Private Cloud " -NewName
"My Cloud"
```

> If you did not provide values for OldName and NewName, you will be prompted for them.

See also

▶ The *Creating a Script from VMM Wizards and Property Pages* article at http://technet.microsoft.com/en-us/library/hh875023.aspx

Storing and running scripts in VMM

A script is a text file that contains one or more Windows PowerShell commands. You can save PowerShell scripts to a folder that will be executed from the VMM command shell, or you can save them to the VMM library and run them using the VMM console.

> For the script to be recognized as a Windows PowerShell script, it has to be saved with a .ps1 extension.

Getting ready

Before you can run a script, check the Windows PowerShell execution policy. The default execution policy in Windows 2012 is Restricted, which prevents all scripts from running.

> In Windows 2012 R2, **RemoteSigned** is the default policy.

How to do it...

After writing a script, you can save it in the VMM library for later use.

Storing a script in the VMM library

Carry out the following steps to save a particular script to the VMM library:

1. Connect to the VMM 2012 R2 console using the VMM admin account that was created previously (`lab\vmm-admin`).

2. On the left-bottom pane, click on the **Library** workspace, expand **Library Servers** in the left pane, and then select the library share that the script is to be stored in.

3. On the **Home** tab in the ribbon, click on **Import Physical Resource**.

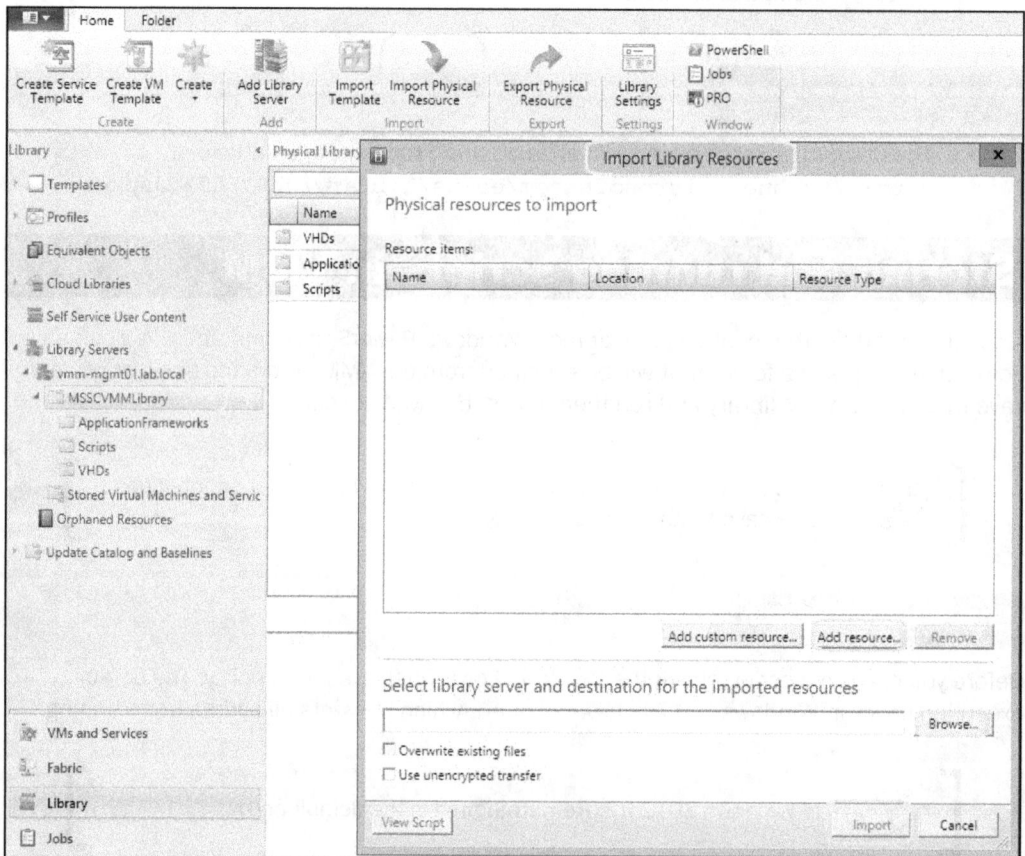

4. In the **Import Library Resources** dialog box, click on **Add resource...**, select a particular library by clicking on **Browse**, and then click on **Import**.

> Alternatively, you can select a script in that share and then click on **Open File Location** on the **PowerShell** tab in the **Windows** group. This opens a Windows Explorer window that will show the location of the library share. Copy your script to the share and then close the Explorer window.

Viewing and updating a script in the VMM library

Carry out the following steps to update a script in the VMM library:

1. On the VMM console that is on the **Library** workspace, select the script and click on **View File** on the **PowerShell** tab.

2. Update the script and then click on **Save**. Close the file.

Running a script from the VMM library

Carry out the following two steps to run a script from the VMM library:

1. On the VMM console that is on the **Library** workspace, select the script and click on **Run** on the **PowerShell** tab.

2. The VMM command shell opens and the script runs.

Running a script from the command prompt

Carry out the following steps to run a script from the command prompt:

1. On a computer on which the VMM console has been installed and the Windows PowerShell execution policy has been set to allow you to run scripts (if you have not done the latter, type in Get-Help Set-ExecutionPolicy in the command prompt), click on **Windows PowerShell** and type in the following line in the command prompt:

   `PS C:\>Import-Module -Name virtualmachinemanager`

2. Then type the following command or script:

   `$vHost = Get-SCVMHost -ComputerName "HyperV02"`

How it works...

Store the scripts in a centralized location, such as a VMM library share, to make them easier to manage, share, and document. You can store, view, update, and run the scripts directly from the VMM library.

If a script is stored on a local server, you can only run it from the VMM command shell (PowerShell). For example, to run a script called `ChangeCloudName.ps1`, run PowerShell and import the VMM module, or open the VMM command shell and type in the script name, as follows:

```
PS C:\Scripts> .\ChangeCloudName.ps1 -OldName "My Cloud" -NewName
"My New Cloud"
```

> If the script is not in the current directory, type in the path to the script.

There's more...

This section covers the topic of working with credentials in PowerShell.

Credentials

When performing certain actions in the VMM command shell, such as adding Hyper-V hosts, you will need to provide credentials.

To accomplish this, you can create a Windows PowerShell `PSCredential` object and store that object in a variable that you can use within a script. To create a `PSCredential` object, use the `Get-Credential` cmdlet, as follows:

```
PS C:\>$Credential = Get-Credential
```

```
PS C:\>Add-SCVMHost "Hyperv02.lab.local" -RemoteConnectEnabled $True
-RemoteConnectPort 5900 -Credential $Credential
```

> You can create a `PSCredential` object programmatically, without requiring any user interaction. However, this method requires that the username and password appear as plain text within the script, which is not recommended for security reasons.

Using VMM Run As accounts

In VMM 2012, it is possible to use Run As accounts to provide credentials for the PowerShell scripts or cmdlets that support the `VMMCredential` parameter type.

Use the `Get-SCRunAsAccount` cmdlet to get a Run As account within a script that provides credentials without the need for user interaction.

The following command gets a Run As account object named `vmm-admin` and stores the object in the `$RunAsAccount` variable:

```
PS C:\> $RunAsAccount = Get-SCRunAsAccount -Name "vmm-admin"
```

Add the SMI-S storage provider with the name, `DellStorageProvider`:

```
PS C:\> Add-SCStorageProvider -SmisWmi -Name "DellStorageProvider" -
RunAsAccount $RunAsAccount -ComputerName "StorageMGMTHost.lab.local"
```

Using the JobGroup parameter

To work with a `JobGroup` parameter, you need to provide a **globally unique identifier** (**GUID**). The following command shows how to create a GUID and store it in the `$JobGroupGUID` variable:

```
$JobGroupGUID = [Guid]::NewGuid().ToString()
```

After creating the GUID, you can add other commands, always specifying the job group GUID. The command will not run with just these steps; a final command is required, which will also include `-JobGroup $JobGroupGUID`.

The tasks carried out by the following sample script are queued and do not run until the `New-SCVirtualMachine` cmdlet is executed. The `New-SCVirtualMachine` cmdlet is the last command, which includes `JobGroup` and initiates the work as shown in the following code snippet:

```
$VMMServer="vmm-mgmt01.lab.local"
$Owner="lab\vmm-admin"
$NewVMname="W2012-Web02"
$HyperVHost="Hyperv02.lab.local"


#Generate a GUID for the JobGroupGUID variable.
$JobGroupGUID = [Guid]::NewGuid().ToString()
```

```
$VirtualHardDisk = Get-SCVirtualHardDisk -VMMServer $VMMServer |
where {$_.Location -eq "\\vmm-mgmt01.lab.local\MSSCVMMLibrary
\VHDs\Blank Disk - Large.vhdx"}


# This is the first cmdlet that uses the JobGroup variable.

New-SCVirtualDiskDrive -VMMServer $VMMServer -IDE -Bus 0 -LUN 0 -
JobGroup $JobGroupGUID -VirtualHardDisk $VirtualHardDisk -VolumeType
BootAndSystem


$HardwareProfile = Get-SCHardwareProfile -VMMServer localhost |
where {$_.Name -eq "2 vCPU Server"}


$vHost = Get-SCVMHost -ComputerName $HyperVHost

$operatingSystem = Get-SCOperatingSystem | where { $_.Name -eq "64-
bit edition of Windows 8" }


# As this is the last cmdlet, use the JobGroup variable

New-SCVirtualMachine -Name $NewVMname  -JobGroup $JobGroupGUID -
VMMServer $VMMServer  -Owner $Owner -VMHost $vHost -Path "G:\VMS\" -
HardwareProfile $HardwareProfile -OperatingSystem $operatingSystem -
RunAsynchronously -StartAction TurnOnVMIfRunningWhenVSStopped -
StopAction SaveVM -DelayStartSeconds 0
```

Cmdlets that you can use JobGroup with

Refer to the following Microsoft TechNet page for the PowerShell cmdlets that can use the JobGroup parameter:

```
http://technet.microsoft.com/en-us/library/hh875035.aspx
```

Using VMM sample scripts

The sample scripts in this recipe illustrate how to use Windows PowerShell for centralized management.

You can use VMM PowerShell cmdlets to automate VMM tasks by executing them from a machine that has the VMM console installed.

The following section contains some samples to add storage and convert the VHD disk format to the VHDX disk format.

w to do it...

an use PowerShell scripts to automate various tasks. The following section will help you
the sample script that counts the number of Virtual Machines per Operating System (VMs
)S).

nting the number of Virtual Machines per Operating System

following script will count the VMs per OS:

```
ort-Module virtualmachinemanager
osts = Get-SCVMHost
each ($vHost in $vHosts){
Get-SCVirtualMachine -VmHost $vHost | Group-Object OperatingSystem |
t Count -Descending | Select Name, Count
```

following image shows the script output:

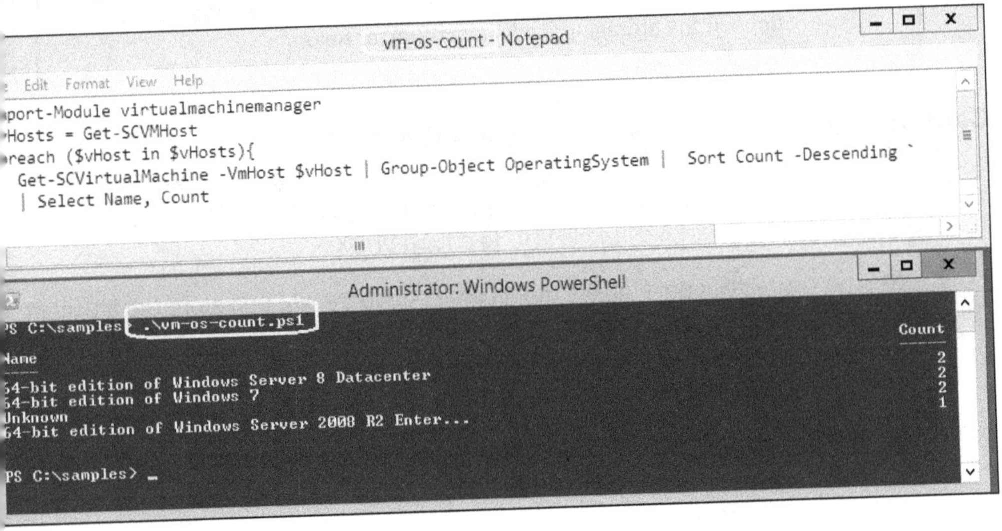

How it works...

ne script starts by importing the `virtualmachinemanager` module. It then creates a
ariable that will store all the hosts.

or each host, it gets all the VMs and groups them by OS property. Finally, it lists the OS and
ne number of VMs associated with it.

ou can change this script to accommodate your needs; for example, you can use it to check
nly the numbers of the machines that are running.

There's more...

Let's have a look at more PowerShell sample scripts.

Adding a storage provider by its IP address

This step will add (integrate) an already installed SMI-S storage provider to VMM. Carry out the following steps to add a storage provider by its IP address:

1. Get the Run As account and store it in the `$RunAsAccount` variable:

    ```
    PS C:\> $RunAsAccount = Get-SCRunAsAccount -Name "vmm-admin"
    ```

2. Add the storage provider with the IP address, `192.168.10.10`:

    ```
    PS C:\> Add-SCStorageProvider -NetworkDeviceName "http://
    192.168.10.10" -TCPPort 5988 -Name "SampleStorageProvider" -
    RunAsAccount $RunAsAccount
    ```

> Make sure to type in the correct `TCPPort` for your storage provider. Consult the storage provider's manual for help.

Converting a dynamic VHD to a fixed VHDX

You can customize this example by adding a parameter that queries for a VM name and searches for all the hard disks to be converted to the VHDX format. Carry out the following steps to convert a dynamic VHD to a fixed VHDX:

1. Get the virtual disk drive object that is attached to the VM and store the object in the `$VirtDiskDrive` variable:

    ```
    PS C:\> $VirtDiskDrive = Get-VirtualDiskDrive -VM
    (Get-SCVirtualMachine -Name "VM-W2012")
    ```

2. Convert the virtual hard disk stored in `$VirtDiskDrive` to a VHDX disk:

    ```
    PS C:\> Convert-VirtualDiskDrive -VirtualDiskDrive
    $VirtDiskDrive -VHDX
    ```

> For this example, it is assumed that the VM has only one virtual hard disk attached and the VM has stopped working.

eating a new virtual disk drive and adding it to an existing tual Machine

can customize this example by querying the VM to find out which slot is free to add to.
y out the following steps to create a new virtual disk drive and add it to an existing VM:

1. Get the VM object and store it in the $VM variable:

   ```
   PS C:\> $VM = Get-SCVirtualMachine -Name "VM-W2012"
   ```

2. Create a new dynamic virtual disk drive on the first IDE channel in the second slot
   of the VM and specify its size as 40 GB:

   ```
   PS C:\> New-SCVirtualDiskDrive -VM $VM -Dynamic -Filename
   "VM-W2012" -IDE -Size 40000 -Bus 0 -LUN 1
   ```

> For this example, it is assumed that the VM already has an attached
> virtual hard disk on the first slot.

esting a dynamic VHD attached to a fixed-format virtual disk ive on a Virtual Machine

r this example, it is assumed that the VM has only one virtual disk drive. You can customize
e script for your needs, for example, by adding a parameter to get the VM name. For more
formation on *Test-SCVirtualDiskDrive*, refer to http://technet.microsoft.com/en-
/library/jj613141(v=sc.20).aspx.

1. Get the VM object and store it in the $VM variable:

   ```
   PS C:\> $VM = Get-SCVirtualMachine -Name "VM-W2012"
   ```

2. Get the attached virtual disk drive and store it in the $VirtDiskDrive variable:

   ```
   PS C:\> $VirtDiskDrive = Get-SCVirtualDiskDrive -VM $VM
   ```

3. If the VM is running, shut down the VM:

   ```
   PS C:\> If ($VM.Status -eq "Running") {Stop-SCVirtualMachine -
   VM $VM -Shutdown}
   ```

4. Test the virtual hard disk stored in $VirtDiskDrive:

   ```
   PS C:\> Test-SCVirtualDiskDrive -VirtualDiskDrive
   $VirtDiskDrive
   ```

See also

- The *Creating a Script from VMM Wizards and Property Pages* article at `http://technet.microsoft.com/en-us/library/hh875023.aspx`

- The *VMM cmdlet online help* topics at `http://technet.microsoft.com/en-us/library/hh875019.aspx`

- The *System Center Virtual Machine Manager R2 2012 cmdlet* reference at `http:technet.microsoft.com/en-us/library/jj654428(v=sc.20).aspx`

Index

Symbols

$RunAsAccount variable 393

A

Active Directory Domain Services (AD DS) 21
administrator user role
  about 212
  user, adding to 214
Advanced Configuration and Power Interface (ACPI) BIOS 277
Analysis Management Objects (AMO)
  installing 365
application administrator role
  about 213
  creating 219, 220
application focus strategy 6
application profile
  about 11, 209
  creating 211
availability options, VM
  about 317
  availability sets 315
  availability sets, configuring on host cluster 317, 318
  configuring 315
  preferred and possible owners 315
  preferred and possible owners, configuring 319
  VM priority 315

B

Background Intelligent Transfer Service. *See* **BITS**
Bare Metal 20
Bare Metal host deployment, fabric management
  about 190
  base image, adding 190
  DHCP server, configuring 190
  host profile, creating 191
  performing 190-194
  PXE server, configuring 190
  PXE server, deploying 190
  Run As account, creating 191
  working 195, 196
Baseboard Management Controller. *See* **BMC**
BITS 39
BITSadmin
  used, for verifying BITS 40
block-level storage devices 174
BMC
  about 20, 265
  configuring 265
BMC protocols
  Data Center Management Interface (DCMI) 265
  Intelligent Platform Management Interface (IPMI) 265
  System Management Architecture for Server Hardware (SMASH) 265

M

MAC spoofing
  enabling 231
management clusters 22
management packs, Operations
        Manager 2012
  importing 357
  installing 354-357
management protocols 20
management server 9
MAP toolkit
  about 7
  URL 7
medium- or large-scale environment 24
memory priority settings, VM
  maximum memory 323
  memory buffer percentage 323
  minimum memory 323
  start-up memory 323
memory throttling 320
memory throttling, VM
  configuring 324
memory weight, VM
  configuring 325
Microsoft Assessment and Planning. *See*
       MAP toolkit
Microsoft Device Specific Module (DSM) 244
Microsoft iSCSI Initiator
       Service 178, 244, 284
Microsoft SQL Server Native Client 80
monitoring, OpsMgr
  extending, with management packs 368
Multipath I/O (MPIO) driver 283
Multipath I/O (MPIO) feature 178, 243
Multivendor hypervisor support
  about 6
  diagrammatic representation 6

N

network adapter
  configuring 174
Network Attached Storage (NAS) 175
networking features, VMM 2012 R2 26
Networking Virtualization (NV) 26
network QoS 152
network settings, VMware ESX host

compliance information, viewing for physical
      network adapter 264
  configuring 262, 263
  verifying, for virtual switch 264
networks, fabric management
  configuring 148
  converged networks, designing for 149
  logical switches, configuring 167
  port classification, creating 167
  port profiles, creating 167
Network Virtualization with Generic Routing
      Encapsulation. *See* **NVGRE**
New-SCVirtualMachine cmdlet 393
No Isolation mode, VM network 161
Non-Uniform Memory Access (NUMA) 282
NUMA, VM
  configuring 315
NVGRE 163, 165

O

object synchronization, VMM PowerShell 382
ODX 226
Operations Manager 2012. *See* **OpsMgr**
Operations Manager 2012 R2 installation
  deploying 353
  discovery and agents, managing 358-360
  management packs, installing 354-357
  management server health, confirming 354
  monitoring, extending with management
      packs 368-373
  performing 346-352
Operations Manager (OpsMgr),
      VMM 2012 R2 252
Operations Manager Report Security
      Administrator profile 367
OpsMgr
  extending, with management packs 368
  proxy settings, configuring for agent 374
  proxy settings, configuring for management
      server 374
OpsMgr 2012-VMM 2012 integration
  configuring 361-364
  maintenance mode integration, enabling in
      VMM 2012 364, 365
  PRO tips, enabling in VMM 2012 364, 365
  reporting, enabling in VMM 365, 366

R

rapid provisioning
  about 247
  used, for deploying virtual machine 248
read-only administrator user role
  about 213
  creating 214, 215
real-world production environment
  correct system requirements,
      specifying 27-29
Receive Side Scaling (RSS) 151
Remote Administrative Tools (RSAT) 68
Remote Desktop Connection (RDC) 68
Reporting Services (SSRS) 351
resources, private cloud fabric
  networking 8
  servers 8
  storage 8
resource throttling
  configuring 320
Robocopy 145
Run As account
  about 21, 99
  BMC category 21
  creating 21
  credentials, creating 98, 99
  deleting 101
  disabling 100
  enabling 100
  external category 21
  host computer category 21
  network device category 21
  profile category 21

S

SAN 243
SAN Copy
  used, for rapid provisioning virtual
      machine 243-245
SAN Copy capable based template
  creating 247, 248
SAN Copy-capable VHD/VHDX
  creating, on host 246

SCAC
  about 331
  connecting 335
  connecting, to private clouds 335
  connecting, to public clouds 336
  connecting, to SVMM 335
  deploying 332-334
scale out feature 241
SCCM Task Sequence (TS) 13
script, PowerShell
  about 389
  creating 386, 387
  credentials 392
  generated script, modifying 388
  JobGroup parameter, using 393
  parameters, adding to generated
      script 388, 389
  running, from command prompt 391
  running, from VMM library 391
  storing, in VMM library 390
  updating, in VMM library 391
  viewing, in VMM library 391
  VMM Run As accounts, using 393
security
  configuring 21
Self Service Portal 11
self-service user roles
  configuring, for sharing/receiving
      resources 221
self-signed SSL certificate, VMM
  importing 255
Serial Attached SCSI (SAS) 19
service
  deploying 240
  deploying, from Services workspace 239
  deploying, from virtual machines 239
  scaling out, in VMM 241
  updating, in VMM 242
service accounts
  creating 68-71
service consumer strategy 6
service-level agreements (SLAs) 153
Service Management Automation 13
Service Principal Name (SPN)
  registering 72

[PACKT] enterprise ✤
PUBLISHING
professional expertise distilled

Thank you for buying
System Center 2012 R2 Virtual Machine Manager Cookbook
Second Edition

About Packt Publishing

Packt, pronounced 'packed', published its first book "*Mastering phpMyAdmin for Effective MySQL Management*" in April 2004 and subsequently continued to specialize in publishing highly focused books on specific technologies and solutions.

Our books and publications share the experiences of your fellow IT professionals in adapting and customizing today's systems, applications, and frameworks. Our solution-based books give you the knowledge and power to customize the software and technologies you're using to get the job done. Packt books are more specific and less general than the IT books you have seen in the past. Our unique business model allows us to bring you more focused information, giving you more of what you need to know, and less of what you don't.

Packt is a modern, yet unique publishing company, which focuses on producing quality, cutting-edge books for communities of developers, administrators, and newbies alike. For more information, please visit our website: www.PacktPub.com.

About Packt Enterprise

In 2010, Packt launched two new brands, Packt Enterprise and Packt Open Source, in order to continue its focus on specialization. This book is part of the Packt Enterprise brand, home to books published on enterprise software – software created by major vendors, including (but not limited to) IBM, Microsoft and Oracle, often for use in other corporations. Its titles will offer information relevant to a range of users of this software, including administrators, developers, architects, and end users.

Writing for Packt

We welcome all inquiries from people who are interested in authoring. Book proposals should be sent to author@packtpub.com. If your book idea is still at an early stage and you would like to discuss it first before writing a formal book proposal, contact us; one of our commissioning editors will get in touch with you.

We're not just looking for published authors; if you have strong technical skills but no writing experience, our experienced editors can help you develop a writing career, or simply get some additional reward for your expertise.

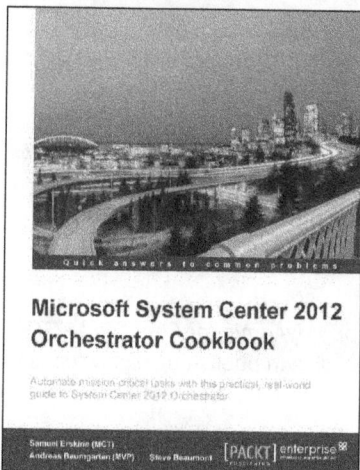

Microsoft System Center 2012 Orchestrator Cookbook

ISBN: 978-1-84968-850-5   Paperback: 318 pages

Automate mission-critical tasks with this practical, real-world guide to System Center 2012 Orchestrator

1. Create powerful runbooks for the System Center 2012 product line.

2. Master System Center 2012 Orchestrator by creating looping, child and branching runbooks.

3. Learn how to install System Center Orchestrator and make it secure and fault tolerant.

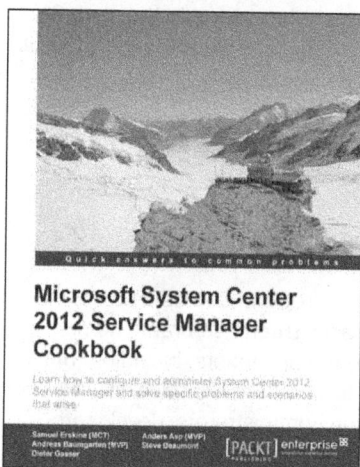

Microsoft System Center 2012 Service Manager Cookbook

ISBN: 978-1-84968-694-5   Paperback: 474 pages

Learn how to configure and administer System Center 2012 Service Manager and solve specific problems and scenarios that arise

1. Practical cookbook with recipes that will help you get the most out of Microsoft System Center 2012 Service Manager.

2. Learn the various methods and best practices administrating and using Microsoft System Center 2012 Service Manager.

3. Save money and time on your projects by learning how to correctly solve specific problems and scenarios that arise while using System Center Service Manager.

Please check **www.PacktPub.com** for information on our titles

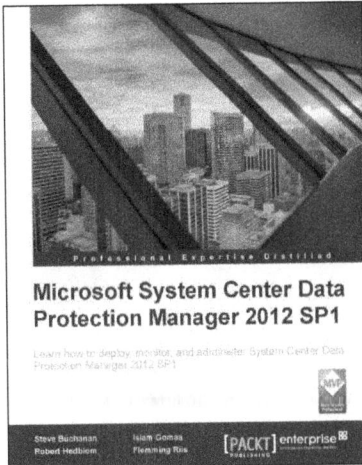

Microsoft System Center Data Protection Manager 2012 SP1

ISBN: 978-1-84968-630-3   Paperback: 328 pages

Learn how to deploy, monitor, and administer System Center Data Protection Manager 2012 SP1

1. Practical guidance that will help you get the most out of Microsoft System Center Data Protection Manager 2012.

2. Gain insight into deploying, monitoring, and administering System Center Data Protection Manager 2012 from a team of Microsoft MVPs.

3. Learn the various methods and best practices for administrating and using Microsoft System Center Data Protection Manager 2012.

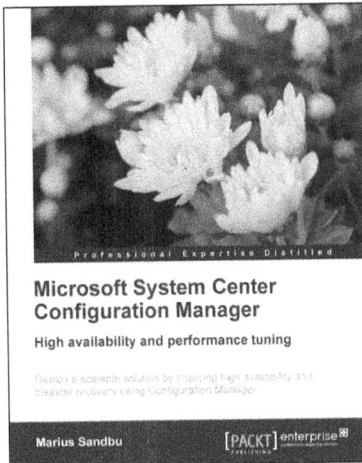

Microsoft System Center Data Protection Manager 2012 SP1

Learn how to deploy, monitor, and administer System Center Data Protection Manager 2012 SP1

Steve Buchanan   Islam Gomaa
Robert Hedblom   Flemming Riis

Microsoft System Center Configuration Manager

ISBN: 978-1-78217-676-3   Paperback: 146 pages

Deploy a scalable solution by ensuring high availability and disaster recovery using Configuration Manager

1. Deploy highly available Configuration Manager sites and roles.

2. Backup, restore, and copy Configuration Manager to other sites.

3. Get to grips with performance tuning and best practices for Configuration Manager sites.

Microsoft System Center Configuration Manager

High availability and performance tuning

Marius Sandbu

Please check **www.PacktPub.com** for information on our titles